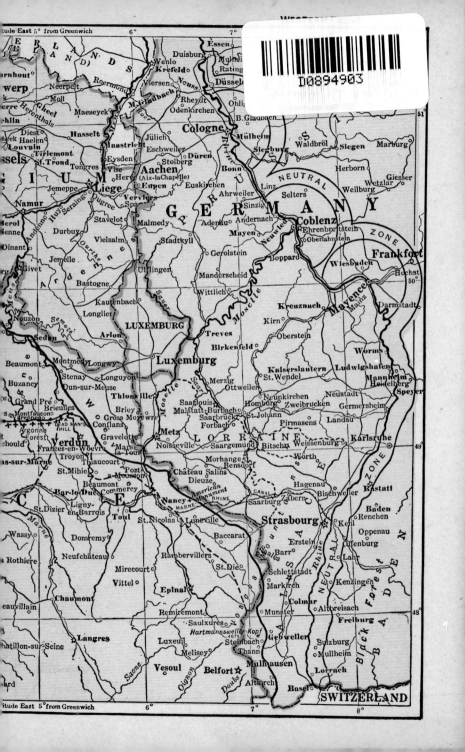

THE LITERARY DIGEST
History of the World War

Compiled from Original and Contemporary Sources: American, British, French, German, and Other

BY

FRANCIS WHITING HALSEY

Author of "The Old New York Frontier," Editor of "Great Epochs in American History," "Seeing Europe with Famous Authors," "Balfour, Viviani, and Joffre, Their Speeches in America," etc.

IN TEN VOLUMES—ILLUSTRATED

VOLUME VI

FOCH'S VICTORIES CONTINUED—THE AMERICANS BREAK THROUGH THE HINDENBURG LINE AND FROM THE ARGONNE TO SEDAN—THE FALL OF CAMBRAI AND THE SIGNING OF THE ARMISTICE—GERMANY'S REVOLUTION—THE KAISER'S FLIGHT—THE SURRENDER OF THE GERMAN SHIPS—THE OCCUPATION OF THE RHINE VALLEY AND WILSON'S TOUR OF EUROPEAN CITIES

September 17, 1918—January 18, 1919

FUNK & WAGNALLS COMPANY
NEW YORK AND LONDON
1920

CONTENTS—VOLUME SIX

ON THE WESTERN FRONT—*Continued*

CONTENTS—VOLUME SIX

ILLUSTRATIONS—VOLUME SIX

FULL PAGES

ILLUSTRATIONS—VOLUME SIX

TEXT ILLUSTRATIONS

ILLUSTRATIONS—VOLUME SIX

ILLUSTRATIONS—VOLUME SIX

MAPS

ON THE WESTERN FRONT

Part XVII
FOCH'S GREAT VICTORIES
(Continued)

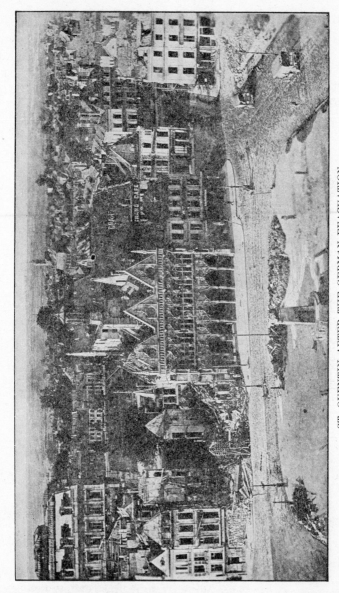

ST. QUENTIN AFTER THE GERMAN EVACUATION

In the center is shown the beautiful Hotel de Ville, and in the forefront of the center what is left of the statue commemorating the siege of 1557 by the Spaniards in the time of Philip II

2

ST. QUENTIN FALLS, BOTH GERMAN FLANKS ARE FORCED BACK, AND BULGARIA SURRENDERS— AMERICANS BREAK THE HINDENBURG LINE AT THE TUNNEL

September 17, 1918—October 3, 1918

MEANWHILE, following the American success in the St. Mihiel salient, British and French veterans on September 17 began another drive in the north against the Hindenburg line in the St. Quentin sector. Sweeping forward on a front of twenty-two miles, they advanced from one and one-third to three miles. The most important aspect of the advance was that it made more certain the eventual capture of St. Quentin which the Germans had been ordered to hold at all costs. As that city had been virtually surrounded on three sides, its fall seemed now only a matter of several days or a few weeks at most. A British assault on a front of sixteen miles from Holnon, west of St. Quentin, to Gouzeaucourt, reached a depth of more than three miles at some points and secured 6,000 prisoners. The blow went far toward wiping out the only remaining bulge that resembled a salient.

The French advance was less spectacular, but equally successful in gaining objectives on a front of six miles, reaching an average depth of one and one-third miles, and adding several hundred prisoners to the record. The French were now less than three miles from the suburbs of St. Quentin. This city, where German troops in 1871 under General Goeben had scored a great victory, was one of the buttresses of the Douai-St. Quentin-Laon line. With the French on the outskirts of La Fère, St. Quentin invested, and with the British battling doggedly for Cambrai, the great Hindenburg system was in danger of being breached at three of its strongest points. Once ousted from it, the Teutons would have back of them no strong fortifications until they reached Maubeuge.

Next day the British made further gains around Gouzeau-court—scene of the engagement in which, late in the autumn of 1917, Col. William Barclay Parsons and his engineers and road-builders, helped to stay the counter-offensive against Byng—and east of Epéhy, while the French, striking south-east of St. Quentin, brought the southern part of their nippers into a still better position for the squeeze. More than 10,000 prisoners and in excess of sixty large guns had fallen into the hands of the British in three days. North-east of Soissons the Germans at this time were counter-attacking viciously against Allied forces holding strategic positions threatening the Chemin-des-Dames. Ludendorff was giving no evidence that he could much longer hold the Hindenburg line, but Foch had produced ample evidence that he could smash it. Allied infantry had become more than a match in quantity and quality for German infantry. Practically all direct connection between St. Quentin and La Fére on the west side of the Oise had now been severed.

In the British advance the Australians had had the hardest fighting. Villages and woods that came in their path had been reduced by encirclement and without great trouble, but trench-lines had to be cleared by direct attack. They took 3,600 prisoners, while their own casualties, including all the wounded, did not number one-half that. As the Australians had been engaged without interruption for four and a half months, their performance stood out as one of the great feats of the offensive. In the first week in May they had begun chipping off bits of the front in the Morlancourt area and continued to do so until the British offensive in the Mont-didier salient, on August 8, gave them an opportunity for an advance on a larger scale. Other Australians at that time were eating their way into German positions at Merris, in the Lys salient. Since then the Australians as one army had been fighting on the southern front. Their drive on September 18 was a worthy climax to their earlier advances.[1]

The work being done at this time by Mangin's army in the Aisne country, owing to more striking operations else-

[1] Cable dispatch from Perry Robinson to The *Sun* (New York).

where, was little chronicled. His soldiers, however, had been making advances after desperate fighting. Skilful maneuver was the secret of his success, German positions being turned from the southwest. The operations ran parallel to those on the equally difficult massif of Thiaucourt, where Humbert's men were pushing steadily toward Lassigny, "nibbling" their way forward by infiltration. Resistance to Mangin was helped greatly by the fact that the Germans were close to the Hindenburg defenses. Counter-stroke after counter-stroke followed every French advance. On the night of September 10 Prussian Guards attacked six times in a vain attempt to win back Laffaux and on the 19th another crack division broke five times against a French unit that

BRITISH OFFICIAL PHOTO.

BRITISH TROOPS WITH THEIR LATEST EQUIPMENT

had just won a farm. It was a pitiless struggle, with little quarter on either side, and fought in ravines and caverns. Grenades that were as deadly as shells were used, and flame-throwers turned darkness into a hell of agony and fire. Mangin's advance was constant, altho it was imperceptible to the outside world; he almost reached Fort Malmaison, key to the Chemin-des-Dames, taken by the French in 1917 and lost again in the descent of the Germans to the Marne. The French were also doing their full share in "nailing" the Germans down to battle from Arras to Reims. Luden-dorff every day grew weaker, here as elsewhere. His chance of constituting an independent mass of reserves was slipping from his grasp.[2]

The British by September 20 were in the midst of wild weather. Even at twenty miles behind the lines there was little shelter for troops, except tents in swamps, groups of huts, slimy dugouts and tarpaulin sheets that could stop up shell-holes in broken houses. Soldiers were fighting and sleeping in wet clothes. Waterproof capes were of slight avail against the storm. Tents were leaky and oozy. Heavy mud and water-holes impeded marching. Steel helmets marching up to line when washed by the downpour gleamed as if with a blue light. Rifles had to be tied about with rags to keep them dry. Great guns went by on cater-pillar-wheels which with their weight sank into soft ruts. Field-batteries were moving along with gunners who hunched forward on mules flaked with mud to their ears. Long roads running through battlefields, such as the Albert-Bapaume road, the Arras road, the Amiens-Péronne road—highways down which so much history had passed in four years—became tracks of yellow mud on which the sun when it broke through clouds shone on rain-washed surfaces. Gangs from labor-battalions were at work filling up shell-holes and smoothing out bumps and gullies made by the heavy traffic of moving armies. Storms broke over dead woods that stood on either side of these highways, etched black against the gray of sky or white of clouds. Out of wet earth, with countless trenches and shell-craters waterlogged, rose the high-jagged walls of fallen houses, bits of churches, abbeys

[2] Cable dispatch from Walter Duranty to The *Times* (New York).

and monasteries, their stones washed white in rain, and masses of broken brick work, from which iron girders stuck out, twisted fantastically. Here once were villages. A pile of rubbish stood where once was a mill, or a sugar factory, or a wayside shrine. Wind howled through these ruins, rain beat down upon them, and British soldiers wandered among them with steel helmets lowered to the storm. Horses and mules were stabled in roofless rooms. Gun limbers were stacked in gardens where flowers grew in a wild chaos of sand-bags and barbed wire.[3]

In sheer duration there had been something astonishing in the Franco-British operations. Begun on July 18 by Pétain's armies, as led by Mangin and Degoutte in attacks on the western side of the Marne salient, they had been pursued without respite, widening methodically toward the north, and all the time swelling instead of diminishing. On September 22, the sixty-sixth day of the battle, there had not been a day without fighting. In that time from what heights had not Hindenburg and Ludendorff fallen, and with them Imperial German pride and arrogance! Since the war-lords of Germany launched their great offensive on March 21 those heavy calculators had no more understood than did their predecessors in 1914 what was meant by the imponderables in war, and especially by one imponderable for which another name was French genius in war.

As Ludendorff, after July 15, sought from time to time to reorganize two armies behind fortification-lines, Foch continuously struck at him until a great turning-point in the war had been reached. It was six months since the Germans launched their great effort, and two since the Allied command recovered the initiative and began to send them back. In conjunction with Austrian defeat on the Piave in June, a slow decline in the submarine menace, a certain degree of recovery in Russia, and news of victories in Macedonia and Palestine, and the continued inpour of American troops, these two months had given warrant for high hopes, tho not yet for an easy, boastful temper. The Entente had taken some 200,000 prisoners, over 2,000 cannon, and an immense amount of war material. Lost ground had been recovered, oppor-

[3] Cable dispatch from Philip Gibbs to The *Times* (New York).

and lack of reserve artillery, and added significantly that "the principle that, even when surrounded, a troop, unless it receives other orders, should fight to the last man and the last cartridge, seems to have fallen into oblivion." News gathered on German frontiers pictured increasing restlessness, discontent and rebelliousness, not only among the civil population but among troops. There were instances of the latter refusing to fire on strikers and other symptoms of a breaking down of the old régime. Prussian morale, that once fearsome product, was falling not only on the circumference of affairs, but at their very center.

The field-fortifications of the Hindenburg line which the Germans had built by the forced labor of prisoners of war and French and Belgian civilians, ran from Lens southward to the Aisne, by way of Quéant, St. Quentin, La Fère, and the St. Gobain Forest, and consisted of elaborate trenches, multiple lines of barbed-wire entanglements, concrete positions for artillery, blockhouses for machine-guns, shelters for infantry, and was protected by flooded stretches of country where means were available for that purpose. Beyond this ran a second line from Lille to Metz, generally parallel to the other as far as Reims, and at distances varying from seven to twenty miles. From Soissons and north of Reims it ran southeastward, joining the old front north of Verdun, and continued from there to Pragny, on the Moselle, south of Metz, where the Americans, coming up from the St. Mihiel salient had just reached it. There were secondary lines attached to the system, notably along the Scheldt from Cambrai north between the Oise and the Serre and northeastward from La Fère along the Suippe above Reims. A third line ran from the Scarpe south of Lille to the Meuse, near Sedan, then southeastward to the basin of Briey, which was protected from the west and south and joined the second line at the Moselle. In the region of Vervins were secondary defense "worms." A fourth line, as yet unoccupied, was intended to furnish a further defense between the Scheldt, near the Belgian frontier, and the Meuse at Givet.

The British advance against the formidable Canal du Nord which began on September 27 was a well-managed maneuver.

THE CANAL DU NORD AND THE TUNNEL

Here the British, on September 27, had an experience comparable to that of the Twenty-seventh and Thirtieth American divisions a few days later. Crossings on the St. Quentin Canal and tunnel, about ten miles east of it, were effected with great difficulty, the canal being 60 feet deep and 70 feet wide, with sloping brick sides. It could be crossed only at certain points, and every yard of it was under German fire

While the whole front became engaged by fire, the real attack was delivered south of the Arras-Cambrai road by Canadians, supported by the Eleventh British Division, with the Fifty-sixth British behind the latter, aided by sixty-five tanks. Every preparation had been made for the attack, the men being well provided with scaling ladders for use in descending and ascending the steep sides of the cut through which the Canal du Nord ran. Most troops, however, appear to have made their way down into the canal and to have clambered up the other side by their own efforts. On the Canal du Nord was a tunnel between two deep cuts, not unlike the tunnel on the St. Quentin Canal where the Americans fought a few days later. The objective of the Canadians, when they had passed the canal, was Bourlon village and wood which had been heavily bombed by gas-shells.

Soon after this event two divisions from the Fourth British Army, and the Twenty-seventh and Thirtieth American Divisions, displayed great gallantry in the direction of Bellenglise—a very difficult position to take. It lay in the bend of the St. Quentin Canal, which after running south from Bullicourt turns sharply to the east toward the Le Tronquoy or St. Quentin tunnel. Some of the troops were equipped with life-belts, others passed on rafts and crossed the western arm of the canal at Bellenglise and to the north of it. Still others went over the canal by foot bridges which the enemy had had no time to destroy. Many, dropping down the sheer side of the canal wall and swimming or wading to the far side, climbed up to assault the German trenches on the eastern bank. The direction of attack was quite unexpected by the Germans, who lost many batteries of artillery which could not be withdrawn before infantry were on them, and large numbers of prisoners as well. So well was the attack designed and carried out and so gallant were the troops, that one division alone took 4,000 prisoners and 70 guns. Further south, the Allies were equally successful. Here they gained touch with the Thirty-second British Division, which had passed through the Forty-sixth Division after it had taken Bellenglise.

North of Bellenglise the American Thirtieth Division, under Major-General H. M. Lewis, having broken through the deep defenses of the Hindenburg line, stormed Bullicourt and seized Nauroy. On their left the Twenty-seventh American Division, under Major-General J. F. O'Ryan, prest on as far as Bony. They met on their way with severe enfilade fire from the high ground, but in spite of it prest steadily on. The fighting on this front of the Second American Corps was very severe, and at many points in the Hindenburg defenses strong bodies of the enemy held out with great obstinacy for many hours, but these were gradually overcome either by the support troops of the American divisions or by the Fifth and Third Australian Divisions, which came up behind the American troops, as they passed over the top of the tunnel and went on farther.

This tunnel was one of the most remarkable engineering works in this part of France. It had been opened by the great Napoleon in 1802. There were wide roadways on either side of the canal itself capable of accommodating several thousand men, and the Germans had dug galleries into the trench work from the east which were nearly as wide and were comfortably arranged for shelter. Beneath the overhead cover of earth the Germans in this shelter had been safe from the heaviest bombardment. There were only one or two places where a chance heavy shell had managed to penetrate. The clearing out of the tunnel was done by the Australians, who had hard fighting and very strenuous work in completing this necessary part of the operation, for the tunnel had extremely strong defenses and many ramifications both east and west back to the German lines, giving opportunities both for escape and reinforcements. In the trenches and down in the tunnel fighting of the most determined character went on while the Australians slowly prest their way onward, clearing out the various points. Live prisoners to the number of 150 were taken, and an immense number of dead Germans were left in the tunnel.[3a]

Of the American share in this work at the St. Quentin tunnel, further details should be given in this history. On September 25, the Twenty-seventh American Division had taken over that part of the St. Quentin front which had been occupied by the Seventy-fourth and Eighteenth British

[3a] The London *Times'* "History of the War."

Divisions, at a place opposite the outpost positions of the Hindenburg line and including points known as the Knoll, Guillemont Farm, and Quennemont Farm. Operating here also was the Thirtieth American Division, the "Old Hickories" from the South. The American position was directly opposite the St. Quentin tunnel and the order was to take that tunnel if it was humanly possible to do so. The problem was first to capture outpost positions and then pass beyond them, and concentrate a full force on the breaking of the Hindenburg line itself. On the morning of the 27th the 106th Regiment began the initial movement of cleaning up these outpost positions. All the strength and morale of the German army lay beyond these points. Loss of them would mean to Germans laying bare of all that was left of the Hindenburg line, the gain of them to the Americans an opportunity to force pressure on that great German defensive wall, still a Rock of Gibraltar of German morale, which was everything that was formidable. The Hindenburg line here consisted of three deep trenches with concrete firing-steps, each trench protected by a belt of barbed-wire entanglements twenty to thirty feet in width. When the first belt of wire was cut, there would be another beyond and still another beyond that. Behind the trenches, acting as a warehouse for fresh troops and a haven for exhausted ones, lay the tunnel. For six kilometers the canal ran through a hill and was constructed of arched brick walls with a broad towpath. Within the tunnel the Germans had filled the canal with boats, in which men were quartered, and had sealed both ends of the tunnel with ferro-concrete walls four feet thick. The tunnel was from ten to fifty meters underground. Access to fighting lines above was through passages and galleries leading up from the tunnel to the trenches.

The 108th Regiment was sent forward at the southern half of the advancing line, and the 107th, the old Seventh of New York, at the northern half. The 108th went through death-dealing fire, and penetrated and held the Hindenburg line from Bony to Bullicourt where, in spite of constant counter-attacks, they held on firmly. The 107th, equally determined, attacked at the northern end when machine-guns planted along every twenty feet of the line sent death fire into their faces and bodies, but they went on with the tunnel as their objective. The 107th tore their way through barbed-wire belts, and were ready to keep on advancing when, no sooner had they conquered one area than fresh German troops rose out of the ground from behind them and fired from the rear, having come up through underground passages connecting them with the tunnel, armed with machine-guns and bombs. They had attacked our men from behind as they were advancing. It became a battle against terrific odds. Time and again the Americans made attempts to clear ground that the advance had gone over, but the constant surging in of Germans from behind made it a grim task. The 105th Regiment was then sent in to stem the German counter-attack. Together with the 107th, it finally overcame the enemy, went ahead, and despite terrific odds some of its elements reached the main line and forced their way into the tunnel from which the retreating Germans were driven out in hordes. Airplanes reported that areas behind the tunnel were thick with running men. The two American divisions, the Thirtieth and the Twenty-seventh formed our Second Corps under Maj.-Gen. George W. Read.

The Germans captured in this battle all appeared broken in body and spirit. When lined up at headquarters they were little better than "masses of limp clothes"—all the fight and the will to war had gone out of them. The plaint exprest by all of them was, "The war is over for the Hindenburg line has been broken." The casualties on both sides were terrific, but the American Army had shown that it, as well as French and British, could break the Hindenburg line. Through the break made by the Americans, the Fourth British Army pushed forward, harassing with terrific fire fleeing columns of Prince Ruprecht's army. The Twenty-seventh Division was then withdrawn from action in order that it might rest and reorganize. During the battle it had captured seventeen German officers and 1,782 enlisted men, aside from a number of field-pieces and hundreds of machine-guns. The armies participating in the battle were the Third British Corps, the Second American Corps, consisting of the Thirtieth, which crossed the canal south of the tunnel, and the Twenty-seventh Divisions; the Australian Corps, the Ninth British Corps, and the Tenth French Army. These were spread along fifteen or more miles, fighting independently on different sectors. After the success was reached the division headquarters of the Twenty-seventh were moved to Busigny, which at that time was the furthest point east held by any divisional headquarters, and close to the enemy's line, which was approximately 2,100 yards distant.[4]

The day after President Wilson sailed a second time for France, on March 6, 1919, nearly 14,000 men of the Twenty-seventh Division arrived in New York. Of these, more than 10,000 came on the *Leviathan*, others on the *Mauretania*. Their reception surpassed, in spontaneous enthusiasm, any greeting ever given to a contingent arriving in that port. More than 15,000 persons were on eighteen ships that went down the bay to welcome Major-General John F. O'Ryan and his division; thousands more lined the Battery walls to cheer the victorious troops, and all day long the streets near the army piers in Hoboken were so crowded with those who hoped to catch a glimpse of some soldier friend that vehicular traffic was stopt. The Twenty-seventh and Thirtieth came home with imperishable laurels because of what they had done in storming the Hindenburg line. On March 25 a formal welcome to the Twenty-seventh took place in New York. It was a demonstration that surpassed the one given to Admiral Dewey when he came home from Manila. Not long afterward the Thirtieth Division landed in Charleston, S. C., where a fit welcome was extended to them also.

Many Germans hid themselves in the great tunnel. Thousands of them refused to come out until a captured German howitzer was placed in the mouth of the tunnel and fired down into it, making a noise as if a mine had been blown up and the bowels of the earth were rent. Before its echoes died away the Germans came rushing out in a mad panic. By this day's work the key to the Hindenburg line above St. Quentin was seized.[5] Near the portals of the tunnel vigorous fighting occurred. Thousands were in the struggle. When the fight was over the mouth of the tunnel was choked with German dead. This action began late in

[4] Lieut.-Col. J. Leslie Kinkaid in The *Times* (New York) March 9, 1919.
[5] Cable dispatch from Edwin L. James to The *Times* (New York).

THE ST. QUENTIN CANAL TUNNEL

the evening and did not end until 8 o'clock next morning.

The Germans had rested their defense in this sector mainly on tremendous fortifications built across three and a half miles where the canal gave them ready-made protection. There was a maze of deep, well-built trenches, countless broad bands of wire, deep and roomy dugouts. Because of its abnormal character the tunnel provided a means of strong resistance to attack. After running through a huge cutting, similar to an enormous railway-cutting, with steep, scrubby banks, the canal enters the tunnel south of Bullicourt. Here and there throughout the tunnel were narrow, uncomfortable shafts running up to exits on the surface. The place had been used by the Germans as a great, unwholesome underground barrack. One grim chamber near the southern entrance was a horrible place after the battle. It was reached by dark stone stairs inside the entrance, winding up through masonry to a narrow brick chamber above the arch, where were four great wheels, apparently connected with ancient machinery of Napoleonic days for winding up and lowering the wooden door of the canal. Here Germans had built a kitchen, and provided bunks for about fifteen men. The bodies of thirteen Germans were found lying there, the dust of the explosion still covering them. One had been thrown into a copper, one behind a wheel, and the rest were on the ground.

One of the most dramatic incidents of the outside battle occurred when the Americans, tired and besplashed, opened their ranks and the Australian units, moving up in support, swept through and became the first wave in a new attack. The storm of cheering that greeted this maneuver rose high above the roar of conflict. There was hard fighting at many places for the Germans had established formidable redoubts in this locality. Le Catelet, the key position to the whole sector between Bullicourt and Bantteux, finally passed into Allied hands.

In the course of this fight for the canal men had to plunge into it loaded with heavy kits and swim across; others used improvised life-boats and bits of plank as rafts. The canal was nearly sixty feet wide and the water ice-cold, but the men got over and clambered up the other side of the cut through which the canal ran before reaching the tunnel, where they trapt the Germans. They had first to go down into the cut and then up the other side, through broken, highly fortified ground. One division, after swimming across, were seen shaking themselves and laughing as they reformed their lines on the eastern bank and, under machine-gun fire, pushed forward into Bellenglise. After escaping from a German barrage, they had to use scaling ladders in climbing the steep sides of the canal. Haig's report, made in January, 1919, on British operations between April and the end of the war, said of the American break through on September 29:

"North of Bellenglise, the Thirtieth American Division, Maj.-Gen. E. M. Lewis, having broken through the deep defenses of the Hindenburg line, stormed Bullicourt and seized Nouroy. On their left, the Twenty-seventh American Division, Maj.-Gen. O'Ryan, met with very heavy enfilading machine-gun fire, but prest on with great gallantry as far as Jouy, where a bitter struggle took place for the possession of the village. The fighting on the whole front of the Second American Corps was severe, and in Bullicourt, Nouroy, Guillemont Farm, and a number of other points, amid the intricacies of the Hindenburg line, strong bodies of the enemy held out with great obstinacy for many hours. These points of resistance were gradually overcome, either by the support-troops of the American divisions or by the Fifth and Third Australian Divisions."

In the midst of this event six chiefs of parties in the German Reichstag were summoned to meet Vice-Chancellor von Payer on September 28, which was about a week after the Americans captured the St. Mihiel salient and the day after that on which the Hindenburg line at the tunnel was assaulted at the canal. Payer probably knew also that Bulgaria at that time was expected to surrender, as she did next day. He said to the six party chiefs: "Gentlemen, I have an extremely painful announcement to make to you. The High Command telephoned yesterday to the Government that it was convinced of the impossibility of winning the war, and that it was necessary, as soon as possible, to ask for an armistice." The assembled deputies were afterward described as "thunderstruck" at this statement, having had no information of an impending catastrophe at the front. One of them ventured to inquire: "Then Alsace-Lorraine is lost?" "Yes, it is lost," replied the Vice-Chancellor. "Posen also, it is probable?" inquired another deputy, to whom Payer responded, "We must try to accustom ourselves to that idea also."

Byng's army and a part of Horne's had now attacked on a thirteen-mile front, penetrating the Hindenburg zone to a depth of three miles, crossing one strip of the zone in its entirety, and taking between 5,000 and 6,000 prisoners. Bourlon Wood, the obstacle before which Byng's offensive of November, 1917, aiming at Cambrai, had faltered, was reached. Cambrai, like St. Quentin and La Fère, since the war began, had been an outpost of the German offensive zone. At this time the Champagne-Meuse valley operations had been linked up with the struggle north and west for Douai, Cambrai, St. Quentin, La Fère, and Laon. Foch's policy was pressure and more pressure on both flanks and on the center of the long German line from the North Sea to Switzerland—continuous application of his forces in order to utilize to the limit his growing numerical superiority. This was strategy which shone by contrast with the German method of concentrated mass-blows at long intervals on widely separated sectors. The effect of a Foch gain anywhere was felt immediately everywhere else. Foch was not conducting several battles but one continuous battle into which all his operations dove-tailed.

When the Allies got astride the St. Quentin-Cambrai railway they seriously restricted the enemy's communications. Important fortified villages were carried. Not even at Bourlon Wood was there much trouble with German infantry. Those found there were easily overpowered except for a few who fought hard. The prisoners taken appeared white and worn, as if they had been living for years below ground and without proper nourishment. Some had been wounded, and had bloody heads, broken arms, and rents in their trousers. These wounded were often seen arm in arm, in couples or with arms on one another's shoulders, a grim and familiar picture in this war. Success attended the British from the start. In the center and on the right they worked steadily behind the Hindenburg front, which was being worn to a frazzle.

By the first of October all signs pointed to a great German retreat in the north of France. At point after point the Hindenburg line had been broken through, and fortress positions taken or surrounded and cut off. While successive blows were delivered at the center, attacks on the extreme flanks, both north and south, were pushed with vigor. One did not need to credit reports that Germans were about to evacuate Belgium, "according to plan," in order to see that their hold upon Ostend and Zeebrugge was seriously im-

© UNDERWOOD & UNDERWOOD, N. Y.

BRITISH REPATRIATING FRENCH CIVILIANS NEAR CAMBRAI

periled. The whole gigantic operation resembled on an immense scale the smaller campaigns against German salients on the Marne and at St. Mihiel. The Germans fought stubbornly, chiefly on the two wings in Flanders and the Argonne, in order to gain a breathing-space for a withdrawal of their main forces. They were very skilful at this kind of retreating, but at the best it entailed heavy losses, both in men, guns, ammunition, and supplies, and was absolutely crushing to German morale in the army and even more so at home.

Haig was watching Lille while the British navy was on guard off Ostend and Zeebrugge, and aeroplanes were worrying German craft in Belgian ports. Horne and Byng, between Cambrai and St. Quentin, had driven in a deep wedge between those towns. The climax of a great battle was near. At the same time Mangin had driven the Crown Prince back from the Vesle to old lines north of the Ailette and east of Courtecon, while a retirement to the northwest of Reims was being hurried. Gouraud had made a striking advance west of the Argonne, capturing Condé Binarville and forcing the enemy's withdrawal into the forest, incidentally relieving Liggett's American force of some of the pressure on its left. Here Americans had been battling against strong enemy reserves originally intended for the Cambrai front and were making slow but steady progress. It was estimated that the Allies had taken in the west close to 70,000 prisoners in six days.

While the battle was in progress along the Hindenburg line, Foch instructed King Albert to launch an offensive in Flanders with his Belgian troops and the Second British Army under Plumer. The Belgians attacked north of the Ypres salient, the British south of it. Rushing through front enemy positions, Gillain's troops penetrated into the main German defenses to a depth of four miles, and by the evening of September 28 practically the whole of the Houthulst Forest had fallen into their hands. Continuing

AMERICANS WITH CANNON BOUND FOR THE FRONT

their attack next day, the Allies captured the Passchendaele Ridge, and descending the eastern slopes of the ridge crossed the Ypres-Roulers railway and then stormed the village of Moorslede, which overlooks the Roulers-Menin road. Later in the day the Belgians pushed to within two and a half miles of Roulers. On the extreme left they captured Dixmude, and extended their front to Zarren and Staden on the Ypres-Thourout road. When Plumer's army, moving on a ten-mile front north and south of the Ypres-Menin road, had pushed the Germans off the Messines-Wytschaete Ridge, the victory was complete. This was the first chance the Belgians had had of showing their mettle since the retreat from Antwerp in 1914, and they had made the most of it. Positions which it took British troops three months to conquer in 1917 were now carried by the Belgians in forty-eight hours. The success was due, not wholly to German weakness, but to the courage of the soldiers and the tactical leading, which left nothing to be desired.

Houthulst Forest had been converted into a tremendous fortress and was the pivot of the whole German line between Armentières and Nieuport. Innumerable redoubts, dugouts, and concrete blockhouses had been constructed. Along every road traversing the forest were doors leading to subterranean shelters, making the whole area resemble a city of cave-dwellers. At every crossroad were signs bearing inscriptions such as "Friedrichstrasse," "Wilhelmstrasse," etc. At each crossroad were four little inoffensive-looking green boxes. Upon approaching these boxes one noticed ugly death-head signs, with the word "danger" painted conspicuously on them. These boxes contained forty pounds of high explosives, timed by the cave-dwellers to explode when the Belgian soldiers entered the forest, but the Belgians arrived sooner than anticipated and were able to remove percussion caps from the mines. More than 1,000,000 shells of all calibers and numerous guns were found along roads in forests after the battle.

One wing had advanced from Dixmude and Merckem, across inundated fields checked with shell-holes, others from Ypres and Bixschoote. They joined north of the forest after three days of terrific fighting. Then the forest was entered by Flemish troops, many of whom were battling within the shadows of the ruins of their own homes. Cold steel played a large part in clearing up the forest. Thousands of prisoners were captured there. Houthulst Forest became a forest no longer. A few trees still stood like nude spars swaying in the wind. Others, smashed and splintered, lay across water-filled shell-holes. When the Belgians plunged out of the Houthulst Forest and off the Passchendaele Ridge they emerged on the great Belgian plain. The railroad from Roulers to Lille was now under their guns.

© COMMITTEE ON PUBLIC INFORMATION

SOLDIERS VISITING THE GRAVE OF A COMRADE

On October 14, King Albert launched an attack with the Belgian and Second British Army, strengthened by a French Corps sent up from the Champagne under command of Degoutte. The Belgian army operated in two wings drawn up east and west of Roulers, with the French between them and Plumer's army on the right. During the first day the Belgian left wing captured Cortemarck and a whole group of villages west of the Roulers-Thourout road, while the French carried Roulers by assault. East of Roulers the Belgians reached the road between that town and Ingelmunster, while on their right Second Army troops captured Le Chat, on the Courtrai-Ingelmunster road, and Plumer's troops occupied Wervicq and Menin. Next day the Belgians continued their advance toward Thourout, while the French pushed along the road to Lichtervelde, hoping to cut off the retreat of the Germans from Ostend. On the right the Belgians secured possession of the railway between Roulers and Ingelmunster, and Plumer's troops entered Courtrai.

The Germans then began a hasty retreat from the coast and down the left bank of the Lys, and British troops cleared the whole river bank up to Harlebeke. Plumer's troops crossed the Lys between Armentières and Menin and reached the outskirts of Turcoing. On the 17th the Belgians captured Thourout and entered Ostend, which had been evacuated by the enemy on the night of the 15th. On the 19th the Belgians entered Bruges and Zeebrugge, and the French Thielt. Altho they lost 12,000 prisoners and more than 100 guns during the first two days' fighting, Arnim got the bulk of his German army and stores away without a *débâcle*. He had been preparing to retreat since King Albert's first offensive on September 28.

Owing to the success of the Flanders offensive and the continuous pressure which Haig brought to bear between Cambrai and St. Quentin, the Germans holding the sector of the front astride La Bassée Canal had found themselves in an enclave with two salients daily increasing in depth on either side of them. To avoid being caught in a trap Ludendorff decided to withdraw from the La Bassée-Lens line—on October 2, when the Germans executed a hasty but well-prepared retreat to positions covering Lille. The retreat was followed up by Birdwood, whose troops occupied Lens. Established on this line, and not wishing to damage Lille by artillery-fire, Birdwood awaited the development of the envelopment movement by Plumer's troops from the Lys and Horne's troops from the Scarpe. After Douai was practically captured, on October 13, and Plumer had begun to cross the Lys on the 15th, the Germans evacuated Lille, and Birdwood on the 17th entered the town.

With hurricane force Foch's army had swept upon the Germans in five simultaneous movements. One million and a half of men had beaten them back. British and Americans had attacked with terrific violence on a thirty-mile front from St. Quentin to the Scarpe. While British and Canadians reached the outskirts of Cambrai, others were speeding forward in the Le Catelet sector. More than a dozen villages were occupied. Haig was astride the Cambrai-St. Quentin railroad and the French were launching a new offensive on a fifteen-mile front from St. Quentin to La Fère and had advanced two miles. In Flanders, Belgians and British had hurled the enemy back on a front of nearly twenty miles. Northeast of Soissons Mangin had broken German thrusts aimed to save the Chemin-des-Dames and reached the highest point of that famous highway, penetrating two miles on a front of seven. The banks of the Ailette were reached at two points below Laon. Further east Gouraud and Pershing went forward more than a mile, capturing Romagne and Brieulles, the French taking Bellevue Heights, Manre and Bussy farm.

No longer was any French department occupied in its entirety by Germans. Foch was fighting five battles simultaneously—a feat unparalleled in the history of war. Each was so timed that one army supported another, each forming an indispensable part of the whole. Grant's idea of a continuous attack by a multiplicity of forces on many fronts was being realized in France. The Belgians were close to Roulers; the British, marching up the Lys, were about to outflank beyond Lille; the Siegfried line at two points, Cambrai and St. Quentin, was going to pieces, the fall of both places considered a question of days only; Le Catelet, the central pillar of the Hindenburg system, was outflanked; Mangin was driving the enemy north of the Chemin-des-Dames; Gouraud was at the gates of Challerange on his way to Vouziers, the key to the lateral railroad communications of the Germans, and several American divisions duplicating American success at Bellenglise, were driving northeast in the Argonne. During a week the Allies took more than 50,000 prisoners. Foch's plan was in full development. Since September 28 both wings of the vast battle-front had been aflame—the one near the North Sea, the other around Verdun—the Germans using their last reserves. With their great superiority in effectives, nothing could stop the Allies, flushed as they were by victory. The whole German military machine was tottering.

From the English Channel to the River Jordan where Allenby was winning thrilling successes the Allies' battle-front was flaming up and all along rang news of victory. There never had been such a far-flung battle-line. Beginning in Belgium it extended to Palestine, and was now in action practically in all sectors. The grip of the Germans on Belgium had been broken and their divisions on both sides of La Bassée Canal were retiring to escape envelopment from beyond Ypres. Germans were getting out of Lille so fast that wheelbarrows and hand-baskets were being requisitioned to take away valuables—many of them stolen goods. Hooglede, Handeeme and La Biset, close to Armentières, were taken. The Allied forces, to whom Degoutte's army from the Champagne front had been added, were gaining both north and south, while British monitors shelled the Belgian coast. St. Quentin fell to the French who took also the Faubourg d'Isle, occupied Moy on the Oise, and advanced to Itancourt. Gouraud's army in the Champagne kept moving ahead along the western edge of the Argonne, and there were signs of a German withdrawal before Pershing's men on the eastern edge. Americans in a week had taken over 120 guns, 750 trench-mortars, 300 machine-guns, 100 heavy guns, and large quantities of other booty.

There could be no mistaking the fact that Foch's battle was reaching a climax. Within a brief period—a month at most—a German retirement out of northern France was assured. German resistance, altho tremendous and sustained in certain sectors, was breaking down in others. In a single day, with insignificant losses, Belgians had retaken all the ground which the British had spent five months and half a million casualties in taking one year before. That could mean only one thing: that the German army, as a whole, was breaking down. The period of maneuvering was over and the moment had arrived when a decision would be expected. In Belgium King Albert and Plumer had been winning another battle of Ypres, while Horne, Byng, and Rawlinson were refighting victoriously the battle for Cambrai. On the Aisne, Mangin was winning the battle Nivelle had lost in

1917 and in the Champagne Gouraud was winning a contest only partially won by Pétain in 1915. Famous fields of other campaigns about Verdun had been left in the rear by Pershing; he was advancing over ground which had not seen an Allied soldier since August, 1914. Many old battle-fields were again being fought over simultaneously; hopes long postponed were •being realized. Foch's armies were going forward, slowly in some places, with phenomenal rapidity in others, but everywhere they were advancing. What was happening was like the break-up of ice in a great river when spring came. Cambrai, Roulers, St. Quentin, Laon, Vouziers—these in past years had been the objectives of campaigns lasting months or separate campaigns that had to be main efforts extending over a whole year.

This stage of Foch's offensive was essentially a battle of converging wings. Belgians and British in the north struck eastward, Americans and French between the Meuse and the Suippe struck north and northwest. If the axes of these movements were drawn they would meet in classic battle-grounds in the Sambre and Meuse triangle. Every gain they made was a threat against the most protruding parts of the German center. The advance of Gouraud in the Champagne in three days varied from six miles at the center, north of Tahure, to three miles on the right, in the Aisne Valley. Standing on a height overlooking the field, a strong impression of the labyrinth of defenses that had been dug there during four years could be obtained. The landscape, for mile behind mile, was a shining white lattice-work of trenches, the interstices of which were patches of dirty marl pitted with shell-craters and littered with wire and the débris of old lines. The trenches were not a succession of parallel lines, but a series of scientific systems, with switches, blockhouses, pill-boxes, machine-gun posts by hundreds, places for gathering reserves, observatories, dugouts cut thirty feet deep in solid chalk and elaborate telegraph and light railway connections. There was here no mountain or forest block like St. Gobain, or the Argonne; there were no possibilities of inundation as in Belgium, no large towns to use as supplementary fortifications; but field-works pure and simple.

While the great battle-line that stretched across western Belgium and northern France dipt down to the Macedonian ridges and turned south to the border of the Syrian desert, into which tattered remnants of the destroyed Turkish armies at the time were fleeing; while there was a battle-line in north Russia, where German-paid troops of the Bolsheviki were being driven back, and one in Siberia where the Germans themselves and their Bolshevist allies were being forced across a continent, the eyes of the world were fixt on one great battle-line that extended from Flanders southeast to

© COMMITTEE ON PUBLIC INFORMATION

AMERICANS USING FRENCH "75s"

the plain of Armageddon. Gouraud, since the attack began in the Argonne, had broken the resistance of twenty-one German divisions. Carlowitz had suddenly abandoned Malmaison, one of the outer strongholds before Laon and the western end of the Chemin-des-Dames, and was retreating behind the Ailette. Mangin steadily pushed his investment of the Malmaison Plateau by a concentric movement from northwest, west, and south, and fought a fierce engagement at Colombe Farm. Famous old landmarks were quickly reached and passed.

29

In one day the Belgian army and Plumer's British army retook ridges southeast and east of Ypres, the capture of which in 1917 had cost Haig a whole summer's campaign. Allied forces routed Germans out of the Hindenburg zone north of the Lys. North and south first-line communications between Lille and the German front from Dixmude to the North Sea coast were cut. The Allies had to move only a few miles north from Roulers to cut second lines, leaving the Germans on two sectors with no railroad connection, except a long, circuitous one through Ghent and Bruges. The break-through on the Ypres front was sensational both in extent and in the ease with which it was effected. It exposed to view the decline in German morale as no other recent operation had exposed it. Allied armies were well to the northeast of Lille and the Flanders end of the Hindenburg line had been smashed even more completely than sectors in Artois, Picardy, and the Champagne.

If the liberation of northern France had alone been the maximum gain of this campaign it would have been remembered as one of the most wonderful in history, for it had broken the German offensive and conquered provinces and cities had slipt rapidly from Germany's grasp. Allied troops in Belgium, French Flanders, Artois, the Champagne, and Lorraine were advancing over country which had been German for forty-seven months, and all chance of a German return to it was gone. Cambrai, St. Quentin, and Lille had been converted into starting-places for an Allied advance to Germany. If the road was still long, the rate of advance was increasing and victory was no longer a matter of debate. From the North Sea to the Moselle the final advance was under way. Ludendorff had thrown the Hindenburg line into the discard. Only a few days before St. Quentin fell, Hertling was saying to the Main Committee of the Reichstag, "The iron wall of the Western Front can not be broken." The Hindenburg line was that "iron wall," constructed at enormous expense in labor and material, the last word in the science of rigid fronts and defensive positional warfare, the strongest defensive on which German armies had ever stood. Now it had crumbled like plaster.

Into "Bochia," as writers at home were beginning to call

the Fatherland, the Germans carried practically all the population of St. Quentin in their retreat from that city. The Germans for four years had been in possession of the town. Before the war it had 56,000 people. "Not an old man, woman, or child has been left; hale or sick. young or old, they have all been carried away," said G. H. Perris,[6] who went into St. Quentin after the evacuation. Nothing more amazing to him had occurred in the war. None but Germans, who scorned the principles of humanity as well as The Hague and Geneva regulations, could have attempted what he saw there. "The carcass of the cathedral" was like an old ruin newly damaged. The vaulting of its apse had gone completely. The splendid Gothic nave, springing over forty feet high, had partly fallen in, with stone and dust littering the floor. Of the stained glass windows and of stone and woodwork, dating back to the twelfth century, only pitiful fragments remained. Parts of a chapel that had survived six centuries and which the Spaniards of Queen Elizabeth's day and the Germans of Bismarck's had spared, were shattered. The frescoes of the choir were open to the sky.

Not far from the Grand Place the elaborate monument of the siege of 1557, with its surrounding statuary, had escaped with only a broken pillar. The façade of the quaint and charming fifteenth century Town Hall, with a gallery of seven arcades, upper balustrade and wooden bell-tower, was intact, but the fine windows were gone, the roof had fallen in upon the Renaissance council chamber, and the floor was encumbered with rubbish. Eighteen months before the Germans had removed from the Lecuyer Museum its famous collection of Quentin de la Tour's pastels. A large château in Renaissance style had been gutted by fire. On entering the town, the Allies had captured a German officer with a motor-wagon loaded with loot he was about to carry off. This was not a case of common vandalism. but a scientific development of the German art of war as wrought into phases which the western conscience had always regarded as crimes. Taking away furniture, machinery, family treasures, and artistic heritages was carried out on a scale

[6] Correspondent of the *Times* (New York).

31

that history had not hitherto known. St. Quentin was only the latest illustration of Prussian devotion to crime.

Only the rush of French troops into St. Quentin prevented the wholesale destruction of the place. French soldiers who dashed in, surprized a German lieutenant and two men in the main thoroughfare with a wagon loaded with destructive material, which they were in the act of distributing where it would work havoc. The material consisted of shells, coupled up in such manner that both would explode with the touching off of a cartridge fixt between them. The greater part of St. Quentin was still intact, but such destruction as had been accomplished had been most systematic. Weaving- and spinning-mills, lace factories and metallurgical works—everything, in a word, which could give St. Quentin the possibility of competing with German trade after the war—had been destroyed. This was the blackest evidence against Germany, so far as St. Quentin was concerned—the annihilation of all the industrial possibilities in a busy manufacturing town of 45,000 inhabitants. On each side of the central thoroughfare the Germans transformed lawns into a cemetery containing about 300 graves of German soldiers in the tidiest condition. Statues had been carried away, museums and picture galleries swept clean. The greatest artistic loss was the theft of world-famous pastels of Quentin de la Tour, which filled two large rooms and were the pride and delight of the inhabitants. The town hall had not suffered much, but the lead roofing had been carried off, as well as the contents of the ancient belfry. In the mayor's room French soldiers discovered that thousands of commercial records, account books, and receipts had been examined with a view to utilizing the information when they resumed trade after the war.

St. Quentin having fallen, the Allies swept forward on wide fronts in five sectors. In Flanders British and Belgians struck new blows southward in an enveloping movement toward Lille and eight villages fell to their arms. The British attacked on both sides of Armentières and carried their lines to within a few miles of the city. The British poured into a sharp salient driven across the St. Quentin Canal, advanced more than two miles, stormed two villages and

GERMANS WELCOMING AMERICAN TROOPS TO THEIR COUNTRY

vi.

cleared the enemy from below Le Catelet. Between Cambrai
and St. Quentin a tremendous battle swayed back and forth.
Smashing attacks and counter-attacks followed in quick succession. Above Cambrai the British broke the resistance of
fresh German forces and drove forward more than a mile.
Unceasing French blows broke through the Chemin-des-
Dames and threw the enemy back on a front of fifteen miles.
Berthelot's army swept ahead two miles and a half, capturing the heights of St. Thierry, which commanded Reims on
the northwest, and several villages. Five thousand Germans
were taken prisoners in this sector in two days, one day's
bag numbering 2,000. In the Champagne, Gouraud took
two villages and entered the outskirts of Challerange.
Americans northwest of Verdun continued their advance up
the Meuse and through the Argonne, where enemy resistance
was especially strong. In a week the Germans lost on the
West Front 60,000 prisoners, 1,000 guns and hundreds of
thousands in casualties. In September the British had
taken 66,300 prisoners, in August and September 123,618
prisoners and 1,400 guns.

With the entrance into battle of Berthelot's army west of
Reims, the entire line from the North Sea to the Meuse was
in action, save for a twenty-mile stretch from around Armentières and from Vimy Ridge to the Arras-Douai road. Everywhere the pressure became unremitting. The Germans were
fighting rear-guard battles. They could not overlook the
threat which was developing on their flank in Belgium and
on their flank in eastern Champagne, where Gouraud's army
was living up to a "methodical progress." Gouraud had cut
the railroad through the middle of the Argonne from Grand
Pré to Challerange and was only six miles from Vouziers.
It was the implacable nature of this advance that the Germans had to fear most. In the beginning of the Argonne
battle Americans had made the most rapid advance—seven
miles. Since then they had pushed forward another three
miles. The French on the other hand had first scored a
three-mile advance, but since then had pushed forward
another eight. It was a question of how much longer Ludendorff could wait for the development of this direct menace
to his eastern line of communications.

ON THE WESTERN FRONT

On October 3 British troops broke through the Hindenburg system in the neighborhood of Fresnoy. Cavalry forces followed and then "whippet" tanks and armored cars. It was a perfect cavalry country. Infantry and masses of machine-gunners poured through the break with the enemy in full flight north. The Allies, now in open country, were threatening Bohain, an important junction of roads and railways. Americans had pushed within two miles of the place. Gouraud was closing relentlessly on the Germans. While attacking the Suippe line he was marching on Machault and Juinville, and had arrived close to the former places. American forces, moving along the right bank of the Meuse, won back places that were famous in the Verdun struggle and got in line with other Americans on the left bank.

On September 29 Bulgaria, under Allied pressure from the Saloniki front lasting only a few short months, surrendered, the terms laid down by the Allies being accepted unconditionally. Bulgaria agreed to break with Germany and Austria, to surrender her arms, demobilize her armies, evacuate invaded territory and give the Allies right of way for military operations on Bulgarian soil against Germany, Austria-Hungary, and Turkey. With this destruction of the pan-German Mittel-Europa dream the German Chancellor and Foreign Minister went out of office. In a letter accepting Hertling's resignation, the Kaiser proposed rather vaguely to let the German people have a larger part in their government. The Entente now realized that the backbone of German resistance could be broken in the west as effectively as the backbone of Mittel-Europa had been broken in the east. It was only a question of continuing the smashing tactics Foch had employed. Actual victory was coming and the end was in sight, whatever the intervening difficulties might be. Turkey could not last long, for her physical link with Germany was definitely broken. The war had resolved itself into a question, not of wearing Germany out, but of beating her in the field and thus destroying the prestige of Prussian militarism at home. At the same time, the long and heroic endurance of Belgium saw deliverance near. The mad and God-defying ambitions of the German

FRENCH CHILDREN WATCHING AMERICANS GETTING A GUN INTO POSITION

Junkers were about to fall like Lucifer. As Bulgaria confest defeat, so Germany would be forced to do; and it would be left for the common voice of mankind to say what should be the punishment of her rulers for their crimes.

The Allied wall in the Balkans could now be shoved up to the Danube and the Save. With an Allied fleet passing through the Dardanelles and into the Black Sea, German treaties with Roumania and the Ukraine would soon totter. Among border-peoples handed over by the Bolsheviki to Germany—in the Ukraine, in Lithuania, in Baltic lands, where the population was chafing under the reimposed rule of German barons—a people's war in conjunction with the Allies promised to flare up. In the west Allied walls were closing in on the Germans at an overwhelming rate. The Belgians had pushed forward another five miles, Americans ten miles northwest; the British east and south; Mangin north and east. Germans yielded everywhere after furious resistance. Never on the Western Front had they been so hard beset at so many vital points. Half a dozen centers of communications were simultaneously threatened—Roulers, Cambrai, St. Quentin, La Fère, and Grand Pré. The Hindenburg line had been filed down thin in most places. A tragic repetition of the "One Hoss Shay" threatened the Germans. Foch, the man who bided his time for four months, and would not let the enemy force him into action where his means were not perfectly adjusted to the end in view, was not the man, however, to plunge forward for a decision recklessly. The price he was paying would bring in due time its value received. This might be in a few days or weeks, or it might not come until winter, but the exhausted German army was going back to the frontier.

Belgrade from its fortress height dominated the Danube, but Nish was the railroad-key to the Balkans. With Bulgarian opposition eliminated, D'Espérey could now cut the only direct railway line from Berlin to Constantinople, leading to the much-advertised road to Bagdad, not yet completed, but parts of which were now within British lines in Mesopotamia. There did remain the Roumanian railways for German use in case her "dictated peace" in that land should prove revolution proof, but none was direct and all were inferior. The great freight route of the Balkans is the Danube. Serbia restored would command the river down to the Iron Gates—where the watch and ward of Bulgaria repentant began. The Berlin to Bagdad route was broken.

Fighting with a freshness that none could equal, with an ardor that only troops new to warfare know, with an intelligence that is given to few, the Americans, altho their artillery, aeroplanes and tanks were almost all French and only the transport, equipment, ammunition and rifles were American, were the great hopes of the Allies—the force that was to swing the balance against Germany. In saying that that hope was more than fulfilled, that the weight in the balance was indeed heavy and decisive, one expresses what every impartial Englishman associated with the American forces in battle can emphatically affirm. America did justice to her greatness. Her sons were the sons of a virile and fruitful nation, and those sons fought with a spirit, a nerve, and a power that saw the end of the war and the defeat of Germany.

In parting with the American Second Corps, after the armistice was signed, Haig uttered no perfunctory encomium when he said:

"On the 29th of September you participated with distinction in a great and critical attack, which shattered the enemy's resistance on the Hindenburg line, and opened the road to final victory. The deeds of the Twenty-seventh and Thirtieth American Divisions, which took Bellecourt and Nauroy and gallantly sustained the desperate struggle for Bony, will rank with the highest achievements of the war. The names of Brancourt, Prémont, Busigny, Vaux-Andigny, St. Souplet, and Wassigny will testify to the dash and energy of your attacks. I am proud to have had you in my command."

Such was this knightly British soldier's esteem for Americans who had helped him win laurels that would long endure. Foch himself testified that the shattering of the vital spur of the Hindenburg line by the Fourth British Army and the American Second Corps in the last days of September "opened the road to final victory." [7]

[7] Principal Sources: William L. McPherson in The *Tribune* (New York), Haig's report on operations from April to November, 1918. Pershing's report to the War Department in December, 1918; The *World*, The *Evening Post*, New York; *The Fortnightly Review* (London), The *Tribune*, The *Journal of Commerce*, The *Sun*, The *Times*, New York; Associated Press dispatches; the London *Times*, "History of the War."

VIII

THE FRANCO-AMERICAN DRIVE IN THE CHAM-
PAGNE-MEUSE-ARGONNE SECTOR

September 26, 1918—October 10, 1918

SIX days after the one hundred and twenty-sixth anni-
versary of the battle of Valmy, and in the same part of
France, Franco-American troops, on a front reaching from
Reims to Verdun, launched at dawn on September 26 what
proved to be the first act in a continued and final Allied
effort to force the Germans out of northern France. Here
in eastern France really had taken place the beginning of
what was sometimes called the Battle of the Hindenburg
Line, leading as it did to the British thrust around Cambrai
on October 8, in which the last defenses of the field-fortress
system were broken. On September 26 the Germans between
the North Sea and the Meuse were substantially on the same
ground that they had occupied when they began their
offensive on March 21. On a front of nearly two hundred
miles they stood behind a defense-system that had been
perfected after two years of work in some places, and after
four years in others. All the points of vantage were theirs.
From Arras to Soissons they had before them a desert
created by their own soldiers during the "victorious retreat" of March, 1917, and it was a desert which challenged
the best efforts of Allied engineers to construct adequate
communication over it for advancing armies. Behind the
Germans, on the other hand, was an undevastated country
with lines of communication well perfected. In solving his
great problem, Foch first opened battle on the two flanks of
the great line, reserving his main thrust on the center for
an appropriate moment in the future. So it was that on
September 26 Liggett's First American Army, in conjunction with Gouraud's Fourth French Army, delivered their
blows on the German left, while King Albert's Belgian Army
and Plumer's Second British Army attacked the German

38

MONTFAUCON

From this point the American advance in the Argonne was continued on September 26

right. Meanwhile, on the St. Quentin tunnel front the Hindenburg line had been broken by American, British and Australian troops.

At Valmy the first of all battles for French liberty had been fought 126 years before. As now, so then, Prussians and Austrians had combined in an effort to suppress liberty in a republic. The French army of 1792, like the British army of 1914, was "a contemptible little army"—at least to Prussian and Austrian eyes—and, like our own "embattled farmers" around Boston in 1775, was not only an undisciplined army but was made up largely of raw recruits—farmers, artizans, and tradesmen—or what it had been the fashion in France in those early days to call clumsy burghers, low-born mechanics, and peasant churls; but they were men who learned at Valmy, as Americans learned at Bunker Hill, that they "could face cannon-balls, pull triggers, and cross bayonets without having been drilled into a machine army officered by scions of noble houses." Frenchmen by their success at Valmy in 1792 were roused to confidence in themselves and in each other, and that confidence "grew into a spirit of unbounded audacity and ambition," so that, with the cannonade at Valmy, there began a long course of French victories which eventually carried the soldiers of France to Berlin and Moscow.[8] It was on Valmy Day (September 20, 1792) that France first assumed the title of a republic.

The field of Valmy lies only twenty miles south of Cernay near the southwestern border of the Argonne. Of decisive battles in world history Creasy counted Valmy one. He thus placed it alongside Tours, Blenheim, Waterloo, and Gettysburg. The Teutons in 1792 had marched leisurely to the Argonne, expecting that they would have an unopposed march, or a mere parade to Paris—much as the Germans thought they could do in 1914 by crossing Belgium. Some 60,000 among those Teutons of 1792 were Prussians, "trained," says Creasy, "in the school, and many of them, under the eye of the great Frederick, heirs to the glories of the Seven Years' War, and universally esteemed the best troops in Europe." With them went 45,000 Austrians,

[8] Creasy's "Decisive Battles of the World."

picked mostly from forces that had served in Austria's war with Turkey, besides some 15,000 soldiers of the French aristocracy and a powerful body of Hessian troops. Longwy and Verdun, almost unopposed, surrendered to them; in fact, they had got through the passes of the Argonne and the way to Paris seemed open to them when they fell upon that conglomerate mass of soldiers from the new-born French Republic, already half defeated from their inexperience, their lack of confidence, and their fear, and the same thing happened as had happened seventeen years before at Bunker Hill.

The Teutons could not break through those raw levies; they unexpectedly found themselves receiving shot for shot; their fire slackened and the spirit of the new France loomed up before their eyes more and more as the battle got into French heads like wine. The full sound of that wild enthusiasm reached Prussian and Austrian ears, a sound with which for the next twenty years they were to keep well acquainted, and they realized, as Goethe, who was with them, afterward said, that something new had come into the world. All the war spirit went out of those trained Prussians and Austrians and their advance was driven back. The battle soon came to an end, never to be renewed, altho the Teutonic leader, the Duke of Brunswick, did linger doggedly in the Argonne for some time longer, eventually to go back to Germany defeated, and the French Republic entered upon its career of unrivaled martial achievement.

A century and a quarter afterward French and Americans were now fighting in the Argonne for the self-same cause as Frenchmen fought under Dumouriez and Kellerman in 1792. It was a never-ending cause, of which the issue in 1918 was the same as the issue in 1792, the same as when French and American soldiers saw Cornwallis deliver up his sword at Yorktown. The Kaiser had called to life again the spirit of Valmy, and in the same region where the hosts of an earlier king and kaiser, 126 years before, had been forced to go limping back to Berlin and Vienna.[9]

East of the Argonne on September 26, or three days before other Americans under Haig in the north broke

[9] Col. Frederick Palmer in his "America in France."

through the Hindenburg line, Americans went forward at one drive to an average depth of seven miles and the French west of it advanced more than four miles. With Pétain in general command of the operation, the French were directed by Gouraud, the Americans by Pershing. In the initial movements twelve towns and more than 5,000 prisoners were taken by the Americans. After terrific artillery preparation, beginning at 11 o'clock at night and becoming intense an hour before daybreak, the two armies swept forward under cover of heavy fog. Germans in retreat left behind them burning villages of which thirty were observed. This devastation scarcely added, however, to the desolation already wrought in that sharply disputed ground where all vestiges of vegetation had long since disappeared. The ground, crossed and criss-crossed in every direction by trenches, had been blown out of shape.

Gouraud was the same general who, after secretly falling back to his second line east of Reims in July, had led the whole German force in front of him into a colossal trap and with dramatic suddenness brought what was to have been a victorious German advance within a stone's throw of disaster. Since then Gouraud's men had been waiting like hounds in leash for the word from Foch when they should strike once more. Castelnau was there in the east also, on the Lorraine frontier, and that name leapt to every lip in Paris as synonymous with victory. It was Castelnau who, in 1914, by his victory at the Grand Couronné, in front of Nancy, snatched victory from under the eyes of the German Kaiser who had gone there in person to witness a success for his heir. As Gouraud's stroke had been the first step leading to the second Marne victory, so was Castelnau's the first in that series of wonderful events which brought about the miracle of the Marne. With Castelnau in command of any section on the eastern border, there was not a French soldier in arms who would not have fought with assurance of victory. Castelnau stood in a group of three or four men over whom Paris disputed as to which might justly be styled the greatest living French commander. He had lost three of his five sons in the war and two fell while fighting under his own command.

FOCH'S GREAT VICTORIES

Vital reasons had pointed to the Champagne and the Argonne as the places where Foch's next large-scale offensive would begin what might prove to be a decisive blow in the year's campaign. Here and on the front between Arras and Ypres were the two sectors of the Western Front along which, except for the easy victory gained by Gouraud in July, Allied armies in Foch's offensive had not yet been engaged. As between the far north and the Champagne-

VARENNES

Varennes lies on the eastern border of the Argonne, and is famous as the place where Louis XVI and Marie Antoinette were recognized after their flight from Paris, arrested and taken back to the city. Carlyle's account of the event is famous among his historical writings

Argonne country, there were in favor of the latter the fact that it lay much nearer Foch's two great centers of energy, Paris and Châlons, and that it was nearer the bulk of the American forces in France whose great rôle was expected to be played between Châlons and Nancy. But beyond these considerations was the fundamental strategic one that the Hindenburg bulge in France could be broken, either on its upper western face or on its southern. A break in the upper west would be disastrous enough, but a natural line of retreat eastward, toward Belgium, would still remain available to the Germans in the south unless there was a break through from the Champagne to the north, cutting across the natural direction of a German retreat.

If ever a Sedan for the Germans could be won, it had to be fought by an Allied army interposing itself between the German Western Front and the Fatherland, which was the reason why Americans now appeared as far west as Verdun and the Argonne, where they could strike hands with the French in the Champagne. One great result of the St. Mihiel victory was already visible. Not eastward in the direction of Metz, where many had been looking—at least not now—but north and west toward Verdun and the Argonne, the next blow had to fall. American troops were able to appear in force in this region largely because the St. Mihiel victory had thrown open the great trunk line from Toul to Verdun, giving increased facilities for the maneuver of such large bodies of men as were needed for Foch's victories.

The direction the advance took was straight northward toward Sedan, some thirty miles away. Sedan was the most important city in this part of the front, more important, indeed, from the standpoint of communications, than Metz itself. Its capture could have paralyzed a great section of the German front in France. From Sedan and Mezières, a little further on, the entire southern section of the German line had been fed and supplied. Having pushed the Germans back to the Hindenburg line in Artois, Picardy, Ile-de-France and western Champagne, Foch now struck in a sector which had been comparatively quiet for two years. It was more than two years since Falkenhayn was defeated at Verdun. It was just three years and a day since Joffre began his Champagne offensive of September, 1915, fought on the same ground over which the left wing of the Franco-American forces were now to advance. Joffre never got as far as the railroad, prudently breaking off a battle which had proved expensive to him, but which in its initial stage yielded 40,000 German prisoners; but Joffre at that time was only "nibbling." Foch in 1918 had larger results in view—results affecting the whole German position in France. By driving a few miles north from the Suippes to Somme-Py he could cut the lateral railroad which had been Joffre's objective. Continuing on to Vouziers, he could cut another lateral rail system, and if he could continue down the Aisne from Vouziers to Réthel, he could not only break all direct east-and-west connections between Laon and the Meuse, but establish his armies on the flank of German positions along the Aisne, thus creating a vulnerable German salient, having near its apex the great Laon bastion. The battle might have been called a drive for Sedan on a front of nearly fifty miles between the Suippe and the Meuse; it was an effort toward Sedan in a sentimental as well as a geographical sense.

The American advance was made between the Argonne and the Meuse, the course being northward along the west bank of the Meuse. Less than twice the seven miles which the Americans covered in their first day's work separated their line from Stenay and hardly ten from Buzancy. The French on the western side of the Argonne advanced half the average distance covered by the Americans but were not held up. They went through first positions for three or four miles and took 7,000 prisoners, which, with the American bag, made 12,000, or not far short of the 16,000 taken by Ludendorff in the first day of his terrific blow on a fifty-mile front in March. If the French could get to Réthel, that greater Sedan which had been a dream might become a reality, unless the Germans meanwhile should have fled from Lille to the frontier as far as the Meuse. It was well not to be carried away by excessive optimism, but Americans could not fail to recall how frequently the seemingly impossible had happened within ten weeks—the outwitting of the Germans on the Marne and on the Somme, the shattering of the "Switch line," the destruction of Turkish armies in Palestine and the break through in Macedonia. The Entente seemed to be on the eve of a great event; even with failure to gain a crushing victory, gains of much importance were assured. The nature of the battle-line showed once more Foch's resourcefulness and his splendid reserve force.

The abandonment by the Germans of positions they had not ceased to strengthen from the time when they first occupied them, revealed a state of high nervousness, symptoms of which had appeared at different points along the front for a month. The American attack was made in what was in a way the weakest section of the German line, from the eastern edge of the Argonne to the Heights of the Meuse. This weakness was due to absence of lines of communications. Between Sedan and Verdun there was only one railroad east and west, only one crossing of the Argonne, which was through a pass at Grand Pré, from Challerange northeast of Reims. Between the Aire and the Meuse there was not a single railroad east and west except such a possible link as Germany might have constructed since the war began.

There was much positive advantage in attacking here. An attack delivered west of the Argonne had limitations before it was launched; a pocket created by the Aisne was a pocket within which fighting could take place, but when the pocket had been taken the Allies could be stopt and the German line generally might remain where it was before. Between the Aire and the Meuse, however, both the American attacking flanks would be well guarded as far as Grand Pré, where the Aire flows through the Argonne. By that time some readjustment of the German line would be necessary.

On the ' day of the Argonne offensive, the British, aided by Americans, struck their new blow on a twenty-mile front in Picardy and took 5,000 prisoners and many guns. In that stroke the Americans who were with the British captured strong defenses on the Hindenburg line before Le Catelet. Half-way between Cambrai and St. Quentin Haig's forces, in a direct thrust at Cambrai, swept forward to within three miles of that city. "We broke the enemy resistance on the whole battle-front," said an official statement, an incident in the operations that soon developed into sweeping success on the northern front.

At 5.35 o'clock on the morning of September 26 there came to American headquarters north of Verdun word that the Missouri observation-post "reports that the troops went over the top with a yell on the minute." Five minutes before Pershing's First Army had struck out against a series of concrete strongholds which the Germans had deemed invulnerable. Ahead of them batteries blazed a trail of demolition, the very destructiveness of which saved thousands of American lives. For three hours the night air was rent by shrieking and bursting explosives. Overhead a half-spent moon shone tranquilly down from a cloudless sky. In valleys that cleaved apart steep ridges in that Verdun countryside, a gray mist clung, thickly veiling and yet intensifying the grimness of death.

From the summit of Hill 304, which had been the scene of much bloody carnage in the Verdun battle of 1916, a correspondent [10] looked out over the battlefield, shrouded in the faint pallor that heralds a dawn, but with the moon supreme. Behind were leaping tongues of flames on every hillside and a din that made one's brain quiver. Ahead, lighted by bursting explosives, was silhouetted a range of heights a mile away marking the enemy line. At 5.30 infantry moved forward, but it was not until half an hour later, when sunrise had brought light, that glimpses of them were obtainable as they swarmed out of mist in the valley, lingered an instant on the hillcrest, and then vanished abruptly on the other side. Advancing column squads spread out widely and climbed upward slowly, with never a

[10] Lincoln Eyre of The *World* (New York).

© UNDERWOOD & UNDERWOOD, N. Y.

PILE-BRIDGE BUILT BY AMERICANS

pause, their progress made gradual by the barrage that preceded them which rolled along not faster than a hundred
yards in four minutes. After the first infantry wave came
a second and then a third in such deliberate, untroubled
fashion that they seemed to have gone miles before the first
clatter of machine-guns was heard striking above the deeper-
toned racket of shells. Artillery impeded them not at all
because reduced to impotence by counter-fire.

Ludendorff had known that something would happen in
this section, but guessed that Pershing would aim at Briey
and Metz instead of the Argonne, and so had left the bulk
of his reserves and guns east of the Meuse. Consequently
the Americans were able to cross the Forges brook, storm
the wood of the same name and seize Drillancourt, Grecourt,
and Dannovoux without encountering artillery opposition.
In the center, north of Hill 304, American troops, supported
wherever possible by tanks, reached Malancourt and Béthin-
court in the first bound. Before noon the Americans were
beyond Cuisy, tho the enemy had fought stiffly in and about
powerfully fortified hamlets. Montfaucon Wood, so strong
as to be almost inaccessible frontally, was outflanked without difficulty, but Montfaucon itself was not taken until
after savage fighting, defended as it was by machine-gunners
instructed to spare nothing, including their own lives. The
last living German was eventually got out of the place, and
soon afterward Nantillers was in American hands. On the
left Liggett's corps, refraining from the costly work of
driving into the Argonne, advanced along the eastern edge
of the forest, machine-gunned infantry units defending
Varennes and Valiquois. It was at Varennes that Louis
XVI and Marie Antoinette were captured in their flight
during the French Revolution and obliged to turn about and
return to Paris.

As at St. Mihiel a fortnight before, the fighting became
open before the end of the first twelve hours, altho no
better trenches existed anywhere on the front than those
constructed by the Germans in this region. Prisoners began
to swarm in as soon as the Americans reached the German
second line. Many hundreds were trapt by the encirclement
of Montfaucon Wood. At Vauquois the Americans were op-

GENERAL PERSHING

49

posed by a Prussian Guard Division, the other enemy divisions being of mediocre quality. The prisoners captured appeared not to be in the least downcast. One gang of fifty or more yelled *"Ja, Ja"* in chorus when asked if they were satisfied with their fate.

It was difficult for one who had not seen the sight to imagine the quantity of barbed wire that had been used and the extent of the burrowing that had been done on this section in four years. There seemed to be wire enough several times to circle the globe, while if all the trenches in the Aire Valley alone could have been put end to end, they might have reached to New York. There were big trenches, little trenches, communicating trenches, simple trenches, and trenches fitted with palatial dugouts and electric lights. One German officer had framed pictures on his trench walls and running water in his quarters. One of the most interesting places taken was Vauquois, where the Germans had extended natural caves into tunnels that reached back under the hill to the north of Montfaucon; the largest place taken, stood on a hill which was a natural fortress put to use by the Germans as a storehouse.

Tanks of American design were employed for the first time in this attack and behaved splendidly. In the fighting for Vauquois they went crawling forward under shelter of a dense smoke-screen protecting infantry in their advances. They dealt so successfully with machine-guns that our men made their entry without difficulty and with scarcely a casualty.[11]

The arrival of the French on the banks of the Py, on the west side of the Argonne, marked the successful termination of the first phase of their attack. Here the line ran almost directly east and west from south of Somme-Py to south of the Cernay woods. The French held Cernay. The line marked an advance of five or six miles over extraordinarily difficult ground covered with trenches and deeply wired barriers. Having broken deep into the Hindenburg line between the Suippe and the Argonne, Gouraud's advance had secured satisfactory results, when the formidable character of the defense was considered. Could Liggett's corps reach Stenay, it would be on the flank of the whole system of

[11] Cable dispatch from Lincoln Eyre to The *World* (New York).

direct German rail and road communications between Laon and Metz and would nearly sever contact between the German armies in the north and those in Lorraine and Alsace. North of Stenay and Sedan the Ardennes Forest intervened to bar east and west communications, while north of the Ardennes there was only a long roundabout connection through Liége to Aix-la-Chapelle and the Rhine.

Another day's advance brought the Americans almost in touch with the German Kriemhilde line at Brieulles, the southern outskirts of which were occupied by our troops. Here American aviators, despite bad weather, had downed sixty German airplanes and twelve balloons in three days. Next day it was raining, with inky darkness in the forest at night, the Germans shelling heavily, pouring forth gas and raking hills with thousands of 77's. When Americans in their advance came upon barbed wire, rifles had to be slung across their shoulders and pliers pulled out to cut the wire, with machine-guns still going and shells falling all around them. Having cut the barbed wire, they often stumbled on other wire concealed in underbrush. German snipers and machine-gun men all this time took their toll. It required stout hearts and real men to stand all this through two and a half miles. Meanwhile it was hard to get supplies and ammunition over roads which had not been used for four years and in which bushes had grown up and innumerable shell-holes been created by mines set off by Germans. For want of roads supplies had often to be carried on human backs. The Hindenburg line reaching to its rear of trenches and dugouts here covered slightly more than four kilometers, and the same was true of it in the Champagne. Engineers performed a colossal task in mending roads.

Perhaps the most dramatic fighting in which Americans were engaged was a battle that lasted through a whole night in the forest where, if one advanced, he would get into an elaborate system of machine-gun posts or dugouts cleverly concealed in underbrush. In that phase of the offensive the task was appalling. Even more formidable was the wire when found woven endlessly among trees. Hundreds and hundreds of miles of it had been strung since two years before. Through it had grown weeds and grass more than three feet high, making the wire more serious by its concealment. Through such a country the Americans fought their way foot by foot. Young in years and experience, in depressing darkness, where death might be ambushed behind any of a myriad trunks of trees, and where the rattle of machine-guns was multiplied and magnified by the forest into a deafening snarl of thunder, every man knew how small his chances were of being looked after by friendly hands if he should fail. Even when stretcher-bearers found him, the task of getting him out was one of daunting magnitude. How the wounded were ever rescued even their saviors scarcely knew. Notwithstanding everything, our troops went through the forest steadily. Even the Germans would have got lost in that bewildering complication of ravines and ridges.

The Americans were also greatly hampered by the mass of shell-craters that studded old battlefields over which transports had to move. Roads across No Man's Land became jammed with traffic that barely moved for hours, and presented a good target for German bombs. But everywhere American endurance was splendid, and especially when exposed to rain, with cold driving winds that had all the rawness of late November in New York. Troops shivered in clothing which was fit only for summer wear. The result was that hurry calls for blankets, woolen socks and sweaters went out, one division demanding 10,000 pairs of blankets. Men often had to fight on empty stomachs because of congestion along roads. Seldom had American troops undergone such trials, and yet they were cheerful and willing to fight more. They had overcome four-year-old defenses that the Germans believed impregnable. The Germans were pushing strong forces forward—some from Metz and others from Alsace—making fierce counter-attacks, so that Americans were not pleased to read the constant assertions in the press that the German morale was gone. It was true that the German soldier was not as sure of himself as he had been, but the graves that marked many hillsides between the Argonne and the Meuse told that he still fought to the death.[12]

For feats of combative engineering, on which the entire

[12] Cable dispatch from Edwin L. James to The *Times* (New York).

issue of the battle between the Meuse and the Argonne depended, credit was given to Illinois troops supported by New York artillery. Troops had to advance from the famous Dead Man's Hill across a deep swamp 200 yards wide. A brook nearby averaged five yards in width and was four feet deep, but it had spread out at this time of the year into a morass on both sides. South of the swamp lay barbed-wire entanglements under the slopes of Dead Man's Hill in a belt forming a barrier 1,000 yards wide. North of the swamp rose a formidable hill, on the right of which, 1,000 yards away was Forges Wood, a stronghold organized by the Ger-

© COMMITTEE ON PUBLIC INFORMATION

ROAD- AND BRIDGE-BUILDING BY AMERICAN ENGINEERS

mans until they believed it impregnable. The American plan of attack embraced the crossing of this morass so that troops could assemble opposite the hill, surround Forges Wood and sweep on in a fast turning movement toward the Meuse. Before midnight engineers crept forward and cut wide lanes through masses of twisted, rusty wire without the knowledge of the enemy, whose sentinels paced the north side of the swamp of Forges Creek. Then in pitch darkness they carried nearly 12,000 feet of duckboards—strongly built ladder-like bridges—7,000 bundles of willow twigs bound solidly with wire, and 5,000 feet of heavy rope, to the very edge of the swamp and waited for the barrage from

New York gunners, who, by prearranged time-table, were told to put a solid wall of bursting shells on the north side of the swamp and·hold the fire there forty-five minutes.

Several thousand American doughboys waited with bayonets fixt in the shadow of Dead Man's Hill for the barrage to begin and the engineers to pave Forges swamp so that they could cross. Promptly the guns opened up, the Americans working in perfect unison, New Yorkers showering shells behind, while Illinois engineers rushed forward behind New York's wall of fire, wading into the morass and stretching hundreds of ropes from one side to the other. They started through muck and waded or swam until everything was laid in accordance with blueprint plans furnished beforehand. Then they entered like ants into an inferno of noise. In the weird light furnished by the bursting shells of the New Yorkers they went forward, ropes lowering them down into the mud by which duckboards were carried forward and laid down and more duckboards placed across the creek itself. The job was finished in less than the specified time, and signals sent back to waiting infantrymen who now went over the top, down into the valley, through lanes of wire, and then over the Forges swamp in single file across the newly laid bridges. In some places bridges disappeared in the mire from the weight of the men, but engineers wading deep in muck held planks under the duckboards, while fighting men passed. Some of the infantry impatiently waded through the swamp itself.

Enemy machine-gun fire was beginning to sound through the barrage when all had reached the other side. As the infantry formed into the first wave the New York barrage, precisely at the end of forty-five minutes, was jumped a hundred yards ahead to make room for the second wave, which was forming. Five minutes later the barrage jumped another hundred yards to make room for the third wave, and then began to crawl up the hill with all waves following. When it reached the hill crest it performed graceful curves into Forges Wood, where the enemy had been waiting for a frontal attack instead of a flank attack and so found the doughboys in waves behind them. The only avenue of escape lay southeast toward the Meuse and here they found American machine-gun barrage playing over ground where they had been expecting the American waves to advance. Cut off and completely surrounded, they surrendered in batches. One dugout alone yielded three officers and seventy men. Isolated machine-gun nests in the woods sputtered gayly in a direction where no American troops longer existed. One lieutenant and his platoon cleaned out five of these nests without a casualty. When Forges Wood was cleared, New York gunners, answering the signal flares, changed their fuses and sent another barrage many kilometers from Forges swamp, the operation a swinging movement, which began on a straight line east of the Meuse, and then swung fanlike against that river. All the objectives were reached at noon, about seven hours after the waves left the swamp. Thousands of prisoners were bagged in this operation. It was so audacious and cleverly executed that the enemy was swept off his feet. Without that engineering feat victory would have been impossible. Villages on the Meuse now fell like ripe plums. The entire ground captured was ground that had seen some of the bloodiest fighting in the German effort against Verdun in 1916.[13]

In Champagne the French enlarged their gains from north of Somme-Py to the western fringe of the Argonne. The railroad junction-point of Challerange, a short distance south of Vouziers, was captured. After the French had completed their domination of the Aire Valley where they were awaiting the arrival of Americans, the big wooded bastion promised to be out of the fighting-line. The Americans were slowly approaching that rendezvous. Just as Gouraud's army had mastered the entrance to the Grandpré defile and Berthelot's had conquered the massif of St. Thierry, news came of the capture of St. Quentin, on October 2. That ancient town and fortress was not only the largest yet recovered from the enemy, but the moral effect of its loss was great in Germany, which for eighteen months had trumpeted it as the "corner-stone" of the Hindenburg line. Old streets sloping up to the cathedral on the eastern height were blazing with fire when French soldiers made their way through the evacuated city, from west to east, passing the town hall

[13] Cable dispatch from Wilbur Forrest to The *Tribune* (New York).

in the center, which seemed intact, but which they did not enter for fear of mines.

American troops in the Argonne on October 3 were keeping up a steady pressure on the enemy, New York troops building light railways through dense underbrush almost up to the enemy's line. The struggle here became the worst ever faced by Americans. Thick belts of barbed wire and nature's underbrush combined with barrage made it impossible to see ten feet ahead. Everywhere was a determined enemy, with modern weapons of war. Men who had occupied stools in brokers' offices a year before, seasoned now by months in open air, outwitted German veterans and advanced by ruses as clever as any with which American pioneers had thwarted aborigines in the Far West. In one place the Germans had set up thousands of feet of wire with steel trusses, but, despite heavy German fire, the Americans found a way over the wire rampart. Stupefied by American ingenuity and thrown back, the Germans sought refuge behind another belt of wire. Belts of wire as thick as wooded undergrowth were again and again destroyed in spite of explosives discharged from long pipes concealed in brush, as our troops made their way in the darkness through the gaps. Old Indian warfare and "dog fighting" characterized that battle—a fight against nature and the Germans, and more especially against the enemy's exact knowledge of every road and path. One captured ravine contained about two thousand miniature houses built over dugouts, and now death-traps, but engineers investigated them and rendered them harmless. Near Varennes the Germans had blown a great hole in the main road and placed four hundred mines along roads that connected with the main road further on. One Cassidy from Ninety-sixth Street and Broadway, New York, here rooted out every mine without a casualty.

Every day saw New York men pushing further ahead, cutting through dense underbrush and barbed wire, and defying German machine-guns.[14] Troops that had had their first taste of trenches in the Lorraine sector and had emerged from a fiery furnace well tempered, now ranked among our shock-troops. Innumerable instances were given to show

[14] Cable dispatch from Wilbur Forrest to The *Tribune* (New York).

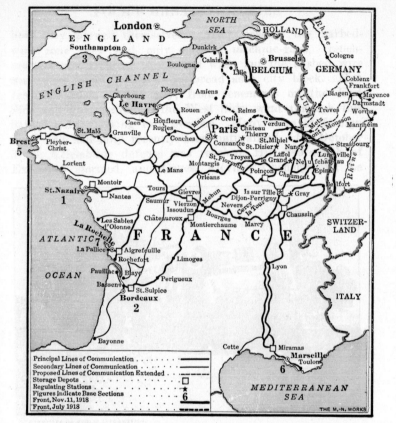

AMERICAN TRANSPORTATION OPERATIONS IN FRANCE

American railway engineers, chief among whom were Gen. W. W. Atterbury of the Pennsylvania Railroad, Col. William Barclay Parsons, Chief Engineer of the first New York subway, and Col. William J. Wilgus, formerly Vice-President of the New York Central, did not build across France a new four-track railroad, as they were widely declared to have done, but they did accomplish in France a vast work in railroad extensions, terminal facilities and equipment. They greatly enlarged ocean terminals at Bordeaux, La Rochelle, St. Nazaire, and Brest, built enormous storage depots at Montoir, Gièvres, Chateauroux, Poinçon, Chaussin, Miramas and Langres, large regulating stations at several points in northeastern France, enlarged and extended existing lines of communication direct from the coast to the battle areas, so as to go around Paris instead of going into it as most French railroads do, and built direct supply lines from supply stations to the actual fighting front. All this work meant, not only the building of roadbeds and trackage, but the importation of locomotives by many hundreds and freight-cars by the thousands. It was estimated that when the armistice was signed these American engineers had put at the service of our armies in France new railroad facilities about equal to three times those of the Lehigh Valley system. The above map of these operations was prepared by Colonel Wilgus, who was the Deputy Director-General of Transportation, and has kindly permitted it to be used in this history

continued to make the strongest sort of defense, with absolute disregard for losses. In the Argonne they hurriedly felled and wired trees, and placed machine-guns before advancing troops, but were driven back until the Kriemhilde line was bitten into so deeply that when fighting occurred north of it the opposing forces would be on equal terms, the Germans having no longer the advantage of organized positions with fortified steel, masonry, and intricate wire defenses. The German troops had been badly pounded. One battalion had only fifty men left. A Prussian Guard Division had to be taken altogether out of the line; another was kept in only by filling it up with Landsturm troops. In a large sense the battle was won by artillery, which had been well placed before the attack started.[15] The German troops were mainly Guards, Jaegers, and other units that had distinguished themselves throughout the war. One division, the flower of the German army, wore a special green uniform with insignia of eidelweiss and antlers on their caps, and the letter "C" in memory of the Carpathians, where their record had been notable.

Despite all the Germans could do west of the forest, Gouraud's men penetrated far into the second battle-zone, where a threat toward Vouziers had been thought dangerous. Some flanking piece of woodland or some other vital point of defense was first smashed by artillery and then infantry were sent forward. Tank-batteries had a superhuman task to perform. In many places steel-protected ravines formed impassable barriers, and everywhere anti-tank rifles and machine-guns of special caliber were ready for use. Batteries of anti-tank cannon were installed at points where the dreaded monsters were likely to appear. Tank crews often sacrificed themselves to help on an infantry advance. On the whole front the enemy was not only resisting to the last, but counter-attacking with fury wherever occasion offered. It was impossible to over-estimate the service rendered to the Allied cause by Gouraud's army, which was fighting a great part of the German reserves at points of vital importance, and was making progress.

[15] Cable dispatch from Edwin L. James to The *Times* (New York).

Gouraud forced a withdrawal of the Germans behind the Suippe, a retirement taking twenty-four hours, in which in some places his men advanced as much as eight miles. Just when it began to look as if he had made an extremely heavy effort without definite gain, the German line crumbled, and he reaped a fine reward for persistence against desperate opposition. Altho Americans east of the Argonne had reached the Kriemhilde line on the right, it was not a part of their plan to drive ahead too far until the line had been evened up in the west. The Germans were making use of every feature of the terrain to conceal their machine-guns. From Romagne to the Meuse the battles of four years had swept the land clean of villages and all natural shelters for guns, but this was not true in the Aire Valley, where each hill sloped down to the beginning of another and each had its little wood. In valleys, bushes gave ideal shelter for machine-gun nests. From Fléville to Landres the Germans had thousands of machine-guns, so that the stiff fight had to continue. Germans still had a salient there. They had not stopt the Allied advance on both sides of the forest, but were keeping a strong force in thick woods, where nests were found in scores of places. German positions became hourly more precarious as the French on the west and the Americans on the east of the forest made their way northward.

When the Americans moved on toward Chéhéry, with strongly protected hills, they ran into a veritable wall of machine-guns. Small tanks did the work of forcing passage. After this, infantry swept up the Aire Valley to the southern edge of Fléville. Following white smoke-puffs of rolling barrage and advancing 100 yards every four minutes, infantry assaulted the Romagne Ridge, and the Kriemhilde trenches. In some places they found little wire, in others surprizingly few trenches, evidences of the haste with which the Germans had repaired an old position. As soon as the first wave stopt, the second passed through. Renewing the attack, strong resistance was met, but troops, split up into small parties, sifted through. Further desperate fighting was expected since the Germans had their backs to the wall and were fighting hard. Our men had a feeling of grim determination to overcome all obstacles, whether of nature, such as wooded ridges, or of man, such as shells or bullets.

While the Americans were sweeping the Germans from the Argonne, railroad engineers behind brought up rations and shells. Troops commanded by Col. William Barclay Parsons, the chief engineer of the first New York subway, who had been among the first American units to arrive in Europe, had already laid standard gage railroad-tracks behind lines needed for the transportation of supplies for the St. Mihiel attack, and with Colonel Parsons was cooperating Col. William J. Wilgus, formerly a vice-president of the New York Central system. American engines were now running trains over the famous Verdun battlefield, hauling heavy shells for monster guns to blast the trenches of the Kriemhilde Stellung. These were the troops who at a critical moment had jumped into the Cambrai battle of 1917 and fought beside the British. They had learned how to lay broad gage tracks faster than infantry could advance.[16]

The ground won in the Argonne revealed living quarters of German officers that were luxurious almost beyond belief. On the northern side of the hill were concrete châlets well furnished, some of two stories, with ornate windows and fronts decorated and painted. Inside were comfortable sleeping-quarters, lockers, bath-rooms, and good beds. One club-house had billiard tables, another a bowling alley, and not far off stood a movie theater seating 500. All were built in a manner impregnable to shell-fire. The southern side of the forest was seamed with trenches and torn with innumerable shells that had fallen there in four years.

Nearly all the Argonne had now been captured. It was one of the notable achievements of the war, and by far the biggest thing our troops had done. They had taken what was long regarded as an impregnable position, one for the possession of which some hundreds of thousands of men had died in four years and two months. The Argonne was the strongest defense on the eastern wing of the great German salient from the sea to the Moselle, and perhaps was

---

[16] Cable dispatch from Thomas M. Johnson to The *Evening Sun* (New York).

to the Germans the most important position of all. Its loss was most serious for them, and to the Allies its recovery had been vital. The whole eastern half of Foch's move up to this time had been held up in the Argonne, and now the Germans had been driven out of it by the First American Army.

The Argonne was about fifty kilometers long. Americans had been told that it could not be taken frontally and so the plan was to advance up the Aire on the east and the Aisne on the west and thus pinch it out. Across this forest, which hid a series of hills and ravines and dense jungles, ran the Hindenburg line, four kilometers deep, with trenches and lines of wire at short intervals for a depth of two and a half miles. Rocks, trees, and holes formed shelters for thousands of machine-guns. Roads had been mined or blown up, so that artillery could not be used with great effect. The Germans were protected by pill-boxes, dugouts, and ready-made positions, running always to the southern side and the crests of hills. On these hills the most of the American advance was made, while the Germans had every cross-trail and road under exact range from guns further back. The forest proper was a veritable hell, but boys from New York had been ordered to go through it. Some days they gained a kilometer, some days nothing. It was a case of cutting a path through wire and then filtering ahead single file. This gave the Germans a chance of which they took advantage to get behind the Americans and engage in bitter hand-to-hand fighting. For eight days progress was piecemeal, but after ten days real success began as the Germans gave way.

Regarding the Argonne as safe, the Germans had long used it as a recreation place for jaded divisions, wearied by fighting on other parts of the front, and as the seat of handsome quarters for officers. But it was not for this that the German command sent three of the seven Prussian Guard Divisions to hold the Argonne, but because this thorn in the side of France was the key to the whole German front from Reims to the Meuse; it afforded strong protection for the Kriemhilde system, where the Germans expected to stop the Americans. Practically no Germans now remained in the forest and on the Meuse Americans were astride this line, having crashed through in three places, winning the biggest victory Pershing gained.[17]

The war of movement had now got into its most active phase north and east of Reims, where Berthelot was emerging from the Champagne into the Aisne country. By the occupation of Condé-sur-Suippe, at the junction of the Aisne and Suippe and a little northeast of Berry-au-Bac, that eastern terminus of the Chemin-des-Dames was outflanked and the fate of Laon hastened. While Berthelot's army was in full movement, Mangin at the western end of the Chemin-des-Dames was preparing to hasten the German retiring movement by direct attack. Dogged pressure and maneuvering skill led to a sudden and dramatic result in the first week of October, when the four-year-old salient before Reims was abandoned—thirty miles wide and eight miles deep—and the Germans fled to the Suippe and Arnes, pursued by French cavalry and infantry. Brimont, Nogent, l'Abbesse, and the Moronvillers hills had fallen without need to fire a shot. Thousands of prisoners and many guns were taken. This was the strongest part of the Crown Prince's line. Its fall was a pure triumph of good generalship and indomitable pluck.[18]

By October 10, Americans got through the Kriemhilde line on a front of nearly four miles. They had smashed the last organized German defenses west of the Meuse, and were advancing northward with only natural defenses between them and the Belgian frontier. The Argonne pocket had been wiped out and a complete junction of French and Americans effected. Americans were moving up with engineers blazing the way through woods and tangled wire. On October 9 an American bombing expedition, consisting of more than 350 machines, dropt 32 tons of explosives on German cantonments, about twelve miles north of Verdun. The exploit marked one of the high spots in the air-fleet operations of the war. In the expedition were more than 200 bombing airplanes, 100 pursuit machines and 50 triplanes. Twelve enemy machines were destroyed. Only one Entente plane failed to return.

---

[17] Cable dispatch from Edwin L. James to The *Times* (New York).
[18] Cable dispatch from Edwin L. James to The *Times* (New York).

Having driven the Germans out of the Argonne proper, the operations of Gouraud and Pershing now became more closely connected, at least in a physical sense, with those of Berthelot and Mangin in the Champagne and with the British and Belgians in Picardy, Artois, and Flanders. They are, therefore, set forth in succeeding chapters as parts of Foch's movements along the whole line which in October forced the Germans to leave France and western

© COMMITTEE ON PUBLIC INFORMATION.

DECORATION DAY AT AN AMERICAN CEMETERY IN FRANCE

Belgium. Marshal Foch, on January 15, 1919, at Trèves, received in audience some American newspaper correspondents during his visit there in connection with an extension of the German armistice and made a little speech to them:

"This is for me a happy opportunity to tell you all the good things I think of the American Army and of the part it played on our side. Your soldiers were superb. They came to us young, enthusiastic and carried forward by a vigorous idealism, and they marched to battle with admirable gallantry. Yes, they were superb. There is no other word. When they appeared our armies were, as you know, fatigued by three years of relentless struggle and the mantle of war lay heavily upon them. We were magnificently comforted by the virility of your Americans. The youth of the United States brought a renewal of the hope that hastened victory. Not only was this moral fact of the highest importance, but you also brought material aid, and the wealth which you placed at our disposal contributed to the final success. Nobody among us will ever forget what America did. And you know what happened on the field of battle since the month of July: first the Marne, then in the region of Verdun. General Pershing wished as far as possible to have his army concentrated in an American sector. The Argonne and the heights of the Meuse was a sector hard to tackle. There were considerable obstacles there. 'All right,' I said to him. 'Your men have the devil's own punch. They will get away with all that. Go to it.' And finally everything went well, everything went so well that here we are on the Rhine."

The graves of Americans who had fallen in France were not overlooked by the French on our Memorial Day in 1919. Services were held in many cemeteries, including those near the battle-lines where our troops had fallen, and those near hospitals where wounds had resulted in death. The most notable events of the day took place at Suresnes, near Paris, and at Romagne, in the Argonne. President Wilson went to Suresnes to make an address while General Pershing went to Romagne, which was near territory where the Americans had suffered their heaviest losses. A battalion of infantry, a battalion of artillery, and a regimental band went to Romagne and similar detachments to other cemeteries. Marshal Pétain had given directions to French troops to pay tribute on that day to their fallen comrades from over seas.

The cemetery at Romagne is the largest American burial ground in Europe. A total of 9,572 officers and men had been buried there by May, 1919, and only 160 of that number remained unidentified. The cemetery lies on the side of a gently sloping hill just outside the town, on a piece of ground that was captured by the Thirty-second American Division late in October, 1918. General Pershing made an address, and each

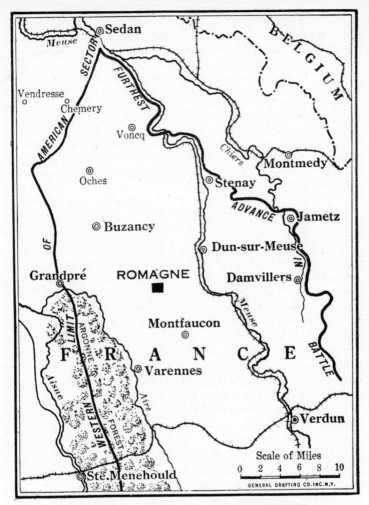

THE ROMAGNE CEMETERY IN THE ARGONNE

Here, eventually, it is expected that 25,000 American soldiers will be buried. Congress will make such ample provision for laying it out and maintaining it that it will ere long become another Gettysburg. On June 12, "without serious debate or amendment," the Senate passed a bill authorizing the appointment of a commission "to acquire an American cemetery in France in which would be buried the bodies of American soldiers who lost their lives in that country during the war." The bill carried with it an appropriation of $500,000 for the establishment of the cemetery

grave was decorated with an American flag and a wreath of evergreen from the adjacent forest. Twenty thousand other men who died in France were eventually to be moved to this cemetery. Americans from every State in the Union were already buried there, their bodies lying in long tiers, in a plot covering approximately thirteen acres. Crosses at the heads of graves bore the names of the men and the units in which they fought. When complete, the cemetery was to cover twenty-five acres. Paths would enable one to reach any grave. Back of the large cemetery was another burial place on a hill where German machine-gunners were waiting in October for Americans while they swarmed over the hill. This cemetery is within sight of war-shattered houses, shelled terrain and unsightly war ruins. Ceremonies took place also in a small cemetery near Montfaucon, southeast of Romagne, where many men of the Seventy-ninth Division fell during the capture of Montfaucon. Romagne and Montfaucon are some thirty kilometers north of Verdun. Eventually 25,000 of our dead were to be assembled at Romagne, so that to this little town in the heart of the Meuse-Argonne battlefield would go, in future years, thousands of American pilgrim travelers. For American fathers and mothers who lost sons in the Argonne it would become a Mecca. A correspondent [18a] wrote from Romagne late in April:

"On our right, on a hillside, we saw what appeared to be a huge engineering work, great excavations, much larger than the cellars of average American homes. These were giant graves, perhaps eight feet deep, and at least forty feet long, the hillside before us covered with them. At least twenty were open, and as many more had been closed. Tools were lying all about, and a hundred or more automobile trucks were standing while negro soldiers and drivers were taking their mid-day meal. Brown-faced and well-weathered white men, whose eyes had the crowfoot wrinkles common to sailors and men who spend their lives under the glare of the open sky, were passing between wooden office buildings or conversing in twos and threes regarding their problems. Army engineers had as their force of workmen 3,600 negroes gathered from many different parts of the United States.

"Little gardens had been laid out and bordered by white-washed

[18a] In a cable dispatch to The *Times* (New York).

stones. In one of the office buildings clerks were keeping records. No banking clerks could have been more careful with accounts than were these white soldier clerks. In the road were great piles of strong and well-built caskets—neat and solid boxes well constructed. 'As you go about the Argonne battlefield,' said one of the engineer officers to me, 'you will see our men with trucks working for miles around, and stakes put up here and there. Each stake marks the grave of an American soldier who was buried where he fell. As the battlefield was sixteen miles wide and over thirty miles long, and as some 26,000 of our boys were killed in action on this field, you can understand what a task we have in gathering their bodies here in this one place. Our scouts have combed every foot of the 430 square miles, from the Argonne to the Meuse, and no soldier whose grave was marked in any way will fail to have a place in the Romagne Cemetery.' " [19]

[19] Principal Sources: Creasy's "Decisive Battles of the World"; The *Times*, The *Evening Post*, New York; William L. McPherson in The *Tribune* (New York); The "Military Expert" of The New York *Times*; The *World* (New York), Associated Press dispatches.

PHOTO FROM AMERICAN RED CROSS.

THE AMERICAN CEMETERY AT ROMAGNE AS
PARTIALLY COMPLETED

IX

LENS OCCUPIED AND REIMS REDEEMED

October 2, 1918—October 8, 1918

LUDENDORFF'S situation in the west called for a more extended retirement than he had yet been willing to undertake. Ever since the Montdidier salient was broken, and his cause definitely lost, he had tried to retire in instalments, but every stand he made was ineffectual. His Hindenburg line, the "iron wall" which Hindenburg himself had boasted "could not be broken in thirty years," was falling to pieces everywhere from Dixmude to the Meuse. Once he could be forced out of his defense-zone—the strongest he had in France—Ludendorff's next natural front would be the Scheldt and the Meuse. He had attempted to postpone his inevitable "strategical withdrawal" to the French and Belgian borders, but each time had failed. By October 2 a great retreat of Germans from northern France and Belgium had set in.

The master strategy of Foch was working out its results. Pincers were closing in on a great salient that extended from the North Sea at Nieuport, through Roulers, Lille and Douai, through Cambrai, St. Quentin and La Fère, west of Laon to northeast of Soissons, along the Aisne to Reims and then eastward as far as the Suippes, while huge French and American armies were waiting in the Champagne and Argonne for the signal that would tell them they were to complete the work at the eastern end of this salient, reaching over about 180 miles. Germans were in retreat on both sides of La Bassée Canal, with British following closely after them, the direct result of the Belgian advance between Dixmude and Ypres, which was one of the remarkable incidents of the war, and closely followed by British occupation of part of Cambrai and complete French occupation of St. Quentin. That was one side of the pincers. The other was in the region of Laon to the north of Reims, where the brilliant advance of Berthelot's poilus had made the position of the Germans untenable, and they were retreating on a wide front. The Germans would soon have to leave the Belgian coast and their submarine bases there. The other great menace, the American army east of the Argonne, had for its function to cut off German retreat to the shelter of Metz, the strongest fort in all Germany. Additional advances by Pershing's men would close this avenue to the Germans, and what disasters would follow no one could predict. Belgians, fighting in a sea of mud, had captured Hooglede and Handzeeme, northeast of Roulers, and were close to Roulers itself. A French army under Degoutte had come up and was at work with the Belgians.

Lens, the heart of the great coal region in northern France, long surrounded by the British, and Armentières, almost equally important as a manufacturing center, were definitely evacuated by the Germans on October 3. Fortified positions between Cambrai and St. Quentin had been smashed, and far off to the southeast Austro-Hungarians in Albania, forsaken by their former allies, the Bulgarians, were in full retreat northward toward their own borders. Germans were slowly but surely being forced everywhere to give ground. Roulers had been entered, and King Albert's men were virtually on the Roulers-Ostend-Bruges railway. The capture of Armentières had brought Lille within striking distance, and the evacuation of Lens had placed Douai, the fortress northeast of Arras, and all the territory between Arras and Menin, virtually in the hands of the British. From Cambrai to St. Quentin, German resistance was still strong, but British, Americans, and French withstood their counter-attacks, smashed old Hindenburg positions and materially advanced their line.

The recapture of Lens and its coal mines gave to Paris the highest hopes of being much better off for winter coal. The memory of two winters to Parisians had survived as nightmares, and would do so for many years in the recollection of thousands. Coal at more than one period during these winters was absolutely unprocurable at any price. In the second half of each winter there was a period of from five to seven weeks of intense cold, when Paris was in such straits that hundreds of persons, even wealthy ones, were compelled to remain in bed all day as the only place affording them anything like warmth. From this point of view the capture of no other place had been more eagerly looked forward to in Paris. Practically the whole of the French coal supply, other than that received from the Briey basin, which was still tightly shut behind German lines facing the American front in Lorraine, had come from Lens, and the adjacent Béthune coal-fields, but the most important field was Lens. The Béthune field, altho for many months under fire of German guns, never had been sufficiently damaged to prevent continuous working, but the output was not sufficient to meet much more than the pressing necessities of French munition works. Thousands of families in the Paris area had been content with a single hundredweight of coal a week, and never had been able to rely on even that much as certainly obtainable.

Measures had been taken long before with a view to rendering the operation of the Lens mines possible once more, with the very shortest delay. It was found, however, that the pits had suffered enormous damage, approaches to pitheads having been rendered impassable by the creation of enormous craters. All the working plant, winding gear, and ventilating appliances had been destroyed and the mine galleries flooded. Many galleries had been blown up at the last moment before the Germans bolted. The work of getting the pits into working order again would be enormous. Lens itself was in the most frightful state of devastation imaginable. Before they were driven out, the Germans carried out destruction on a very large scale. Apparently their intention was to make even the very ruins disappear. Mines were exploded in the middle of many streets and at crossings, leaving enormous craters. Unlike most British and American mining towns, Lens had been a veritable garden city, where nearly every miner lived in his own house surrounded by a garden. It was now a picture of inexpressible desolation. The German object was evidently to cripple the French coal industry for the benefit of German trade. At Armentières the same policy was pursued. Armentières was the headquarters of the French table linen manufacture, with a turnover amounting to $20,000,000 a year. By destroying the linen factories the Germans evidently had hoped to get the French trade in these goods for their own manufacturers, whose principal centers were in Westphalia and Hesse.

The bill the Germans would have to pay for their wanton destruction in France had already been increased many millions by the deliberate damage they had done to the collieries of the Lens field. Of some 10,000 houses which constituted Lens—formerly a workingman's paradise—not one remained standing. Every house had been deliberately razed and the gardens ruined for a long time to come. Mines in every case had been flooded. The pumping alone would require two years to restore. It was estimated that the pits contained something like 100,000,000 cubic yards of water, which would have to be brought up from a depth averaging 1,000 feet. The machinery necessary was estimated at 50,000 horsepower.

Next day the British broke through the last fortified line of the Hindenburg system between St. Quentin and Cambrai and poured out into the open beyond, the foe retiring in front of them. A desperate three-days' battle for the Fonsommes-Beaurevoir line ended in Allied favor. The British gathered in 5,000 prisoners and numerous guns and advanced five miles. Haig reported "complete success." The final breach was made by the Second Australian Division. The great German base at Laon now seemed doomed. Le Catelet was in Allied hands. In Flanders the Germans had given up La Bassée. The great retreat took on added impetus on October 4 on both sides of the Belgian frontier and in the section east of the Cambrai-St. Quentin line. Tremendous fighting continued. Back of the German lines all roads and railroads became choked with transports moving eastward. In the Lens-Armentières regions the British, close on the heels of the Germans, advanced several miles until they were only six miles from Lille. North of the Belgian border Belgians and French pushed forward until their troops were on both sides of Roulers, destined soon to pass into their hands. The retreat from Lens and Armentières was of tremendous import as it was practically an admission that the great battle on the Cambrai-St. Quentin line was nearing its inevitable conclusion. There were plenty of signs that the Germans were preparing for a general retreat, but they intended to make it in slow and orderly fashion, accompanied by the withdrawal of guns and supplies to prepared positions, probably along the line of the Meuse, where Ludendorff intended that the Germans, in new and strong positions, should hold the Allies during the winter.

The British entered the outskirts of Montbrehain and reached Fresnoy-le-Grand. Six powerful attacks were made by Germans east of Le Catelet, after which German dead covered the ground in places literally in piles. New signs of demoralization were noted here and on other sections of the front. This extended even to the artillery which is usually the last affected. In Flanders conditions were worse for the Germans. Naval authorities looked for an early abandonment of the entire Belgian coast. Big guns had already been removed and the coast was under heavy bombardment by British war-craft. The country behind the German front was all ablaze. Germans were working frantically to get their supplies away from the dune country. Blows in Flanders and about Cambrai bore quick results. The enemy was in the midst of a retirement from the Lille salient, from Lens, La Bassée and Armentières. Ludendorff could not hope long to retain Lille, or positions directly north and west of it. That sector was his strongest fortified stretch in northern France and had been the scene of some of the bitterest fighting of the war. Here French and British in other years had sacrificed thousands of lives in vain efforts to take Lille. Both French and Haig had tried unsuccessfully to breach the German defenses, but they were now taken without a fight. Strategically, Lille was of immense importance to the enemy; besides being a railway center, it was the junction of highways running from Courtrai, Tournai, Valenciennes and Douai, and the key to various defensive systems. Ludendorff's job consisted now of saving his armies, not of holding territory. He was trying to escape Foch's blows just as a pugilist tries to evade punishment from his antagonist.

FOCH'S GREAT VICTORIES

So far Ludendorff's retreat was most accentuated in the north, where the successes of the Belgian Army, the French under Degoutte, and Plumer's Second British Army had turned the German salient west of Lille into a man-trap. Belgians, French and British had driven in behind Lille to the north and northeast, reaching the Lys below Warneton. They had also reached a line running north from Menin through Roulers. Portions of Plumer's forces were only two miles north of Turcoing, which was six miles northeast of Lille, on the main road from Lille to Ghent. Ludendorff's downfall had been a story of salients. He had spent four months and used up the élite divisions of his army, driving salients into Allied lines in France, and when he came to a standstill, was occupying a series of exceedingly dangerous pockets. In getting out and back again behind the Hindenburg line he had lost 260,000 prisoners and 3,700 guns since July 18. Then his failure to hold the Hindenburg line in Flanders, Picardy, and the Champagne east of Reims had led quickly to the creation of two new German salients as vulnerable as those of Montdidier and the Marne. He could not escape the Allied noose unless he drew quickly out of the Lille sack, so he had evacuated Lens and Armentières.

By October 5 the Germans had evacuated the Moronvilliers massif and Fort Brimont. One of the strongest

THE RUINS OF LENS

positions of the whole front had fallen into French hands
without fighting . A possible menace to Gouraud's flank had
been removed and his whole line brought level. Further
west, Berthelot's army was stabbing hard at the enemy retreating from the center of the great salient. Mangin was
gaining ground despite a heavy fire of gas and high explosives. Debéney's troops had made a brilliant local attack
above St. Quentin, and carried the heights southeast of
Chardonvert, taking 450 prisoners. Reims was now redeemed.

In an advance of about six miles along a front of about
thirty east and west, the Cathedral City was at last freed
from the dreadful bombardment under which it had suffered
almost daily for four years. For the first time in that long
period, the remnant of the city's civil population was resting in peace, the Germans retreating toward the Suippe and
the Arnes, having abandoned powerfully fortified positions.
Fort Brimont, from which Reims had been shelled, and the
massif of Moronvilliers were occupied and Nogent l'Abbesse,
east of Reims, completely encircled. Advance guards in
close touch with retiring Germans passed beyond the line of
Orainville-Bourgogne-Béthenville. Further east the French
held the Aire along its course, and crossed the Suippe at
Orainville and the Aisne at several points, reaching wooded
heights to the north. Further west, almost south of Laon,
Italian troops took Soupir, and, driving the Germans before
them, reached plateaux northeast. Fires in Laon indicated
that the Germans were about to abandon that stronghold of
their system and probably with it the St. Gobain massif.

The Chemin-des-Dames defenses, to which the Crown
Prince's armies had retreated after their defeat in the
Marne salient, were now flanked at both ends by the French.
It had been slow and painful work to get a footing in this
stretch of high ground, but their efforts had succeeded at
last. Mangin had been hammering at the western end practically from the time when the Germans established themselves there after their retreat from the Marne. Reports
from all Allied war offices showed that the offensive was
being kept up at all points from the sea to Verdun.

The last shell fell upon Reims on October 4, after which
the Germans retired over the hills to save the guns that had

fired the parting shots, one of which hit the cathedral. A few more stones fell from the ragged edge of an old breach in one of the arches of the ceiling. Another cloud of dust and smoke rose out of the skeleton structure, and the German effort at destruction ended. Threatened by the enveloping movement of Gouraud's army, the Germans were compelled to retire from an impregnable fortress northeast of the city, which for four years had been in their hands, and were now in retreat miles to the north. Altho in this war the Germans never had had a foothold in Reims since 1914, their lines ever since the first great advance of that year had run almost through its suburbs. Year after year the city had been subjected to devastating and senseless shelling from batteries at Brimont and Moronvillers. The wanton destruction of the cathedral was only second in influence to the invasion of Belgium in revealing to the world the ruthlessness and brutality of the German military leaders. Altho not completely destroyed, Reims had suffered terribly in four years. Many buildings had been ruined, and streets formerly full of life had become almost deserted. Its complete redemption was hailed with joy throughout France, not only because it restored to the nation an industrial city of much importance, but because it was an unmistakable indication that the grip of the enemy upon northern France was rapidly weakening. Three months before, Reims was a French salient projecting sharply into German lines. Now it was miles behind the battle-front.

It was hard to realize that this wrecked and ruined city was once the place for the coronation of French kings, or that it was the nation's religious center. A once prosperous city of more than 100,000 population had become a panorama of broken brick, stone, and mortar. Its civilian population began to trickle back in small groups to find not a single shop or factory open. There were some 25,000,000 quarts of champagne stored away in the wine-cellars, 7,000,000 having been confiscated from their German owners. The Germans had done to Reims what no amount of money could repay. Everywhere was evidence that they used incendiary bombs, seeking to destroy by fire what they could not reach with bullets and shells. South of the cathedral was the archiepiscopal palace, containing apartments used by kings in dressing for coronations and the hall in which royal banquets were held. It was shell-riddled and burned. For three days before the Germans dropt back from their circle of forts around the city, they had saturated the entire area with mustard-gas, and so had demonstrated once more how they could neither lose nor play the war-game fairly. Business and residential sections had been robbed of all form of life, theaters torn to their foundations, cafés wrecked, department stores demolished. Reims was once the throbbing heart of a plain bounded by vine-clad hills which yielded the community great wealth. French barbed wire still ran through its streets, zigzagging across them, and showing that the French intended, if the Germans ever broke their outer defenses and passed the inner line, to fight every step of the way rather than let go of the historic town.[20] Reims was a ruin. Around the center and near the cathedral only remnants of walls were standing. While the cathedral walls stood there were great holes in them, as well as in the ceiling. Inspection revealed broken columns, and large detached pieces of stone that hung in midair as if by some invisible force. Here and there a fragment of a detail of the exterior remained to enable future visitors to perceive what a glory the building must once have been. It could never be completely restored.

American troops operating with the French in the Champagne advanced their lines and captured St. Étienne. German lines were withdrawn on a twenty-eight mile stretch. The ground across which the Americans had fought was remarkable for strength. The completeness of their victory was attested by mounds and heaps of captured material; concrete pill-boxes, now shattered and helpless; intricate trench-systems almost equivalent to forts; tiny woods which had been converted into machine-gun nests with great thicknesses of barbed wire, roads destroyed or torn into great gaping holes by mines. Fields for miles on either side of the main advance were shell-marked as few places were in France. Munition boxes, heaped to the size of houses, attested the haste of the German retreat. In spite of all diffi-

[20] Cable dispatch from Raymond G. Carroll to The *Sun* (New York).

culties the Americans had advanced steadily and were in a good part responsible for the victory since they acted as the fulcrum of an Allied lever which tipped up the German line for more than twelve kilometers at the western end.

American Indians fought on this front and the Germans found the redskins not a whit less stubborn than paler Americans. On October 8 in the hills of Champagne, the Prussian Guard met warriors representing thirteen Indian tribes who looked down on St. Étienne. A company of them had been fighting with the Thirty-sixth Division, made up in part of

COURTESY OF THE MARINE CORPS RECRUITING PUBLICITY BUREAU

NEAR BLANC MONT RIDGE

Maj. George K. Shuler, whose Marine command in October, 1918, took this Ridge, which lies north of Reims, stands looking toward the Ridge during a visit made afterward

Texas and Oklahoma Rangers. With the French this division was removing the German menace to Reims. The company was full of men with Indian names that were the despair of the regimental paymaster, who never could keep track of Big Bear, Rainbow Blanket, Bacon Rind, Hohemanatubbe, and 246 others, Creeks, Sioux, Seminoles, Apaches, Wyandottes, Choctaws, and Mohawks. Collectively they owned many square miles of the richest oil and mineral lands of Oklahoma. Thousands of dollars in royalties were piling up for them at home every day. When the fight ended, the Prussian Guards were rushing over the hilltops, casting away rifles, knapsacks, and canteens, sacrificing everything for speed. The Indians had had as their first task the reduction of a group of machine-gun nests on a slope. They came out of a forest in woodsmen style, dodged into shell-holes that looked up to where the enemy was entrenched, and reverted to Indian tactics, showing contempt for machine-gun fire, lifting their hands above the rims of shell-holes, intent only on searching with keen eyes for the exact points from which the enemy was firing. Having sighted these points, they slung their rifles over the tops of the holes and fired deliberately and as coolly as if they were shooting deer. In the first hours of battle they encircled and took almost a dozen strong machine-gun positions in spite of German shell-fire.[21]

[21] Principal Sources: William L. McPherson in The *Tribune* (New York), The *Evening Post*, The *Sun*, New York; The *Stars and Stripes;* The *Times*, The *Evening Sun*, New York; Associated Press and United Press dispatches.

X

HAIG SHATTERS THE LAST OF THE HINDENBURG LINE AND CAMBRAI FALLS—AMERICANS ON TWO FRONTS

October 8, 1918—October 11, 1918

HAVING made Ludendorff anxious for both his flanks, Foch, on October 8, delivered his master-stroke between Cambrai and St. Quentin. Aided by Debéney's French army between St. Quentin and the Oise, three British armies, those of Horne, Byng, and Rawlinson, now began there the greatest British achievement in the war, in which past disappointments were banished and old defeats avenged. In three days the British drove straight through twelve miles of the Hindenburg line on the front where it was strongest, and pushed out into the open country beyond. By October 12 they were at Le Cateau, the fall of Cambrai was assured, and the Hindenburg line had become a memory. The British thrust was a final thrust, the decisive battle of the war, and its consequences were immediate. It recalled a remark as to the British in great wars—that they never succeed in winning more than one battle, but that battle is the last. They again broke the Hindenburg line, and drove a wedge deeply into the German front. The Germans, both in Lille and between the Oise and the Aisne, including Laon and the St. Gobain forest and facing Reims, were now in a state of military desperation, for something drastic had occurred. The Allied center had performed its mission. Few people in Great Britain then realized what on October 8 their Third and Fourth Armies had accomplished, when in the darkness of a wild autumn night they attacked on a twenty-mile front and broke through the last defense of the Hindenburg system. It was a fitting climax to a fortnight of bitter, but ever victorious fighting, through a labyrinth of fortifications. With the British here was the Thirtieth American division.

In three weeks Foch had upset the equilibrium of the whole German front from the North Sea to the Meuse. He had compelled a retreat from the Hindenburg line, with all its various annexes, insured a retirement out of all French territory west of the Meuse, liberated Belgium west of the Scheldt, defeated the German army in a battle for which they had themselves chosen the ground, and for which they had prepared during four years. With the liberation of Belgium and France. accomplished, many thousands of men and women who had endured slavery for four years realized that for them the long night was over.

Foch's battle was one of the world's few enduring military triumphs, its consequences as great as those of Leipzig. Germany's dream of world-power had been as certainly terminated in northern France as the great French Emperor's was more than a century before in Saxony. Foch's October battle extended over a front reaching from the sea to Verdun which was twice as long as that of the first Marne, hitherto the longest of battle-lines. It was fought by not fewer than 4,000,000 men; was immediately followed by the evacuation of more than 7,000 square miles of French and Belgian territory, and by a retreat as unmistakable as that of Napoleon. Germany's problem now was how to prevent an invasion of the Fatherland and an overturn of the Prussian dynasty. It was similar to that which faced Napoleon when he failed to solve his problem and was in consequence driven to abdication and exile. The task before William II was not lighter.

The merit of Foch's strategy lay in his ability to expand the pressure over a very wide front, and multiply partial thrusts until the enemy was never able to get his breath or anticipated in which direction the next blow would fall. The Germans had undertaken to destroy their antagonist by a few terrible blows, which Foch had parried or dodged, and then he began to play with the Germans. Having put them on the defensive at the second Marne, he worried them at the third Somme, and made their ultimate defeat beyond question in the battle of the Hindenburg line. Never was the superiority of French to Germany military science more perfectly revealed. French, like German, strategy, was

CANADIAN WAR RECORDS

STREET SCENE IN RUINED CAMBRAI

based on Napoleonic principles, but the Germans only imitated Napoleon, while the Allied Commander-in-Chief interpreted him.

The Foch strategy had to be seen as a whole if one were to appreciate it. Foch used everywhere all the resources he had. Under him were coordinated operations in Palestine and Macedonia with operations in Flanders and Champagne. The result was the most wonderful climax ever acquired in a military campaign. Damascus, Beirut, Aleppo, Uskub, Nish, Lille, Douai, Cambrai, and St. Quentin all fell, if not at the same moment, at least in rapid succession and within a short time of one another. The world, German as well as

Allied and neutral, received a sudden impression that a simultaneous collapse had taken place in all the various elements of which the proposed German world empire was to be composed. In the second week of September that empire had reached, on the south, to the Jordan and the Euphrates, and northward had touched the North Sea on the Belgian coast. By the end of the second week in October it came to a stop on the Danube and was rapidly receding from the Belgian coast toward the German frontier. Its Austrian fraction was crumbling into ruins and its Bulgarian and Turkish departments existed no more. Belgium and Serbia were emerging from German submersion; France was rapidly being cleared of German occupation. For the German mind the whole world had suddenly been turned upside down— but for the rest of us it was assuming its normal position.

This for the British was the third battle of Cambrai. Fifty months before on ground now within reach of British artillery had been fought the first battle as a consequence of an enforced stand by Smith-Dorrien's half of Great Britain's Expeditionary Army, then making its heroic retreat from Belgium to the Marne. Faced with destruction, the British hardly more than 30,000 strong, had met the brunt of Kluck's army in full advance, and then, defeated, had successfully withdrawn. It was perhaps the most critical day of all days in the retreat from Mons to the Marne, but Smith-Dorrien had saved his force. Three years later Byng won and then lost the second battle of Cambrai, on ground that was now in British hands, and which narrowly missed being for the British one of the great victories of the war. That battle revolutionized methods in war; it established the tank and confuted the idea that no penetration of positions was longer possible in war. The third battle of Cambrai was a major circumstance in the far more considerable battle of northern France. Cavalry were crossing fields where many of Britain's "Old Contemptibles" were sleeping their last sleep. French peasants had been told in August, 1914, that the British would some day return, and now they had returned. It was the last and decisive circumstance in the far-flung battle for the Hindenburg line in which Ludendorff was beaten, the Hindenburg line turned on either flank and broken in the center. What remained to be decided was the condition in which the German armies would reach Belgium and the Meuse.

The Germans since September 26 had lost a battle which, in numbers involved and in extent of active front, was the greatest of the war. Between Cambrai and St. Quentin Allied attacks had fallen like hammer-blows. In the Champagne the army of Gouraud was eating into German positions like a cancer. Gouraud's westermost point of thrust was approaching the eastern wing of Berthelot's effort, and

ASSEMBLING AN AMERICAN LOCOMOTIVE IN FRANCE

a sharp swing back of the German lines from Reims toward the Aisne and Réthel was being forced. A German withdrawal from the St. Gobain positions and Léon would soon be under way. The fact that probably more than 260,000 German prisoners had been taken since the beginning of the Foch offensive imprest the general reader as interesting, but, for the moment it was not the important fact. Greater winnings and more immediate results were in sight, because we were thinking now, not in terms of German attrition, but of

German collapse. The Allies had captured since the middle
of July on all fronts virtually three-quarters of a million
men; for, besides captures in the West, they had put out of
the fighting a Bulgarian army of probably three hundred
thousand men and a Turkish army numbering close upon
two hundred thousand. The Americans were coming on by
hundreds of thousands every month, while the French class
of 1919 was awaiting entrance into battle and the class of
1920 was accepting the call to the colors. Great Allied
forces had been released in the Near East for service against
Germany, provided Foch should decide that this was where
they could be best employed.

The whole battle-front formed a salient between Nieuport
and Verdun—a huge arc of a circle whereof a line drawn
through Courtrai, Valenciennes, Hirson, and Mézières was
the chord. These four towns were junction-points through
which the principal enemy communications passed. Foch
was reducing the salient in logical fashion by pressure on
its sides. That accounted for the violence of the fighting
between Cambrai, St. Quentin, the Champagne and the
Meuse. To assure himself against interference from flanks
Foch, using Americans, had first obliterated the pocket of
St. Mihiel, which made Verdun and the Meuse perfect cover
for his right. Then he launched the army of Belgium on
the extreme left to protect the flank of the main British
operations. The striking success of the latter blow, delivered with unexpected strength in an unexpected quarter,
opened further possibilities of enormous importance—nothing less than a threat to enemy communications from the
whole region between the sea and St. Quentin. Already a
part of the German communications between the Belgian
coast and the interior had been interrupted, and an ac-
centuation of the threat to the Bruges-Ghent-Brussels line
would force an abandonment of the litteral. Such an event
would be one of the bitterest blows Germany could receive;
as greatly diminishing her already waning submarine campaign, and wresting from her a coveted position on the
shores of the English Channel, which had been one of her
principal objectives in the war.

Pressure of the most terrific kind was being applied at

all points. The Central Powers now had to give up the Balkans, Turkey had to get out of the war on the same terms as Bulgaria, and the Allies were in position to invade Austria-Hungary because it was not far from the Serbian border to Budapest, but before that city was reached Austria would have to crumble. Germany's retreat had involved giving up positions she had strengthened during nearly four years of occupancy. Belgian operations in the north proved it was not necessary to drive the Germans out of France foot by foot, since clever flanking movements could accomplish it in another way, with a minimum waste of human material. German forces were steadily retiring, or being thrown back by assaults along the whole wide front. North of St. Quentin troops had again broken into the Hindenburg system of defenses, crossed the Scheldt Canal between Crèvecœur and Le Catelet, and taken a section of the line on the plateau of La Terrière, while the Germans were retiring from the high ground east of the canal. The entire Champagne front was giving way before terrific blows of Berthelot and Gouraud. Great tongues of flame were shooting up from Douai and fires had been started in Cambrai, where the Germans blew up stores they were unable to save, and destroyed things of no military value. General devastation of the country ensued. Village after village east and southeast of Cambrai and Douai was ablaze. The Germans even set fire to the wreckage of ruined houses. The homes of the peasant poor in which they might have lived again went up in flames.

The Thirtieth Division of the Americans, which was sometimes called the "Old Hickory" Division, in helping to break the Hindenburg line between Cambrai and St. Quentin, advanced twelve miles into enemy territory, took scores of villages and hundreds of prisoners. This division was at the apex of the wedge Haig was driving between German armies north and south. It was composed chiefly of men from the mountain districts of Tennessee, North Carolina, and South Carolina, who had always proved splendid soldiers. Constant use of firearms due to frequent feuds had made them natural fighters. In previous wars they had not always proved amenable to discipline, but they displayed the utmost coolness and bravery.

ON THE WESTERN FRONT

The balance of strength at the front had now changed in favor of the Allies to the extent of approximately 1,000,000 men; and this process would continue until the end of the war. A diminution of the enemy's forces was the key to what had been happening recently in France and Flanders. The Germans, unable to make good their losses, were forced to reduce their line. When Foch hurled them back from the Marne to the Aisne they had attempted to shorten their fronts on the Somme and in Flanders; but before they could do so, in their own time and in their own way, they were anticipated and defeated by Haig. They then hoped to stand for the winter on the Hindenburg system, and once more were defeated by the skill of Allied leadership.[22] Ludendorff's only hope of staying in France lay in an armistice granted by the Allied governments. All his positions were crumbling. The British break through between St. Quentin and Cambrai had imperiled his whole front north to Douai. Since then the British had advanced east through the Le Catelet gap as far as Montbrehain, and had turned at right angles north, capturing Aubencheul-aux-Bois and pushed on toward Lesdain, five miles southeast of Cambrai; they were only four miles from the highroad between Cambrai and Le Cateau. Rawlinson was in the rear of Cambrai, which had been enveloped from southwest, west and north. A general retirement north of Valenciennes and on the line of the Scheldt was imminent.

Below St. Quentin at several points Ludendorff's situation was still more difficult. Berthelot's advance northwest of Reims and Gouraud's west of the Suippe had made this salient ripe for pinching and by October 7 it had been pinched. The Germans abandoned Fort Brimont and all other heights from which, at their leisure, they had from time to time shot Reims to pieces, their retirement so precipitate that the French line east of Reims was advanced north about eight miles. Franco-American forces in this region were driving toward Machault and Juniville, the latter town only six miles south of Rethel. Before Rethel was reached what was left of the La Fère-Laon-Reims salient would have become valueless. What happened east of Reims

[22] Cable dispatch to The *Times* (New York) from Gen. Sir Frederick Maurice.

would soon happen south of Laon. German armies between Laon and the Argonne would be forced to retire northeast over congested roads, and as they retired all direct communication between them and the German armies east of the Meuse would be severed. The menace of this demoralizing retreat brought at this time from the Kaiser a strategic offer of peace by "discussion," which was the only obstacle Berlin had left to throw in the path of the peace-by-victory strategy of Foch.

German military critics now spoke of Foch's "demoniac energy," of the scientific, calculating mind that was at work on the Western Front. It was not a Bersark that had broken loose, for in the very torrent, tempest, and as Hamlet might have said, whirlwind of the Allied attack, there was a temperance that gave it smoothness. There always was something impressive about the smooth working of real success. It was the fundamental achievement of Foch that almost in an hour he had reduced the mighty German army to the position of Russians and Roumanians against Hindenburg and Mackensen. Demoniac energy—and intelligence—were at their height between July 15 and July 18, when Foch imposed his will on Ludendorff. There was no longer a doubt of Foch's superiority, both in strategy and tactics, to the German commanders opposed to him.

It was Joffre who had selected Foch in the autumn of 1914 to foil the determined effort of the German High Command to get to the sea. It was then that Foch began that association with British generals, Sir John French, Smith-Dorrien, Haig, Byng, Rawlinson, Allenby, and others—which ripened into esteem for their efficiency and faith in their trustworthiness. All came to admire him, as officer, gentleman, and comrade. He never failed them in emergencies and they never failed him. They were for him to a man when the question of a unified command had to be settled and they could serve under him, knowing that he represented not only the best of France, but that he was a consummate master of the art of war. Foch never had visions of a great destiny. In the simplicity of his life he had not been different from the body of his countrymen. But he had always nourished ideals, had known and believed in ethical values, and was soundly patriotic and devout. He may not have prayed as much as "Stonewall" Jackson did, but he was given to prayer before battles. He believed in the efficacy of prayer, and regarded the German "will to victory" as a barren phrase. This formidable soldier was a man of soul and imagination, and as the French army had both soul and imagination Foch knew that it was invincible.

Evidence accumulated that the Germans contemplated an early evacuation of Belgium. Their military documents had been removed from the Lille district and everything portable taken out of the country east of the Hindenburg line. Boats on the Scheldt had been taken over for transport of ammunition and war supplies eastward through Belgium. Most of their heavy guns protecting the coast had been removed, together with stores of munitions. While in possession of the Belgian coast they had been within easy reach of London with their Gothas, the distance being only about a hundred miles, but from Antwerp, which might be their next stand, the distance would be doubled. As the Allies would have anti-aircraft guns between Antwerp and the coast further raids on the British capital would be virtually out of the question. Should the Germans fall back to Antwerp, the Rhine Valley would be within comparatively easy raiding distance for Allied fliers. Thus, retirement from the coast would be a hard blow to German pride. Pan-Germans had insisted upon the retention of these ports as the first necessary step in attaining the German dream of world power.

There had been discord for months at German Grand Headquarters. Hindenburg had been in nominal, but Ludendorf was in actual command. The latter's failure had apparently encouraged the former to repudiate the Ludendorffian strategy. Not until the war ended would the world know who was responsible for one of the most fatal enterprises in military history—the German West Front campaign of 1918. Ludendorff's burden of accountability to the German people would be doubled if it should be established that he had devised the campaign. It was a gamble in which all that Germany had in military prestige and power was recklessly squandered. Had the Germans in March elected to stay on Hindenburg lines, they would not now

CAMBRAI AS THE GERMANS LEFT IT ON FIRE

BRITISH OFFICIAL PHOTO

SOME OF THE RUINS OF CAMBRAI

have been begging for peace. Allied unity of command would probably not have been achieved. The flow of American troops to France would not have been accelerated. The Macedonian front would not have crumbled. Germany would have had troops to spare to defend Macedonia and Palestine, and to keep Bulgaria and Turkey at least nominally contributing members of the Quadruple Alliance. She would also have had enough troops left to develop and organize her power in the conquered Russian provinces—perhaps to exploit those provinces to her own military benefit.

Germany's real hope lay in solidifying her grip in the East and in playing for a deadlock in the West. Hindenburg had favored that policy in the previous winter and so read the future better than Ludendorff. If he had now urged a more rapid German retirement in France, he had read the present better than Ludendorff. Under the Hindenburg plan the German armies could have retired to the French frontier at a minimum cost, but under the Ludendorff plan an armistice had to be sought in order to secure their safe and economical withdrawal. The German retirement from France was already under way. Events in the Champagne bore no other interpretation. Along the British front the fighting was still on the Hindenburg line, if we were to think of that line as a dozen or more miles wide. But the war of movement had not yet been fully attained. In the Champagne the German line had gone, and the war of movement there at least was in full swing.

Never before in the war had the Germans, looking at the situation as a whole, been in such desperate plight in a military way, and never before had the Allies fought with such *élan* and such uniform success. Military circles were agreed that the purpose of the German resistance was to afford their army a chance to fall back without disastrous loss to a new line of defense, through Lille to Valenciennes, Maubeuge, Avesnes, and Hirson on the Belgian frontier nearly east of St. Quentin. However, it was not likely that the Germans would be able to hold any of it. Perhaps a line, starting from the Dutch border, would run through Ghent and then to Valenciennes. It was no secret that Foch had completed operations preliminary to a tremendous effort which was to achieve a decisive stroke. He had maneuvered the enemy into positions which he desired them to occupy when the time arrived to overwhelm them at a place where further retirement would present a maximum of difficulties. Tremendous losses, increasing threat to communications and lack of material had placed the German army where its defeat on a colossal scale was impending.

It was doubtful if any powerful government had ever

© COMMITTEE ON PUBLIC INFORMATION   FRENCH OFFICIAL PHOTO

PRISONERS CAPTURED BY THE FRENCH IN A NIGHT RAID

undergone quite the humiliation which Germany had suffered. Even when it asked its government to make an official appeal for an armistice, the appeal was immediately scouted by all the Powers concerned. Public opinion was almost absolutely unanimous in the countries addrest that the request was a trick and Germany's profest readiness to accept Wilson's terms of peace a sham. Two of Wilson's fourteen stipulations had covered the restoration of Alsace-Lorraine and the setting up of an independent Poland; but the *Lokal Anzieger* of Berlin promptly served notice that those two points, in spite of an acceptance of the terms, would be ruled out in the discussion. In other words, when the German Government "accepted" Wilson's program as "a basis for peace negotiations," it intended to reserve the right to knock out any part which it did not like.

The genius of the German people had been described as attaining its richest fruition in its army, where was found an expression of all the great qualities which German modesty had been fond of monopolizing—loyalty, discipline, laboriousness, forethought, education. The Germans had put into their army the best of themselves—and now that German army had been defeated. That was the truth which events in the last six months had borne in upon German consciousness. Had Germany been starved into submission, had she been driven into defeat by exhaustion of man-power, had she succumbed to revolution from within, there would have been a measure of consolation for the War Lord and his adjutants. But Germany stood defeated through none of these weapons. She had been beaten by a weapon of her own choice and worship, the sword, which she had labored absorbingly for forty-four years to make sharp and true. Ultimately Germany's man-power was bound to dry up, her food supplies would vanish, her people would rise against their masters. But the simple fact was that none of these causes had yet operated, except in a minor degree, in the historic period from March 21, when Germany almost had victory within her grasp, to early in October, when Germany confest defeat.

Germany had faced her opponents in the west on March 21 with an army which we now know was stronger than the Allied armies then were by a quarter of a million men. At the end of the May offensive she was stronger, according to some observers, by half a million, and she was stronger in war material. Besides her own, she had a goodly portion of 2,700 cannon captured from the Italians at Carporetto and guns and munitions presented to her by the Bolsheviki. She had the advantage of a united command. By all tests, men, material, leadership, and morale, the Kaiser was assured of victory. But instead of victory William II met defeat, and the change was brought about by no miracle. It was doubtful whether the fighting forces of the Allies on July 15 outnumbered the Germans so heavily as the Germans outnumbered the Allies on March 21. And yet the Allies were now compelling Germany to sue for peace. This astounding result was brought about by stedfastness, prodigies of energy, unity, and inspired leadership. What the German army set out to do and failed to do, the Allied armies, with no superior initial advantage, accomplished.

Always as if praying that something would save him from a knockout, Ludendorff was retreating from the Lille salient, sidestepping at the St. Gobain massif, clinching at Cambrai, the Champagne and the Argonne. The British were holding their breach between Cambrai and St. Quentin, while tanks reconnoitered the open country. The Germans delivered six powerful counter-attacks in twenty-four hours, but the only result was to pile high the German dead, while the British stood firm. Prisoners said they had been told to hold at all cost while a new line running through Valenciennes was being built. Before the British armies could be seen the whole front ablaze with villages on fire. On the Belgian coast Germans were blowing up dugouts and removing heavy guns pell mell. Cambrai was taken on October 9, the final blow being administered by Canadian troops. "On the battlefield between Cambrai and St. Quentin we occupied positions to the rear, thereby giving up Cambrai," said the official Berlin confession. Cambrai was taken in an irresistible rush, after an unparalleled preparation with artillery fire by guns that stood almost wheel to wheel. It was the junction of no less than five railways and a pivot for the great German offensive that began near the end of March. The Germans had had no greater loss since the fateful July 18, when Foch struck his first blow. The advancing Allies, however, were aiming at other objectives than Cambrai, which was only a sign-post on their movement to the Belgian frontier. From Cambrai thirty miles northeast in a straight line was the fortress of Maubeuge, against which Kluck sought to pin the British Expeditionary Army in the first month of the war. Ten miles further on was the frontier. The British were now headed for Le Cateau.

So rapid were their movements that it was difficult to keep track of the front from day to day.

Canadian and British troops came together in the center of Cambrai entering from north and south. Many Germans had escaped, but hundreds who had been held there to launch a counter-attack were either killed or captured. Some were still in deep cellars, two stories underground, and in tunnels which the Germans had dug during their occupation. These were routed out and sent back to cages. South of the city armies rapidly overcame opposition. The Germans started to retreat soon after the attack began, and the front line for twenty miles began to move eastward. Airplanes, with which the sky was literally crowded, reported that Wambaix had been taken, and then Harcourt. Other tidings came of villages falling before the Allied advance, Selvigny, Caullery, Ligny, Montigny and Maretz, all quickly reached and passed, and soon the British were closing in on Caudry and Bertry. After the Cambrai-Le Cateau road was crossed, the railway between St. Quentin and Bertry was cut. It was clear that the enemy had been badly smashed, with British and Americans standing on the threshold of a wide, open country. Fast "whippet" tanks and armored cars performed valuable service in pursuing fleeing Germans, killing many and rounding up a large number. They smashed strong points held by rear-guards waiting for cavalry.

Philip Gibbs [23] drove through the whole depth of the advance made since August 8, every mile of it haunted by memories of bloody fighting, landmarks of broken brickwork, dead trees, or twisted iron, a place where British troops had done deadly things. Along roads and in ditches lay dead horses, overturned gun-limbers, and smashed guns. He had never seen a road so strewn with dead beasts, not even the Menin road in Flanders. Every yard showed shell-holes. Beyond were little towns quite unscathed by war and beautiful to see by eyes tired of all this ruin, with their whitewashed walls and red-tiled roofs. It was delightful to find them out there beyond that forty miles of misery, but it was more astonishing to find inhabitants in houses and shops, still smiling after four years of agony. They stood

[23] Correspondent of The *Times* (New York).

in little groups, staring with joyful eyes at the passing of British soldiers and British transports. Women would surround any soldier who could speak a little French and pour out gratitude for their deliverance.

The Germans left Cambrai a smoking ruin, and probably had never perpetrated a more ruthless or more premeditated act of vandalism than their destruction of that city. When the Canadians first entered, the great public square, the Place d'Armes, was virtually intact, the Allies having refrained from shelling it, but now it was a mass of ruins, due to explosions which began at 9 o'clock in the morning and continued all day in every part of the town. These explosions were due to incendiary bombs having time fuses attached, and were followed immediately by outbursts of fire. In one short street a dozen houses simultaneously burst into flames. The town hall, bishop's palace, and other buildings were blown to pieces. The cathedral escaped with its ruined chancel, but fire was found lapping the base of

PRINCE MAXIMILIAN OF BADEN

The Imperial Chancellor, who in October succeeded Count von Hertling and, on behalf of Germany, requested President Wilson to obtain from the Entente Allies an armistice

the great belfry tower. As the hours went by that day the universal character of the destruction was realized. It caused the sun to be obscured partly until it seemed like a fiery ball in a mass of smoke, and the thick dust of falling walls. Father Therez had remained in the city all that time. He was a priest of the Church of St. Druon. Two days before he had been ordered by the Germans to leave but refused because he had to attend to a dying woman. The Germans threatened to shoot him, but he persisted and after they went away cared for civilians who had hidden themselves for ten days in cellars.

Cambrai, sacked and burned by retreating Germans, was about the only illumination the American people then required for an intelligent reading of the German proposal of an armistice, and the maiden speech of Prince Max (the new Chancellor) in the Reichstag as to what he called the "remaking of the German soul." The new attitude of the Kaiser and his army was morally the same as that of wretches who had been shouting "*Kamerad*" and then shot in the back French and British soldiers to whom they surrendered. With one arm raised in supplication for peace, Germany was continuing, with the other, the inhuman outrages that had already made her rulers infamous.

We heard at this time an explanation, attributed to a high officer in the German army, that the wanton destruction of towns and cities was necessary "because it was the only way to stay the Allied advance." This was a larger development of the dastardly crime of placing French and Belgian women and non-combatants in front of German troops as a protection against fire. This destruction of French towns revived demands for the assessment of material loss on German cities and towns. No wanton destruction of German property was proposed, but the burden of restoration was to be transferred from the unhappy victims to the brothers and sisters of the German perpetrators of the outrages.

Cambrai being lost, Douai was uncovered. The British were now well in the rear of Douai and could easily envelop it from the southeast. When it fell the whole German line north through Lille to Courtrai would be turned. Ludendorff had not far to go to reach the Scheldt, from Antwerp west to Ghent, and then south through Tournai to Valenciennes. South of Douai and Cambrai the situation, was different. Here the deep German salient, of which Laon was the apex, was being steadily narrowed into a sack. It was already threatened by the advance of the British, Americans, and French east of Cambrai and Le Catelet. Following up the thrust, the Allies reached Bertry and Busigny. Bertry was only four miles west-southwest of Le Catelet. As Bohain was only eight miles northwest of Guise, the Allies were already on the point of breaking the line between Guise and Le Cateau. When they did this, they would have turned the whole west side of the Laon salient. Ludendorff's chief problem now was to extricate himself from the Laon trap. Gouraud's drive in Champagne was pressing armies toward the north and northwest. German lines of retreat were thus converging on congested roads. The crisis of the retreat would come when the La Fère-Aisne valley front gave way and the German armies became entangled in their rush for a new winter line which Ludendorff probably hoped to establish from Valenciennes east to Mézières and then up the Meuse, covering the Briey iron district to the neighborhood of Metz.

Besides what Americans had done to help Haig in breaking the Hindenburg line, the American army on the Meuse-Argonne front now was doing its ·best to add to the difficulties of the German retreat. It had pushed up the east side of the Meuse as well as the west side, in order to close the Meuse crossings. American troops had made a junction at Cornay, on the Aire River, at the northeastern tip of the Argonne, with a French column coming east through the Grand Pré gap, north of the Argonne. An American offensive on a large scale east of the Meuse, directed at the envelopment of Metz from the northwest, was still to be reckoned with. Ludendorff might succeed in establishing his new line from Valenciennes to Mézières and Sedan. But the preservation of his connections from Sedan to Metz might prove a heart-breaking problem for him after the American offensive in the Verdun section got going.

German armies in the north were in full flight. Cavalry was hustling them in what virtually amounted to a rout. So fast was the retreat that columns of Allied troops in parade formation passed through numerous villages, completely out of contact with the Germans. More than 10,000 prisoners and between 100 and 200 guns were captured in one day. Twenty-three German divisions—more than a quarter of a million men—were severely handled. The maximum depth of the advance was between eight and ten miles. Behind them the Germans left the country devastated, burning towns and villages as they went. On October 10 the retreat covered a thirty-five mile front between the Scarpe and the Oise, south of St. Quentin. The remnants of thirty broken divisions were going at full speed, cavalry closely pursuing them. Behind followed infantry marching rapidly in columns of fours through evacuated villages.

Haig reported that the whole Hindenburg system had been cleared on a thirty-five mile front and that the Allies were "operating far beyond and to the east." There was much confusion within enemy lines. Before two British armies elements from no fewer than twenty-nine divisions were identified along the twenty-mile fighting line. Such a concentration of troops seemed almost incredible until it was realized that some of these divisions had been engaged almost continuously since August 8, and many were mere shadows of old organizations. The ground was covered with dead men and horses. Many Germans were buried under tons of earth in collapsed dugouts. No rest had been given them. In addition to barrages falling on them, as they vainly tried to stem the onrush, British and American guns were hammering their rear lines, paying especial attention to roads. As darkness fell, the sky was dotted with British airplanes hovering over smoking and flaming battlefields or dropping bombs. Throughout the day they bombed roads, barracks, massed troops, and batteries. As the Germans fled from place to place fires began to break out behind them, and the ground rocked with terrific explosions as ammunition which they had no time to save was destroyed. Everything combustible in the area around Caudry, Inchy, Le Cateau, St. Benin, St. Souplet, Vaux-Andigny, and Bohain seemed to have been set on fire. Towns elsewhere were burned, north and south, as if the Germans were determined to lay the country in absolute waste. Airmen reported that "explosions were occurring in place after place." [24]

[24] Principal Sources: The *Tribune,* The *Evening Post,* The *Times,* New York; William L. McPherson in The *Tribune* (New York); The *Sun,* The *World,* New York; General Pershing's report to the War Department, Associated Press dispatches.

XI

LAON, LA FÈRE, AND LILLE TAKEN, AND THE BELGIAN COAST SET FREE—AMERICANS IN THE ARGONNE

October 12, 1918—October 28, 1918

IT was still evident that, if Haig could force the Germans back on a line running through Valenciennes, they would have to retire from the St. Gobain Forest and evacuate Laon, and ultimately all their positions on the upper Aisne. A favorite headline in German newspapers was, "We are staking everything." The German High Command was literally doing this in order to postpone, as long as possible, the evil day when an order for a general retreat should become inevitable. In the colossal battle still going on it was not for them any longer a question of local successes, or the defeat of one army, but the fate of four armies, those of Hutier, Bernhardi, Carlowitz, and Arnim, which, stretching from St. Quentin to the Aisne, were prest closely by British and Allied armies under Haig, Debeney and Mangin. On every front armies were yielding position after position and waiting with what composure they could for the day when, their flanks having been turned, they would have to retreat with all their material through a country which could provide a road and railway facilities adequate for the retreat, not of four armies, but of only one. Should they wait too long four of their armies would be between the hammer and the anvil, and two million men would have to retreat in desperate haste between Valenciennes and the Meuse, when a yard of space on a muddy, rutted road would become as precious to men as if it was paved with gold. Men would have to fight merely to get marching room.[25]

[25] Cable dispatch from Walter Duranty in The Times (New York).

The American First Army was still pushing north up the Meuse Valley east of the Argonne, where it had penetrated that part of the German secondary line known as the "Kriemhilde Stellung." The Germans had set fire to Dunsur-Meuse, which Pershing was approaching on both sides of the river. If Montmedy were taken, German armies in the north would be practically severed from those in Lorraine and Alsace, inasmuch as the only good railroad connection that would be left was a long and circuitous one by way of the Rhine, Aix-la-Chapelle, Liége and Namur. When a retreat actually began no one could tell where it would end or what it would lead to. The once invincible Ludendorff had been everywhere outmaneuvered. It was not pretended that his successive withdrawals had been voluntary or elastic; they had involved permanent losses exceeding half a million men, including 250,000 prisoners, thousands of cannon and thousands of machine-guns. The retreat by October had broken the spirit of the German people; a radical internal crisis was at hand. All reasonable men desired the speediest possible conclusion of the war, but before that day came the Teutonic war-lords had to be beaten on the very ground they had themselves chosen for the war in the very seat of their pride, in order that the superstition of their supreme ability as soldiers should be destroyed.[26]

The retreat under way was on a vast scale, with more men, guns, and war materials than history ever saw moved before. The one great problem of the German High Command was to keep a clear space between receding waves of Germans and onrushing waves of Allied avengers. East of Cambrai the British extended their gains, and further south the French advanced so far past St. Quentin that they seriously threatened the German hold on the St. Gobain massif. East of St. Quentin the French reached Mézières-sur-Oise, making an advance of five miles. Two thousand prisoners and a large number of guns were captured. American troops participated in the advance. Together with the British and Colonial divisions with whom they were operating, they had now got entirely through the Hindenburg defensive maze and were in the open country

[26] Cable dispatch from G. H. Perris to The *Times* (New York).

beyond. French and Americans had worked their way through defensive positions between Reims and the Meuse. Along the Argonne front had been encountered a defensive system twelve miles wide, tangled everywhere with barbed wire and bristling with machine-guns. Inch by inch the Americans had cut their way through and were now pressing on in the general direction of Sedan. Already they had reached Cornay, on the Aire, where they formed a junction with the French.

This advance of the French and Americans with that of French and British Colonials north and west endangered still further the German hold on Laon and La Fère, two cities to which the Germans were clinging with a desperation born of despair. Laon and La Fère were hinges for all German movements in northern France, but they could not hold out much longer as the French were pressing eastward from St. Quentin on one side and from Reims on the other. The best fighting material now left in the German armies was concentrated between St. Quentin and Cambrai and around Laon. On all parts of the front, behind their lines, the Germans were burning the French villages through which they were being driven. As the flames rose there sprang up also in France and England an ever higher wave of indignation which was rapidly assuming the shape of a demand for retaliation in kind against these Prussianized barbarians in that not far distant day when Allied fighters would be on German soil.

BRITISH EAST INDIAN TROOPS IN CAMP ON THE WESTERN FRONT

ON THE WESTERN FRONT

The great British victory on October 8 had attained a deeper sway than any previous offensive in the last half year. In two days the British had advanced nearly twelve miles in the direction of Le Cateau, and the effects of this penetration in the center were being registered north and south. The German line was yielding east of Lens, and Douai might soon join Cambrai and St. Quentin behind the Allied front. South of St. Quentin the French were occupying the entire western bank of the Oise. They had taken Mézières and, linking up northward with the British, would soon be in Ribemont and had Guise and Wasigny in immediate prospect. From Cambrai a great wedge had been driven into German positions, threatening toward the north, Valenciennes; toward the south, Laon and the Aisne Valley. A German retirement from the Laon salient was only a question of days. The British arm was swinging eastward across the great trunk railways upon which the Germans had to retire toward the Belgian border. When the Allied line reached Wasigny and Guise, a matter of three to five miles, the railway between Valenciennes and Laon would have been cut and connection between the Germans north and south of the Oise severed.

Now, it was the armies Gouraud and Berthelot which sent the enemy reeling back, and now, it was those of Rawlinson and Byng. The capture of Berry-au-Bac made the menace to the Germans on their left wing more acute than ever, and soon the peril would be acute on their right. The ominous thing for the Germans was that as the battle went on, the fury of the blows increased. Rawlinson and Byng had been fighting for two full months, but the blow which they delivered on October 8 was heavier than any of the others. When Haig had crossed the Oise around Guise, and the French the Aisne between Neufchâtel and Château Porcien, the end would be clearly in sight. By the end was meant the driving of Germans to the Belgian border. New American attacks east of the Meuse in the general direction of Montmédy and Longuyon were in preparation for a final stage in the great battle, which was expected to carry war into the enemy's territory. It was Foch's intention that, when the Germans got back to the line running from

Lille to Montmédy, they would find Americans and French waiting for them.

Prisoners along the front filled cages to overflowing, while dead Germans and dead German horses covered the ground everywhere. English, Scotch, New Zealand, French, and American troops that had participated in the advance escaped with light losses. Among hundreds of German dead in the Argonne an unusual proportion were found with only a single bullet wound, bearing out reports of the remarkable use the Yankees made of their rifles, against German machine-gunners. Staggering under the impact of a combined British, French, and American blow, the Germans were on the verge of utter route. In retreat eastward they were abandoning everything that would retard their flight, while Allied cavalry was cutting and slashing at their heels, and infantry was marching in the wake of horsemen in column formation. British and Americans on the outskirts of Le Cateau were approaching Solesmes. Southward, the French were bearing down on Ribemont. Allied progress had extended northward to the Scarpe. Detachments were reported to have entered Vitrey en Artois and Arleux, and to be headed for Douai. Inspired by the German Government's request to President Wilson for an armistice, of which they knew only as much as was contained in the Kaiser's order of the day, German divisions between Cambrai and St. Quentin were making one of the feeblest fights known since the Somme became a battlefield.

By October 11 Douai was flanked and was being evacuated by the Germans, whose retirement extended down through the Laon region at the great elbow in the line, and thence eastward beyond the Meuse where American troops were making life for them almost unbearable. Between Douai and St. Quentin the retreat became so rapid that pursuers frequently lost touch with the Germans. In the Champagne and as far east as the Meuse the retreat was to the north and at a slower rate as it gave more resistance. The French and Americans were aiming at the Valenciennes-Lille railway which ran east from Mézières to Metz. When this road was cut the whole German position in France would have to be evacuated. The British had now left Cambrai far behind and were pushing eastward from Le Cateau, crossing the Seille and making a maximum advance of five miles on a front of about thirty. Italian troops under Mangin had reached the Chemin-des-Dames in the region of Courtacon, which was being abandoned as rapidly as the Germans could get away. There was every indication that the massif of St. Gobain, from which the German big gun had shelled Paris, near the western end of the road, was no longer tenable. Its capture by the French was regarded as a

© UNDERWOOD & UNDERWOOD, N. Y.

A ZINC FACTORY NEAR DOUAI BEFORE IT WAS DESTROYED
BY THE GERMANS ON LEAVING THE CITY

matter of days, altho for years it had defied all efforts of the Allies to wrest it from the Kaiser's troops. The enemy front in this region, under assaults from Mangin's army and the army operating northwest of Reims, was seriously shaken despite energetic German resistance. Gouraud's poilus were driving the Germans toward the Suippe. In the Argonne Americans and French had captured a part if not all of Grandpré where they effected a junction. Practically all the Argonne Forest was in the hands of the Allies. The Germans had been compelled to abandon an enormous quantity of stores. The American First Army in clearing the forest had taken about 7,000 prisoners in three days. Ten thousand French—men, women and children—had been liberated by the Allied advance.

Cavalry joined in Gouraud's pursuit of Germans on October 11 and were the first to enter La Neuville. French and American troops at some points gained seven miles, Americans, notwithstanding a heavy bombardment of the region with mustard-gas shells, took Machault. Gouraud's troops advanced to the river Retourne, over most of its length, and took Savigny-sur-Aisne, only two and a half

© UNDERWOOD & UNDERWOOD, N. Y.

ZINC FACTORY NEAR DOUAI AFTER IT WAS DESTROYED

miles south of Vouziers, which was in flames, as were Guise and villages south of Laon. In the Champagne, the French and Americans, joining hands north of the Argonne in the Grandpré Gap, occupied the Grandpré station, while patrols entered the town itself. Northwest of Verdun Americans cleared out a little pocket in the direction of Sivry which had held them up a long time. Heavy artillery firing began west of the Meuse, started by Americans before daylight, while other Americans struck German lines east of the Argonne and captured villages. The ridge of Dame Marie was stormed after hard fighting, and more than 1,000 prisoners taken. Fighting infantry swept through the northern portion of the Argonne for nearly five miles with little opposition. By this advance they got a firmer grip on territory north of the broken Kriemhilde line. Gouraud, in conjunction with Berthelot, was steadily overcoming resistance from strong rear-guards, supplied with machine-guns. Counter-attacks were frequent, but the artillery-fire was generally confined to lighter pieces, as if the Germans were evacuating their big guns. Opposite Mangin they were resisting with strong artillery support, machine-guns and infantry. They evidently trusted to the fastnesses of the St. Gobain Forest to bar Allied progress, while they completed their evacuation along three lines of railroad still available from Laon.

All the big and little kings, grand dukes, and reigning princes in Germany were summoned to Berlin at this critical time as if to sit in an inquest on Ludendorff's strategy. His staggering losses in the colossal gamble had not yet been liquidated. That was the real situation for the council to deal with. The masquerade of "democracy and parliamentarism" in Germany which was being staged for impressionable pacifists outside of Germany was now dropt as a side issue, the great question being how to get German armies back to the Belgian border, and then across the Rhine. If they could be got back under the safe conduct of an armistice, as a preliminary to peace, Germany might continue her subjection to Hohenzollernism, whatever camouflaged form of government she might establish. But if they did not get back, spas in Switzerland promised to be crowded with German kings, grand dukes and dukes of lesser degree, all experiencing a state of exile. While Ludendorff, the quartermaster, was at this council, his armies were continuing their "victorious retirement," the Allies taking Le Cateau and closing in on Guise, British and American troops being only six miles away. The French had crossed the Oise below Guise and were approaching the town.

South of Laon the French had cleared all but a small section at the eastern end of the Chemin-des-Dames—that between Cerny-en-Laonnois and Craonne. The Germans were on the point of evacuating the forest of St. Gobain, now nearly surrounded. After it went Laon would go. In Champagne Gouraud's army was within two miles of Vouziers. East of Laon each German army had now to shift for itself in retreat northeast toward the Belgian frontier. Nowhere since the beginning of the war did Germans show less of their old fighting spirit than south of Cambrai, where Haig forced a gap in their lines. After they were beaten on the Marne in July, they had withdrawn virtually at their own gait, offering obstinate resistance every mile of the way. But now east of the Scheldt they were thrown into disorderly retreat, and British troops in their advance over a wide area encountered no opposition. The picture of British regiments marching rapidly forward in columns of fours through villages that the Germans had evacuated was not that of an army facing serious obstacles. The enemy was in plain flight.

No one could foresee from day to day where Foch's plans might lead. On the Meuse, in the Champagne, in Picardy and in Flanders, his armies were fast crowding the Germans back. French and Americans north of the Argonne held Vouziers at their mercy, and along the entire Champagne front were pushing northward. The French had almost cleared the Chemin-des-Dames. From south and north French and British had cut in behind Laon. In their rapid advance through Cambrai and Le Cateau the British penetrated within ten miles of Valenciennes. The occupation of Douai and Lille was a matter of days. Clear to the North Sea the German front was cracking. A break through by the Allies in the Argonne, in Champagne or in Picardy would cut railroad lines of communication of first importance to the Germans and spell disaster. Their whole position from the sea to Verdun had been shaken and their only hope of safety lay in a general and more rapid retreat. Beaten and demoralized, outgeneraled and outfought, they had now to quit France as best they could.

According to German legends, somewhere in Thuringia, in a deep cavern of Kyffhauser Mountain, guarded by a flock of hoarse-crowing ravens, sat Frederick Barbarossa, his flaming red beard grown deep into the fissures of an old stone table. The ancient legend had it that, in the extreme hour of Germany's need, this hero would arise and gird on his crusader's sword and step forth once more to save his land. One could well imagine at the present crisis a delegation from the Kaiser, in frock coats and shiny hats, Herr von Kühlmann, Professor Delbruck, Admiral von Tirpitz, and Herr Scheidemann, arriving at the cave's mouth and timorously laying before the hero a memorandum of Germania's necessities and an appeal on behalf of Pan-Germanism for his aid. One might wonder what the old man's answer would be, he who had stalked across the world conquering it, not for Teutonism, but for the medieval conception of a League of Nations, of which Petrarch sang, and which was called the Holy Roman Empire. It was probable that he would growl back at these strange, frock-coated successors of a mighty era, and that for their like he would not stir, as Thuringian rock-fastnesses echoed and re-echoed his deep-growling contempt.

On October 12 President Wilson marched at the head of the American Division at a great Liberty Loan parade in New York, and received an ovation such as no President had ever before been accorded. He took his position ahead of the American contingents at Seventy-second Street and remained with the parade until the head reached the disbanding point in Washington Square. Police estimated that more than 500,000 persons cheered him on his way down Fifth Avenue. Some twenty odd nationalities were represented in the parade. On that day Teutonic legions in Europe were on the run, and Pershing's hosts in France numbered nearly 2,000,000. American troops were fighting from Flanders to the Vosges, and the President in a memorable note had just made a counter-thrust against a much-heralded German peace offensive. In these circumstances Mr. Wilson was greeted as a victorious President who had met a great obstacle and overcame it. The total subscriptions to this Liberty Loan were announced at the end of October over $6,800,000,000. The subscribers numbered over 21,000,-000. The largest previous subscription ever recorded anywhere to a public loan was $4,900,000,000 made to the British Government's loan of February, 1917, but that loan was separated by more than a year from any other single great subscription, whereas the United States Government had already obtained, in two "loan drives," actual payments of $7,978,000,000 in the twelve months before this $6,000,-000,000 loan was offered. That it should have been so handsomely oversubscribed, under all these circumstances, put the episode in the place which it ought to occupy, as a sequel to what our country had done in placing a powerful and effective fighting force in France at the exact moment when it was needed, in upsetting the submarine program by furnishing new ships and in breaking the menace of famine among our Allies.

After overcoming machine-gun posts, French advance-guards occupied Vouziers on October 11 and found that the Germans had burned a great quantity of stores and munitions. From the eastern border of the Argonne to Guise the whole countryside had burst into flames. German savagery was wreaking the vengeance of despair on towns and villages. It seemed as if the military chiefs were trying deliberately to put a barrier of hatred before the olive branch that had been so eagerly proffered by the German civil authorities.

The British advance on October 13 brought them to the gates of Douai. To the south the French had blotted out La Fère, Laon, and the greater portion of the St. Gobain Massif. It was generally forecast that the loss of these positions would make it impossible for the Germans to hold the Meuse line. Gourard's army had reached the bend of the Aisne south of Rethel and Château-Porcien and Rethel, an important base, were directly menaced. The French were only a little over twenty miles from Mézières, from which the Crown Prince a few days before had removed his headquarters in haste. The whole Laon salient, in fact, had given way. By crossing the Oise at many points above La Fère the French had cut direct connections between Laon and Guise. The latter city was the southern anchor of the line which Ludendorff was now trying to hold. All the way from La Fère to the Argonne the Crown Prince's group of armies were in hurried retreat and the fall of Douai had lain Valenciennes open to attack. The big German fighting machine was beginning to function awkwardly and painfully. No line of safety for it was in sight, even on the French and Belgian border; hence Germany wanted a truce.

In accordance with his strategy of continued action on all fronts, Foch now struck at the weakened German line in Flanders. Ludendorff's inability to hold the Belgian coast, or to stay on in the Lille salient, had been evident ever since the Belgians, British and French struck east from Ypres in September and reached the line of the Lys River and the road between Menin and Roulers. The drive toward Courtrai and Ghent was now resumed. On a twenty-mile front, curving from Comines, on the Lys, to a point above Roulers, British, French and Belgian troops broke through German positions. Roulers was quickly taken and an advance of five miles or more was made east and southeast of that city. There remained only one route —a very indirect cne—from Lille and Courtrai to the Belgian coast, by way of Ghent, and that line was under fire from Lendelede. Courtrai was twelve miles northeast of Lille. The envelopment of Lille from the north was approaching completion and a German retreat in the north to the line of the Scheldt was inevitable. This retreat would not only free the great French industrial centers of Lille, Roubaix, and Tourcoing, but liberate Bruges and the entire Belgian coast. On the southern front the French had advanced seven miles north of Laon and cut the Laon-Guise railroad. Guise and Rethel were about to fall. Without waiting for an armistice the German armies in this sector were everywhere heading in confusion toward the Belgian frontier.

A thrilling race was under way between Germans fleeing out of the Laon pocket and the Allies closing in from the northwest, along the Oise and from the southeast, along the Aisne. Two lines of railway paralleling two principal highways were open to the Germans from Laon. One ran north along the valley of the Serre through Verins to Hirson; the other northeast, through Rozoy to Rumigny and Mézières. The uncertain factor was how big a start the Germans had had out of Laon. The city had been entered without resistance, which meant that the Germans had left in sufficient time to make up a handicap of about ten miles against Allies pressing in from the flanks.

One of the last great German strongholds in France was in the hands of the Allies when the St. Gobain Massif, which formed the corner-stone of the enemy's defensive system, was wrested from the invaders on October 12. With the fall of this region both Laon and Le Fère were occupied. Having passed these cities, the French and Italians were advancing on the whole thirty-five mile front between the Oise and the Aisne. The Allies were thus within less than twenty miles of the vital enemy center of Hirson, at the western tip of the Ardennes, seizure of which would definitely have split the German armies. French troops, advancing eastward in the Guise region, were about seventeen miles from Hirson, while those pushing northeast from Laon were within eighteen miles of it.

Peace talk continued to pervade the air, but it was falling on deaf ears as far as armies in the field were concerned. Instead of a relaxation in the fighting, new hostilities, on what seemingly was a major scale, were being carried out by the British, French, and Belgians in Belgian Flanders. The greatest resistance of all was faced by Americans on both sides of the Meuse where vicious counter-attacks were being delivered, their fierceness indicating that fresh forces had been brought into the fray.

Laon was outwardly little damaged. The cathedral and other public buildings were intact, but houses and shops had been completely emptied of their contents. Thousands of inhabitants who had borne the enemy yoke for nearly four years complained of the compulsory labor to which every able-bodied adult and youth was subjected. Mangin had a great reception when he entered the town, children wearing tricolor ribbons and waving extemporized flags, and old folk laughing and crying in their joy at being delivered. Mangin had freed 6,000 from slavery—people who had been not only despoiled of their household goods, money, and other possessions, but robbed of their time. Requisitioned labor had been paid for, not by the Germans themselves, but in orders on the Mayor, so that Laon paid for the labor done by its own citizens for the benefit of the Germans. No discrimination was made between persons of different classes and conditions. All had to bend to the German will. The pillage of Laon began early in the war with the arrival of the first troops, who looted every house and building that was not inhabited, and later extended the pillage to houses that were inhabited. Pillage reached its height on the departure of the General Staff of the German army on whom responsibility was clearly fixt. All the furniture in the City Hall was taken, that in private houses being "requisitioned" sometimes and sometimes simply taken. Five million eight hundred thousand francs ($1,160,000) in cash was the sum exacted from the town, part of it under the guise of a "contribution" and part as fines.

The principal resistance on the entire front was experienced north of the Argonne, east of the Aire. Here the Americans were fighting along with French, both on their right and left flanks. How great was the importance attached by the Germans to holding back the Americans was shown in an order of Marwitz, commander-in-chief of their Fifth Army. "It is on the unconquerable resistance of the Verdun front," said this order, "that depends the fate of a great part of the Western Front, perhaps even of our nation." "The object of this attack," the order continued, "is to cut the Longuyon-Sedan line, the most important artery of the Army of the West. Moreover, it is the enemy's intention to render it impossible for us to exploit the Briey Basin, on which our steel production largely depends."

The crossing of the Aire was performed under great difficulties. When engineers attempted to throw a bridge across the fifty-foot stream they were halted by hand grenades from Germans in trenches not more than one hundred yards away. Our engineers worked repairing crossings as fast as German shells damaged them. The American sector was the key to the German line from west of Laon to east of the Meuse. This made it one of the vital spots of the whole front from the sea to the Moselle. If the Americans once got through here all German communication through Mézières would be imperiled. While

Mézières was not directly north of the American Army, our advance meant that this center would have to fall, which in turn meant that the foe would lose his supply lines at least on a third of the whole salient from the sea to the Moselle. This would force a retirement all along the line. The Germans knew they had to hold back the Americans to avert a military disaster.

In spite of drenching rains, Belgian, French, and British armies continued their drive in Flanders. Belgians pushed north and captured Thourout, eight miles due north of Roulers and ten miles east of Dixmude. It was a strategic point of great importance, since it lay at the apex of an equilateral triangle, one side of which ran northeast to Bruges and the other northwest to Ostend. From Thourout the Belgians could threaten the entire rear of the German positions on the North Sea coast. They had to advance four or five miles further northeast to bring the Ghent-Bruges-Ostend railroad under fire and this was the main supply-line of the coast garrisons. The British had reached the outskirts of Menin and pushed to within two miles of Courtrai and thus were drawing a net around Lille from the north and northeast. In the meantime British forces west of Lille were closing in on that city. In the Laon sector the French, in pursuit of the Crown Prince of Prussia's armies, had almost reached the Serre, which flows east into the Oise a little north of La Fère. Debeney's army, marching northeast, had cleared the south bank of the Serre for some distance east of the Oise. Mangin's army, marching north, was aiming at Crécy-sur-Serre, about eleven miles northeast of Laon. Further east Berthelot's army had passed Sissone and Gouraud's army was across the Aisne at nearly every point except Rethel. The way was still clear for the retreating Germans. But they could not shake themselves free from Foch's pressure without incurring grievous losses. The Allied attack in Flanders on October 17 netted 10,000 prisoners and 200 guns. Next day a new victory brought Allied soldiers to the gates of Courtrai.

Nobody who had not seen the amount of transport needed for a single army corps could realize the immense accumulations needed to support the great armies Germany had in the field. Their communication lines behind the battle-front had long been barely adequate and were sorely strained by a growing shortage of grease, a deterioration of rolling-stock, and the impossibility of maintaining the roadbed at par. The situation grew worse as huge losses of guns and munitions weakened the front. Wounded men in scores of thousands had to take up the space on trains, and the time needed for other operations. The inevitable followed; the Allies broke the "impregnable" fortifications built to protect the arteries through which flowed the life-blood of the German army. By the capture of the St. Gobain Massif and the Hindenburg and Champagne positions the Allies had rolled the Germans back upon their communications. What that meant was failure and defeat. Not only were many railroads and highways under Allied fire; not only were important junctions and depots within easier reach of deadly bombing planes, but an overburdened transportation system had to carry a double load—the material of retreat, in addition to everything needed to maintain resistance.

It was a hopeless task and each new blow by the Allies gave further proof of it.[27] As long as the enemy held the Laon plateau and the massif of St. Gobain, he was solidly entrenched in France and a constant menace to Paris. The Laon plateau was the foundation-stone of the central pivot of his whole ·aggressive and definitive effort on the Western Front. Now that he had been compelled to give it up, France began to sing her magnificat. For Germany the loss marked the end of a dream of fifty years' duration. For France it was the end of a prolonged, agonizing nightmare. The rest of the German line would have to follow suit. That the last living German would be out of France within a month was the universal belief of Paris. We might now expect at any moment to see the Germans quit Lille, the largest French city they had oc-cupied, evacuate all the region between Lys and the Scheldt, retreat from the Belgian coast and stand behind the Scheldt from Condé in France to Ghent.

[27] Cable dispatch from Walter Duranty to The *Times* (New York).

Far from improbable was a rumor attributing to Hindenburg the initiative in Germany's plea for an armistice. German sources of munitions and other war materials were beginning to fail. After all her melting down of captured cannon, church-bells and door-handles, she had reached the end. Hindenburg's policy of blood and iron had collapsed for lack of blood and iron. The story of the tanks was corroborative on this point. Germany had failed to build tanks of her own to meet Allied tanks. Instead she had opposed machine-guns to the Allied moving fortresses. Germany had never been averse to borrowing Allied ideas. She had borrowed the submarine and the airship, the method of breaking through, and the method of surprize. It was hard to escape the conclusion that she lacked the raw material necessary for tank-building.

To the American army between the Meuse and the Argonne had fallen the least share of the glory that came with sharp break-throughs and rapid pursuits, but that army had its share in the glory that came from a vital task manfully accomplished. The American army had to face the stiffest German resistance because American success threatened the Germans with a quick fatality. The whole Allied forward movement from the North Sea to the Meuse was the swinging back of a huge door, with Belgians, British, and French pushing irresistibly against the broad surface of the door, while the Americans on the Meuse were hammering at the hinges. If the hinges gave way that meant German disaster. Before the German frontier was reached, the door in the north would have to swing back eighty miles from Ostend to Antwerp, sixty miles from Courtrai to Brussels, sixty miles from Solesmes to Namur, fifty-five miles from Rethel to Mézières. But less than twenty miles from where the Americans stood would bring them to Montmédy and Longuyon, which meant .the cutting of German communications and the loss of the Briey region. That was why German resistance was so desperate in front of Liggett's men. Having seen at Château-Thierry what they could do in the way of keeping a door shut, Foch had given the Americans the chance of showing what they could do in the way of bursting a door open.

Whatever the future might have in store for Germany, she was already passing through the valley of humiliation. Resolutions adopted by Conservatives in the Prussian Diet announced the coming of "the hour of the Fatherland's greatest distress." Defeat had entered the German soul, and was carrying with it bitterness and despair. Expressions of the German press were amazing in admissions of impending and unavoidable disaster. Old Prussia, the Junker *Kreuz Zeitung* mournfully acknowledged, was no more, "having been pierced to the heart by the sword of Socialism and Democracy." Most extraordinary language was used respecting the penalties Germany might have to pay. One paper called upon Germans to prepare themselves to think of Alsace-Lorraine as hereafter "outside the framework of the empire." Another pictured a coming Slav power, stretching southwest from Danzig—implying that this port was to cease to be German. Another said that the only refuge left for Germany was a place in the League of Nations, altho even there she could only hope to enter as "a belittled Germany." "Prussia is dead," said one Berlin paper, to which the New York *Times* replied, "Prussia is not dead, Prussia is playing possum." Germans were not meeting Armageddon with either dignity or nobility. There was something puerile in the complaining. We had seen the French threatened for four years and some months with irremediable ruin, but standing, undaunted as if in the shadow of the great national catastrophe. We had seen the British "with their backs to the wall" called upon by Haig to fight to the end. Invaded and menaced Italy had been seen standing up under a hurricane of blows without whimpering. But military Germany defeated became a Germany poor in spirit. The world could have had more respect even for people stained by cruelty and crime, if they had behaved more like men when the hour of retribution came.

On October 14 was begun the second stage of the American battle for the remaining portion of the Kremhilde line from Grandpré to the Meuse, the conquest of which would ultimately force the Germans back to the Mézières line. Control of the Côte Châtillon was the key to great stretches north and northwest. The hill was the last of three keys, all of which had been bitterly defended. The capture of Grandpré was accomplished under terrific hardships and with a heroism not hinted at in the brief official announcement of the taking of this stronghold. Grandpré lay on the north bank of the Aire and on the slope of hills leading up to the heights of the Bois de Bourgogne. It was heavily defended by machine-guns. In a blinding rain on October 17 our engineers got two new bridges across a swollen stream. While machine-guns and light artillery prevented reinforcements from getting into Grandpré, infantry advanced from the eastward and, after bloody hand-to-hand fighting, cleaned out the Germans. With enfilading fire from a stronghold further east, our troops occupied two hills commanding the Bois des Loges. Still further east they took Musarde Farm. The day's advance helped to take the pocket of German positions in the Forest de Soult that formed the strong defense between the Fourth French Army and the First American Army and was an all-important railroad center to the heart of what was known as the main artery of the western army.

The haggard and worn appearance of rescued French people told plainly enough of the hard life they had gone through. The pathetic eagerness with which they took off their hats in salute to any one in an officer's uniform, was eloquent of the discipline under which they had lived for four years and of the dragooning they had endured under Prussian militarism. Caudry, Le Cateau, and Bohain were all manufacturing towns in which the population lived almost entirely by lace-making and other textile industries. Here the German invaders wrecked looms and other weaving machinery. Many factories were smashed and broken just for the mere pleasure of seeing the wreckage; there was no visible motive for it. The populations were convinced it had for its sole purpose an intention to destroy the industries of France. Death by shooting was the punishment for numerous offenses, including that of giving aid to British prisoners or destroying crops. At Caudry a girl of fourteen was sent to prison for twenty-one days for giving a British soldier a piece of bread. French peasants

117

spoke with tear-filled eyes of the barbarities inflicted. Many soldiers died from weakness and starvation. When poor fellows were so feeble they were unable to walk, it was a common sight to see German soldiers, under instructions from Prussian officers, prick them with bayonets or beat them with rifle-butts. Observing French kept records of all these affairs, with the names of the Germans who had a part in them.[28]

French cavalry on October 15 were approaching Thielt, seven miles from the Ghent-Bruges Canal, the canal itself being only ten miles from the Dutch border. By this time the German retreat had become so rapid that French, British and Belgian infantry lost touch with them in the center. The despoilers of all that country had been driven from a large section which they had occupied since the early days of the war. They were in full flight from northern Belgium. Beaten disastrously, threatened with utter defeat, they were leaving the country with the utmost speed on a wide front. Half of Belgium had been recovered, including the naval bases in the north. Antwerp, far to the east, offered the next line of defense for the Germans, who were suffering from the inherent faults of Ludendorff's strategy in the spring and early summer. Ludendorff had promised them victory by the use of shock-divisions at given points formed by depletions of other points. Attack after attack had been pushed home but to the point of German exhaustion, and then the Allies were able to bar the road. When Foch saw that the German army was sufficiently exhausted, he struck, and since then (July 18) Ludendorff had had no respite. Instead of intermittent offensives launched after long preparations, the Allied attacks were continuous. Germans to whom a victorious end of the war was promised before August, had been hammered incessantly for three months and compelled to make wide and costly retirements.

No less serious to the Germans was the shortage that had ensued in their material. Numerous captured orders bore witness to their lack of munitions. The words "strictest economy" recurred with ominous frequency. In three

---

[28] Cable dispatch from Perry Robinson to The *Sun* (New York).

months the Allies had destroyed or captured over 5,000 cannon—a full quarter of the total artillery force of Germany. At the same time forced "combing out" of workmen from German factories had seriously lowered production and this weakness was becoming daily more pronounced and dangerous. Germany's last hope was an armistice. Nothing else remained to avert further disaster, or its alternative complete surrender.[29] When the First American Army, which had earned fame at St. Mihiel and was now pressing the Germans through the Kremhilde line, was barely two months old, a Second American Army appeared

[29] Cable dispatch from Walter Duranty to The *Times* (New York).

THE AMERICAN FLAG ON MT. BLANC

Chamonix's Mayor and others are saluting it. This peak of the great mountain mass has been named after President Wilson

in the field and it was not to be long before a Third American Army would make its appearance. In the meantime there was to be no cessation in the flow of American troops into France. The growth of the American forces in eastern France had enabled Foch to withdraw a French army from his center and send it to Flanders, where, in conjunction with Belgians, British, and a few Americans, it formed a group under the supreme command of King Albert.

Had it not been for the work of the American Relief Committee, the people of Laon and other invaded regions would long before this have suffered actual famine. The Germans had turned to their own advantage this philanthropic work. By combining it with their system of requisitions, taxation, and fines, they were able to procure labor from the French without cost to themselves. At the same time they had been appropriating all the natural and accumulated wealth of the country. As far as possible, people were compelled to change French coin or notes into German paper money. Able-bodied men, under pressure of fines, were compelled to labor at a pittance which the municipality was required to pay in municipal notes. Under a pretense of continuing French taxation on the old scale, the whole community was subjected to a levy, ostensibly to pay the costs of a German administration, altho in a civil sense there was no administration, no public service, no social organization, and no protection. The municipality had to issue several millions of francs of paper money on its own credit for these purposes. People were compelled to sell to the Germans for their nearly worthless paper copper utensils, and all other articles particularly wanted. The town was twice fined $25,000 because aviators had thrown bombs on it. Laon was situated on a lonely hill and fell simply by threat of envelopment, without fighting. Only a hundred German soldiers were found there. Hence there had been no military excuse for its destruction.

Ostend, which had been a submarine base and German naval stronghold for four years, was occupied on October 17 by Allied forces who came from the sea, the land and the air. King Albert and Queen Elizabeth soon entered the city. Bruges, fifteen miles east of Ostend and the key to the whole coast line, was entered by Belgian cavalry advancing from both sides. When Zeebrugge was abandoned, the Belgian coast had been practically cleared of the enemy who were fleeing toward new defenses behind Antwerp. Douai had now been entered by the British, Lille had been occupied, and Courtrai taken. More than twenty villages in Belgium were taken on October 17. The fall of Lille took from the Germans the last of the bastions which for years had held up their defensive system from the North Sea to Switzerland. After Cambrai, Laon, and

THE LILLE STATUE IN PARIS

The crowd had gathered after hearing news that Lille had been evacuated
by the Germans

St. Quentin, Lille completed the list. It was the largest city the Germans had held in France. Since it was taken early in the war, it had never been greatly threatened by the Allies. Before the war it had a population of nearly 200,000, and sent products to every corner of the earth.

After the fall of Menin and Courtrai, Lille could not be held. With Roubaix and Tourcoing it had been a prize so rich for the Germans that its relinquishment was obviously dictated by imperative military reasons. It presented a sad spectacle. In August, 1914, some hundreds of houses near the principal square had been destroyed. Explosions wrecked many others. Masses of débris still filled some of the streets. The municipal theater and schoolhouses were destroyed. It had been stript of copper, tin, wool, and mattresses. Besides paying fines amounting to more than 90,000,000 francs, it had suffered from wanton robberies. The whole city took on a delirium of joy over its deliverance. There still remained 120,000 inhabitants, but the Germans had carried off all the male population more than fourteen years of age. News of its deliverance aroused deep and quiet joy in Paris. Flags were hung out, and a crowd of refugees from the region paraded to the Lille statue in the Place de la Concorde, where they sang the "Marseillaise" and decorated the statue with Allied flags.

The fine old city, with its broad avenues and streets and parks, in which all the leaves were turning to crinkled gold, was everywhere draped with the flags of Great Britain and France, flags these people had kept hidden when it had been a prison offense for any French civilian to be discovered with one. One of the terrors of the German occupation had occurred just before Easter in 1916, when 8,000 young women were forcibly seized and sent away to work in fields hundreds of miles from their homes, a reign of terror for every girl in Lille and for their parents. Different quarters of the town were chosen for the conscription. With machine-guns posted at each end of the street, families were ordered to gather in doorways when German officers came around and made an arbitrary choice, saying to one girl, "You," and to another "You," and then ordered men to take them away. Some of these girls were dragged out of their beds and carried off screaming. They were from all conditions of life. Now and then one escaped by threatening to kill herself rather than go, for it was to enter upon a life of misery and horror for any girl of decent instincts. One afterward described how she had spent six months in this forced labor, had had no change of linen in all that time and had slept on a truss of straw in an old barn, with men who were put into the same barn with girls.

All the machinery was removed from great textile factories which had made the wealth of Lille. From Lille,

Roubaix and Tourcoing millions of pounds worth was taken. What could not be taken was smashed. It was a deliberate plan to kill the industry of northern France. Again and again citizens declared that the Germans were "robbers." They "stole everything we had that was worth anything to them," was often said, "old brass, our metal of all kinds, our linen, clocks, draperies. They even took the bells out of our churches, and that is why there are no bells ringing to-day because of our deliverance."

Lille, on October 28, opened wide her gates in formal reception to a division of the Fifth British Army. She paid a supreme tribute of gratitude to Great Britain for her release from the heavy hand of German bondage. No victors could have had better reward. When Lille was freed, the British had chivalrously stept aside and requested French troops to be the first to enter the capital of the Department of the North. The British Division selected to represent the whole army, in entering Lille, consisted of Territorials who had played a gallant part in driving the invaders from the city. These troops marched from one end of the metropolis to the other, amid wildly cheering throngs. Thousands of Allied flags covered buildings. Everywhere red, white and blue were predominant in the national colors of France, Great Britain and the United States. Lille had few American flags to use, but housewives applied themselves industriously to making them, and so the sister republic across the sea was generously represented.

Douai, in its waste and desolation, was a sad sight. The streets were filled with furniture and articles of all kinds. It was as if all the insane asylums had been opened and madmen in their fury had taken delight in destroying everything. The material losses were incalculable. The stained-glass windows in the Church of St. Peter had been smashed and the great organ broken up. Religious ornaments were scattered about the floor. The city hall, where the German commandant had his quarters, was sacked. Most of the paintings in the museum were taken away.

Roubaix and Turcoing celebrated their deliverance as if the day were an American Christmas, New Year's Eve, and

Fourth of July rolled into one. Tears of joy intermingled with shouts of laughter while the population sang, danced, and waved flags. The two cities, near neighbors, went wild with emotional joy. There were kisses, hugs, and handshakes for every British soldier who entered. On the windows housewives pasted pictures of French and British military celebrities torn from magazines. The swashbuckling Germans had gone, leaving in their wake as much ruin as they could effect. Nearly every home had been sacked, and things that could not be carried away were destroyed. Piqued at being forced to leave the towns, they went to extreme lengths to defile, destroy, and steal. Roubaix and Turcoing were systematically burglarized, Roubaix suffering the most. These Germans cut fine leather seats from chairs, ripped pictures from frames, and took

SOME OF THE RUINED PARTS OF LILLE

cloth coverings from mattresses. They went through fine old homes with the idea of seeing how much they could wreck. In many places they went into houses and deliberately broke up everything they could lay their hands upon. For miles around Roubaix and Turcoing the countryside was singed and scorched. with the red heat of war. Broken-up cannon, bursted rifles, pieces of shell, barbed wire, bayonets and other equipment of soldiers were scattered all about. There were miles of mangled fields where shell craters were so thick that it was impossible to tell where one began and the other left off.[30]

[30] Principal Sources: General Pershing's report to the War Department; The *Times*, The *Sun*, New York; William L. McPherson in The *Tribune* (New York); The *World*, The *Evening Post*, New York; Associated Press dispatches.

XII

BELGIAN LANDS AND CITIES RECOVERED

September 29, 1918—October 30, 1918

ALL northwestern Belgium by the middle of October was being rapidly cleared of Germans. British and Belgian forces had occupied Zeebrugge and Heyst, crossed the Ghent-Bruges Canal, and reached the Dutch frontier where about 15,000 Germans, cut off from their retreat by the advance from Ecloo, had withdrawn into Holland and been interned. Soon Thielt fell and then Solesmes. Since the Belgians and British began operations in Flanders, on September 29, in order to force back the German left wing in the Champagne and Argonne, they had made an advance of more than thirty miles over a thirty-six mile front, and had cleared all of western Flanders, as well as the Belgian North Sea coast, of Germans. Here and in northern France, where French and British were cooperating, with some assistance from Americans, a chain of noble cities within a few days had been recovered—Ostend, Bruges, Lille, Douai, Roubaix, Turcoing, Courtrai—all of which had been under German domination since the invasion of August, 1914.

In the final operation for recovering Belgium, Americans had a part. Not only was Pershing able to continue the battle in the Argonne, but our Thirty-seventh and Ninety-first Divisions were hastily withdrawn from our own front and dispatched to help in Belgium. Detraining in the neighborhood of Ypres, these divisions advanced by rapid stages to the fighting line where they were assigned to places adjacent to French corps. On October 31, in continuation of the Flanders offensive, "they attacked," said Pershing, "and methodically broke down all enemy resistance." On November 3 the Thirty-seventh completed its mission by driving the Germans across the Escaut River and firmly establishing itself along the east bank. By a clever flanking movement troops of the Ninety-first Division captured Spitaals Bosschen, a difficult wood extending across the central part of the sector, reached the Escaut, and then penetrated into the town of Audenarde. It was at Audenarde in 1708 that Marlborough gained one of his victories over the French. These divisions, said Pershing, received high commendations from their corps commanders for their dash and energy.

On entering Ostend, British and Belgians found that the

SOLDIERS' QUARTERS IN DIXMUDE

old warship *Vindictive,* which the British had sunk, in April, in the harbor to make it useless as a German sea-base, was still lying aslant across the mole. Before leaving, the Germans had sunk three more vessels, including a mail steamer and a dredger, but there was still room for small craft to pass in and out. Ostend itself was little damaged. Fine summer hotels, familiar to thousands of tourists before the war, were still standing, but harbor-works, like the mole and the sea-front, had been elaborately organized for defensive purposes. In Ostend were still living 25,000 out of 45,000 people, practically all of whom were massed on the sea-front, when, on a late October day, the King and Queen of the Belgians landed with Sir Robert Keyes in a motor-launch from his flagship and were greeted with overwhelming enthusiasm. As they went through the streets, they were closely prest by cheering crowds, eager to touch their garments and kiss their hands so that at times they could hardly move. The King wore the uniform of a Belgian officer, the Queen an oilskin coat and cap, and as they walked together arm in arm, every one was singing either the "Brabançonne" or the "Marseillaise." [31]

Ostend, however, had narrowly escaped the fate of Noyon, Cambrai, and dozens of other towns that had been destroyed. For this a reason was found. Some German soldiers who had been left behind, with orders to explode mines and wreck the town, were discovered helplessly drunk. The mines had already been placed in position but on finding themselves released from control, the German soldiers, instead of exploding the mines, had laid themselves out for a royal debauch, the effects of which were at a climax when the Belgian soldiers dashed in. After the drunken Germans were sobered up by methods more effective than kind, they were told they must immediately put their planted mines out of action. Several objected on the ground that they would be shot if found guilty of such "treachery." "You'll be shot if you don't," was the reply. Whereupon the Germans saw the wisdom of compliance, and within an hour or two all the explosive machinery had been rendered harmless. The inhabitants had suffered greatly from scarcity of clothes. Fifty dollars had become the price of a pair of shoes of the poorest quality, and $200 the price of a shoddy suit. Children and many adults were wearing bright-colored slippers, made from carpets and curtains, with wooden soles. All milk, eggs, and vegetables had been commandeered. Meat had long been a once-a-month luxury. Before America entered the war supplies had been ample, but from the time when she entered the Germans took the overseas food and gave the people poor German food in exchange for it.

[31] Cable dispatch from Philip Gibbs to The *Times* (New York).

The Germans left behind in Belgium a series of sea-front fortifications all the way from Zeebrugge to Nieuport, one continuous line of redoubts, reinforced concrete dugouts, trenches and barbed-wire entanglements, with gun pits about every fifty yards. They had carried off many guns, but had left a large number behind. Zeebrugge had become a city of barbed wire, concrete, steel, and ruins. From the breakwater to points about a mile inland were five barbed wire lines, each having four or five rows. The dug-

© PRESS ILLUSTRATING SERVICE.

SCENE IN OSTEND DURING THE GERMAN OCCUPATION

outs and blockhouses had been craftily camouflaged. Huge guns still stood guard over the breakwater, pointing across the sea toward England. At the entrance to the locks lay the two ships sunk by the British in the gallant action of April, the job thoroughly done. The entrance was completely blocked except for about ten yards on either side, while the breakwater, still unrepaired at the point near shore where it was blown up, proved further the success of the British foray. From Ostend to Zeebrugge the shore line was one continuous fortress where guns stood silhouetted against the sky. One concrete blockhouse, 90 by 30 feet, remained unfinished. The Germans had started other work on new fortifications as late as one month before they left.

The German bombardment of Courtrai damaged many houses by piercing holes in walls and roofs, scarred the noble old church of St. Martin and broke most of the windows, but no great ruin was effected. The town with all its wounds was still standing, but robbed of its copper and wool and even its mattresses. It had been loaded with requisitions and fines, and all its industrial machinery for clothmaking was taken away or destroyed. The Germans with hammers had broken much of the machinery to bits. The officers had been arrogant and brutal to people who received them with courtesy, hiding their hatred and coercing themselves into politeness. Houses had been robbed of furniture and valuables, and food sent for citizens by the International Relief Committee had been seized, and the men in their conduct toward women had been abominable. Philip Gibbs [32] saw the entry of the Belgians and British into Courtrai, but it was not a joyous entry like those into Lille and Bruges, or into some other towns. Civilian crowds greeted any Englishman whom they saw with cheers and embraces, but its 25,000 to 30,000 people had suffered too much for complete reaction. Men doffed their hats to Englishmen with gravity and a kind of dulness, as of a people long stunned by misery.

Bruges was essentially unharmed. Down its long straight avenues of trees, then in autumn foliage, richly colored like gold and crimson banners went Mr. Gibbs soon after the Germans departed. The most beautiful of old Belgian towns, a fairy-tale city in fact, still had its great belfry, celebrated by Longfellow, towering high above ancient houses with stept gables. The spires of three tall churches rising into a blue sky were reflected in canals crossed by small stone bridges. War had not changed the aspect or damaged the beauty of its ancient architecture. It was as if one "had stept out of the horrors of this four years of war into the Flanders of the sixteenth century, on some pageant day when the city was celebrating a festival of joy after the raising of a siege."

[32] Correspondent of The *Times* (New York).

YPRES CATHEDRAL BY MOONLIGHT IN 1918

131

From every house floated Belgian and English flags. Balconies that had been carved five hundred years before were draped with Union Jacks and the Belgian colors. All the people were in the streets massed in crowds outside the city hall with its lace-work front of stone, before the Grunthuis or around gates with fat old towers, looking like giants' castles in fairy-tales. Every child and many women carried banners. Everywhere was color. Soldiers had garlands on their helmets, flags and flowers on their guns. The crowd swayed and surged in streets and squares, and gusts of cheers rose. Not once in all those four years had any man or woman in Bruges received any news of the outside world, nor any letter from relative or friend, nor any knowledge of life or death from those they loved outside. Bruges had been fined enormous sums on various occasions, and everything made of metal that could be found had been taken away. The town had been searched four times for copper. It had been robbed of every scrap of machinery. The Germans paid for nothing except food and drink, and then only in paper money.

The town itself was intact. That President Wilson had saved Bruges was the universal opinion. His reply to the German armistice note, in which he protested against the devastation that was still carried on, was received in Berlin before Bruges was abandoned by the Germans and had caused a marked change in the German attitude. Ten days before the Germans left, some two-score leading citizens had been notified that they would be removed as hostages and had been taken to the railroad station for the purpose when suddenly, after the Wilson note, a counter-order came for their release. At the same time the Germans carefully refrained from injuring buildings or works of art and confined their destruction to the arsenal and German depots. A high Prussian officer admitted it had been decided to spare the invaded territories henceforward as far as possible.

The Stars and Stripes happened to be the first Allied flag that was raised in Bruges. It was hung in the Central Square by an American artist, S. Arient Edwards, who had been living in Bruges for five years. Anticipating the evacuation, he had arranged with the proprietor of a house opposite his own apartment to hang the flag across the square. As soon as the Germans had gone, he dashed across the street early in the morning in his dressing-gown and had the flag up five minutes later. He also hung out a copper kettle that he had kept hidden for four years from the Germans. At first people did not understand his reason for the copper kettle, but when they "caught on," a display of brass and copper followed at many windows. Utensils in great numbers came out that had been walled up in cellars for four years. Copper pots and much fine linen hung with flags were proudly decked with rosettes of Belgian colors. Portraits of the King and Queen were seen everywhere.

On October 25 the King and Queen made their state entry into Bruges, the Queen riding on the left of the King, on his right the young Prince Leopold in the uniform of his regiment of Carbineers. Every soul in the city was in the streets or at windows and balconies, people who had waited four years for the return of the King, who had stayed with his army in that narrow strip of western ground which was all that remained of his kingdom, and whose coming would symbolize to them the restoration of their liberties. While he reviewed his troops, people held back in a hollow square, but when he mounted the steps of the Governor's House, they broke all bounds. Tens of thousands surged around him, cheering that tall figure, as he looked down with his hand at salute to a joyous and wonderful scene. From a hundred old houses long banners floated. It was a splendid day in autumn. Trees along the canals and the walls of houses rising above stone bridges were alike brilliant in flags and the glory of dying foliage. Bruges looked like a picture in some old illuminated book. The belfry rang out a joyous carrillon, while from tall churches, built like dream-castles above gabled roofs, came the booming of deep-toned bells with the singing notes of belfry chimes. The voices of far-off centuries seemed to mingle with the shouts of living men. [33]

Mr. Edwards gave a vivid description of the entry of the King and Queen, who, on the central square were formally received by the burgomaster with a solitary gendarme, one Georges Joye, for escort. Joye, who had been in Bruges all the years the Germans had been there, had refused to give

[33] Cable dispatch from Philip Gibbs to The *Times* (New York).

up his uniform and his old-fashioned rifle despite fines and imprisonment, and had refused to reveal their hiding-place until the Germans abandoned all attempts to overcome his obstinacy. As he stood there in the square alone with a fixt bayonet, the King and Queen shook him by the hand and congratulated him. Mr. Edwards described a visit which the Kaiser had made to Bruges some months before. The finest house in town was made ready for him. At the expense of the corporation it was repainted and redecorated. Hundreds of thousands of marks were spent on it for a visit that lasted fourteen days. For his entry the streets were cleared of all civilians and sentries were posted at every corner. Just before noon, the imperial car, driven at high speed and preceded and followed by two other automobiles, dashed across the square. Mr. Edwards caught a glimpse of a "wax-pale face, with shoulders hunched in a military greatcoat, his right hand twitching nervously at a white mustache, and looking like an aged man, opprest unbearably by the shadow of retribution."

Walter Duranty [34] visited Zeebrugge, the port of Bruges, the principal center of the German submarine campaign against the North Sea and British coast. As many as forty submarines had often been assembled there in huge basins—to say nothing of torpedo-boats, three of which still remained with their smokestacks projecting from the water, where they had been sunk to avoid capture. The arsenal had been used as a repair shop for submarines, but had suffered terribly from the activities of airmen. Everywhere it was dotted with deep dugouts. Tunnels along shore, literally miles long, had been constructed to protect workmen and crews against menaces from the air. The Germans had often said the port was to become the State property of Germany, and was to be made a second Hamburg, through which would pass the trade of Belgium and northern France. They had begun a vast scheme of dock construction to double the port's area. Scores of houses had been pulled down to provide necessary space. Five floating-docks had already been built and the number of cranes, dock-buildings, and repair-yards increased tenfold. Everywhere was a litter of planks and charred rubbish. Cranes that had been dynamited hung grotesquely over the

[34] Correspondent to The *Times* (New York).

water. One giant with a capacity of 25 tons had been blown from its base into the dock. Along the coast sandhills separating the highroad from the beach were honeycombed with battery-positions, succeeding one another without interval. Hundreds of guns were seen, from six to twelve-inch guns, and tons of big shells. Everywhere one saw long muzzles turned seaward.

Mr. Duranty told of the short and riotous life that German

AT THE VENDÔME COLUMN IN PARIS

With all danger to Paris past, workmen are seen engaged in removing piles of dirt that had protected the base of this column with its bas-reliefs from German shell attacks. The lowest front of the picture shows the street level. In 1871 the Vendôme column was pulled down by the commune, but was restored afterward

submarine officers lived in Bruges. One saw repeated what some of the Flemish Little Masters have portrayed as the excesses of Alva's Spanish infantry or of the reckless mercenaries that followed the Condottieri. But those exploits, while they had anticipated, yet at their worst had far from equaled, those of their twentieth-century successors. *U*-boat men were the spoiled darlings of the German forces in Belgium. While on shore they were allowed practically unlimited license. Their pay, already very high—the lowest grade of officers received 800 marks monthly—was almost doubled by supplementary allowances for active service. Promotion, for those who survived, was exceedingly rapid, and decorations were rained upon them. High awards of prize-money were given for Allied warships sunk, and on a sliding scale, according to tonnage for merchant-ships. The finest houses were at their disposal, and the cream of the famous Belgian wine-cellars was "requisitioned" for them. The favorite amusement of officers ashore was to have an orgy of champagne, terminated by the demolition of crockery and furniture. Fine old mansions sometimes were set on fire as a result of such bouts, but, instead of being punished, the officers had a fresh dwelling offered them.

One such house belonging to a millionaire grain merchant became a headquarters and club for U-boat men, the basement transformed into a palatial rathskeller, the walls of which bore cartoon frescoes, with riming mottoes, colored brass lamps and flags from Allied vessels. In one room cartoons were mostly directed against England. One represented John Bull being blown into the sea, in the foreground an immense champagne bottle, fired from a submarine and hitting John Bull, as he stood over the cliffs at Dover. Another showed the anguished head of John Bull peering over the bows of a steamer named the *Butterdampfer,* which was being towed into Zeebrugge by a submarine. Altho the draftsmanship was clever, the vulgarity of tone was typically German. No less characteristic were the mottoes under drawings. The whole house had been stript of furniture and pictures, and all the wine in the cellar, over 10,000 bottles, had been drunk.

The U-boat officer's dress became slovenly; he did not bother to shave, and he indulged in incessant bursts of drunkenness. His temperament, formerly gay and sunny, as time went on was apt to turn gloomy and morose. During the summer men became subject to hallucinations, of which the worst was that the submarine was nothing but a huge floating coffin. This "coffin fear," as the U-boat men called it, became a common feature of their lives—a form of nerve-trouble akin to what doctors call claustrophobia, or fear of a shut room.

A Belgian civilian doctor said he had treated many cases of morphine and other poisoning among boys, who did not dare to reveal their practise of the vice to their own medical officers, or to the admiral. They might stagger and fall in drunken ribaldry, with the lowest women on either arm, break windows, or molest civilians; they might even insult officers, but they were never punished. These pirates of Bruges had a beautiful, quiet, medieval city for their revels. Condemned to the nerve-biting life-in-death of the submarine, their occupation growing more dangerous every month, they consoled themselves with the old philosophy of men doomed to death. In the case of professional murderers like these, one was reminded of the final drink of the eighteenth-century highwayman just before he was hanged at Tyburn.

That part of Belgium now liberated had suffered little in comparison with other parts of the country or with northern France. Western Flanders virtually was intact north of the Lys and east of the old battle-line, but from Nieuport to south of Ypres, was territory which for six or more miles on either side had been a battle-ground for four years, and had become a "dead man's land." East of that region, however, were villages untouched by war, and luxuriant farms. West of the line was ground which British and Belgians had held for four years, where many villages and towns had been destroyed by German shells. Furnes was only an empty shell of tottering walls, and Pervyse merely a geographical name. A post bearing the name was the only thing to show where Ramscapelle had stood. In this region poison-gas had killed all vegetation and trees stood gaunt and bare.

When the German retirement from Flanders began, it was estimated that 250,000 refugees would seek safety in Holland, but only a small fraction of that number arrived. Nearly all who crossed through the wire gates were French, from Valenciennes, Douai, Cambrai, and Quesnoy. The stream trickled in slowly; at first several hundreds only each day, but by the end of October the number had increased to some thousands. There were two main streams some thirty miles apart. One point of entry was where the Dutch provinces of Brabant and Limburg meet, the other was across the Meuse in Maastricht, the capital of Limburg where fugitives were registered by military authorities and had to undergo a physical examination. The spectacle of weary, travel-stained victims toiling through mud and rain was always moving, but the sufferings of old and infirm men, of women, of children on a 150-mile tramp became peculiarly intense. Some of the French civilians were on the road for a month, others for six weeks or two months. All spoke of the kindness of the Belgian people who willingly shared food with them. The refugees often slept at night on the bundles they carried. They comprised all classes. Grandmothers of 80 or 90 braved the inclement weather in wheelbarrows pushed by the most able-bodied. The articles carried included birds in cages, chickens, rabbits, and kitchen utensils. From fatigue the weaker ones often died on the way; others succumbed soon after reaching Holland. Many suffered from grip and bronchial affections. The worst cases received immediate assistance at hospitals and convents.

Many pathetic incidents occurred. One was that of a young mother with the dead body of her six-months-old baby clasped to her breast, the baby having died four days previously, the mother refusing to have the body buried in soil held by Germans. An old woman from Cambrai traveled for three weeks in a chair tied on a cart and had scarcely reached neutral soil when the cart was overturned and she was killed. To distribute the fugitives the Government ordered burgomasters in provincial towns to accommodate them to the extent of 2 per cent. of the populations. To these centers they were taken on special trains, each carrying 1,000 persons. Dutch villagers on the frontier rendered efficient first aid to refugees, altho food was not as plentiful as in 1914. At Maastricht great crowds welcomed the refugees by singing the "Marseillaise" and the "Brabançonne."

With King Albert and the Belgian army marching back into their own land, history was again made dramatic. With a large area of Belgian territory cleared of Germans, the Belgian Government expected shortly to be in Brussels, when the world would see the ending of the long tragedy, the conclusion of a great world-drama. Serbia, which gave the Teutons an excuse for the war, had been first a few weeks before to pluck her soil from under the foot of the trampler, and now

Belgium, whose wrongs had drawn Great Britain into the war, awakened the pity and indignation of the world, and whose loss of everything but her honor and her soul had been a standing affront to Germany, was on the point of becoming once more mistress of her own house. Men of an older time and simpler faith might have exclaimed at the spectacle: "This is the Lord's doing, and it is marvelous in our eyes."

Seldom had the world seen so astonishing an exhibition of poetic justice. There might be differences about other things, but there was only one mind about Belgium. She was the martyr country, for whose rescue and restoration the cru-

© COMMITTEE ON PUBLIC INFORMATION.

CONVALESCENT AMERICAN SOLDIERS AT A BASE HOSPITAL

sading spirit of the Entente nations had been enlisted. Men and women everywhere had been ready to fight and die for her, with something like the mystic ardor that, in far distant centuries, inspired Crusaders bent on reclaiming the Holy Sepulcher. Not the least gratifying part of the whole event was that the great vindication had come about, not by trick or bargain. Belgium was not to be, in Hertling's phrase, "a pawn" on the German chess-board, to be given up and evacuated on conditions, to be tied by this obligation and by that pledge; not as the result of a negotiated withdrawal but as a hasty clearing out of savages at the point of an avenging sword. A wonderful reversal of earthly fortune, an historic act of human justice, lay before us. Belgium, after four years of defiance of German brutality, was looking upon the authors of that brutality as brought low by the undeceived and watchful gods.

There was unrestrained joy in Ghent after its liberation. It was the last Belgian town to be rescued before the armistice. The Germans had clung to it as the pivot of their retreat, holding the canal in front of it by machine-gun fire. It was not until 2 o'clock on November 11 that the last among them went away. Twelve Belgian soldiers had first entered at 7 o'clock. A few minutes afterward all the streets were filled with citizens shouting, cheering, and embracing soldiers and each other. Bells rang out from the churches and old belfries pealed carillons. When Belgian troops marched in with artillery people covered them with flags and overwhelmed sounds of music with shouts of *"Vive la Belgique."* To the British the welcome was almost embarrassing. In cafés people rose with cries of *"Vivent les Anglais,"* clapping of hands and singing "God Save the King." Down many streets Belgian boys and girls were dancing arm in arm, singing "It's a long, long way to Tipperary" as if it were one of their own folk-songs. French lorries came through laden with young poilus under their tricolor and had an enthusiastic welcome. Ghent, with its tall Flemish houses of red brick and stept gables, in many parts was unchanged since Charles II of England lived there in exile. Still stood its old Hôtel de Ville and Palais de Justice with their rich sculptures by Flemish craftsmen; its churches, cathedrals and belfries, whose bells had rung through centuries of joy and grief.

For the first time in five winters the people, when darkness came, lighted their lamps and had open shutters. From windows all over the city streamed out bright beams which as novelties lured one as candle-light does a moth. Bright stars and a crescent moon were in the sky, silvering Flemish gables and frontages between black shadows and making patterns of lace in the Place d'Armes below trees with their autumn foliage. In lights and shadows people danced and sang until midnight; in baker's dozens, with linked arms, men and girls singing in deep voices and in high voices. One song came as a constant refrain between all others, "The Marseillaise," which was sung in crowds as well as in small groups of soldiers and students. One man was seen walking alone down a deserted avenue singing the French song of liberty all to himself, brandishing a stick, his voice ringing out with a kind of ecstasy and passion with the words: *"Allons, enfants, de la patrie! Le jour de gloire est arrivé!"*

Next day, when King Albert made his triumphal entry into his city, vast cheering crowds assembled, the sun shining with a golden light upon old roofs and crowded balconies from which banners hung. King and Queen came riding in with the young Prince, escorted by Belgian, French, and British generals. White flowers were thrown from balconies, petals falling about like confetti. When the royal trio took a position in the Place d'Armes, cheers in storms swept round them. There was a march past of Belgian troops who had fought on the Yser in mud and blood and now had flowers in rifles and on helmets but looking like veterans as they marched under their heavy packs. The Queen, a simple figure, was in a light habit with linen cap. Next to her was the tall King, his face bronzed and hardened from four years in the field. It was a great day for Ghent and for the courage that had carried a great people to victory.

To the pealing of bells in the great cathedral and the cheers of massed crowds, the King, after the armistice was signed, made a State entry into Antwerp. The noble old city, with its broad streets and squares and big public buildings, was decorated across highways with streamers and flags. Physically the people had not suffered, but their joy at liberation, the enthusiasm with which they greeted King Albert, was proof enough that they had suffered in a mental way. Thousands had gone to prison for trivial offenses, or for refusal to pay fines. Among the crowds were figures belonging to the past, as one sees them in old Flemish pictures. Franciscan friars, with cowls turned back so that one saw their shaven crowns, raised themselves on the tips of their sandaled feet to get a glimpse of the King. From latticed

141

windows under high gables round about the cathedral, nuns poked out their heads, laughed and cheered and wept a little as Belgian soldiers carried their colors past the King. Commissaries of police in cocked hats exhorted people to keep to their lines; but they closed in by wild rushes when the King and Queen came in motor-cars behind a cavalry escort, their cars laden with flowers. From scores of windows more flowers fell, so that they drove through a flurry of red and white petals. All over Antwerp bells were mingling in a strange clashing melody; from the belfry of the cathedral the chimes of the gay carillons came tinkling down, playing the "Marseillaise." [35]

When the last German troops left Brussels, extraordinary scenes were witnessed around the North Station, from which most of them departed. Wishing to have money to take home with them, they had sold everything they owned or had stolen. Some laid out objects on the sidewalk and cried their wares for sale, in loud voices. Among articles offered were blankets, clothing, and shoes, as well as wool and copper goods that had been taken from the inhabitants of the city. On November 17, the last detachment of German troops having left during the night, the streets were profusely beflagged with Belgian and Allied colors. The first troops to arrive were greeted with intense enthusiasm. A ceremony proclaiming the liberation of Brussels took place in the Grande Place, which was packed with citizens and former prisoners, windows and balconies crowded. The excitement reached its zenith when a procession was formed, headed by an old banner that had come down from the revolution of 1839, and so was a symbol of Belgian liberty.

On November 22, King Albert halted his white horse at the Flanders gate of Brussels, and Burgomaster Max stept from the throng of municipal councilors to greet him. During the burgomaster's short speech of welcome and the King's reply, the Queen raised her hand from time to time to shelter her eyes from the sun, which was dazzling in a cloudless sky where scores of airplanes wheeled about like gleaming birds. It was a striking picture that the soldier-King made, sitting motionless on his horse. Not a word

[35] Cable dispatch from Philip Gibbs to The *Times* (New York).

of the ceremony could be heard on account of the thunderous cries of the assembled multitude, which never ceased; the enthusiasm delirious, indescribable. Fully a million people must have lined the route through which the procession passed. They were everywhere—on the housetops or perched on ledges from the first story to the fourth, attached by ropes to windows. Each lamp-post bore two or three. On a telegraph pole at the Flanders Gate was a boy hanging insecurely by his sash, and somehow managing to wave and cheer without breaking his neck. Altho his words were lost, the King's face showed deep emotion as he replied to the burgomaster, and gestured twice strongly with his right hand. Two paces behind him was Prince Albert of England in the uniform of the Royal Air Force, the Belgian Prince and Princess just behind. In the grandstand to the rear of the Burgomaster stood a number of American and British officers.

When the short ceremony was ended, the King and Queen turned their horses to greet a party of Allied generals on horseback, and then, as the procession moved forward, it seemed as if the dense noise increased, had that been possible. King Albert entered Brussels along a narrow street where flags made an avenue of color and flowers fell about him. The Princes and their sister rode abreast with Leopold in the center, a slim boy in the plain khaki of the Belgian poilu. On Leopold's right was Charles, a stocky youngster, in the uniform of an English naval cadet. Princess Marie was on the left, a smiling child in a gray dress, her golden hair in fuzzy plaits beside each ear. As she saw a youth on a telegraph pole she laughed and waved her hand to him. The crowd yelled delightedly, and the youth responded with such energy that nothing but a miracle averted a fall. The enthusiasm was frantic. The cobblestones of the road became nearly hidden by a carpet of flowers. The first soldiers to appear were Americans, who received a magnificent ovation. As they in war-worn khaki swung by, there were tears running down the cheeks of Belgian officers. Here was a thrilling contrast; once these had been deserted streets of houses with covered windows, shrouded like faces in mourning, and no sound to break the silence, save the interminable tramp of hobnailed boots or the stern command of an officer; now moving with one Allied detachment after another—French, British, Belgian, American—amid the delirious cheers of the delivered population.[36]

King Albert entered his capital in brilliant autumn sunshine for this climax to this long Belgian drama. He had recovered his capital, while the villain who stole it was a fugitive, hiding behind the skirts of a woman, Queen Wilhelmina of Holland, awaiting whatever fate the Allies might decide to deal out to him. Wilhelm's empire had crumbled, but Belgians were marching with their Allies to German soil. British cavalry was cantering past Waterloo to Cologne; Americans were approaching the Rhine across Luxemburg; Strassburg was flinging out tri-colored bunting in preparation for another triumphal entry on November 24, and the French were hugging Alsace-Lorraine to their bosom. The background of the setting was Versailles, where decorators were touching up, for use at the Peace Conference, the château of Louis XIV, where forty-eight years before the German Empire had been proclaimed, and at this Peace Conference was to be sealed the fate of Germany.

Four years before King Albert had been forced to withdraw his little army before the oncoming waves of Germans, and resign Brussels to the tender mercies of a brutal foe. To the minds of many recollections were called up of a famous cartoon in *Punch* in which the Kaiser standing above King Albert was saying to him, "Well, you have lost everything," to which Albert replied, "Not my soul!" Albert's kingdom had been restored to him while the Kaiser had lost his, to become a fugitive from the wrath of his betrayed people. Europe had been filled with the dust of tumbling Teutonic thrones, but Albert retained his crown, with the love of his people and the admiration of the whole world. Nations united in congratulating this King upon the redemption of his capital.

The royal party proceeded to the Palais de la Nation, where they received a tremendous ovation. Then followed a review of Allied troops which formed a line ten miles long. Flowers were thrown as the procession made its way along boulevards lined with dense throngs, the noise of cheers

[36] Cable dispatch from Walter Duranty to The *Times* (New York).

ARRIVAL IN BRUSSELS OF KING ALBERT AND QUEEN ELIZABETH AFTER THE GERMAN EVACUATION

The King and Queen are seen on horseback in the center of the picture. Belgian, British and American soldiers with flags surround the plaza

VI.

rolling continuously across the city. American troops, with British and French contingents, marched with the Belgians. Observers who had seen many great ceremonies had never seen so vast and varied a crowd or one so carried away by a tumult of sound. The King was at the head of his army. One end of the procession was far down the Ghent road when the other was passing along the Rue Royale. At one place 500 young women, in soprano chorus, sang the Belgian national song. Near them stood a pathetic group of as many

© COMMITTEE ON PUBLIC INFORMATION.

A WRECKED MESS-KITCHEN

wounded men. The roads outside of Brussels were thronged by thousands of liberated prisoners moving homeward and passing outward. There were soldiers with many kinds of guns and vehicles from dog-drawn machine-guns to armored cars, cannon, and touring-cars. Among the pedestrians were women who had walked thirty miles. Unending groups of liberated civilians mingled with the stream.

Nobody stayed at home that day. The city spent large sums on the decorations, including flags, streamers, and statuary of symbolic meaning in wonderful stucco and works of art that might deceive the elect. A skilful sculptor had wrought heroic figures of Edith Cavell and others murdered by Germans. Just before the King arrived, people brought out chairs, tables, ladders, and buckets on which to stand. Members of the royal family were mounted upon beautiful animals sitting so high as to be seen even by those far back in the crowd. The first stage of the journey ended at the Palais de la Nation, where the King descended from his horse to be present at a session of Parliament that would be historic. Belgian, American, and British national anthems were played, one after another, without intermission, for six hours. Brussels had suffered little from physical injuries during the war, or, thanks to the American Relief Commission, from any extreme hunger.

In Belgium it had been a custom among the well-to-do to collect wine as other people collect books, stamps, or pictures. Every prosperous citizen had a cellar of fine burgundy that was his special pride. Nothing suited the Germans better than to possess this wine. Often they would make a sudden visit to a home, demanding wine, and wo to the man who offered a protest or resistance. Imprisonment or a heavy fine was mercilessly inflicted if the Belgian hid anything Germans wished to seize. All the same, an astonishing quantity of wine had escaped them, walled up in cellars or concealed in the unlikeliest hiding-places. The watchword had been, "Hide everything rather than give it up; risk any penalty rather than yield to the Germans." One family slept for three and a half years without sheets or mattresses in order to keep them from the hands of the invaders. They buried brass doorlocks, kitchenware, and lamp-fittings under courtyard paving-stones. [37]

After the last ceremony of the day, when, in the yellowing twilight the King passed through immense crowds in the Grand Place to the Hôtel de Ville in order to receive an address from the burgomaster, the people gave themselves up to a night of carnival. It was a Flemish "kermesse," in which rich and poor, nobles and peasants, high officers and simple soldiers were mingled in equality of rank in a brotherhood of joy. In this folly of the crowds there was the light-

[37] Cable dispatch from Walter Duranty to The *Times* (New York).

heartedness of children dancing to the love of life and the comradeship of humanity, of many nations linking arms across the frontiers of spirit, and the laughter often of women who had dried the salt of their tears. In the open square people danced all night. They clapped their hands and made merry rings around English or American, Belgian or French soldiers, an act that stood for hero-worship to others, whirling about them cheering and singing. It was a moonlit night, and these whirling masses, in a white shadowy glamor, pranced in squadrons down broad avenues under leafless trees and eddied through streets of shops and restaurants, sparkling in electric lights. In these crowds were soldiers of all the Allies.

It was an international night, a festival of victory. French, British, Belgian, and American soldiers hovered about among thousands in queer black uniforms, or in strange combinations of military and civilian clothing, who had tramped into Brussels from prison-camps,—Italians, Russians, Portugese, English, Scottish, Irish, Welsh, Australians, Canadians, all of whom had since been fed and housed by Belgian people. In every village on roads leading to Brussels was enacted some little drama belonging to this war-history, but mingling curiously in one's mind with old memories of another chapter, when, one hundred years before, British soldiers had marched down some of these same roads, and through some of these same villages on their way to the field of Waterloo. British cavalry then went over one of these roads, and now British cavalry were again traversing that road, and for the first time since that June day in 1815, when British horsemen rode out toward Hougomont and La Haye Sainte over fields haunted forever by ghosts of Wellington's army who were there to decide the fate of Europe. One's imagination conjured up the figure of Wellington on his white horse, that hard, hook-nosed face of his staring over those same fields. The voices of French soldiers moving now along these woods seemed to bring back a memory of their great-grandfathers, who, a hundred years before, had shouted *"Vive l'Empereur! Vive l'Empereur!"* as a stout little man rode up on his horse to see the final ruin of all his imperial dreams, as he exclaimed, *"Tout est perdu. Sauve qui peut."* [33]

[33] Cable dispatch from Philip Gibbs to The *Times* (New York).

ON THE WESTERN FRONT

King Albert and the Belgian royal family made their official entry into Liége on November 30 at the head of troops who had conducted the heroic defense of that town in August, 1914. The King and Queen, with General Leman, the defender of Liége at that time, were cheered enthusiastically by crowds. Almost at the same time a Belgian cavalry brigade entered Aix-la-Chapelle, in Germany, at the request of German authorities. It was the Belgian Army's defense of Liége and its surrounding forts in the first two weeks of the war that gave time for other Allied forces, French and British, to be thrown into the war and so save Paris. The Germans had not expected opposition in Belgium, but General Leman's stubbornness held them up for several days. He was afterward captured by the Germans and had been a prisoner until the middle of December, 1917.[39]

[39] Principal Sources: The *Evening Post,* The *Times,* New York; Associated Press dispatches.

XIII

THE FRANCO-AMERICANS MOVE ON TOWARD SEDAN AND THE LOWER BELGIAN BORDER—LUDENDORFF OUT

October 15, 1918—October 30, 1918

WITH her allies deserting her, Germany's armies by the middle of October were being driven into two bottlenecks, sullen under constant defeat and demoralized by their leaders who, before the end of the month, were suing for peace and an armistice. And yet caution was necessary in speaking of the possibilities of a Sedan for the German army—at least in the popular sense of that word, as a victory over an enemy completely trapt. Such a victory was hard to conceive in modern warfare, because of the huge size of armies and the great length of battle-lines. At Sedan in 1870, MacMahon surrendered 83,000 men, or perhaps one-fifth of all the French forces. In 1915 the Germans, in pursuing the Russians from the Dunajec to the Pripet marshes, had claimed a million prisoners, one-fifth of the active Russian army. Nevertheless, there was no Sedan in the East, because four million Russian fighting men and a battle-front still remained in being.

Given plenty of room to retreat in and vast numbers of men to bear the strain of loss by capture, any modern army could avoid a Sedan. The Germans, since July 18, had lost more than 300,000 prisoners, or about four times the number of men whom MacMahon surrendered, and the German prisoners were close to one-sixth of Germany's active fighting men; but the Germans had not been trapt, and hence there was no Sedan. What really gave Sedan its connotation was, not the numerical size of the victory, but its effects. At Metz, Bazaine surrendered twice as many men as MacMahon gave up at Sedan, but at Sedan the French Emperor gave himself up as a prisoner; in other words he abdicated, and at Paris the immediate result of Sedan was a revolution and the establishment of a republic. In a real sense, however, the Allies had now won a Sedan. Franco-Americans were soon to secure the town, and the Germans had been compelled to admit defeat as they saw tottering the throne of the Hohenzollerns. Foch

© COMMITTEE ON PUBLIC INFORMATION.

AN AMERICAN OFFICER WATCHING
GERMANS SHELL A TOWN

had won back from the Germans what the first Sedan lost to France— namely, Alsace-Lorraine, and an admitted leadership among continental nations. When Napoleon III handed over his sword to Germany France gave up to Germany her primacy in Europe. So now the Germans had handed back that leadership to France when they admitted that Germany had become a "belittled Power." If the Allies had not scored a tactical Sedan, they had won a strategic and moral one because Germany was asking them for terms of surrender.

On October 18, three months had passed since Foch launched his counter-offensive against the Marne salient. From every foot of territory gained in their spectacular drives of the spring and summer the Germans had been hurled back. The Hindenburg line, to which they had retired as a refuge from Foch, had been pierced, shattered, and left behind. From the Belgian coast to the Meuse a few miles of trenches were all that remained intact of an elaborate system

150

which was supposed to be absolutely impregnable. Between Cambrai and St. Quentin British and Americans were fifteen miles beyond the Hindenburg line; in Champagne the French were twenty. The battle-front at its nearest point was forty miles from Château-Thierry, where the Americans had won undying fame only a few weeks before, and a full forty-five from Amiens. Paris, which the Germans thought almost within their grasp, was seventy-five miles from the battle-front. More than 4,700 square miles of French and Belgian territory had been redeemed, including several large cities and hundreds of towns and villages. Well-nigh all the French territory once held by the enemy had been reconquered. Three months had sufficed to turn what the Teutons thought certain victory into a stupendous and far-reaching defeat. The great retreat by October 18 had taken on an accelerated pace and spread far to the south from Zeebrugge, close to the Holland frontier, to the Laon district, on a front of about 120 miles, over most of which the Germans were giving way. With the collapse of Germany, occupation of the Belgian coast was now complete. Germany's dream of an invasion of England across the North Sea was ended. The Germans, in fact, were approaching the last ditch where they would have to stand if they were to prevent an invasion of Germany, along the Belgian frontier west of Aix-la-Chapelle—in other words, at the very place where they entered Belgium in August, 1914.

On October 17, working their way along the valley of the Aire in the face of a stiff machine-gun fire, the Americans entered Grandpré, advanced through the valley which runs to one side of the formidable, menacing Bois de Bourgogne, and reached the edge of the Boi de Loges, the most formidable obstacle between them and Buzancy. They had solved one of their most difficult problems and completed one of their greatest achievements in a campaign aiming at Sedan, still ten or more miles away. Despite a steady downpour of rain, cheerfulness continued. The Germans, dismayed by the tenacity of the attacks, had been rushing up men from Metz, companies consisting of only fifty men in some instances and battalions having only 120 bayonets. During three weeks they had used approximately

180,000 fighting men, with enormous losses, against America's First Army. Despite this the First Army had forged steadily forward against a concentration of machine-guns. The importance of the American operation was measured, not so much by the ground gained, as by its effectiveness in drawing large numbers of Germans from other sectors where they were needed.[40]

Of all their conquests in France there now remained to the Germans little save a long, but comparatively narrow, frontier tract between Valenciennes and Metz, within which were two small, altho important, salients. One of these was in the east where Americans and French were pounding at positions in the Grandpré hills, a northern extension of the Argonne Forest, held most obstinately by some of the best remaining German troops, because an Allied break through between the Aisne and the Meuse would have cut the Germans off from their road of retreat into Luxemburg and thrown them into the forest maze of the Ardennes. The other salient was between Le Cateau and Rethel, and was less important tho more dangerous to the German troops holding it. Accordingly, its abandonment, or at least the abandonment of a corner of it between the Oise and the Serre, was begun on October 18, under threat of envelopment by French troops. West of the Oise Hutier was desperately resisting the push of Debeney toward Guise.[41]

On October 22 Foch's armies drove forward from the Dutch border to the Aisne, despite increasing German resistance. East of Cambrai, Haig was within two miles of Valenciennes. Allied forces put out of action the greatest lateral German supply-line in the west, which was the Valenciennes-Hirson railroad. King Albert's Belgians and Plumer's Second British Army had thrown the Germans back at every point. In heavy fighting through wooded country along the Scheldt, reaching the river on a ten-mile front and crossing at several points, they swept forward toward Ghent and to within three miles of Eecloo. Americans aiding the British crossed the Sambre and Oise Canal under heavy fire and inflicted tremendous losses on the enemy in

[40] Cable dispatch from Edwin L. James to The *Times* (New York).
[41] Cable dispatch from G. H. Perris to The *Times* (New York).

futile efforts to halt their advance. North of Le Cateau repeated German attacks launched against British positions
were beaten back. Everywhere Haig's forces held their
gains. French fought the enemy back east of St. Quentin,
between the Serre and Oise, taking the villages of Richecourt
and Mesbrecourt. In the Champagne repeated enemy attacks broke down under a withering 'fire. The Americans
attacked north of the Argonne, taking the Bois de Rappes
and Hill 299. These were both points of strategic importance on the western end of the American line north
of Grandpré. They were cleared of the enemy within
three hours, despite unusual machine-gun opposition. On
October 22 the British penetrated Valenciennes, advance
troops pushing their way into the western suburbs of the
last great German stronghold in northern France.

Since Pershing's men launched their first attack in the
Argonne on September 26, they had put out some twenty
German divisions, including some of the best in the German
army, such as three of the five Guard divisions and the
Twenty-eighth, known as "the Kaiser's own." In front of
them were some eighteen more divisions, and others were
being brought up day by day. The Germans were fighting
these Americans under orders to hold at all costs the lines
which protected the Luxemburg gateway, the most important artery of the German army. If the Mézières-
Luxemburg railroad system could be reached, or put under
gun-fire, all communications from the German front from
before Laon to the Meuse would fail.

The taking of the Argonne positions had been one of the
events of the war. The task performed was the hardest,
bitterest, and least sensational task of Foch's whole far-
flung battle. Pershing had gladly accepted the commission,
knowing it would be no such picnic as the reduction of the
St. Mihiel salient was. That the German command could
make stiff resistance only reflected the more credit on the
American First Army for the progress it made and the
large proportion of German available strength that it used
up. Fully one-sixth of the German rifle-strength was
thrown against the Americans in one week. Only four German divisions were in front of the Americans when the at-

tack began, but these had been reinforced by fully thirty more, which unquestionably Ludendorff could have used to advantage elsewhere had it not been for the American attack.[42] Without the pressure exerted by our incessant attacks between the Argonne and the Meuse, Ostend, Bruges, and Lille might still have been in German hands. So said one of the military chieftains of France to an American general.

When Hoffmann von Fallersleben wrote his "Deutschland über Alles" in 1841, he did not embody in it anything like the aspirations of that full-blown Junkerism which in more recent days had seized upon it and made the song the slogan of a world domination. Only in one direction—and that excusably—had the poet laid himself open to a charge of imperialism. That was when he claimed for the German people space between the Meuse and the Niemen, between the Adige and the Belt. The Germany of 1841 did virtually touch the Meuse, north of Aix-la-Chapelle, and it touched the Belt and Niemen at Königsberg, while Austrian Germans were ruling in Italy as far as the Adige, but modern Junkers chanted Fallersleben's old geography only in a symbolic sense. For the Meuse they had substituted the mouths of the Meuse, which meant Holland and Belgium; for the Memel they substituted the Gulf of Finland and the Dnieper and beyond the Belt their ultimate plans ran to the Arctic. Instead of the Adige as their furthest south they had gone to Bagdad and the Persian Gulf.

That mad program of domination now lay prone, a pitiful wreck. There was no longer any question of a German Mittel-Eurasia from the North Sea to the Persian Gulf. At either end of the huge Junker map, Allied shears had been at work. First they had gone to Mesopotamia. Then after a long pause to Palestine and Bulgaria, until the southern terminus of the Berlin to Bagdad dream had been pushed far back westward to the Danube. Without loss of time, the Allied shears had then cut through at the other end of the map, and the Flanders coast became a German memory. With Great Britain as the arch-enemy of ambitious Prussianism, the dream had been that two pistols would be

[42] Cable dispatch from Edwin L. James to The *Times* (New York).

directed against her power, one from Flanders at her heart in Europe, the other from the Persian Gulf at her possessions in India. Both weapons were now in the scrap-heap. After the Bulgarian collapse, the Junkers would have been happy could they have kept their "Deutschland über Alles" within the modest limits of the Meuse and the

SECRETARY BAKER IN FRONT-LINE TRENCHES

Danube, but in October even the Meuse was in danger, and the French force in Serbia had reached the Danube.

Two great German rivers were the Rhine and the Danube. Along their currents it was the destiny of the Teutonic Junker-thought to expand; in one direction, toward the North Sea with domination of the Atlantic; in the other, toward the Near and Middle East. But parts of the two mighty streams had first to be conquered—those leading down to their mouths. Then Teuton *Weltmacht* could debouch on great ocean highways, but all that grandiose dream had become a thing of the past. The cutting of the navigation on the Danube along the frontier of Serbia was a dramatic reminder of a closed chapter for Junkers. The great river was strewn with the wreck of their ambitions. The Danube was virtually blocked to them at Budapest, and was menaced further north around Pressburg by the new-born Czecho-Slovak nation, while on the Rhine it was a foregone conclusion that the French would establish their own "watch" upon it. Junkerism had set out to navigate the two waterways onward to ocean waters, but Junkerism was about to end in losing even the middle course of both.

The hardest battle in which Americans had taken part was raging northwest of Verdun late in October, where the armies swayed backward and forward in a desperate struggle as attack followed attack in quick succession. The Germans struck determinedly on the line west of the Meuse in an effort to retrieve losses of earlier days. They hurled masses against Pershing's positions at Grandpré and other points, only to be cut down and thrown back with frightful losses.

On October 24 the British won a notable victory on the Valenciennes front. The Third and Fourth Armies, with American aid, stormed forward on a seventeen-mile front below the Belgian frontier, advancing at some points three and a half miles. Ten villages and several thousand prisoners were taken. Haig had approached the northern reaches of the Valenciennes-Hirson line, had cleared Raismes Forest and the west bank of the Scheldt and thrown back the Germans toward the Mormal Forest. Haig reported that resistance had been overcome on a twenty-mile front. Seven thousand prisoners and more than one hundred guns had been taken. North of Valenciennes the territory before the Scheldt was being rapidly cleared up. Valenciennes was reported evacuated, except for small German outposts. The French had made an important advance between the Oise and the Serre and at the Ferrières Farm. Americans east of the Meuse had advanced five-eighths of a mile on a two-mile front, completing the capture of another wood, and west of the Meuse the Grand Carré Farm was occupied. On October 27, north of Laon, the French swept forward on a front of fifteen miles, clearing difficult ground between the Oise and the Serre and reaching the outskirts of Guise. Ten villages and important heights were wrested from the enemy. Nearly four thousand prisoners had been taken in three days. In all forty German divisions had been used against the Americans in the Meuse-Argonne battle. Between September 26 and November 6, we had taken 26,059 prisoners and 468 guns on this front.

On October 29 had been reached the end of a hundred days of successful operations under Foch. In an equal period Napoleon had landed from Elba, regained France, fought and lost Waterloo, and so taken the final step which led him to St. Helena. In the same length of time, Foch had captured upward of 400,000 prisoners and not fewer than 5,000 guns. His armies had liberated more than 8,000 square miles of French and Belgian territory. In winning the battle of the Hindenburg line, he had won the war, this on the confession of Germany herself. Not only had there been a supreme victory in the west, but in Syria a British army under Allenby, acting in strict coordination with Western operations, and under command of Foch, had broken the military power of Turkey and liberated Syria, Mesopotamia and Arabia—sealing the doom of the Osmanli Empire. In Macedonia another army, commanded by a French general, Francinet d'Esperez, but composed of contingents from many nations, had achieved a tremendous battlefield success, compelled the surrender without condition of Bulgaria, abolished Mitteleuropa, and was advancing to the Danube, sweeping before it the last vestige of German control in the Balkans and carrying the doom of Austria-Hungary. The whole gigantic German conception, the colossal German scheme, which for four years had threatened democracy with ever-growing might and with ever-expanding frontiers, had been abolished. German armies in retreating were leaving behind them the wrecks of that world empire which at one time seemed well-nigh realized, but was now shattered forever.

Foch had broken the German legend of invincibility, had eliminated the prestige of the German military machine. A simple French soldier, the soldier of a republican nation the most of whose life had been devoted to teaching the act of war—a mere academic person, a professor as Wilson was, had utterly demolished, not alone the much-lauded German army, but the very legend of German militarism. Six months before men were talking of the possibility that Ludendorff would reach Calais and take Paris and now they were seriously discussing the terms of German surrender. On the military side, Foch might hereafter rank with Cæsar, Frederick and Napoleon, but on the moral side he would surpass them all, since he had done for humanity and civilization what the others did for themselves in the pursuit of great power. Foch rather as a Washington had written a new and splendid chapter in military history. Germany had been beaten by her inferiority of resources as well as by her inferiority of leadership, while Foch had had all the tools he needed. He had the divisions to maneuver with, the guns with which to blast his way through, the tanks with which to defy German machine-guns, abundant airplanes and ample means of transport.

Germany, by all the signs men could see, had reached the end of her resources. Her situation had been made serious from failure to get raw material. Captured German orders showed that she was suffering from shortage of horses and artillery, and from lack of war-material of all sorts. Forced "combing out" of workmen from her factories had seriously lowered her power of new production. She was no longer able to recoup herself for losses. There was a dearth of the particular kind of steel used in the making of guns. Germany's ability to keep on fighting had been largely a matter of resources, but now the French coal-mines around Lens and Loos had been recovered, and Pershing was striking at iron-mines in the Argonne and was within artillery range of those around Metz. Besides these losses, her hold on the mineral resources of the Balkans and Asia Minor had been broken.

"Germany will not accept a peace of violence," said Prince Maximilian on October 23, after application had been made for an armistice, "because the Germans are a proud people, accustomed to victory." Prince Max forgot that since July 18 Germany had ceased to keep the habit of victory. Moreover, it had become a grave question why Germany should now expect the consideration which she had never shown to any of her victims during those fifty odd years when she really had the victory habit. German armies were no longer inflated with an overweening sense of German military prestige, or any proud consciousness of German invincibility. They had been fighting for three months without once making a break in Foch's record for inflicting upon them disaster after disaster. They had been swept out of the strongest defense-lines which their masters of the art of war had been able to construct, and they were going back to the Rhine in utter defeat. When their military autocracy was willing to raise the white flag, then would Germany have to pocket her pride and enter upon that peace of penance and reparation which the Entente world held to be a political and moral necessity.

Without warning came on October 20 welcome news that Ludendorff, First Quartermaster-General of the German army, and virtually its Generalissimo since March 21, had resigned. In accepting his resignation, the Emperor decreed that the Lower Rheinish Infantry No. 39, of which Ludendorff had long been commander, should bear his name. His resignation was overdue. He had failed much more than either of his predecessors who had been in control at

AN AMERICAN NAVAL GUN WITH A RAILWAY MOUNT
Guns of this type were used against the Germans in the last weeks of the war. They have a range of thirty miles

German Grand Headquarters—Moltke or Falkenhayn. His name would remain associated with the most disastrous year in Prussian military annals since Auerstadt and Jena. In military partnership with Hindenburg he had always been the ruling power and Hindenburg the show-window figurehead. Evidently the German Government had held Ludendorff accountable for the western failure. His resignation showed that. His military reputation had perished under the test which his retreat imposed.

The effect of Ludendorff's resignation on the German people, who were already suffering from recurrent shocks in a disturbing crisis, could scarcely have been overestimated. Despite the failure of his ambitious project to seize Paris and the Channel ports, and the subsequent reverses which overtook his army, his military prestige for weeks had remained high. Germans for the most part continued to have faith that he would ultimately extricate them from military disaster. But now their faith had experienced one of the rudest shocks of the war. His fall was the fall of the third great German military figure in the war. The younger Moltke—justly or unjustly, but probably unjustly—had paid the price of failure in the original German plan of campaign in France. Falkenhayn, who succeeded him, lasted nearly two years; but disappeared at the end of August, 1916, when the failure of the great battle of Verdun was sealed in the battle of the Somme, and the lesson was driven home by the intervention of Roumania. There was no sign of Hindenburg's removal; altho he had lately celebrated his seventy-first birthday amid signs of public indifference, and enthusiasm about him had evaporated. Ludendorff went because he was responsible for the western failure; it was notorious that Hindenburg had been opposed to the military plan of 1918, and that for a long time he had practically stood aside.

The Hindenburg-Ludendorff combination had supplied one of the most curious chapters in German propaganda. Journalists had vied with one another in describing them as "inimitable twins" and in lauding their incomparable skill in organizing for victory. For a long time the German public really believed in Hindenburg, but the initiated

were always aware that Ludendorff was supplying the brains
of the partnership. It had often been said that, when it became necessary to throw back the unexpectedly rapid Russian
invasion of East Prussia in 1914, Ludendorff was first choice
for commander, but that he himself asked for Hindenburg
as his nominal chief. Since then Hindenburg and Ludendorff had been inseparable until their recent differences of
opinion. For two years Ludendorff's opinion had carried

© COMMITTEE ON PUBLIC INFORMATION.

STERILIZERS USED IN ERADICATING VERMIN FROM CLOTHING

weight in all military decisions and in all military interference with imperial policy. Again and again he was described as the real master of Germany. Great, therefore,
was his fall. He was still only fifty-three years of age. In
1914 he had just become a major-general, in command of
an infantry brigade. He was with the first German troops
which crossed the Belgian frontier, and was the real captor
of Liége. For two years he controlled all operations against

Russia, and thereafter controlled all German strategy in the west as well.

The passing of Ludendorff was something more than the exits of Moltke and Falkenhayn had been, but like them, he had failed to bring off the great decision, and, like them, was doomed, as all unsuccessful generals are doomed by failure. Ludendorff had been more than an unsuccessful general; he had been a symbol and the final hope, of German militarism, which had staked all on him. When he failed the military autocracy fell with him, much as Sedan blew the last vestiges of the tinsel glory of the Napoleonic tradition out of French imagination. Ludendorff was the last and most distinguished victim of superior French strategy. He had paid the debt of 1870 to France with a vengeance. For Wörth, Gravelotte, and Sedan, France had to her account the First Marne, Verdun, the Second Marne and now the great retreat. The military tradition of the French Revolution had again mastered that of Frederick the Great. Moltke had met Joffre, Falkenhayn had met Pétain, and now Ludendorff had met Foch. The German collapse was written on the very heavens, its most striking sign the disgrace and retirement of Ludendorff.

With Ludendorff died Germany's last military hope. With her man-power approaching exhaustion and with her finances and natural resources under an intolerable strain, there was nothing for her but to bow to the inevitable. Bulgaria, Turkey, and Austria, had taken the path of a separate peace, casting themselves upon the mercy of the Entente Allies. The evidence was clear that Germany's humiliation was at hand. "The day" had plainly come—not *"Der Tag"* of boastful and wicked militarists, but the day which men and women in France, Great Britain, Italy, and the United States had been longing for through years of heroic endurance and sacrifice unutterable. It was the day when the spirit of Germany had to break; when the bitter conviction had to enter her soul that the whole plan of rule and gain by force and greed which she had pursued for sixty years was a horrible mistake, and that the great gamble of the war of 1914 had been lost.

On October 30 it was announced that General Groener,

the Prussian War Minister, after an audience with the Emperor, had been made the successor of Ludendorff. Groener was regarded as the greatest organizing director that Germany had. He was chief of the military railway service when the war broke out and for a long time afterward. He not only distributed the troops on Western and Eastern Fronts, but moved large bodies from one to the other when circumstances demanded. In November, 1916, Groener had been made head of the Department of Munitions, and was thus practically director of labor and manufactures for the empire, in which office he produced astonishing results, visiting munition and other plants and making eloquent speeches on speeding-up work. In December, 1916, when only forty years old, Groener was at the height of his fame. He was called the third man in Germany's military triumvirate, the others being Hindenburg and Ludendorff. His services were apparently now needed in solving the problem of getting German troops back to their homes.

The *Frankfurter Zeitung,* in its issue of October 27, said Ludendorff had been removed from the Western Front "on the day on which his terrible strategic error, the last and greatest of his mistakes, came to light." According to its knowledge, the responsible leadership of German measures of defense had not been in Ludendorff's hands since the time when the Supreme Command had called for the desperate step of "offering an armistice." Since then the retreat and the rearrangement of the German defensive front had been the work of another general. This statement meant to the London *Times* that Ludendorff "was removed at the end of September," which was a week or ten days before the British and Americans under Haig won the great victory on the Hindenburg line.[43]

XIV

LAST SHOTS OF THE WAR IN WHICH THE FRENCH AND AMERICANS TAKE SEDAN AND THE BRITISH MAUBEUGE AND MONS

October 31, 1918—November 11, 1918

IN four weeks the American army had seen one of the hardest-fought and most bitterly contested of the war's battles. They had drawn into it more than thirty, and perhaps forty, German divisions from other parts of the front, and so had helped on the advance which the British, French and Belgians were making further west and north. Among the divisions the Germans threw in were three of the five Prussian divisions of Guards and the Twenty-eighth, Fifty-second, Thirteenth, and Thirty-seventh, that were reckoned among "the Kaiser's best." This formidable German resistance had been put up to guard the great lateral communication-line running from Mésières to Montmédy, Sedan, and Longuyon. In four weeks the American army had captured more than 20,000 prisoners, and in addition to 127 large guns, many machine-guns, anti-tank guns and ammunition. They had fired more than 2,500,000 rounds of artillery-ammunition, at times running as high as 150,000 a day. They had used more than 1,000 cannon of all calibers, not including captured guns, which, using German ammunition, had been turned against the Germans. They had brought down 230 airplanes and 23 observation balloons. This record was made in adverse weather, with only three really good flying days. In addition, the bombing service had made many successful sallies behind enemy lines by day and night, dropping more than 80,000 pounds of high explosives. In one expedition more than 200 airplanes were used, making the largest airplane concentration on a single event ever known.

Forty thousand engineers, working day and night, had

rebuilt needed roads, using stone from destroyed villages
and incidentally wiping off the map the last vestiges of
villages which for four years had existed only as dismal and
scattered piles of stone. Hundreds of yards of barbed wire-
entanglements had been bridged because they could not be
cut. Roads, sunk almost into obliteration through four
years of neglect, and often impassable two days after they
were used because of black soil that would not stand up,
had to be repaired with the greatest labor, the engineer
force in many cases carrying supplies on their backs be-

THE MEUSE ABOVE SEDAN

cause trucks could not be moved up. A road over the
Forges swamp had to be built by laying logs and sticks in
corduroy style in mushy swampland while the men engaged
in the work were under fire.[44]

In Belgium, at the end of October, there was little fighting except by artillery wings, while around Valenciennes
engagements between British and Germans savored more of
outpost encounters than pitched battles. Farther south the
French continued their process of leveling the old salient

[44] Cable dispatch from Edwin L. James to The *Times* (New York).

between St. Quentin and Rethel. Notwithstanding violent resistance additional progress was made by Debeney's troops. On some sectors the Germans were slowly retreating, but patrols nowhere permitted them to get out of contact with them. Aside from artillery and machine-gun activity there was little fighting for some days on that part of the front held by the Americans from the Meuse to Grandpré. Germans had been heavily bombing American positions with shells of all caliber, including gas projectiles, with Americans answering shot for shot. New big American guns were violently shelling German positions far behind the lines, taking under fire towns of strategic importance. Conflans, west of Metz, the principal junction point of communication with the big fortress on the Moselle, and Spincourt and Dommary-Baroncourt, also important railroad junctions, came under particularly heavy fire. In addition, American aviators lent their aid in the process of blasting away enemy positions.

While the Americans were driving away east of the Meuse, they were exerting equal pressure along the heights of the Aire, beyond Grandpré. Here the French, on the left, were pushing on beyond Vouziers and starting the formation of a salient with the American left as a peak. Heavy German artillery-fire revealed an uneasiness regarding the safety of the Briey iron-fields. The Briey district would be affected by any big gun bombardment of the Longuyon railway, the direct line over which German supplies had to be hauled. Guns were carrying shells twenty-five miles from points five to ten miles behind the American lines. These guns were of much larger caliber than the German guns which for weeks had fired on Paris. The latter were nine-inch guns, the American sixteen-inch. Debeney's troops, operating northeast of Laon, were advancing steadily toward Hirson. in order to cut railway communication with Metz. At Guise the French were fighting in the streets, and had captured the barracks and hospital south of the château.

The maxim, "tho the mills of God grind slowly, yet they grind exceeding small," might have been applied to the retributive progress made by the end of October by the

First American Army operating north of Verdun. With strength, and ardor unquenched by villainous weather, physical fatigue, or the sight of death in hideous forms, the Americans were gradually grinding down the German power of resistance. On either side of the Meuse, Prussianism was battling with a fury born of despair. Its finest soldiers had been slaughtered in droves, in order that their hard-prest comrades in the west and north might escape the trap in which they would be caught were Pershing's divisions to forge ahead too fast for them. Nineteen German divisions were still striving with dogged desperation to bar the Americans' advance. At several points one American battalion was forcing backward four German battalions, which, taking into account the proportionate strength of units, meant three or four Germans to two Americans. In six weeks our army had captured close to 40,000 men, more than 300 guns, and about a thousand trench-mortars and machine-guns. It had also freed several hundred square miles of French territory, and killed or wounded perhaps 150,000 Germans.

Nowhere had the enemy punished any American division so severely as to impair its fighting efficiency; while of enemy divisions at least a dozen had been rendered unfit for service.[45] Long-range, big-caliber American guns were shelling important German communications running through Longuyon, Montmédy, Sedan and Mézières. This system running through Luxembourg formed one of the two gateways between Germany and the American army, the other clearing through Liége. To protect this road Germans had thrown in the best of their army. Our front line was now some thirteen miles from the railroad. An advance of a few more miles would bring the road within accurate range of guns of which we had hundreds available.

With the Germans then seeking through President Wilson for an armistice with the Entente Powers, representatives of these Powers had met in Versailles on October 31. The last to arrive for the conference was Foch who came alone, without aid or orderly. Numerous uniformed officials of the Allied nations, with councilors, prime ministers, and personages of high estate, had lent dignity to the scene.

[45] Cable dispatch from Lincoln Eyre to The *World* (New York)

Automobiles had gone gliding over asphalt and cobblestone streets, bearing world-figures, some carrying high staff-officers in dazzling uniforms, others naval chiefs in blue-black, variegated with gold stripes and patterned according to their country's orders. Now and then limousines with distinguished civilians rushed by, claiming right of way. At the Trianon Palace, where they met, deliberations could be conducted as if in the quiet of a woodland dell. With the great palace and grounds still kept up as in old days, the Trianon, nestling in clusters of giant trees surrounded by a picturesque park, and resplendent with flower gardens and serpentine walks, stood almost within its shadow.

At the gathering on October 31 guards of French, British, American, and Italian soldiers stood on duty at various posts. Within a radius of some hundreds of yards nobody was allowed to pass unless able to produce the necessary official papers. On decisions to be reached at this conference much of later Entente military movements was expected to depend, these in turn depending on the outcome of the German request for an armistice, and especially on the question as to German acceptance of the terms which Foch, representing the Entente, would be authorized at this gathering to impose.

On November 1, the First American Army attacked on a front of over fifteen miles north of Verdun, its right flank on the Meuse, and drove a wedge into the heart of the German position. The resistance was weak at first, but stiffened in the course of the day into heavy fighting. When night fell infantry had made a good advance into the Bois de Barricourt, a dozen or more villages had been taken and 3,000 prisoners. Next day Valenciennes was captured by the British, Canadian troops under General Currie, who had met fierce resistance in the outskirts, being the first to enter the city. Advance detachments, pressing beyond Valenciennes, entered St. Saulvé on the road to Mons and progress was also made southeast of Valenciennes. Some 4,000 prisoners were taken. Counter-attacks were made with the help of tanks, but they broke down utterly. The weather was heavy; in a thick veil of mist could be seen black slag mountains, not unlike Egyptian pyramids, with factory chimneys faintly outlined above them. Dead horses, horribly mangled, lay at the roadside. Along the Scheldt Canal lay Valenciennes, an attenuated city, which one could see from end to end, with churches and factory chimneys high above the roofs.

Best known as an ancient city of lace-makers, Valenciennes had been famous for a thousand years because of its history and the men and women who were born within its walls. It had suffered many sieges, captures and conflicts; it had been the prize of robber-princes and warring empires. There, 500 years ago, was born Sir John Froissart, the gallant knight and medieval war-correspondent. The solitude of the city was oppressive. Altho liberated there were no manifestations of joy in Valenciennes. "Oh, my God!" said an old woman, "those devils have gone at last! What have they not made us suffer?" "Sir," said her husband, "they have stolen everything, broken everything, and have ground us down for four years. They are bandits and brigands!" Another woman put her hand to her heart in a breathless way as she said: "For four years we have suffered. It would take four years more to tell you all we have suffered. Mon Dieu! Mon Dieu!"

"We are some of those who escaped," said another man. "Escaped from what?" asked Philip Gibbs. The man pointed to a poster on the wall, which was an order for the mobilization of all men between 15 and 35; they were to present themselves to the German commandant under severe penalties, in order to be evacuated through the German lines. This order was dated October 31, and the mobilization was to have taken place on November 1, which was the day before the capture of the city. On October 3, 20,000 people had been forcibly expelled from the city, in the direction of Mons, leaving 5,000, who were employed by the Germans in municipal service—maintaining fire and water supplies, washing, and other work. The German rule had been hard, with continual requisitions, fines, and imprisonments. The fines increased in severity as Germany became more and more in need of money. In the early days private individuals had been fined 100 marks or so for trivial offenses; in the last days of the German occupation they had to pay as much as 2,000. The requisitioning extended to copper, mattresses, wool, and wine. Less than a month before their departure German soldiers completed their sack of the city, by going to each shop and filling their bags with

MOUZON, ON THE MEUSE, NEAR SEDAN
Here was fighting between Germans and Americans of the Second Division, including Marines, on the morning of the signing of the armistice

Valenciennes lace, linen handkerchiefs and clothes. The people had been poorly fed, only those who had money being able to obtain anything beyond the necessities of life. Butter was 40 francs a pound, sugar 25 francs, and chocolate 80 francs. The people were encouraged to work in market-gardens and grow potatoes and cauliflowers, but the Germans requisitioned all they produced.

In those early November days, when Germany was trembling under the defections of her allies, her own disasters in the field and the revolution at home, one of the greatest battles of the war was raging on both wings of the Western Front, where Foch was hammering at vital lines of communication. In Flanders British and Belgians were forcing the crossing of the Scheldt, the last natural obstacle that barred the road to Brussels. In the east Americans were winning marked successes while Gouraud kept them freed from menace on their left flank. On November 3 Franco-Belgian troops reached a line within five miles of Ghent. Further north French and American forces had occupied Audenarde, and Americans were battling their way across the Scheldt. Valenciennes, free of German machine-gunners, lay well behind the consolidated British line. But its outskirts were in ruins and the city itself was a sad sight until the center of the town was reached—there practically no damage had been done. The Grand Place with the beautiful Hôtel de Ville, except for trifling marks from stray bullets, was intact. Groups of civilians gathered here and there, some viewing the damage helplessly, others trying to reestablish their homes. Little children were playing in the ruined streets, with dead Germans lying unnoticed beside them.

Pershing's troops captured Buzancy on November 2, having pushed on seven miles southwest of Stenay. At times the German retreat was so rapid that in order to keep in touch with them motor-trucks had to be used by the Americans in pursuit. Loss of positions below Stenay forced a wide-sweeping German retirement to the Mons-Maubeuge-Hirson-Mézières line. Meanwhile trucks loaded with doughboys were seen rushing over crowded roads and going north

COURTESY OF THE MARINE CORPS RECRUITING PUBLICITY BUREAU

A VILLAGE ON THE MEUSE, NEAR SEDAN

after the retreating Germans. Half a hundred such trucks went off loaded with doughboys armed with rifles, some of them perched on hoods, with machine-guns mounted above drivers' heads, fighting men standing often on tiptoe as they went roaring northward on a grand hunt. In five weeks the Americans in this section had inflicted losses of more than 100,000 on the Germans, including 30,000 unwounded prisoners. After leaving Buzancy the Americans swept ahead between four and six kilometers before they could get into contact with the enemy. The Germans simply were not fighting; they were only getting out of the way. Those five weeks of grueling battle were the bloodiest in which American troops had fought. The German command threw against them, in point of numbers, almost one-fourth of the entire German available force on the Western Front. Of 180 German divisions Americans had faced more than 40.

Early in November the Freya Stellung was passed for almost the entire length of its battle-front. This made the fourth German defense-line that the Americans had shattered since September 26—the Hindenburg, Volker, Kremhilde, and now the Freya Stellung. Comparatively open country was now ahead of them and in open-country fighting Americans could do their best. Division after division arrived, went into action and melted away under the storm, until forty German divisions had been used. It was a great feat the Americans performed, obscured at the time by great feats performed by British and French elsewhere. It lacked the brilliance of the British work in breaking the last of the Hindenburg line, which was one of the great triumphs of this war, but it surpassed greatly all that we could have expected or hoped for in our first campaign.

Grandpré, an old town far behind, was now in ruins. It had changed hands five times. North of the road stood its ancient citadel on a hill where lay German dead and American dead in disarray. Americans had charged this hill from the east and in hand-to-hand fighting had vanquished the enemy. Perhaps two hundred dead lay in the small area of the citadel, with broken rifles, dented helmets, broken bayonets, wrecked packs, and dead covering the ground. In the Bois des Loges, where Germans and Americans fought for two and a half weeks, lay hundreds of dead unburied. One soldier lay with his pick in his hand. Four dead Germans were about him.

Before the war Buzancy had 3,000 inhabitants, all now

gone, and only sorry ruins were left of a once pretty town, defiled beyond conception. The streets had been given German names and so had the shops. Everything worth carrying away was gone. What had not been taken had been destroyed with true German vandalism. In a beautiful château was a library strewn around with leaves from priceless books. Filth lay in rooms where officers of high degree had lived. What chinaware had not been carted away was ruthlessly broken. Germans had devoted the last few hours

A MOTORCYCLE DISPATCH-RIDER

to defiling what they had not destroyed. A beautiful old church that had been used for a barracks contained masses of filth and rubbish. Empty wine bottles stood upon the altar and an overpowering stench hung about the whole place.

North of Verdun German resistance had been thoroughly broken. Americans had passed beyond Stenay, on the west bank, and were striking for Sedan. The advance soon got within a mile and a quarter of Beaumont, or six miles northwest of Stenay, and on November 6 was only ten southeast of Sedan. When Sedan was reached the German line coming down along the Belgian border would be dislocated. Beaumont was only eight miles from the main railroad connecting Metz and Thionville, through Montmédy, with Sedan. Mézières and Hirson on the German life-line were under fire and when they fell German armies would be cut into two practically isolated groups, one north of the Ardennes barrier and one south of it. Foch was driving the Germans against a wall, so far as defenses of their holdings in France and Belgium were concerned.

On November 5, the day after President Wilson transmitted to Germany the terms upon which the Entente Allies had decided to grant the request for an armistice, the British, southeast of Valenciennes, broke through German defenses based on the Mormal Forest and the Sambre river and canal and Le Quesnoy, after being nearly surrounded for several days, fell with its garrison of 1,000 men. Haig's forces, pushing far beyond it, reached the northeastern corner of the Mormal bastion, or a point only two miles southwest of Bavay, which was close to the Belgian boundary, nine miles west of Maubeuge. The British had passed the railroad that ran through the forest from Le Quesnoy to Avesnes, and were in a position to cut the railroad running along the Belgian border from Bavay to Maubeuge and Hirson. Germans were in full retreat along the whole French battle-front, with the exception of the region of Rethel, where a strong rear-guard was covering a railway that was one of the arteries vital to Germany. On a front of more than sixty miles the French had thrown the Germans back an average of six miles. The French from Champagne, as well as the Americans from the Argonne, were now getting close to Sedan, which the French and not the Americans were to be the ones actually to take. On their right and left Americans and British were still advancing. Unless all signs failed the final great retreat had begun. The question now was whether the enemy would be able to reach the Meuse and make a stand.

The British had achieved a great victory south of Valenciennes, about Le Quesnoy and Landrecies. Le Quesnoy was a medieval town, defended by high ramparts, inner and outer bastions, and garrisoned by over 1,000 Germans, who had orders to defend it at all costs. New Zealanders, determined to take Le Quesnoy, set out to assault it frontally as soon as the attack was launched with a bombardment. They stormed the outer ramparts in old-fashioned style, using scaling ladders, and made breaches through the walls, as in the ancient days of men-at-arms, but with more peril because of machine-gun fire which swept them from the inner defenses. When they had gained a part of the outer ramparts they could get no further, and new tactics had to be adopted. One body of men went round Le Quesnoy on the north and another on the south, until the town was completely surrounded by New Zealanders, and the German garrison was called upon to surrender in messages dropt inside the town from British airplanes flying low above it.

In the Oise-Serre region the French on November 5 made an advance averaging five or six miles, taking Vervins, and driving the Germans back on Hirson. A similar gain was made north of the Aisne. Americans north of Verdun were still going forward at full speed. Divisions of the First Army operating on the west bank of the Meuse pushed ahead a couple of miles and reached Chémery and Maisoncelle, just below Rancourt and only seven and a half miles south-southeast of Sedan, which was now in plain view from the captured heights. On the east side of the Meuse Pershing's forces cleared the bank to a point north of Dun-sur-Meuse, so that the campaign for Sedan was rapidly moving to a climax. The place where Napoleon III surrendered McMahon's army in 1870 had been a name of ill omen in French memories for nearly fifty years, but now it was to become a glorious name in French and in American military annals, if only the French with our help could take it before an armistice, then in progress, intervened. On November 6 the Americans were within six miles of it.

The crossing of the Meuse and the capture of Dun by Americans was one of the most gallant feats in the operations northwest of Verdun. The crossing involved the forcing of a way over a 160-foot river, besides a half-mile stretch of mud and a 60-foot canal, all in the face of enemy fire, and involved besides swimming and pulling men over with ropes. Grappling irons had to be used to scale the walls of the canal where machine-gunners were posted with scores of batteries on adjoining hills. While the Americans had the choice of crossings anywhere within five miles, they actually were limited to one point, where two-thirds of a mile of mud lay between the river and the canal. At all other points the Germans were firmly entrenched. Here they had not protected themselves with trenches because they never dreamed the Americans would be daring enough to try to make the passage. This crossing was made a short distance north of Brieulles.

Close to where the swimmers crossed, engineers threw over pontoon-boats and a tiny foot-bridge. Some of the pontoons were destroyed by the enemy, but the bridge remained intact and added materially to the constantly increasing numbers of men arriving on the west bank. Soon after dark the first brigade was across the first barrier, and more men were ready to make the journey. Then came the second, which was the crossing of the kilometer of mud stretching between the river and the canal. Under withering fire the Americans floundered through this mud, their feet sinking into it so that their pace was slowed down to a laborious walk. Next came the crossing of the deep canal, with steep sides and Germans at the top of the eastern edge. Swimmers again got into action and plunged through notwithstanding the fire and scrambled to the top, where they divided their attention between driving off the enemy and helping non-swimmers across. The Germans gave way without much resistance.

The German retirement continued elsewhere on the whole front. The British were less than fifty miles from Namur. French and Americans were well-nigh astride the Metz-Sedan railroad, hardly twelve miles from Mézières, and only sixty-two miles from Namur, which was assuming the character of a swiftly narrowing gateway through which German forces in France, nine armies strong, would have to retreat. Hampered by lack of motor-transport, the Germans were being crowded along such roads and railroads as were still open to them, but never free from the deadly assaults of Allied aircraft. Some weeks before Foch had said: "I

KNIGHTS OF COLUMBUS BEFORE THE MADELAINE IN PARIS

have not yet had my battle,'' but the operations now in progress justified a belief that the Marshal's hour had come at last—provided an armistice did not intervene. The American force was almost in the shadow of the Ardennes, that wide, deep belt of heavy woods and broken hills through which flows the Meuse northward toward the sea. If Sedan could be reached, not only would the railroad be cut, but several important branches would be severed. Just west of Sedan was Mézières, where another connecting link from the north came into the main stem and was in as great danger as Sedan. This line constituted the greatest menace to Germany, and, if cut, promised to bring a real disaster.

The approach of French troops and our troops to Sedan was to France something more than a revival of the bitter memories of forty-eight years before, now all but abolished by the victories of four months. It promised to be a significant and decisive detail in a new Sedan, ten times greater than that which extinguished the tinsel empire of Napoleon III and imposed upon France almost half a century of humiliation. The Germans were facing a situation which was critical from the Scheldt to the outskirts of Metz. In the west, British armies had broken through the last permanent line of German defenses and were advancing toward Bavai and Maubeuge, and nearing the first British battlefield of the war, the Mons of unhappy memory. Here the Germans had both their flanks in peril and their center exposed. Any local collapse would bring general ruin. Any failure on either flank would precipitate a colossal capture of German troops and a substantial elimination of the fighting forces of the German Empire. It was with this situation in their eyes that the German Government and the German people had to receive the armistice terms they had asked for, and which were now ready for them to receive from the hands of Marshal Foch. The greatest Prussian disaster since Jena and the possibility of a new Sedan, a German one this time, was in full view—and Pershing's army was sure to be in at such a death.

On November 7 the troops of the Forty-second (Rainbow) Division, which included men from twenty-six States of the Union, among them men of the old Sixty-ninth New York, marched down long slopes that led to the Meuse, and in the distance beyond them lay the roofs and walls of Sedan. Along the river bank where they were lay the little village of Wadelaincourt, seemingly deserted. Rain fell and gray clouds hung low. Not a single gray-coated German was seen. Slowly platoon commanders, young second lieutenants, just out of college, went forward, with men in little groups of eight or ten, carrying rifles and hand grenades as they passed through Wadelaincourt and came within sight of Sedan, the goal of six weeks of straining effort by American arms. First patrols made their way into outlying houses on the west side of the Meuse, from where they could see across the river Sedan, a straggling French city, built for the most part of gray stone, with the towers of churches rising above. Through the rain columns of smoke drifted up slowly from different parts which were on fire. Sedan was filled with Germans struggling to get away with guns and transports. The bridge across the Meuse had been blown up and the Meuse had become twice its usual size, its marshy banks now broad sheets of water. From northern heights guns sheltered in woods began to fire heavily on the Americans, but next day American aviators flying over Sedan could not see a trace of Germans, the town having been evacuated.[46]

In reaching Sedan the Americans showed, not so much military science, as martial spirit, and that became a large factor in Germany's desire for peace. The Forty-second Division actually outran its communications; it advanced twenty-five miles and more in five days. The First as well as the Forty-second participated in the fighting at Waldincourt and on the heights south of Sedan. Whether it was the First or the Forty-second who first saw Sedan one could not find out by asking either division. Betting at army headquarters favored the Rainbows. While they were racing for Sedan, a French division which had been ordered by Gouraud to advance, found that the only usable highway was already blocked by hurrying Americans ahead of them in the western outskirts of the town. The Second Division sent back word late the same night that it also had seen Sedan, having moved up along the Meuse, not knowing

<hr />

[46] Cable dispatch from Thomas M. Johnson to The *Sun* (New York).

tha. it was in a rivalry for the honor. The Americans, having had a look at the place from a distance, withdrew from before it, leaving the French to take possession of the town. One company of Americans, however, remained with the French, as a matter of courtesy, in making the entry.

Whatever may be said in years to come as to which division got so near Sedan first, one could positively declare that if the entire Fifth German Army had tried to hold the heights of Sedan, it would have had a great struggle with the 165th, 166th, 167th and 168th Infantry of the First Division; with the Fifth and Sixth Regiments of Marines, and with the Ninth and Twenty-third Infantry of the Second Division, while regiments of the Sixth Division were right behind. Every bridge and culvert on the river had been blown out, and where there were no bridges or culverts the retreating Germans had blown out stretches of road. One stretch of 200 yards had nine holes, each of which was big enough to hold a house. Engineers by rushing work bridged these holes, but it was a formidable task.

Sedan was in very good condition with the exception of the damage caused in the northern part by fires set by Germans two and three days before. There had been practically no fighting in the city, the Allied plan having been to avoid that if possible.[47] An advance of more than thirty-four miles had now been made by Americans since the offensive in the Argonne was begun on September 26. Meanwhile British, French, and American troops, elsewhere on the front between the Scheldt and the Meuse, were pushing the Germans out of the small section of France which they still occupied. It so happened that Sedan was entered on the very day the German armistice delegation was dispatched to the front. Germany's army was now all bottled up, with only one avenue of escape—that through Liége. Among the troops that helped to take Sedan were the Forty-second (Rainbow) Division, including the old Sixty-ninth New York; the Seventy-seventh (New York), Seventy-eighth (New Jersey and New York), Eightieth (Pennsylvania), Thirty-second (Michigan and Wisconsin), Ninetieth (Texas and Oklahoma), the First, Second, Third and Fifth Regulars, Eighty-ninth

[47] Sedan dispatch from Edwin L. James to The *Times* (New York).

180

(Kansas and Nebraska), Twenty-sixth (New England), and the Twenty-ninth (New Jersey). It was a fine thing for the French and Americans to achieve this success after five weeks of bloody and disheartening fighting in which they had to break the best German resistance that the Kaiser could put against them. History looked down that day from heights to where the Stars and Stripes were raised above the sleepy little city, in which Napoleon III surrendered his last army, and his pinchbeck empire vanished overnight with

A GERMAN FUNERAL ON THE WESTERN FRONT

news of his capitulation. Meanwhile the French drove on-ward toward the Belgian border, almost reaching it from the neighborhood of Hirson, their advance covering as much as ten miles at various points. They were east of La Capelle, and had taken Rumigny. Southeast of Mézières they were as much as within ten or twelve miles of the Bel-gian line, while the British continued their advance toward Maubeuge.

No mortal could imagine what the German retreat meant in terms of traffic and in human energy, unless he knew the mechanism of modern war. It meant the surging forward of motor-truck columns and transport wagons for scores of miles back from the new front, for when one link of the chain was extended all that chain had also to be dragged ahead—a chain made up of hundreds of thousands of men with all their material. Big guns had to be got into motion, crawling over narrow roads on caterpillar tractors. Tanks had to find new hiding-places. Roads became merely narrow channels down which mud-splashed battalions on the march had to crowd to one side to make way for endless columns of field-batteries, motor-busses and motor-trucks, swaying perilously along deep and muddy ruts on the edge of greasy ditches. Staff officers and headquarters men had to shift their lodgings from village to village. Pontoon bridges had to be carried mounted on heavy wagons. Airdrome equipment had to be packed for removal, not to mention field-kitchens. Ammunition columns had also to move and a whole army of road-menders. When all these things had to happen troops could advance only a mile or two from day to day.[48]

From the Belgian frontier to Metz the German was entering his last ditch, and France was practically freed of his presence. He had become condemned to fight for his life in Belgium, which was the final retribution for his invasion of that country—for turning his plighted word into a "scrap of paper." German militarism was to be destroyed on the very ground where it had committed its foulest crimes. While one-half its forces were retiring on Waterloo, the other half was in flight from Sedan. If the occupation of Sedan had occurred twenty-four hours before it did, so great an achievement would have been the signal in America for nation-wide rejoicing. As it was, the announcement was overshadowed by a premature report of the acceptance by the Germans of Foch's armistice terms, and a resultant extraordinary celebration. The occupation of Sedan had brought a line of communication vital to the German army into Entente control, and created a situation intolerable for armies depending on it for support. With that line now unavailable Germans in Belgium and north-

[48] Cable dispatch from Philip Gibbs to The *Times* (New York).

ern France were endangered to a far greater degree than they had ever yet been. German armies had to move because they were simply driven out; no pretense was made—not even in clever Berlin bulletins—that they were withdrawing voluntarily.

The British on the same day renewed their push eastward toward Maubeuge and Mons, while the French continued their advance northward and beyond the Meuse, forming a junction beyond Mézières with Franco-Americans from Sedan. East of the Meuse Americans reached the Woëvre Forest and made an advance in the neighborhood of Haraumont and Brandeville. When the British were south of Tournai, the Germans started to withdraw. Pressing after them the British crossed the Scheldt and occupied Condé and several villages along the Condé-Mons Canal. Further south British troops got across the main road leading north of Maubeuge. The Allies had now all but closed the north and east "bottlenecks" through which the Germans had counted on making their escape from France. It had become a race—with Germany to get out, with the Allies to head them off east of Sedan. Roads became choked with fleeing Germans hurrying away in every conceivable kind of transport, those unable to ride either walking or running, their whole effort being to get out. After two or three days more of pushing forward, Allied troops would find themselves out in the open, the British beyond all waterways north and northeast of Valenciennes and making their way over level country west of Brussels, with French in the plains fronting the forest of the Ardennes, and Americans out in the Woëvre west of Metz. In those great stretches of open country the Germans would be deprived of all the natural defenses, hills, ravines, and forests, that had enabled them to delay the Allied advances. Military observers were a unit in belief that, once the German armies were prest beyond the French frontier their retreat would become a rout.

Germany was beaten not only on the front but at home. While her envoys were digesting Foch's armistice terms during the seventy-two hours allotted them, their country was crumbling to pieces; the revolution had begun. On the whole front the pursuit was relentless, the German no longer having a stomach for resistance. Gouraud held the west bank of the Meuse from Sedan to the outskirts of Mézières and had liberated scores of villages while Americans had virtually cut the final line of the German defense. Germany's dying effort was tragic as well as ludicrous. While men in front lines were fighting to the last ditch, rear areas were congested with transports, galloping toward Metz and elsewhere, in an attempt to save as much booty as possible from the wreckage. Germans who had set forth in 1914 to make France their booty were retiring with vegetables under their arms plucked from French gardens, or with carts filled with garden-truck, chickens, and household trinkets which they had stolen. From Longuyon to Conflans a solid line of wagons, camions, and cannon was going southeastward in the direction of Metz. The road leading from Conflans was a mass of galloping cannon-limbers. By November 9 the British were closing in on Mons. Further south they were surrounding the fortress of Maubeuge, which Joffre had tried to hold in 1914, but could not because of high-power German artillery such as had already subdued the Belgian fortresses of Liége and Namur. South and southeast the French were up to La Capelle and Hirson. Tournai and Maubeuge were captured on November 9, the latter just south of the Belgian frontier. After four years and three months of war, the British were advancing toward ground where in August, 1914, the "Contemptibles" first saw the flash of German guns and, fighting desperately, retreated. Now they had passed through towns which in 1914 saw them staggering, bleeding, and beaten under fierce German onslaughts. Flushed with many victories, they would never again taste defeat while the Germans were to know nothing else.

Gouraud made an official entry into Sedan on November 10. Disorder was in the ranks of the far-off retreating German army. Booty increased in importance as the pursuit went on. Several railroad trains, batteries of artillery, immense ammunition dumps and stores, and wagon trains fell into Gouraud's hands, together with a large number of prisoners. Everywhere French troops were within a short day's march of the border, and could have completed the liberation of

AT THE MOMENT OF VICTORY

French soldiers going into "No Man's Land" after the signing of the armistice

VI.

French soil had not the roads become encumbered by traffic
and the booty Germans left behind. French cavalry did
cross the Belgian border north and east of Hirson, an important German position. Considerable gains were made
along the whole front of about thirty miles from the junction of French and British armies to the Meuse east of
Mézières.

The fact that November 10 might be the last day of the
war had no recognizable effect on military operations along
the American front. Our men were fighting from Sedan
east to the Moselle near Pont-à-Mousson. The important

GERMAN SOLDIERS RESTING AT NIGHT FALL

town of Stenay, on the Meuse, where the Crown Prince had
made his headquarters, and after the Germans had endeavored to hold by hundreds of machine-gun nests and
terrible artillery and hand-to-hand barrages from hills beyond Stenay, was taken. It was the last town in the
Americans separated by miles billions of francs, the cost
issued—much said and had one in "German payments,"
and had on the western Meuse Heights positions
chain of the "Kriemhild" wall one of the Argonne were
crushed."

Still others . . . . 157 %

French soil had not the roads become encumbered by traffic and the booty Germans left behind. French cavalry did cross the Belgian border north and east of Hirson, an important German position. Considerable gains were made along the whole front of about thirty miles from the junction of French and British armies to the Meuse east of Mézières.

The fact that November 10 might be the last day of the war had no recognizable effect on military operations along the American front. Our men were fighting from Sedan east to the Moselle near Pont-à-Mousson. The important

GERMAN SOLDIERS RESTING AT MARS-LA-TOUR

town of Stenay, on the Meuse, where the Crown Prince had made his headquarters, and which the Germans had endeavored to hold by hundreds of machine-gun nests and terrific artillery and machine-gun barrages from hills beyond Stenay, was taken. It was the last town that the Americans captured. Berlin's bulletin of that day—the last issued—merely said that the enemy "followed our movements" and that on the eastern Meuse Heights and the plain of the Woëvre "many attacks of the Americans were repulsed."

Still unable as they were to tell the truth, German militarism in its death agony clung also to its savagery. A deluge of high explosives and poison-gas was poured on Mézières where 20,000 civilians, men, women and children, were penned like trapt rats without the possibility of escape, the broad stream of the Meuse cutting them off from French soldiers. For the moment no succor was possible. Incendiary shells fired a hospital. Wounded were taken to cellars in which the whole population was crouching. While cellars might give protection from fire or melinite, they were worse than death-traps against the fumes of poisonous gas. So a murderous order was given, and faithfully German gunners carried it out. The civilians in the town had no gas-masks and no chemicals to save lives, and so had to submit to this martyrdom—the final testimony that mere civilization was a thing apart from Prussianized Germany at the close of the war.

Almost coincident with the signing of the armistice, Mons capitulated before pressure from the British and Canadians who drove the Germans out through the same gateway by which Bülow and Kluck had hurled their armies against the "Contemptibles" in 1914. The population of Mons paraded the streets, cheering madly for their deliverance in cries which must have reached the ears of Germans outside the walls. The celebration and rejoicing in the afternoon made the old town vibrate, while bands and pipers led marching thousands. On the road to Mons were columns of marching troops, bands playing ahead of them, almost every man with flags on his rifle, the red, blue, and white of France, the red, yellow, and black of Belgium. Flowers were in their caps, and they had red and white chrysanthemums given by people who cheered them on their way in many villages which had been liberated from the German yoke. For the British the war ended at Mons, just as at Mons it began for them four years before.

The Canadian Division which had the satisfaction of fighting its way into Mons received a great reception in the city, which contained 40,000 inhabitants. The scene in the main square, when the long-silent chimes once more played the "Brabançonne" and other Allied hymns, was one of the most touching in their experience. During the last month it had been more than evident that discipline no longer prevailed in the German army. Soldiers, instead of goose-stepping and offering wooden salutes before officers, began to ignore discipline and officers completely. Officers seemed to disappear as by magic, and the behavior of men was more and more independent. For three weeks the Germans had been in flight without order, loading wagons with loot, often of the most useless character, such as dog-kennels, bird-cages, chairs or tables with legs missing, collected anywhere or anyhow.

Philip Gibbs [49] described how, in villages round about Mons, after the fall of that city, people surged in narrow streets and English laughter rose above the chatter of women and children. British soldiers were still on the march with guns and their old field-cookers. Motor-cars streaked through streets, dodging traffic now and then; rockets were fired and gusts of laughter came from officers, who were shooting off pistols into the darkness to celebrate the end. From dark towns like Tournai and Lille rockets rose and burned with a white light. Aviators flew like bats in the dusk, skimming tree-tops and gables, doing Puck-like gambols above a tawny sunset, looping and spiraling and falling in steep dives which looked like death for them until the planes flattened out and rose again. These boys who had been reprieved from the menace that was close to them in every flight shot off flares and rockets, which dropt down to crowds of French and Flemish people waving to them from below. Late in the night came sounds of singing and laughter from open windows in towns which had been long shuttered, with people hiding in cellars. British officers sat down to French pianos, romped about the keys, crashed out chords and led a chorus of men who wanted to sing some old song.

On leaving Mons, Mr. Gibbs dodged a hundred mine-craters, blown up by the enemy along the road, and now entangled in the tides of traffic. He had traveled far through liberated country. Before that he had determined to get to Mons on the day of "cease firing!" Moving one way for miles he saw a pageant with endless tides of British infantry, cavalry, artillery, and transport, the flutter of flags above them. In the opposite direction there moved another tide, and that, too, had its flags and its banners. It was the pitiful, heroic tide of life composed of thousands of civilians who that morning had come back through German lines, men from 15 to 60, who had been taken away from Cambrai, Courtrai, Lille, Roubaix, Tourcoing, Tournai and Valenciennes, besides hundreds of towns and villages in the wake of the enemy's retreat. To the very end the German command had conscripted this manhood for use as forced labor, but also to prevent them from serving Allied armies.

On all roads through Mons thousands of women were making their way home burdened with luggage. Men bore packs so heavy that they bent under them, exhausted as they were by long trekking, with only food enough to keep alive. Each man had added some straws to his camel's weight by thrusting flags into his pack, not one flag, but four or five, so that, as he trudged with bent head, they fluttered above him. There were armies of boys and crowds of elderly men in black coats and derby hats with mud up to their knees, stains on their backs where they had slept on filthy straw. Groups of a dozen or more pushed hand-carts, made roughly out of boxes, and holding bags and packs. Thus they made their way through the British troops, and every now and then stopt round their carts to raise their hats and shout *"Vivent les Anglais!"* or to grasp the hands of British Tommies and say, "Bravo! Bravo!"

Women showed the courage which had never departed from them through all the years of tragedy. Hot and spent by a long journey, their hair had become uncoiled, their skirts bedraggled in mud, but they had an eager look and strained forward at the ropes of carts with the vision of their homes luring them on mile after mile to Tournai and Lille. Mr. Gibbs met many people in Mons who remembered the first battle as if it had occurred the day before. Little groups stood around telling of those days seeming now so far off and pointing out places where the British fought in the streets before they made up outside a line from which they had to fall back in retreat before overwhelming forces. Some of those old "Contemptibles" had survived and were now in Mons again, among them the Fifth Lancers, who had been chosen to enter with the Canadians. Poor old Tommy had had a rough time, and had hated it, but had been patient and long-suffering, full of grim and silent courage, not boasting about the things he had done, not caring a lot for glory, not getting much

COURTESY OF THE MARINE CORPS RECRUITING PUBLICITY BUREAU

A VILLAGE ON THE MEUSE
In the old building facing the river, Germans were sniping on the morning of November 11

chance for dash; but he had done his job, and it had been well done.

There was poetic justice in the war ending where it did— at one extremity of the battle-line, with the British in Mons —at the other, with French and Americans in Sedan, both names of terrible memories. At Mons began the desolation of English homes. Sedan stood for the fall of France from the first position in Europe after which for more than forty years she had bowed under the threatening German shadow. When, in November, 1918, the British marched into Mons and the French into Sedan, it seemed as if the war could not do otherwise than end. It was the dramatic climax of the play, the downfall of the criminal at the scenes of his crimes, the triumph of the wronged at the place where the wrong was committed.

At dawn on November 11 there was no hint on the Meuse of a cessation of hostilities, in accordance with the armistice which the Germans had signed with Foch in his railway car near Senlis. Americans attacked in force at 8 o'clock, the onslaught preceded by a tremendous barrage which was returned in kind. For three hours Americans swept forward, hurling themselves against wire-entanglements, under a devastating return gun-fire. Then, at exactly one minute of eleven, like a calm following the crash of thunder at the clearing of a storm, guns on both sides abruptly ceased firing and the silence was more startling even than the deafening roar of the barrage had been. Again the skyline figures were suddenly silhouetted, cautiously at first, but growing bolder along the line, until they stood upright. These were Germans. The Americans were less cautious. As the barrage died away, ending in a husky rumble in the distance, runners sprang along the firing-line, and dough-boys leaped from trenches, fox-holes and shell-craters, splitting the unaccustomed silence with a roar of voices like an outburst at some great closely contested game of base-ball in a world series. The defeated Germans joined vociferously in the cheering and the World War was ended.

While one minute before eleven it would have meant death to show oneself above shelter, not more than a minute after the hour the rolling plain was alive with cheering, shouting, care-free men. Soon both Germans and Americans were seen moving carelessly along that narrow stretch of ground they had so fiercely been fighting over, some of them shy and awkward in manner, like embarrassed schoolboys. This first advance was followed by offers from the Americans to the Germans of cigarets, chocolate, and chewing-gum, and from the Germans offers of hot coffee, bread, and sausages. Orders forbidding fraternizing had been strict, but the novelty of the situation overcame prudence, and doughboys surreptitiously visited German dugouts. Along the barbed wire at a road crossing there soon began a brisk barter in souvenirs, the Germans bewildered by the number of Americans who spoke German. At Stenay Americans had picked their way across the flooded river, entered and delivered the town at the very moment when the fighting ended. In the rear every one knew that the war was to stop at 11 o'clock, but in the front line no one except the officers knew. Doughboys knew nothing except that their orders were to attack. The Americans fought to the last minute. At 10.40, at 10.50, at 10.55, they were still fighting. Everywhere on the line in France was the same sudden and profound silence as the hour struck and guns for the first time ceased the terrible chorus from the North Sea to Switzerland.

Over hills in the east which had been the scene of bloody warfare almost constantly since the conflict began, and the scene of perhaps the world's most bitter battle where the Crown Prince had so long tried to take Verdun, there fell an almost unearthly calm. Where the roar of a million shells had often torn the air, one could have heard a sparrow twitter had the war left any sparrows there. Torn, twisted, and tortured was that land. Of all the woods no tree was left whole; of pretty villages only blackened and stark bits of moss-covered and shattered stones; of roads there was not a trace. Somber shadow and silence were over all and would have seemed ominous had one not known it was harmless now. Soon the landscape was filled with cheering men. No Fourth of July in the United States ever saw such fireworks as threw red, green, and blue streaks across that foggy sky. Far away was poor, torn, suffering Verdun, now suddenly turned into a place of victory. Gathering darkness that night hid its wounds and one saw the French tricolor and the Stars and Stripes flying from house-tops and parapets made visible by searchlights. At the top of the grizzled fortress walls a band, half French and half Yankee, played all the tunes it knew. Through the streets marched rejoicing Yankees and their Allies.[50]

[50] Cable dispatch from Edwin L. James to The *Times* (New York).

XV

AMERICANS IN THE WAR—DIVISIONS THAT SERVED
AT THE FRONT, THEIR ACHIEVEMENTS AND
THEIR LOSSES—PERSHING AND SOME OF
HIS GENERALS—FOCH IN VICTORY, AND
PÉTAIN'S FINE APPEAL TO
HIS SOLDIERS

April 6, 1917—May, 1919

AMERICA in this war had landed 2,000,000 men in France
at the time of the signing of the armistice. She had at
least 2,000,000 more in preparation for going over. At the
front some 600,000 and perhaps 750,000 of her men had served
on the fighting-line. These figures relate to land operations.
Those on the sea, in which our navy participated against
submarines, are outlined in a later chapter of this volume,
Part XVIII, Chapter IV. As to which among the twenty-
five or thirty divisions that reached the front in France
saw most service, some observers held that the Second
Division, composed of the Fifth and Sixth Marines, the
Ninth and Twenty-third Regular Infantry, and the
Twelfth, Fifteenth and Seventeenth Artillery Regiments,
did the most fighting, but others, especially the First
and Forty-second, would not have agreed with that
opinion. First in the trenches had been the First Division,
and in every battle it had given an excellent account of
itself. The two divisions, First and Second, had both arrived in France in the early autumn of 1917, when the
American uniform was yet unknown on the Western Front.
They had been hastily gathered together and sent over-
seas in response to an urgent demand following the visit
of Marshal Joffre. While the First went more quickly into
training, the Second was used at once for all sorts of work,
such as building railroads, landing coal, and other prosaic
tasks. Between times it was getting military training, but
its officers were mostly experienced men and the skeletons
of its regiments were composed of old army men. Not until

AMERICANS IN THE WAR—DIVISIONS THAT SERVED
AT THE FRONT, THEIR ACHIEVEMENTS AND
THEIR LOSSES—PERSHING AND SOME OF
HIS GENERALS—FOCH IN VICTORY, AND
PÉTAIN'S FINE APPEAL TO
HIS SOLDIERS

April of 1917—May, 1919

AMERICA in this war had landed 2,000,000 men in France
at the time of the signing of the armistice. She had at
least 2,000,000 more in preparation for going over. At the
front some 600,000 and perhaps 750,000 of her men had served
on the fighting-line. These figures relate to land operations.
Those on the sea, in which our navy participated against
submarines, are outlined in a later chapter of this volume
(Part XVIII, Chapter IV. As to which among the twenty-
five or thirty divisions that reached the front in France
saw most service, some observers held that the Second
Division, composed of the Fifth and Sixth Marines, the
Ninth and Twenty-third Regular Infantry, and the
Twelfth, Fifteenth and Seventeenth Artillery Regiments,
did the most fighting, but others, especially the First
and Forty-second, would not have agreed with that
opinion. First in the trenches had been the First Division
and in every battle it had given an excellent account of
itself. The two divisions, First and Second, had both arrived in France in the early autumn of 1917, when the
American uniform was yet unknown on the western front.
They had been hastily gathered together and sent over-
seas in response to an urgent demand following the rise
of Marshal Joffre. With the First went accompanied by much
training, the Second was used at once for all sorts of
small mobilizing railroads, hauling coal, and other purposes
of war. Between times it was getting military training but
its ranks were mainly expanded up, and the Second
division regiments were composed of old enlistments, not until

199

March did the Second leave its training-camps and go with the French for a six-weeks' training in the trenches on the heights of the Meuse southeast of Verdun.

When the Germans started their "victory" drive late in March, Pershing offered Foch anything the Americans had in France that could be of any use. The First Division was taken at once from the Toul sector and sent to the Montdidier region, and the Second, after a short period of intensive training, to the Somme region. It was the First that took Cantigny. The Second was about to go into line when the Germans, late in May, changed the Entente plans by driving southward from the Chemin-des-Dames to the Marne, and reaching Château-Thierry, when the Second was at once put into camions and rushed to the scene of battle at Château-Thierry where the Germans were threatening Paris as they had not threatened the French capital since the fall of 1914. Just west of Château-Thierry, on June 1, the Second was thrown into the across the Paris-Metz highway at the point where the Germans were nearest Paris, and there in the Belleau Wood, the Fifth and Sixth Marines of this division won undying fame by stopping the German rush. They had no artillery on the first day, because their guns had not yet come, and they had no food except emergency rations. Moreover, their ammunition was not all that it might have been and yet they effectively checked the Germans at the Bois de Belleau, and for eleven days fought against repeated German attacks and repelled them. On the last day of May the machine-gunners of the Third Division, rushing into Château-Thierry after a sixty-hour trip in camions, also aided in stopping the Germans. For days afterward the Second Division prevented the German advance. On the last day of that month the Ninth and Twenty-third Infantry, seeing with others of the Second at Vaux, greatly improved the Allied prospects.

The Second was not again heard from until July 18, when Foch electrified the world by his brilliant counter-thrust and Château-Thierry became part of the great Marne victory. The most important blow, indeed, the first blow, in this offensive, was delivered south of Soissons. Here tonight the First and Second Divisions, with the famous French

March did the Second leave its training-camps and go with the French for a six-weeks' training in the trenches on the heights of the Meuse southeast of Verdun.

When the Germans started their "victory" drive late in March, Pershing offered Foch anything the Americans had in France that could be of any use. The First Division was taken at once from the Toul sector and sent to the Montdidier region, and the Second, after a short period of intensive training, to the Somme region. It was the First that took Cantigny. The Second was about to go into line when the Germans, late in May, changed the Entente plans by driving southward from the Chemin-des-Dames to the Marne, and reaching Château-Thierry, when the Second was at once put into camions and rushed to the scene of battle at Château-Thierry, where the Germans were threatening Paris as they had not threatened the French capital since the fall of 1914. Just west of Château-Thierry, on June 1, the Second was thrown into line across the Paris-Metz highway at the point where the Germans were nearest Paris, and there in the Belleau Wood, the Fifth and Sixth Marines of this division won undying fame by stopping the German rush. They had no artillery on the first day, because their guns had not yet come, and they had no food except emergency rations. Moreover, their ammunition was not all that it might have been, and yet they effectively checked the Germans at the Bois de Belleau, and for eleven days fought against repeated German attacks and repelled them. On the last day of May machine-gunners of the Third Division, rushing into Château-Thierry after a sixty-hour trip in camions, also aided in stopping the Germans. For days afterward the Second Division prevented the German advance. On the last day of that month the Ninth and Twenty-third Infantry, acting with others of the Second at Vaux, greatly improved the Allied prospects.

The Second was not again heard from until July 18, when Foch electrified the world by his brilliant counter-thrust and Château-Thierry became part of the great Marne salient victory. The most important blow, indeed the vital blow, in this offensive, was delivered south of Soissons. Here fought the First and Second Divisions, with the famous French

Moroccan Division betwen them, and an advance of eight kilometers, made on the first day, rendered possible the eventual reduction of the salient that was menacing Paris.[51]

When Pershing started his drive to reduce the St. Mihiel salient on September 12, the Second Division had a place in the hardest of the fighting along the southern side of the salient, where the heaviest German resistance was expected. Again the Second made good, smashing through in record time. After this battle the Second disappeared from battle not to reappear until October 2 and then where it was least expected—in the Champagne with Gouraud's Fourth Army, which was driving north to free Reims and break the German hold on that region. On the first day, in the region of Somme-Py, the Second broke through the German line for six kilometers, leading in the attack. In succeeding days they greatly aided Gouraud in breaking the German hold on the hills of Champagne and liberating Reims, for which the Kaiser's heart had bled often and freely. When Pershing, on November 1, started the drive which took the Americans eventually to Sedan, the Second was in the line fronting St. Georges against a position which had held the Americans at a standstill for two weeks. It broke through for five kilometers on the first day, and, leading other divisions, was responsible for the German *communiqué's* first admission during the war that the German line had been broken. Such in brief outline were the performances of the Second Division in helping to save Paris, reduce Reims, and reach Sedan.

The Forty-second (Rainbow) Division, which had left the United States just a year before, that is on October 18 and following days, had been involved in all the larger actions in which the Americans were engaged. After reaching France it underwent a period of training in a back area, and on April 1 took over a sector in the Lunéville region, being the first American division intrusted with a divisional sector. Having held for three months an active but stationary front of fifteen kilometers, it had been sent to the Champagne where, with Gouraud's army, it helped in the great exploit of meeting the German drive of July 15 north of

---

[51] Cable dispatch from Edwin L. James to The *Times* (New York).

MAJ.-GEN. GEORGE W. READ
© HARRIS & EWING.

MAJ.-GEN. JOSEPH T. DICKMAN
U. S. OFFICIAL PHOTO.

MAJ.-GEN. WILLIAM M. WRIGHT
© HARRIS & EWING.

MAJ.-GEN. CHARLES H. MUIR

MAJ.-GEN. CHARLES T. MENOHER
© CLINEDINST, WASHINGTON, D. C.

MAJ.-GEN. ADELBERT CRONKHITE

MAJ.-GEN. WILLIAM G. HAAN
© UNDERWOOD & UNDERWOOD, N. Y.

MAJ.-GEN. FRANK J. HIMES
© PRESS ILLUSTRATING SERVICE.

A GROUP OF AMERICAN MAJOR-GENERALS

Suippes, when Gouraud held up fierce onslaughts. From the Champagne the division went to Château-Thierry, where it distinguished itself in crossing the Ourcq, capturing Sergy, Seringes, Villiers-sur-Fère, and Nesles, and making an advance of sixteen kilometers. After receiving replacements, it then went to the Toul sector, where it took part in the reduction of the St. Mihiel salient. Having made an advance of twenty kilometers, it turned its sector over to newer troops and went to the Argonne, where it was assigned to the piercing of the Kremhilde Stellung at its apex in the region of the Côte de Châtillon, where it took Hill No. 288 after being told the thing could not be done. This American division had fought and taken prisoners from twenty-six German divisions, including three Prussian Guard and one Austrian division, and prisoners from nineteen independent German units.[52] During the 224 days in which it was stationed at the front it was in action 180 times. The remainder of the time it spent in moving from front to front or waiting in reserve close behind the front.[53]

Whether it was a unit of the One Hundred and Sixty-fifth Infantry, or the old Sixty-ninth of New York, which was first to cross the Ourcq, in July, 1918, was first to reach the Vesle, and first to get over the Rhine into German territory, became at the end of the war a matter of some discussion. So also the Twenty-seventh Division, composed of New York National Guard troops, and the Thirtieth, or "Old Hickory" Division, composed of militia from the Carolinas and Tennessee, made rival claims as to their respective parts in helping to break the Hindenburg line in October, and the One Hundred and Sixth and One Hundred and Seventh Infantry as to the part they had played in breaking certain segments of the line. Twenty-one American divisions, totalling more than 650,000 fighting men, had participated in the action beginning on September 26, and known variously as the battle of the Argonne and the battle of the Meuse, but which history might still call Sedan—the battle that combined with British and French efforts at this

[52] Cable dispatch from Edwin L. James to The *Times* (New York).

[53] Statement made by Brig.-Gen. Douglas MacArthur in *The Army and Navy Journal,* December, 1918.

time, on other fronts, definitely ended the world's bloodiest war. The reduction of the St. Mihiel salient in the middle of September had cut off at one stroke a menacing projection toward Verdun and weakened the enemy by threatening Metz. With the conclusion of the St. Mihiel action, the steady inflow of American forces that consequently set in caused a displacement of power as between Allied and German armies.

Including men who served in the later part of the Argonne battle, it was said there was hardly a county, or perhaps a township in the United States that had not had at least one representative in it and that every State from first to last had had a division, or some part of a division in the fighting. Altogether 650,000 Americans had been engaged in the Argonne. At the beginning of the battle the troops who took part, with a few exceptions, had not completed their training. Two divisions had never been under fire before, and only two—the Seventy-seventh and Twenty-eighth—had taken part in engagements that could have been called serious, these two having just come from the Marne salient where they fought from the Vesle to the Aisne.

None of our troops who had been at St. Mihiel were at the launching of the Argonne offensive, tho some came in afterward. Veteran divisions were therefore missing from the first assault; however, all had had some trench experience and all possest artillery—the Eightieth, or "Blue Ridge Division," which was under General Adelbert Cronkhite; the Thirty-third, of Illinois, under General George Bell, Jr.; the Thirty-fifth, of Missouri and Kansas, under General Peter M. Traub; the Seventy-seventh from New York City, assigned to the Argonne Forest proper, and under General Robert Alexander. Other divisions that served in the Argonne by the time Sedan was reached in November, were the Thirty-seventh, or "the Buckeye Division," under General Charles S. Farnsworth; the Seventy-ninth from Virginia and Maryland, under General Joseph E. Kuhn; the Ninety-first or "Wild West Division," from the Pacific Northwest, under General William H. Johnston; the Ninetieth, under General Henry T. Allen (which was relieved by the Fifth Division under General Hanson E. Ely from October 12th to 22d); the Fourth, or "Ivy Division," under General M. L. Hersey (relieved by the Third or "Marne Division" under General Preston Brown on October 19); the Third Division under General Preston Brown (relieved by the Fifth or "Red Diamond," under General Hanson E. Ely on October 27); the Thirty-second under General William G. Haan (relieved by the Eighty-ninth or "Western," under General Frank L. Winn, on October 20); the First Division under General Frank Parker (relieved by the Forty-second, or "Rainbow Division," under General Charles T. Menoher, on October 12); the Twenty-eighth or "Keystone Division," under General William H. Hay (relieved by the Eighty-second or "All American Division," under General G. B. Duncan, on October 9); the second under General J. A. Le Jeune, and the Seventy-eighth under General James McRae, Twenty-sixth under General Frank E. Bamford, and the Twenty-ninth under Charles S. Morton. Other American divisions, often best known by their fancy names, were the Thirty-fourth, called the "Sandstorm Division," from New Mexico, under General J. A. Johnston; the Thirty-sixth, "Lone Star Division," from Texas, under General W. R. Smith; the Forty-first, or "Sunshine Division," under General R. Coulter, Jr.; the Eighty-first, or "Wild Cat Division," under General C. J. Bailey; the Eighty-eighth, or "Clover Leaf," under General William Wiegel, and the Ninety-second or "Buffalo," under General Charles G. Ballou.

© COMMITTEE PUBLIC INFORMATION.

MAJ.-GEN. E. M. LEWIS
Commander of the "Old Hickory" Division

Many divisions remained in line in the Argonne so long that they required nerves of steel to stand the strain. Some were

sent in a second time after having had only a few days of rest.
The First, Fifth, Twenty-sixth, Forty-second, Eightieth, and
Ninetieth were in the line twice. Many acts of individual
prowess occurred. A notable one was credited to Sergeant
Alvin C York, of the 328th Infantry in the Eighty-second Division, who at the head of a detachment of seven men, killed
in the Argonne twenty Germans, took 132 prisoners, including
four officers, and put thirty-six machine guns out of business.
York received the Congressional Medal of Honor and the
French Croix de Guerre. His home was in Pall Mall, a mountain village in Tennessee, where he was second elder of a
Christian Science Church. On his return in May, 1919, York
was married in Pall Mall in the presence of 3,000 people. In
the Eighty-second Division also was the 325th Infantry, in
which was Captain Frank Williams, a former deputy sheriff in
Montana and Wyoming, where he had won twenty-odd fights
with cattle thieves. On Hill 182, in the Argonne, Williams
killed five Germans, and with a machine-gun company won the
hill in a five-hour fight. The division in 26 days captured 845
prisoners. Its killed and wounded amounted to 215 officers
and 5,794 men.

The Eighty-second, known as the "All American Division,"
had 26 days of continuous fighting in the Meuse-Argonne. It
was organized at Camp Gordon, Georgia, and was under command of Major-General Eben Swift, its men coming from
Georgia, Alabama, and Tennessee. It served under the British
for five weeks in the summer of 1918, was then transferred to
Toul where it participated in the St. Mihiel drive, having
1,200 casualties, and captured the towns of Norroy and Van-
deries. Then it went to the Argonne, where it was continuously
on the front for 26 days. One of the Eighty-second's attacks
was made north of Fleville, where it penetrated an outpost
line of the Kremhilde-Stellung.

The Seventy-ninth had first entered the line on September
14, 1918, at a point only half a kilometer distant from the
famous Dead Man's Hill. It was assigned to the capture of
Montfaucon, which had been in German hands since 1914.
Commanded by Major-General John E. Kuhn, it was made up
of drafted men from Pennsylvania, Maryland, New York,
West Virginia, and the District of Columbia. General Kuhn

was afterward made a Commander of the Legion of Honor. In Montfaucon, after its capture, the division found a house with a periscope running above its roof from a concrete, bomb-proof cellar. The periscope gave a view of all the Allied lines on that side of Verdun and had been used for observation purposes by the Crown Prince during the great siege of 1916. Dugouts were found with luxurious lighting systems, and large quantities of beer, wine, and fresh cabbages.

The First Division, with General Charles P. Summerall in command, went into the Argonne to give relief, first to the Thirty-fifth, and then to the Seventy-seventh. Some of the men in the Seventy-seventh comprised what was known somewhat mysteriously as the "Lost Battalion"—this battalion having been for a time separated in the forest from the remainder of the division. Later the Forty-second relieved the First. The Forty-second took the Côte de Châtillon, one of the brilliant incidents of the campaign. Its work led to a break in the Kremhilde-Stellung. The Thirty-second, commanded by General William S. Haan, also did brilliant work. The Forty-second lost in the Argonne 380 killed and had 2,895 casualties. The Thirty-second had 474 killed and 5,019 casualties. One battalion of the Eighty-second lost all but 190 of its men and served in the sector 25 days. The division had 1,000 killed and 6,700 casualties, and at one time had only 4,500 men fit for duty. It was one of the divisions that reached the Kremhilde-Stellung as early as the sixth day. The fighting in the Argonne was described by Frederick Palmer as "a dozen Belleau Woods made into one."

The Forty-second was first to reach the outskirts of Sedan. Being on the left of the American line, it was nearest to Sedan when the Meuse was reached. Next came the Seventy-seventh and then in order going east, the First, Second, Eighty-ninth, Ninetieth and Fifth. The two latter had, however, crossed the Meuse, the Ninetieth at Stenay, the Fifth at Sassey and Dun-sur-Meuse, whence it had proceeded northeastward through the Forest of the Woevre to Juvigny. Meanwhile, further south, other American divisions had crossed the Meuse—the Seventy-ninth, Twenty-sixth, Thirty-seventh, and Twenty-ninth. The report that the Rainbow Division actually entered Sedan was, however, an error. It entered Wadelincourt, a

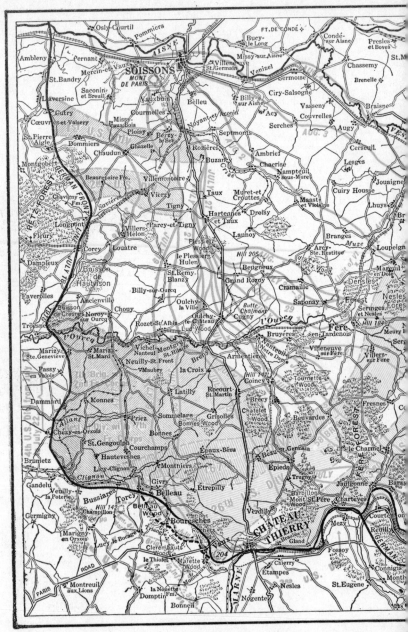

WHERE THE AMERICANS, BEING 30 PER CENT. OF T

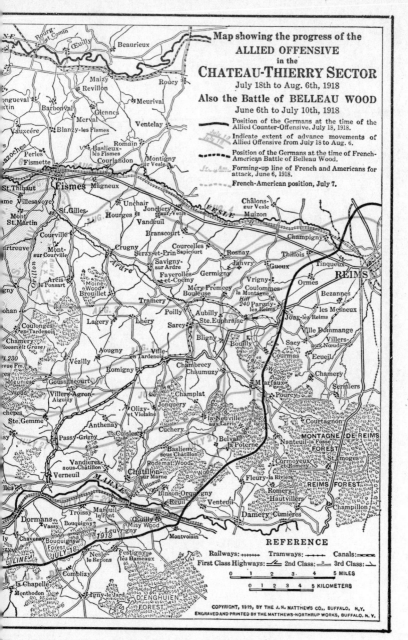

Map showing the progress of the
ALLIED OFFENSIVE
in the
CHATEAU-THIERRY SECTOR
July 18th to Aug. 6th, 1918

Also the Battle of BELLEAU WOOD
June 6th to July 10th, 1918

Position of the Germans at the time of the Allied Counter-Offensive. July 18, 1918.

Indicate extent of advance movements of Allied Offensive from July 18 to Aug. 6.

Position of the Germans at the time of French-American Battle of Belleau Wood.

Forming-up line of French and Americans for attack, June 6, 1918.

French-American position, July 7.

REFERENCE

Railways: ┼┼┼┼┼   Tramways: ┈┈┈   Canals: ═══
First Class Highways: ══ 2nd Class: ─┴─ 3rd Class: ─┴─

0   1   2   3   4   5 MILES

0 1 2 3 4 5 KILOMETERS

COPYRIGHT, 1919, BY THE J. N. MATTHEWS CO., BUFFALO, N.Y.
ENGRAVED AND PRINTED BY THE MATTHEWS-NORTHRUP WORKS, BUFFALO, N.Y.

ED FORCES, FOUGHT FROM JULY 18 TO AUGUST 6, 1918

suburb on the other side of the river. It was the French who first entered Sedan. On the night of November 10 the Second and the Eighty-ninth divisions accomplished a crossing of the Meuse about thirty miles up the Meuse from Sedan. The Eighty-first, sometimes called the "Stone Wall Division," and sometimes the "Wild Cat Division," had been trained at Camp Jackson, South Carolina, and was commanded by Major-General Charles J. Bailey. On September 19, it reached St. Die in the Vosges area, early in November, was south of Verdun, and on November 6 took over ground that had been held by the Thirty-fifth and attacked the fortified villages of Moranville, Grimacourt, and Albacourt. In three days' fighting the division had 167 men killed and 11 officers, with 1,032 casualties.

The Fourth Division, commanded by Major-General George H. Cameron, organized in North Carolina, took a vital part in the Marne salient counter-thrust and in the Argonne offensive, losing in casualties a total of 12,940 men. Its first active service took place in July in the neighborhood of La Ferté-Sous-Jouaire. In the Marne salient campaign it had a share in the battle for the Ourcq and at Sergy, whence it proceeded to the crossing of the Vesle. In the Argonne it took part in the first blow struck northwest of Verdun, and altogether was in action 83 days.

The Seventy-eighth Division arrived in France on June 8, 1918, and after training with the British joined the Americans on the eastern frontier. It comprised men drafted from northern New York and New Jersey. In September it went to the St. Mihiel salient to relieve the Second and Fifth Divisions, and in october relieved the Seventy-seventh in the Argonne, where it remained active until November 5, being associated particularly with Grandpré. Between November 2 and November 5 it occupied several villages during a rapid advance. At one time nine enemy divisions, or what was left of them, faced the Seventy-eighth in the Argonne. It lost in killed, wounded, and missing, 4,990 men, of whom the dead were 16 officers and 785 enlisted men.

Of the commanders who served as Pershing's chief lieutenants, little was heard in America while the war was in progress. Nor was much heard of the work of particular divisions. That Americans had done things at Seicheprey, Cantigny, Chateau-Thierry, Belleau Wood, St. Mihiel, the St. Quentin Canal and Tunnel, and in the Argonne, became widely known, but as to what divisions had been engaged we knew little or nothing, and so of leading generals. Frederick Palmer [53a] first imparted real knowledge among us in these matters. "Liggett, Bullard, Harbord and Summerall," said he, "were to Pershing what Sherman, Sheridan, Thomas and Hancock were to Grant and Jackson, Longstreet and Stuart were to Lee." James J. Harbord, who was Chief of Staff to Pershing when he went to France, afterward became a Brigadier-General, in command of the Fourth or Marine Brigade of the Second Division, taking the place of General Doyem, who had gone home ill. Harbord, tho not a Marine himself, soon acquired the full confidence of the Marines under his command, and when the Marines were rushed against the Germans on the Marne, it was Harbord who took the offensive in Belleau Wood. After Belleau Wood Harbord was made a Major-General and given command of the Second Division, of which the Marines had formed a part and which formerly was commanded by Gen. Omar Bundy. In the great drive of July 18 the Second Division shared honors with the First, serving alongside French divisions in Mangin's army. The First and Second Divisions, in the Marne salient, lost in casualties about 50 per cent. of their men.

Lieut.-Gen. Hunter Liggett had been assigned to command the First Corps. When the March offensive began, his best divisions were sent from Toul to the Picardy front, where they took Cantigny. They were then ordered to the Marne front, where they made a stand on the road to Paris. Liggett, in the Marne counter-offensive, came into close association with the French, and in the Meuse-Argonne battle his corps had the left front, which was in or near the forest itself. Our Second Army was commanded by Robert L. Bullard, who had previously commanded the First Division in the Toul sector and then at Cantigny. Sometime before Foch's stroke of July 18 Bullard was placed in command of the Third Corps. In the advance to the Vesle he had with him the

Seventy-seventh and Twenty-eighth Divisions. Bullard was in the St. Mihiel advance, and afterward was sent into the Argonne, where he had the right flank.

Charles P. Summerall and John L. Hines were both promoted rapidly, from division to corps commanders. Summerall, who had been in the march on Peking, was at Toul and Cantigny, in the drive on Soissons in the Marne salient, and in the Argonne—"a lieutenant," says Colonel Palmer, "after Bullard's own heart, Cromwellian in his downrightness and driving initiative and his devout, crusader's faith in his cause and his men." Hines, with much service elsewhere, also commanded a corps in the Meuse-Argonne. Before it had ever been in action, Joseph T. Dickman took the Third Division to the defense of the Marne at Chateau-Thierry, where he, at the Surmerlin River, "held like a stone wall," after which he helped to drive the Germans northward from the Marne. After the armistice he commanded an Army of Occupation on the Rhine comprising the First, Second, Third, Fourth, Fifth, Twenty-sixth, Thirty-second, Forty-second, Eighty-ninth and Ninetieth Divisions.

Maj.-Gen. George W. Read commanded the Second Corps, including the Twenty-seventh and Thirtieth Divisions, which made the famous advance across the Hindenburg line at the St. Quentin Canal and tunnel. Gen. Adelbert Cronkhite, of the Eightieth Division, was a man of much hard common sense. Henry T. Allen led the National Army Division with much dash and courage, William Wright led the Eighty-ninth along the Meuse, William J. Haan led the Thirty-second against the heights of the Ourcq and in the Argonne, and Charles T. Menoher, said Colonel Palmer, "stamped his vigorous character on the Rainbow Division."

America's contribution to winning the war could not be properly measured by the work of her armies on the Western Front. Those armies bore themselves handsomely on all occasion, and their influence in the final battles was considerable, and yet the actual share borne by American troops in the war, judged either by numbers actually engaged or by losses in comparison to those of the other chief belligerents, was comparatively small—those killed in battle, or who died of wounds, being, as reported down to June 10, 1919, only

46,500, and the total casualties only 298,000, while the corresponding figures for at least three other Entente nations reached seven figures. America's chief contributions were moral, financial, and industrial, but in the course of another year we would have had in the field the greatest army of any nation, and our war power would have been unquestionably preponderant; but, as it stood, our military effort had to be judged as "an incomplete but splendid fragment." [53b]

Revised totals, showing American major casualties, prisoners and guns captured, were made public by the War Department on July 5, 1919. The number of major casualties shown was more than 59,000, of prisoners captured more than 60,000, of artillery pieces and machine-guns, captured more than 12,000. Replacements totaled approximately 357,000 men, two divisions, the First and Second, regulars, calling for replacements of several thousand more than the full strength with which they entered the battle-line. American units advanced a total of 767 kilometers, the greatest advance by any single division being 71½ kilometers made by the Seventy-seventh Division. A kilometer is approximately five-eighths of a mile. The major casualties suffered by divisions were as follows:

Div.	Cas't's.	Div.	Cas't's.	Div.	Cas't's.	Div.	Cas't's.
2	5,260	77	2,692	91	1,702	93	489
1	5,248	5	2,504	82	1,592	7	326
28	3,890	79	2,389	90	1,585	81	270
3	3,617	27	2,194	89	1,525	92	211
32	3,213	78	1,825	80	1,355	6	122
4	2,986	30	1,772	37	1,250	88	66
42	2,950	35	1,772	20	1,117		
26	2,864	33	1,738	36	869		
Total							59,393

Following are the numbers of artillery pieces captured:

Div.	No.	Div.	No.	Div.	No.	Div.	No.
2	343	3	51	37	34	28	16
89	127	4	44	42	25	82	11
5	98	77	44	35	24	36	9
33	93	90	42	29	21	78	4
80	88	91	33	32	21		
30	81	79	32	26	16		
Total							1,257

[53b] The London *Times'* "History of the War."

© PAUL THOMPSON.

FOUR AMERICAN ACES ON ARRIVAL HOME

From left to right these men are: Lieut. Douglas Campbell, Capt. Edward V. Rickenbacker (the leading American ace), Maj. James A. Meissner, and Lieut. Paul F. Baer

The machine-gun table follows:

Div.	No.	Div.	No.	Div.	No.	Div.	No.
3	1,501	89	456	79	275	65	85
2	1,350	30	426	37	263	28	63
5	802	33	414	29	250	78	43
80	641	77	323	90	230	4	31
42	495	82	311	32	190	7	28
91	471	36	294	26	132		

Total 9,073

Following are the numbers of prisoners captured:

Div.	No.	Div.	No.	Div.	No.	Div.	No.
2	12,026	4	2,756	90	1,876	35	781
1	6,469	91	2,412	80	1,813	77	750
89	5,061	5	2,405	37	1,495	36	549
33	3,985	27	2,355	42	1,317	78	398
30	3,848	3	2,240	28	921	79	392
26	3,148	32	2,153	82	845	7	68

Total 60,063

A table showing the number of replacements sent to each division was as follows:

Div.	No.	Div.	No.	Div.	No.	Div.	No.
2	35,343	26	14,411	79	6,246	78	3,190
1	30,206	77	12,728	33	5,413	92	2,920
3	24,033	5	12,611	27	5,355	6	2,784
18	21,717	91	12,530	29	4,977	30	2,384
90	4,437	35	10,605	80	4,495	81	1,984
32	20,140	82	8,402	7	4,112	88	731
4	19,599	89	7,669	36	3,397		
42	17,253	37	6,282				

Total 356,954

The number of kilometers advanced by each division included in the tabulation was shown in this table:

Div.	No.	Div.	No.	Div.	No.	Div.	No.
77	71½	32	36	90	28½	27	11
2	62	33	36	4	24½	28	10
42	55	89	36	36	21	92	3
1	51	91	34	78	21	29	7
3	41	37	30¾	79	19½	81	5½
26	37	30	29½	82	17	7	¾
80	37	5	29	34	12½		

Total 767

The several divisions embraced in these tables, including replacements, constituted a total of 1,140,000 men participating in battle. The full fighting strength of a division was 27,000 men. We had put forth about twice the man-power that the North supplied in our Civil War, but this was to be measured in the light of a far greater population. Among each one hundred Americans five took up arms in the World War—a goodly showing—but in the Civil War ten in every hundred served. As about 2,400,000 men served the North in the Civil War, a proportionate consideration of the man-power of the country in the two wars would show nearly two to one in favor of the Civil War. With a total of 4,800,000 men gathered into the armed forces of the United States between April 6, 1917, and November 11, 1918, an American effort in the World War, proportionate to that put forth in

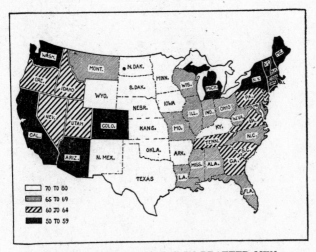

70 TO 80
65 TO 69
60 TO 64
50 TO 59

PERCENTAGES OF STATES IN DRAFTED MEN

The map shows the percentages of men who passed the physical examination, by States, the highest record being made by States west of the Mississippi and by Kentucky

1861-1865, would have meant nearly 10,000,000 fighting men. Herewith are reproduced a map and three diagrams to show the sources of our man-power by States and our losses in lives compared with other belligerent nations.*

Colonel Ayres's "Summary" sets forth other interesting data. Two of every three American soldiers who reached

---

* From "A Statistical Summary of the War with Germany," prepared by Col. Leonard P. Ayres and issued by the War Department in July, 1919.

France had some part in battle. The number who reached France was 2,084,000, and of these 1,300,000 saw active service at the front. Of all the divisions that reached France, twenty-nine were in active combat service. Seven were regular

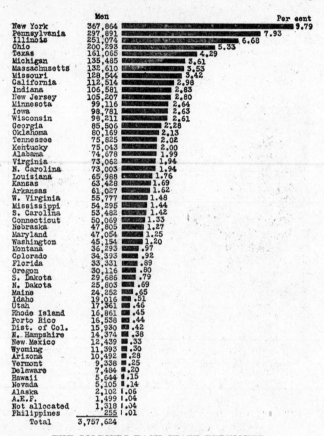

	Men		Per cent
New York	367,864		9.79
Pennsylvania	297,891		7.93
Illinois	251,074		6.68
Ohio	200,293		5.33
Texas	161,065		4.29
Michigan	135,485		3.61
Massachusetts	132,610		3.53
Missouri	128,544		3.42
California	112,514		2.98
Indiana	106,581		2.83
New Jersey	105,207		2.80
Minnesota	99,116		2.64
Iowa	98,781		2.63
Wisconsin	98,211		2.61
Georgia	85,506		2.28
Oklahoma	80,169		2.13
Tennessee	75,825		2.02
Kentucky	75,043		2.00
Alabama	74,678		1.99
Virginia	73,062		1.94
N. Carolina	73,003		1.94
Louisiana	65,988		1.76
Kansas	63,428		1.69
Arkansas	61,027		1.62
W. Virginia	55,777		1.48
Mississippi	54,295		1.44
S. Carolina	53,482		1.42
Connecticut	50,069		1.33
Nebraska	47,805		1.27
Maryland	47,054		1.25
Washington	45,154		1.20
Montana	36,293		.97
Colorado	34,393		.92
Florida	33,331		.89
Oregon	30,116		.80
S. Dakota	29,686		.79
N. Dakota	25,803		.69
Maine	24,252		.65
Idaho	19,016		.51
Utah	17,361		.46
Rhode Island	16,861		.45
Porto Rico	16,538		.44
Dist. of Col.	15,930		.42
N. Hampshire	14,374		.38
New Mexico	12,439		.33
Wyoming	11,393		.30
Arizona	10,492		.28
Vermont	9,338		.25
Delaware	7,484		.20
Hawaii	5,644		.15
Nevada	5,105		.14
Alaska	2,102		.06
A.E.F.	1,499		.04
Not allocated	1,318		.04
Philippines	255		.01
Total	3,757,624		

THE SOLDIERS EACH STATE FURNISHED

army divisions, eleven were organized from the National Guard, and eleven were made up of National army troops. American divisions were in battle for two hundred days and engaged in thirteen major operations. From the middle of August, 1919, until the end of the war the American divisions held during the greater part of the time a front longer than was held by the British. In October American divisions held 101 miles of line, or 23 per cent. of the entire Western Front. In the battle of St. Mihiel 550,000 Americans were engaged, as compared with approximately 100,000 on the Northern side in the Battle of Gettysburg. The artillery fired more than 1,000,000 shells in four hours, the most intense concentration of artillery

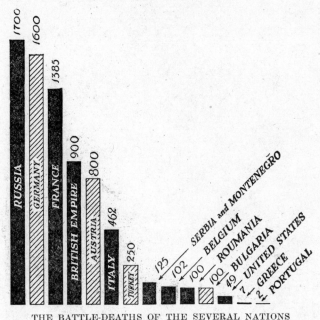

THE BATTLE-DEATHS OF THE SEVERAL NATIONS
The figures represent thousands. The total battle-deaths of all the armies engaged were officially placed at 7,582,000

fire ever recorded. The Meuse-Argonne battle lasted forty-seven days, during which 1,200,000 troops from first to last were engaged. Of every one hundred American soldiers and sailors who served two were killed or died of disease during the period of hostilities. For every man killed in battle seven were wounded. Five out of every six men sent to hospitals on account of wounds were cured and returned to duty. The war cost America $21,850,000,000, or approximately $1,000,000 an hour, and of the total $13,930,000,000 went for army expenses. The casualties in the Meuse-Argonne battle were 120,000 officers and men. Our battle-deaths were about 50,000; our wounded totaled approximately 236,000, and deaths from disease down to April 30, 1919, were 56,991.

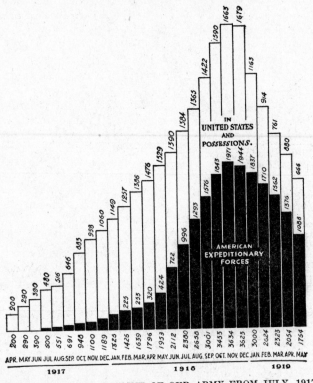

IN UNITED STATES AND POSSESSIONS.

AMERICAN EXPEDITIONARY FORCES

THE GROWTH AND DECLINE OF OUR ARMY FROM JULY, 1917, TO MAY, 1919

The diagram shows the size of our forces, month by month, including all who were in service at home and those serving in France, the figures representing thousands

Had any Napoleonic campaign surpassed that of Foch as a military achievement? British, French, American, Italian, Belgian troops all perfectly controlled by a single hand, all used with exact coordination, had been made to contribute to the uttermost of their possibilities. In less than four months Foch had won a supreme victory; he had smashed the German machine, plucked it bodily from its defenses and flung it out of France. As the struggle ended, we in America had a right to recall with pride that our own army had been the final reserve flung onto the battlefield, where in the face of obstacles which are not even yet understood it rose to supreme heights. Before the achievements of the French and British on the same field the world should forever stand in awe. That agony of four years preceding the late dawn of victory had been borne by them with such a courage and devotion as made all praise seem feeble. But if the Americans came late, they came in time. Our contribution was very small in comparison with that of France and Great Britain, but it was a contribution without which victory in 1918, if not in 1919, had been impossible. Our soldiers, from Seicheprey and Cantigny to Sedan, had played a large rôle in a great victory that surpassed the wildest dreams of the Entente.

Foch at the last had been tempted by a great ambition, but had nobly thrust the temptation aside. Had he decided to continue hostilities ten days longer he might have brought about the surrender of the entire German army and won the greatest of all victories, but he renounced that great victory deliberately and with his eyes open, because continuation of the struggle would have cost a certain number of French, British and American lives, at a time when it had been in his power to make peace on terms that meant victory. Such at least was the contention of more than one competent writer after the signing of the armistice. It was for this reason that the terms of the armistice were exprest in terms of decesive victory. Foch knew that the Germans had no illusion about their military condition as one in which they had nothing left with which to negotiate. It was for them to surrender or be destroyed. Foch's snare had been laid and the net was being drawn closer about the enemy every day. He was narrowing rapidly the only gap through which a million and a half of Germans, with their cumbrous transportation, could have effected their escape. Most of their trunk lines were in his hands, or under fire of his guns. Some other man with a lust for glory would have found a way to defer the negotiations for an armistice while he struck the blow that would have ended all.

Foch was never greater than in the hour when he decided

SERGEANT YORK'S ARRIVAL HOME
The meeting with his mother at
Pall Mall, Tennessee

that he would choose the lesser victory rather than shed the blood of thousands more.

Not inferior in nobility was the spirit of Pétain, in that hour of supreme victory. As commander of the French armies he addrest an order of the day to his troops eulogizing their tenacity and energy during the four years when France "had to vanquish the foe, in order not to die," and then asked those now going forth under the terms of the armistice to occupy German territory not to permit their resentment over German violence and barbarism in France to lead them astray; they were to "respect persons and property." "After having beaten the adversary by arms," said he, in words that deserved to go into anthologies, "you will impose upon the enemy the dignity of your attitude, and thus the world will wonder what to admire more, your conduct in victory or your heroism in battle." [54]

[54] Principal Sources: The *Tribune*, The *World*, The *Times*, The *Evening Sun* (New York), Associated Press and United Press dispatches, Frederick Palmer, "America in France" (Dodd, Mead & Co.).

ON THE WESTERN FRONT

Part XVIII

FROM THE ARMISTICE TO THE MEETING OF THE PARIS PEACE CONFERENCE

THE FIRST ARMISTICE DAY CELEBRATION

Not until late in the afternoon was it made known that the news of the
signing of the armistice was premature. The upper scene is on Fifth
Avenue, New York, near the Public Library; the lower in Madison Square,
New York

214

I

ALL THE CENTRAL POWERS SIGN ARMISTICES WITH A REVOLUTION IN AUSTRIA

September 29, 1918—November 11, 1918

WITH Bulgaria begging for an armistice late in September, with Turkish forces in Palestine virtually annihilated, Americans and French pressing on victoriously in the Champagne and the Argonne, and British advancing in the direction of Cambrai, Prussianism everywhere on the defensive, or in retreat, and our Fourth Liberty Loan Campaign launched under most inspiring conditions, President Wilson could have desired no more suitable opportunity for giving, as in October, in his armistice correspondence with Germany, point and emphasis to the great doctrine that this was a people's war which could be ended only by a people's peace. Official Germany had as yet no conception of that truth. It was still living in the days of the Congress of Vienna when nationalities and peoples were bartered about like cattle. It still believed possible a negotiated peace, in which diplomatists would adjust the differences of governments, arrange the strategic requirements of great powers and begin a new game of imperialism under the rules of the old.

Germany was in a critical situation. She had brought a crisis upon her political life and there was only one way in which she could save herself. Her people had been deprived of capacity for settling the issue themselves, and so it had to be done for them by the Entente, not so much for their sake, however, as for the safety of other nations. Changes in the German Government might, it seemed, come at any moment. Socialists and Center party leaders had sharply criticized the government in debates following Chancellor Hertling's peace speech. Scheidemann had declared that the Brest treaty stood in the way of a general peace and that the chief success of the submarine warfare had been to draw America into the conflict, while another leader, speaking for the Catholic Party, had stated that Ludendorff, not Hertling, was running Germany. A parliamentary Germany, of which the Kaiser now gave out some vague promise, could undoubtedly be better dealt with by the Allies than an autocratic Germany; France, Great Britain, and the United States had all declared this repeatedly. Indeed, they could afford to be more lenient and even generous in making peace with the German people— or a government directly representing that people—than with the House of Hohenzollern. But this did not alter the fact that the old fundamentals would still have to be insisted upon. Restitution, reparation, guaranties—these were conditions which a reformed German Government as well as a Hohenzollern autocracy would have to meet.

Bulgaria had signed an armistice on September 29, accepting unconditionally all the terms the Allies laid down which virtually rendered her incapable of any further operations. Three days later Prince Maximilian of Baden was announced as the new German Chancellor succeeding Hertling. It was the second time he had been put forward as a candidate for the office. When Dr. Michaelis fell, in November, 1917, Moderates, Socialists, and Radicals brought out Prince Max, but before his name had reached the Kaiser he declined for "dynastic reasons." His appointment now promised a new peace move. Prince Max was declared to have been the first man in German public life to declare that the empire could not conquer by the sword alone. In the downfall of Hertling, the seventh Chancellor since the empire was created, optimists saw a victory for the popular party, since Hertling was driven from office because of his failure to redeem promises made in the name of the crown. He had become a badly worn creature in the hands of the military party, without whose approval both he and the crown were now impotent.

Prince Max was in reality a sop thrown to South Germans when Prussianized Germany's difficulties had become too great to be brushed away by a political device, or by any one man. The whole question of rule by the people had come to the front in Germany. When the Kaiser went so far as to assent to the general doctrine of a ministry responsible to the Reichstag, he at once let out the impounded waters and no man could tell where or how far they would flow. Parliamentary government in Germany had long been opposed, and even shuddered at, by the Prussian oligarchs. In now conceding its desirability, they were sealing their own doom.

Prince Max being from Baden, was from one of the liberal strongholds of Germany. He had made moderate speeches, and was known as a wealthy Junker who had begun to see the ruin of his class through further prolongation of the war, and so he wanted peace; but he was essentially a reactionary who could make overtures with one hand to the Allies, and oppose bitterly with the other any change in Germany's internal condition. The fact that von Payer remained Vice-chancellor showed that the Kaiser's new government was not one bit better than the last. While a so-called pacifist had been set up as Chancellor, behind him were the same military directors who, having failed in their military push, were now anxious to conduct a peace push. "When the Devil was sick the Devil a saint would be."

The Kaiser, in the guise of a reformer of the Prussian parliament, did not inspire great confidence either in his own country or elsewhere. The world knew that he and the Junker leaders loathed the thought of parliamentary reform. In pretending to yield something, they threw out only a sop to still popular clamor until the tempest passed. Wilhelm was not the first Hohenzollern who had made in his hour of need liberal promises that he had no intention of keeping. King Frederick William III, when struggling against Napoleon, had stimulated his people to heroic deeds with the promise of a constitution, but when Napoleon was overthrown, shamelessly broke his word. So again, Frederick William IV, in bowing before the demands of the revolutionists of 1848, solemnly swore that he would lead a liberal movement in Germany, and later, when the danger passed, placed himself in the hands of reactionaries and drew up the mockery of a constitution which still persisted in Prussia ever afterward.

The Hohenzollern monarchy was threatened with a crisis such as it had never known before. It faced the anger of a weary and desperate people, a people it had misled and betrayed. There began to arise at Potsdam intense fear of collapse with the coming of defeat, a fear that the people would thrust aside leaders responsible for the country's plight and take into their own hands both the making of peace and the remodeling of the government. So the Kaiser, shaping his course upon the example of his ancestors, sought to allay the storm with a pretense of constitutional reform. His efforts were not taken seriously, for the Hohenzollern word had too often been broken. And yet Germany, on October 5, as if her word would be taken in Entente countries, sought peace in her own name instead of Austria's. The text of a note forwarded by the new Chancellor, Prince Maximilian, to President Wilson through the Swiss Government was as follows:

"The German Government requests the President of the United States to take in hand the restoration of peace, acquaint all the belligerent states of this request and invite them to send plenipotentiaries for the purpose of opening negotiations. It accepts the program set forth by the President of the United States in his message to Congress on January 8th and in his later pronouncements, especially his speech of September 27th, as a basis for peace negotiations. With a view to avoiding further bloodshed, the German Government requests the immediate conclusion of an armistice on land and water and in the air."

Consciousness of approaching defeat had not yet sunk deep enough into the Teutonic mind to divest it of a characteristically Prussian type of arrogance. Only six months before, exponents of German opinion had been talking in terms of huge indemnities and large territorial acquisitions. Vanquished nations were to be bled white and Germany was to vault easily, and inevitably, into a position of world-supremacy. Now the talk, official and unofficial, was less truculent, but it was not, in any essential respect, less arrogant. The Kaiser in a statement of his own at the same time deigned to announce that he had "resolved once more to offer peace to the enemy," but wished to have it understood that he "would only extend his hand for an honorable peace.'' Thus a potentate, who had earned, as no one in all history had earned the contempt and loathing of mankind, had the assurance to pretend that he was in a position to ''offer'' something to his foes except abject surrender. He had the insolence to ignore the fact that a hand such as his extended for any purpose save supplication would be spurned by the nations which intended to dictate the terms on which the war would end. What the new Chancellor said did not greatly matter. His assumption that President Wilson occupied a position of sufficient detachment to act as a mediator between Germany and her enemies was not particularly felicitous and a reference he at this time had made to an ''unbroken'' German line in the west was of the same grotesque inexactitude as an allusion by the Kaiser to his ''unbeaten'' fleet. Between them, the two men merely gave another illustration of the utter futility of discussing peace terms until Germany was beaten to her knees—of bestowing even passing notice on overtures intended mainly to protect the Hohenzollern dynasty from the wrath of the German people.

Berlin still thought that the American public would seize upon the slightest pretext to end the war. It looked upon Wilson as a philosopher within the range of whose broad ethical statements the German Government could roam about at will, seeming to accept his principles while intriguing to escape the application of them. Allied peoples, as reflected in their press and by their leaders, were a unit in demanding in reply to the German request for an armistice unconditional surrender. There was no discordant note. In the United States the maneuver was denounced in many spirited speeches. Senator Lodge, leader of the Republicans, declared that to grant an armistice would mean to lose the war and all we had fought for. Senator McCumber, of North Dakota, introduced a resolution that before an armistice was granted Germany must disband her armies, surrender her navy and all her war weapons, agree to pay for all the damage she had done in occupied territory and give France back Alsace-Lorraine, with an indemnity such as France had to pay Germany in 1871. London suspected the move to be a trick, aimed at breaking down the fighting spirits of Foch's armies. In any case an armistice was regarded as out of the question, because it was also out of the question for German armies much longer to stay in France. Every day they were yielding to Foch's pressure. "Victory first, then peace," was the way French civilians, returning to their shell-wrecked homes in northern France, exprest themselves on the subject. The same idea ran through the Allied armies, where men who had seen their comrades die felt that they would have died in vain unless victory became absolute. President Wilson at first sent no reply to Prince Max, but rather an inquiry, through Secretary of State Lansing, for more precise information.

In dealing with the new German peace offensive, he employed the same tactics that Foch had used in breaking the German military offensive—a counter-offensive. His decision, in substance, was that the United States would not participate in any peace discussion in which the terms laid down by the President were merely "a basis for peace negotiations." Before he would present the German proposal to the Entente, terms must be accepted, and nothing left to negotiation but the practical details of their application. Nor would he associate himself with a German request for an armistice while German troops occupied invaded territory, and by that he obviously meant to include Russia. If Germany wished him to act as a messenger in carrying to the European Allies her request for an armistice, she had first to withdraw her troops from other people's territory and get back to her own soil, and if the German Government wished to talk peace, it must demonstrate that it was acting for the German people and not "merely" for the German autocracy or, as he exprest it, for "the constituted authorities who had conducted the war."

Germany's object of this peace offensive was to convince the German people that their Government was wholeheartedly for peace, even on President Wilson's terms, and that the blood-guilt for further prolongation of the war would rest upon the Allies with their "will to destruction." The purpose was undertaken in order to steel German morale for an inevitable German retreat and for the defensive warfare which the Imperial Government said it had henceforth to wage. The President simply shifted the issue back to Germany, and left the German Government to get out as best it could from a trap it had carefully set for the United States and the Allies.

Bad as was the military situation at the front for Germany, conditions were far worse behind the lines. Otherwise the proposal she made for an armistice would never have been made. Had it come from a reputable, responsible government, it would inevitably have been accepted by the United States and the Allies. It was the notorious character of the German Government and its faithless attitude toward all its engagements which impelled the President to withhold a reply until certain definite questions were answered by the Imperial Chancellor. A Government which had set forth to dominate the world and had never before talked of peace, except in terms of a German victory, now pleaded with the President to bring about an armistice and to take in hand the restoration of peace on the basis of his own program. When a Government traveled thus far on the road to surrender, the world could rest assured that the German people had gone much further. Unless all signs were misleading, Prussianism also was approaching its Sedan.

Whether the Kaiser abdicated or not, the end of the Hohenzollern dynasty was fairly in sight. The Electors of Brandenburg and their successors had been the architects of modern Germany, but when the qualities that had made the Hohenzollern line great and those that had made it base became united in one man, as they were in William II, the ruin of Germany had been achieved as Hohenzollern work. Napoleon had a prophetic insight, when he said: "As long as this house reigns, and until the red cap of liberty is erected in Germany, there will be no peace in Europe." Pope Leo XIII, after a personal interview with the young German Emperor in 1888, made a statement that had been remembered ever since: "This young man is obstinate and vain, and it is to be feared that his reign will terminate in disaster."

Germany's reply to the President was made on October 12, above the signature of the new Foreign Secretary Solf.

Germany "accepted the terms laid down by President Wilson in his address of January 8 [1] and in his subsequent addresses on the foundation of a permanent peace of justice." She was "ready to comply with the proposition of the President in regard to evacuation," but suggested "a mixed commission for making the necessary arrangements concerning the evacuation." Germany now had a new government "formed by conferences and in agreement with the great majority of the Reichstag." She had a Chancellor "supported in all his actions by the will of this majority," and speaking "in the name of the German Government and the German people."

While the official text of this reply was on its way to Washington, the Kings and Princes whose states made up the German Empire were meeting in the throne-room of the Kaiser's palace in Berlin, their hurried entry into Berlin from all corners of the empire being described as unprecedently spectacular, in the sense that never before had the ruling Princes of Germany been convened in so short a time. Abandoning the pomp and ceremony that usually attended such visits, many of them had gone to Berlin in high-powered automobiles, while others had chartered special trains. When their arrival was known to Berliners great excitement resulted. Peace became the sole topic of discussion. Not the least striking of the rumors that got afloat was one that the Kaiser had abdicated. It persisted for some days until officially denied.

President Wilson on October 14 informed Germany that it "must be clearly understood that the process of evacuation and the conditions of an armistice are matters which must be left to the judgment and advice of the military advisers of the Government of the United States and the Allied Governments, and the President feels it his duty to say that no arrangement can be accepted by the Government of the United States which does not provide absolutely satisfactory safeguards and guaranties of the maintenance of the present military supremacy of the armies of the United States and of the Allies in the field." Furthermore, the nations associated against Germany could not be

[1] The "Fourteen Points" address of January 8, 1918.

expected to agree to a cessation of arms "while acts of inhumanity, spoliation, and desolation are being continued which they justly look upon with horror and with burning hearts."

In conclusion the President found it necessary, "in order that there may be no possibility of misunderstanding," very solemnly to call the attention of the Government of Germany to "the language and plain intent of one of the terms of peace which the German Government has now accepted." This was contained in the address of the President at Mount Vernon on the Fourth of July, 1918,

© COMMITTEE ON PUBLIC INFORMATION.

PRESIDENT WILSON READING HIS FOURTH OF JULY ADDRESS
AT MOUNT VERNON

and was as follows: "The destruction of every arbitrary power anywhere that can separately, secretly, and of its single choice disturb the peace of the world, or if it can not be presently destroyed, at least its reduction to virtual impotency." The President added that "the power which has hitherto controlled the German nation is of the sort here described"; that it was "within the choice of the German nation to alter it," and that the words quoted constituted "a condition precedent to peace, if peace is to come by the action of the German people themselves."

Steps for the organization of Austria on a federalized

basis were proclaimed by Emperor Charles on October 18, but the plan did not include the union of Austrian Poland with a proposed "independent Polish state," and the city of Trieste and the Trieste region were to be treated separately, "in conformity with the wishes of its population." Other political action of more far-reaching importance to Austria-Hungary and to the future of the Central Powers was taken on the same day, when the Provisional Government of the new Czecho-Slovak nation declared its independence. Prof. Thomas G. Masaryk, who had been serving as President of the Czecho-Slovak National Council, on that day presented to the State Department in Washington, and dispatched to the Entente Governments, the text of a declaration of independence in the form in which it had been adopted at Paris by the Provisional Government.

The offer by Kaiser Karl of autonomy for the Czecho-Slovaks was therefore late in coming and was less important as a sign of repentance than as a confession of defeat. The Czecho-Slovak Declaration had not only promptly countered Kaiser Karl, but it was something that might serve for Jugo-Slavia, for Poland, for Italy, and unredeemed Roumania, whose claims on Austria had received recognition from the Allies and from the United States. Hungary, moreover, which had always been a grudging partner of Austria, at the same time declared her independence of Austria, except for a "friendly union." There had been a time when an offer of "local autonomy," democratically defined and honestly fulfilled, might have made Austria-Hungary an endurable political system in the eyes of her maltreated "subject races"; but neither to Budapest nor to Vienna were these races looking now for the determination of their future. They proposed to have something to say about it themselves.

It became known on October 19 that the German decision to reply affirmatively to President Wilson's note was taken at a dramatic meeting of the Crown Council in Berlin, where Ludendorff made a gloomy report on the military situation—the situation being such that Germany might be invaded within a few weeks. On the same day President Wilson replied to the Austro-Hungarian note of October 7, which was essentially the same as the German note of that date asking for an armistice, and also referred favorably to his fourteen peace points. The Austrian proposal as to peace terms was refused because events since they were named had altered the attitude and responsibility of the American Government. The President gave plain notice to Vienna that mere "autonomy" for the Czecho-Slovaks, the Jugo-Slavs, and other opprest peoples of the Dual Monarchy could no longer be regarded by the American Government and its Allies as a basis for durable peace. These people having declared their independence the Vienna Government would have to deal with them directly.

To all intents and purposes the realm of Emperor Charles scarcely existed any longer. The opprest nationalities had claimed their independence and no power in Budapest or Vienna was able to say nay to them. Delegations from the non-German nationalities of the Emperor had met and announced their complete severance from the Austrian states, and made a demand for the union of all Serbians, Croats, and Slovenes in a great kingdom of Jugo-Slavia. In many parts of Bohemia a republic had been proclaimed. It was even asserted that on the day on which an independent Jugo-Slavia was proclaimed, an independent Hungary would be heralded at Budapest.[1a] Meanwhile Austria's army was melting away; it was taking the road that the Russian army took, but taking it in perfect order. In fact, a great revolution was under way, and a great dream was being realized. One of its immediate aspects was that it promised soon to leave Germany alone as the only existing autocracy in Europe.

President Wilson showed a master hand in his reply to Austria's note. Its main request—for an armistice and peace negotiations—he quietly put aside, in order to point out the folly of imagining that the United States and the Allies could act that day as if nothing had happened since January 8. Among events of high importance that had occurred, Mr. Wilson singled out only one—the Allied recognition of Czecho-Slovak belligerency and the justice of the nationalistic

[1a] Statement made in The Essen *Zeitung*. Amsterdam dispatch from George Renwick to The *Times* (New York).

aspirations of the Jugo-Slavs. This had wholly altered the situation as it stood on January 8 when he named his fourteen terms. Austria was proposing a kind of federalized government with local "autonomy," but the President adroitly said that now it was not for him, but for the peoples involved, to decide what action the Austrian Government should take. Into the consciousness of the Teutonic rulers was penetrating the truth that Mr. Wilson meant what he said about a halfway peace being intolerable, and about an armistice being unthinkable if it impaired in any way the military supremacy of the Allied armies. It was that supremacy which was settling Germany's fate. The sooner and the more completely she bowed to the inevitable obviously would now be the better course for her.

The German Foreign Minister, in due course, sent a message to President Wilson in which Germany profest to accept all the conditions for an armistice and an eventual peace that had been laid down by the President. He indicated her willingness to evacuate occupied territory under an agreement to be reached by the military chiefs in the field—obviously meaning her own chiefs as well as those of the Entente. All submarine commanders, Solf said, had been ordered to cease their attacks upon passenger-vessels. Denial was made that lifeboats and passengers had ever purposely been destroyed, or that any authorized atrocities had been committed by German troops. It was declared also that Germany had now a parliamentary form of government, responsible to the people. The German Government wanted an armistice which, while securing the evacuation of France and Belgium, would guarantee the present "actual standard of power" of both armies in the field, which was obviously the exact purpose the German High Command had in view in originally seeking a cessation of hostilities because it would save Germany from losses that would be inevitable if her present retreat were continued, and would restore the prestige of army chiefs with the German public by enabling Hindenburg and Gröner to deliver safely on German soil what was left of their armies. It would also cover up the faults in German strategy for which the German field-forces were now paying the penalty.

The German military clique was not yet ready to admit defeat. It still controlled the Government in Berlin and still aimed at solidifying German resistance by means of specious proposals of "peace with honor." Germany had lost the war and had to recognize the fact, but when she talked about "honor" she talked about something she had lost long ago—all through the war years since she invaded Belgium—and which no peace terms could ever give her back. These German professions about peace could not be trusted by the Entente Powers because the "convictions" of Germans were always subject to alteration through any change that might occur in the war situation. That was what happened with the Reichstag peace resolution of July, 1917. As soon as the war situation in Russia entered a new phase, that resolution was shamelessly thrown overboard, and the Reichstag openly trampled upon it by ratifying the Brest-Litovsk and Roumanian treaties. It was the same Reichstag in whose excellent intentions and firm resolves the Entente Powers were now asked to confide.

"Not peace negotiations, but surrender"—these words were the keynote of President Wilson's final reply to the German appeal on October 23. He reminded Germany that the power of "the King of Prussia" was still in unimpaired control of the empire; that the nations of the world did not trust the mere word of those who had been the masters of Germany's policy; that the United States would not deal with any but veritable representatives of the German people, and that if our Government "must deal with the military masters and the monarchial autocrats of Germany now, it must demand, not peace negotiations, but surrender." With the idea of surrender and a dictated peace strictly in view, the President had decided to take up with the Allied Governments the question of an armistice, the terms of this armistice to be imposed by Marshal Foch acting with Generals Haig, Pétain, Pershing, and Diaz, and other military advisers of the Allied Governments who would submit to Germany the terms, provided they considered an armistice possible from the military point of view. Bulgaria having been utterly defeated, Allied troops were about to occupy Adrianople and make their way to Constantinople. Two Brit ish divisions and one French were already on the River Maritze on the night of October 30–31 ready to seize the northern bridges. The bridge at Ipsala was in Allied possession, while in the rear the First Greek Corps was echeloned between Cavalia and Drama, ready to take part in the general advance.[2]

Great Britain, on October 30, officially received peace proposals from Turkey which were tantamount to unconditional surrender. The terms included free passage of the Dardanelles by the Allied fleet; immediate repatriation of British war-prisoners; occupation of the forts of the Dardanelles and Bosporus as necessary to secure the passage of Allied warships to the Black Sea. The far-reaching effects of Turkey's surrender—which would open up to the Allies a new route to Russia, release strong forces from Palestine and Mesopotamia for other fronts, effect a complete transformation of the naval situation in the Mediterranean, and sweep the Black Sea clear of ships taken by Germany from Russia, combined with the Austrian collapse, brought the World War to a nearer conclusion than the most optimistic observers had thought possible a few months before.

Germany's military *débâcle*, even should last-ditch counsels prevail, now appeared imminent. She had no fresh divisions in the real sense of the term. There had been instances within a fortnight of fighting German divisions that had been unable to muster a thousand rifles out of a regular establishment of 6,750; in one case a division was reduced to 783 rifles. The total shortage of rifles in the German establishment was estimated at over 550,000. The reserves in German depots were less than 350,000, including the greater portion of the 1920 class. Germany's losses in guns on the Western Front since July 15, when she had 18,000 guns of all calibers in action, amounted to 33 per cent. Yet nothing like general demoralization had set in; German resistance could still be prolonged if the German people favored it, and even if peace should fail to come by way of Versailles. The armistice with Turkey was signed at Mudros, on the Island of Lemnos, in the Ægean Sea, on October 31. Gen-

2 Statement of Lieut.-Gen. Sir George F. Milne in The *Gazette* (London).

THE HOUSES OF PARLIAMENT AT BUDAPEST
Here legislation for the new Hungarian Republic was carried through

eral Townshend, the British commander, who was captured at Kut-el-Amara and had been a prisoner in Turkey since January, was liberated by the Turks in order to inform the British Admiral who commanded in the Ægean Sea, that the Turkish Government desired to enter into negotiations for an armistice. A week later the armistice was signed.

Military insurrections broke out in Vienna and Budapest on October 30 and the people and troops acclaimed a Republic. At Budapest the troops were armed with machine-guns and munitions, and had possession of one railroad terminal. They were acting in agreement with the Hungarian National Assembly which expected to take over the administration of the government. Officers had torn the imperial cockade from their hats, and the imperial standard had been hauled down from Parliament House. The Emperor Charles had left Vienna and was in the Royal Palace in Godollo, fifteen miles northeast of Budapest. A crowd stormed the military prison at Budapest and released political and military prisoners.

From the ruins of Austria-Hungary, the Czecho-Slovak Republic had been the first of new states to rise, but Bohemia now appeared on the map as an independent country of about 12,000,000 inhabitants and with an area, roughly five times that of Belgium. A republic was solemnly proclaimed and the military authorities handed over their functions to the National Council, the army having become a sort of gendarmerie. Prague was beflagged for the occasion, and her enthusiasm was boundless. Great demonstrations exprest the joy of the people who acclaimed the Entente and America. Everywhere monster meetings were held. Patriotic speeches proclaimed the linking up of the new State with the cause championed by the Entente and America. The last moments of Austrian supremacy in Bohemia had been reached. In Prague a tremendous crowd gathered around the John Huss monument. Amid continuous cheering a young man climbed up to an Austrian eagle and tore it down, the crowd quickly trampling it to pieces. Early in October the union between Hungary and Croatia, which had lasted for ten centuries, was declared null and void, and the union of independent Croatia with the rest of Jugo-

Slavia proclaimed. With these events the ramshackle Austrian Empire was ceasing to exist and the Austrian commander on the Italian front applied to General Diaz, the Italian commander-in-chief, for an armistice on October 31. The application was forwarded to the Supreme War Council at Versailles, and within a few days the ancient and hated monarchy, faced with complete internal anarchy, signed an armistice under the terms of which she virtually surrendered. Italy then occupied Trieste, Pola, and the Trentino.

Next day Count Tisza, the former Hungarian Premier, was killed by a soldier. Tisza, who was a typical Magyar magnate, was probably the best-hated man in Hungary. Political opponents of his own rank had fought duels with him; those of inferior rank had tried to assassinate him. He was a powerful man, both physically and mentally; his patriotism, while limited to the magnate class, was of the ambitious sort, its aim being to promote the greatness of Hungary. Austria and even Germany he regarded as mere pawns in his game. He had made use of the late Archduke Francis Ferdinand by having him agitate for a triune monarchy in place of the dual monarchy, to be made up of Germans, Magyars, and Slavs, believing that a new government would thus be centralized at Budapest rather than at Vienna. The whole Austrian Balkan policy of preventing the Balkan States from growing strong enough to form a league for the benefit of Russia against Turkey was his. Tisza, as Premier in Hungary in 1914, was quick to see the opportunities offered by the assassination of the Archduke Francis Ferdinand, and was believed to have arranged privately with friends at the Wilhelmstrasse in Berlin the famous conclave of the Kaiser's military family at Potsdam on July 5 where the plans were made for a united German and Austro-Hungarian action in case Russia intervened to save Serbia. Altho Count Berchtold was then the Austro-Hungarian Foreign Minister, the ultimatum to Serbia, as delivered by Baron von Gieslingen, the Austro-Hungarian Minister at Belgrade, was believed to have been largely Tisza's work.

Austro-Hungary broke up into a group of independent states, some of which were of a strongly Socialistic nature.

A National Assembly in Vienna adopted a constitution for the German part of Austria "in which no place was left for the crown." Those who expected to head the new government were mostly Socialists. Count Michael Karolyi announced that the Hungarian National Council had taken over the government of Hungary.

Austria-Hungary started the world conflagration by attacking Serbia. Never was war made on a more frivolous pretext. The Jingoistic statesmen of Vienna and Budapest took up arms in order to strengthen their hold on the subject peoples of the dual monarchy, and now retribution had come. Emperor Charles, the last of the Hapsburgs, was in flight from his capital, where a Socialist Republic had been proclaimed; the Austrian Empire split into fragments, had completely disappeared as a great power and as a member of the European Concert. The red flag floated over the Parliament building in Vienna, and Kaiser Wilhelm stood alone brandishing his "good German sword." All his allies had fallen away from him. The whole structure of Mitteleuropa had collapsed. The southern border of the Pan-German world empire ran now only twenty miles south of Dresden and only 130 miles south of Berlin. A new Czecho-Slovak state had been interposed as a barrier between Saxony and German Austria, and its existence had cut the Berlin-Vienna railroad—an indisputable sign that the long alliance between the Hohenzollern and the Hapsburg monarchies had been dissolved. In Emperor Charles' dominions all centralized authority had disappeared. People of the several parts of the empire were celebrating their liberation. Slovakia was free, Galicia was free, a southern Slav state was being organized at Agram, and Hungary had announced her independence.

History was being made with such lightning-speed that people failed to comprehend the full significance of changes, any one of which would have startled the world five years before. The terms granted to Turkey had almost automatically called into being an independent Arabia, an autonomous Armenia, a free Palestine, with Syria and Mesopotamia as French and British protectorates, and Persia liberated forever from the pressure of German intrigue and

Turkish penetration. The terms also prepared the way for the transformation of the great city on the Golden Horn into a free port, and for the opening of the historic highway of the Dardanelles and the Bosporus to the world's commerce. The terms of the Austrian armistice had dissolved the dual monarchy into its constituent elements, and with them had emerged two new nationalities—the Czecho-Slovaks and the Jugo-Slavs. From a time far beyond the memory of living men Austria had been among the proudest of nations; she had exhibited greater pride, with less reason for it, than had perhaps any other of the Powers. She now surrendered upon terms more humiliating than any ever before submitted to by a nation of any pretensions whatever to importance. A complete surrender had annihilated her as a belligerent, and put it out of her power to offer further armed resistance to the will of her foes. That had been the primary purpose of the terms imposed upon her. No terms after an unconditional surrender could have reduced her to impotence and harmlessness more effectually than those to which she now yielded. She was to cease hostilities by land and sea. Her armies were to be totally demobilized and withdrawn from the Western Front, where she had cooperated with Germany. Half her material equipment was surrendered. She evacuated all territory invaded by her since the beginning of the war. More than that, she was to withdraw behind lines fixt by the terms of the armistice in a series of delimitations which would restore to Italy territory rightfully hers but which had long been included within the frontiers of Austria.

A condition of the armistice of terrible import to Germany, and which hastened a decision of that empire to accept the inevitable, was one which opened to the Allies "the right of free movement over all roads and rail and waterways in Austro-Hungarian territory," and yielded up to their use the necessary means of transportation. Strategic points in Austria-Hungary were to be occupied by the armies of the Associated Powers, wherever they might deem this necessary for the conduct of military operations or for the maintenance of order. All German troops were required to leave Austro-Hungarian territory within fifteen days, or be interned for the duration of the war. Allied prisoners of war were to be given up at once, but Austrian prisoners held by the Allies would not be given up. Austrian ships of war, including submarines, were to be surrendered, or concentrated in ports designated by the Allies and disarmed. Austrian territorial waters were to be opened to the warships of her enemies and be made free, including the Danube and its tributaries. Nothing had been omitted or overlooked that could be considered essential to making Austria powerless.

Germany's three allies, Bulgaria, Turkey, and Austria-Hungary, had now laid down their arms, ceased hostilities and accepted terms which made it impossible for them to renew the war. The iron ring had closed about Germany once more. When it first encircled her, with Russia guarding the eastern frontier, her empire was still formidable. She had great armies, an abundance of munitions, resources sufficient to sustain her, and her people, buoyed up by hope of victory, were united and obedient to her autocratic will. Since then the Allies had made dreadful inroads upon her man power. She had become short of munitions, her material and financial resources had been greatly reduced, and her sore straits were made evident by political convulsions within her borders and the acceptance of, or the pretense of accepting, constitutional changes which profoundly modified the position and power of her Emperor. Against an increasing host of foes, she stood alone. There was no help for her from any quarter. Germany had to surrender, and surrender soon. From the terms imposed upon Austria she could judge of the severity of those which she would have to accept herself.

Germany's collapse was more moral than military. She still had her armies intact, altho diminished in numbers, and they were still fighting on enemy soil. Hindenburg still commanded more than two million men. The military status was robust and hopeful compared with that of the Southern Confederacy in the latter part of 1864 and early 1865. But Davis and Lee fought on, and not until Grant had shattered the defenses of Richmond did they hoist the white flag. The difference was that the South fought an honorable

AMERICANS FROM CHÂTEAU-THIERRY MARCHING THROUGH PARIS

The equestrian statue represents Washington, who is pointing his sword toward the Avenue du President Wilson

war, that Lee was not only a superb soldier but a chivalrous gentleman. The South had no such evil conscience as Germany had. German leaders and people knew they had conducted a brutal, hideous warfare, filled with unexampled crimes until in the German military class the title of officer had become completely dissociated from the title of gentleman.

As Germans of all classes saw the war approaching their own soil, they recoiled in terror from the thought of bearing what they had made France and Belgium, Poland, Serbia, Russia, and Roumania suffer. So they cried out for that mercy which the coward always asks but never grants. They revolted at taking their own medicine, were willing to descend to any humiliation rather than defend themselves to exhaustion as the South did, as the Boers did, as France did in 1871. Germany could have held out longer even with Austria-Hungary gone, had there been anything heroic in the composition of her leaders. She chose rather to avoid a just retribution by groveling at the feet of those on whom she had vented her barbarism, and by the end of October a financial panic seized Berlin. Ordinary paper currency of the empire vanished so that the municipality had to issue emergency currency. In spite of appeals to depositors from German banks runs on banks continued. People of means in Dusseldorf fled from the city when they heard that German Headquarters would be established there as soon as the army was forced across the Rhine. Working people in Cologne, seeing factories closing and rich fugitives crowding trains, indulged in violent demonstrations for peace.

President Wilson transmitted to Germany, on November 4, the armistice terms as finally agreed upon at a meeting of the Supreme War Council in Versailles. Would the once arrogant nation which set out four years and three months before to conquer the world, now actually sign a surrender which left her politically bankrupt, and even without the slightest salve of "military honor"? President Wilson forwarded the armistice terms to Marshal Foch whom they reached on November 5. Foch was then ready to deliver them to Germany, whenever she sent properly accredited representatives to him with a white flag asking for them.

The Allies had agreed, as Germany declared in advance she also would agree, to Wilson's fourteen points, but one was added respecting Germany's obligation to make good her ravages in occupied territory and on the sea; to which President Wilson also assented, and it was further agreed that the Peace Conference should define more precisely what was meant by "freedom of the seas." The Allies imposed an armistice upon Germany which left her, in a military sense, at their mercy, but announced beforehand that the peace terms which they would exact would be, in general, those to which Germany had profest a willingness to submit.

The President's note was the last link in a chain of developments leading up to acceptance, or rejection, by Germany of the armistice terms. No one pretended to estimate the stupendous German penalties involved in these terms. The damage done to civilians in France alone was so great that André Tardieu, of the French High Commission, estimated that it would take twenty years and 100,000 workers to restore France. All the destruction of a wanton character in Belgium, France, Serbia, Roumania, Montenegro, on the seas and in air-raids, was to be provided for. Figures of fabulous size, tens of billions of dollars, were needed in attempting to estimate it. Dispatches from Amsterdam soon said that Germany not only had climbed down, but had climbed all the way down. The dismissal of Ludendorff had virtually been a condition precedent to peace, and to all appearance he had resigned because of his hostility to political changes and in particular to any transference of authority from the military command to the civil power. For two years he had been a sort of small Napoleon, overshadowing Hindenburg, and more powerful and arbitrary, altho working behind the scenes, than any Chancellor since Bismarck. His retention would have made any but a defiant reply to the armistice peace terms hypocritical and worse than useless. Now that he was gone the final collapse could not be long delayed.

While waiting for the German delegates to come to him and ask for the armistice, Foch did not cease his pressure on the demoralized enemy any more than Grant eased up on the Confederate forces in the last days before Appomattox. The whole Western Front from Ghent to the Meuse was kept aflame, the Germans being squeezed rapidly off the little they still held of French soil. When, on November 6, the German Government dispatched delegates to the front to receive the armistice terms from Foch, British armies were almost up to Maubeuge, had cleared the Mormal Forest, and driven forward to the outskirts of Hautmont, two miles southwest of Maubeuge, and the French and Americans were in sight of Sedan. Germany also knew that another offensive would be launched on the Lorraine front on November 14 by 600,000 men under Castelnau. American and French troops had been concentrated between Briey and Château-Salins, supported by 3,000 guns of all calibers and 300 tanks on a front of forty-five miles. The German commander on this front had available approximately only 160,000 men, with 1,000 guns. The Allied attack would have carried the war into German Lorraine and Rhenish Prussia and threatened to cut from its base the German army in Belgium and the Ardennes. The German command had averted that catastrophe by pleading for an armistice. Entente success in this territory could not have made victory more complete than it already was, because Germany accepted all the Allied conditions. Foch deemed it useless to cause further shedding of blood, because Germany was already in a desperate plight and ready to surrender.[3]

Information came to light in February, 1919, concerning the great attack in Lorraine that was to have come on November 14. It was to force the capitulation of Metz. Many fully expected that the Allies would take 600,000 prisoners before the end of November and perhaps more, if the pursuit of the German army could be pushed rapidly enough. This had been the reason for the mobilization of large bodies of calvary around Toul and Nancy behind the front to be attacked. The Germans had no reserves left, and the Lorraine front was held by only four German divisions. The force opposed to them comprised nineteen French divisions and six American divisions, which were equivalent to twelve French divisions. As soon as the first thrust was

[3] The *Excelsior* (Paris).

made, all the American troops of the First and Second armies were to become involved in supporting attacks along the front all the way to Sedan. The American divisions selected to make the first attack on November 14 were the Fourth and Seventh of the Regular Army; the Twenty-eighth and Thirty-third, veteran guard divisions from Pennsylvania and Illinois; the Thirty-fifth from Kansas and Missouri. Two National Army Divisions, the negroes of the

© UNDERWOOD & UNDERWOOD, N. Y.

WHERE THE ARMISTICE OF NOVEMBER 11 WAS SIGNED

On the right is the train in which the Germans came, on the left the train of Marshal Foch, in which the signing took place. The forest is that of Compiègne, and near Senlis

Ninety-third and the Middle Westerners of the Eighty-eighth, completed the seven divisions.

In a forest near Senlis, on November 8, Marshal Foch delivered to the German delegates the terms as fixt by the Allied Conference in Versailles. A courier with these terms was sent by the German delegates at once to Spa, in eastern Belgium, near the German border, where the Kaiser and the German High Command were waiting for him. Foch had refused to grant a German request for an immediate cessation of hostilities, and fixt the time for a reply from Germany at seventy-two hours later, which meant 11 A.M. on Monday, November 11. After the courier returned from his journey of 200 miles, the envoys again met Foch at his headquarters in the railroad car in the forest. Senlis was a little French town, far removed from the echo of battle, but now nothing more than a row of gutted houses, having been wantonly burned by the Germans in 1914. It was a strange experience for Senlis whose main street had been ruined by German incendiaries to see French military automobiles containing the German envoys passing through on their way to Foch's car on an errand of national humiliation. Doubtless they all recalled that tragic day in September, 1914, when their mayor and several fellow-townsmen were shot by the Germans, and nights when the earth shook to the crash of bursting German air-bombs and the thunder of answering batteries in the Ludendorff offensive of 1918.

Since Queen Louise after Jena was sent with a rose in her hand to plead with Napoleon for Brandenburg, no such humiliation had ever come to Germany. Representatives of a proud and Prussianized empire had come under a white flag to accept the terms of an armistice imposed by a Marshal of France—an ultimate demonstration of the fact that a military decision had been reached. At the same hour British armies were in Belgium approaching Waterloo, French and American soldiers had recovered the Argonne and Sedan. The soil of France was all but freed. The hundred-year-old military tradition of the German army, the tradition of Waterloo, Sadowa, and Sedan had been so far destroyed that the world would no longer listen to superior German military leadership. Confident of its strength, assured of its weapons, arrogant beyond anything in history, the great machine which had challenged to mortal combat the unorganized forces of civilization, and thrust its sword through all the covenants and commands of civilization, now lay prone in the dust. Bursting upon an unprepared and unsuspecting world, it had been checked, despite its incredible strength, on the Marne, at Ypres, at Verdun, in Picardy, at the Hindenburg line, and in the North Sea by the British fleet. As the German Empire had been built up by the sword, so now it had been destroyed by the sword. In a cycle of disasters, it had seen its old legend destroyed, its leaders outgeneraled, its soldiers outfought, and of all that tremendous and arrogant tradition of invincibility nothing was left. For all serious-minded men it was a solemnizing spectacle, a work of retribution. What Germany had sown she had reaped in a terrible harvest. The orphans and widows of Belgium and France had called into being a greater power than all the legions of whom the Kaiser had boasted for thirty years.

Prince Maximilian had not run up the white flag because in the privacy of his study he had made up his mind that it was time for the Central Powers to quit. He had acted under the "iron compulsion" of the German High Command which knew that the alternative to armistice was another Sedan. The demand for terms and the authority for signing them had really come from Hindenburg himself. The German delegates were to ask for concessions on nine points, but, so ran the order received by Erzberger by wireless, "even if you do not succeed in obtaining concessions on these points, you must sign the armistice." Thus upon the supreme issue, Hindenburg in November, 1918, was in full agreement with Foch and knew that Germany had lost the war. Erzberger in February, 1919, quoted Hindenburg's wireless message in the National Assembly at Weimar. The applause with which he was rewarded was in part an expression of sympathy for his humiliating task; in fact, a manifestation of relief for having heard the truth at last. After four years of pleasant fictions, culminating in *Niedergang*, even the bitterest truth now seemed almost palatable to Germany.

On November 8 the nervous tension of years of war was suddenly broken in America by a false report that Germany had that day signed the armistice. Joyful enthusiasm pent up through the long ordeal broke forth only to be lost on a "fake." All over the country sirens, whistles and bells rose in a resounding clamor about one o'clock in the afternoon, carrying news of the supposed signing and the cessation of hostilities. Men and women of all ages and all stations, in every part of New York and many other cities, with unspoken accord, suddenly stopt business and poured out into streets to join all that afternoon and until midnight in a delirious carnival of joy beyond comparison with anything ever seen before. The false report went to villages, small towns and great cities, where celebrations as enthusiastic as those in New York took place. Afternoon papers which carried the false news were snatched off the stands by eager crowds. No attention meanwhile was paid to the less romantic reports of a steady advance of Allied armies, of the taking of Sedan by French and Americans, or of the outbreak of a revolution in Germany. It was not till late afternoon that papers declared the report false. Even then the celebrating went on just the same until far into the night. The United States had got into the war last, and now it was getting out first.

The peace jubilation had merely come off ahead of schedule; that was all, and what did it matter? We were on the verge of peace, at any rate. Even if the German Government had been inclined to fight longer internal discontent would have soon forced a peace or a revolution. An extensive mutiny had occurred in the Kiel fleet and an uprising had put Hamburg into revolt. Mutineers wanted peace, and if they could not get peace they would bring about anarchy. What the crowd was celebrating on November 8, 1918, was not a newspaper "fake" but a great historic fact, one which it and all Americans had been longing for an excuse to celebrate ever since Foch drove the Germans back; ever since Bulgaria fell; ever since Turkey prayed for peace; ever since Austria crumbled, and an excuse had come in a false newspaper report. Believing it, New York blew its lid off with a reverberating bang. The nightmare that had hung over the world for four years had been torn to fragments and victory was here with the blessings of peace in her train. It did not make any difference that the fighting might go on for a time—the end was before our eyes, and it was the end that the civilized world had longed for from the first. Germany was defeated, and whether it took her hours or months to say so was of small consequence compared with that. When Germany sent the Erzberger Commission as suppliants to Foch she had already surrendered.

By the terms of the armistice as signed November 11, the Allied Governments and the United States retained the power to dictate, without further argument, the final conditions of peace. It was equally certain that the peace would be a peace without amnesties for the Kaiser, his war ministers, his naval ministers, his army commanders, or his military governors, who were primarily responsible for outrageous deeds committed under their authority or by their

BRITISH OFFICIAL PHOTO.

GERMAN HEADQUARTERS AT SPA

The picture shows the entrance to the grounds which were afterward used as headquarters for the International Armistice Commission. A German sentry is still guarding the gate, and a German automobile, flying a white flag, is coming out of the grounds

orders. These criminals in high places could have been under no misapprehension as to the kind of justice that awaited them. Of the meeting of the commission at Foch's headquarters in the railway car, no details were published in England or America, but ten days later one of the German Commission wrote for the *Vossiche Zeitung* an account of the journey from Spa to Senlis, the meeting with the Allied Commission and the signing of the armistice. As given below the account evoked comment as a concrete illustration of the German as a bad loser:

"When on November 8th we reached the French lines, coming by motor-cars from Spa in the November fog, carriages were ready to convey us to the unknown place of negotiations. The motor-journey, with French officers, lasted ten hours. It appears to me probable that it was intentionally prolonged in order to take us right and left through the ruined province, and so prepare us, by our own inspection, for what hate and revenge would demand of us in the form of the sharpest possible conditions. A Frenchman silently pointed out the ruins and then mentioned a name—"*Voilà St. Quentin!*" In the evening a train stood ready for us somewhere. The blinds were drawn, and when we awoke in the morning the train stood still in the middle of a wood. We know now that we negotiated in the Forest of Compiègne. We did not know it eight days ago. Possibly it was a precautionary measure for us also that we were not taken to the city. Perhaps they feared the acts of violence on the population's side, for the hatred accumulated in its heart was unbounded. We were in a wood, without houses or tents, entirely shut off by troops. Only two trains stood on the railway—one was Foch's and that of his companions, the other was ours. In these two trains we lived, worked, negotiated. Our train was provided with a sleeping-car, a large saloon, and a restaurant car, and was very comfortably fitted up. We were amply supplied with everything necessary. The officer who had the supervision of our train caused everything we wanted to be brought. We have nothing to complain of, either, in the way in which the guards, of whom there were a large number around our train, greeted us; the great hatred and revenge which they seem to cherish against our country found expression only in the form of negotiations and the sharpness of the conditions.

"Those of us who were soldiers wore uniforms, with the Iron Cross. The introduction of the half-dozen French officers with whom we negotiated was a formal ceremony. Marshal Foch, who only showed himself twice, at the beginning and at the end—a severe, calm man—bestowed on us no word in the courtly tone which formerly distinguished the most chivalrous nation, nor did his officers. He received us with these words, '*Qu'est-ce que vous désirez, Messieurs?*" and invited us to sit down in the large working compartment with tables and maps. As each spoke in his own language, and everything translated, the reading out of the conditions alone occupied two hours. It is an invention that Marshal Foch replied to us that there was no question of negotiations but only of imposing conditions. However cool his behavior, Marshal Foch showed himself by no means tactless or brusque, as General d'Esperey did toward Count Karolyi at Belgrade.

"We went back to our train. As we were still commissioned by the old Government, and were by no means charged to sign everything unconditionally, we divided the various points under Herr Erzberger's guidance into three categories—military, diplomatic, and naval conditions—and negotiated thereafter separately with the members of the enemy Commissions, which consisted exclusively of officers. All these officers exhibited the same cool bearing, untempered by any humane word, which Marshal Foch had assumed. One could at the most observe somewhat more politeness from the chief than from his General Staff. The British Admiral took his tone absolutely from the French.

"We really had nothing to negotiate; we pointed out the technical impossibility of some of the conditions. We might, indeed, send cipher telegrams to Germany via the Eiffel Tower, but we were cut off from all connection with the world in this lonely wood. Marshal Foch himself went away twice, apparently to Paris, and couriers could bring newspapers in two hours. Thus our enemies were able to give us the Paris newspapers of Sunday morning, the newspapers in which the Kaiser's abdication was announced. We read no smile, no triumph on their faces, but we looked into their hearts. Our work was really undisturbed by the Revolution. Our letters of credit, which were signed by the 'German Government,' retained their validity. We could also already speedily consult with Herr Ebert and soften somewhat, by small concessions from the enemy, the new Government's unconditional subjection. Just before the end of the second and last general sitting, we produced our protest in German, which has been published, but were eventually obliged to sign the document forced on us with its inhuman conditions."

With just a touch of dramatic fervor and a slight raising of his voice, President Wilson, before the Senate and House of Representatives, on November 11, read the armistice terms which Germany had been forced to accept. At first there was a faint hand-clapping, then a cheer or two, and finally cheers until men on the floor and in the gallery got on their feet cheering without restraint this official statement that America and the Allies had won the war for freedom and justice. It was a dramatic moment. Drastic conditions were laid down for Germany. Among the more important were the following:

"The evacuation of Belgium, France, Alsace-Lorraine and Luxemburg, within fourteen days. The surrender of guns and equipments, including 2,500 heavy field-guns, 30,000 machine-guns and 2,000 airplanes. The evacuation of the left bank of the Rhine and a neutral zone to be maintained on the right bank of the Rhine. The surrender of rolling stock in occupied territory. The abandonment of the Bucharest and Brest treaties. The surrender of 160 submarines and larger war-craft. The reparation of all damage done, and restitution of the Russian and Roumanian gold taken by Germany. The evacuation of all Black Sea ports. The restoration of all Allied and United States merchant vessels. The existing blockade conditions set up by Allies to remain unchanged and all German merchant-ships found at sea to be liable to capture. The disarmament and internment at neutral ports of 6 battle-cruisers, 10 battleships, 8 light cruisers, and 50 destroyers. The immediate repatriation without reciprocity of all Allied and United States prisoners of war. The freedom of access to and from the Baltic to naval and mercantile marines of the Allied and associated powers. The concentration and immobilization in German bases of all naval aircraft. The duration of the armistice to be thirty days with option to extend. It can be terminated by either side on forty-eight hours' notice."

Much had been reproachfully said of "eleventh-hour repentance" and other eleventh-hour futilities, but eleventh-hour events derived from Germany's signing of the armistice a new and different suggestion—hostilities in the World War had ceased at the eleventh hour, and not only this, but ceased on the eleventh day of the eleventh month of the year.

The outpouring of emotion that followed the receipt of the false news of peace made no reduction in the volume of the demonstration which greeted news of the actual signing of the armistice in Foch's railway car on November 11. If on this day the spirit was somewhat different, the jubilations over the real surrender somewhat more standardized and lacking the millennial-dawn spirit which possest everybody when the premature report held currency, it was a celebration whose like we shall scarcely ever see again. The first demonstration had been a sort of rehearsal for the second. What happened in large cities was what happened the world over—in towns, cities, and small villages. Typical of many villages was a description of what occurred at Unadilla, in east central New York, where the Methodist church bell was rung at 4.30 A.M. and the Episcopal bell at 4.45—the latter by the rector himself. An Italian shoemaker got out his cornet and woke people up going through the village playing ''Marching Through Georgia,'' while other citizens went along shouting ''Wake up,'' until all rose, put out their flags and lighted up their houses—all this in fine starlight on a fogless morning followed an hour later by sunrise in a cloudless sky.

Accounts from London and Paris, no less than from Lima in Peru, where people had not participated in the war at all, read much like descriptions of the demonstration in New York, which was not unnatural, for there had probably never been an instance in the history of the world where so large a percentage of the human race was thrilled simultaneously by the same emotion. In London when King George drove along Fleet Street on his way to the Mansion House, crowds struggled to approach his carriage and shake hands with the head of Imperial Democracy. Church bells pealed merry chimes. Sounds were heard from ''Big Ben'' at Westminster, whose tones had not been given out since early in the war. Such was the din in East End streets that few Cockneys could hear the sound of Bow-bells. The King in uniform, accompanied by the Queen and Princess Mary, drove in an open carriage, escorted by half a dozen mounted policemen, whose chief task was to clear the way. He was making a royal visit to congratulate the Lord Mayor and the citizens of London. His coming, quite unexpected by the crowds, was a truly royal progress. Everywhere soldiers were supreme; American boys in khaki had the time of their lives. From St. Paul's to Oxford Circus and from Whitehall to Victoria Streets, streets were full from curb to curb with laughing, jostling, happy people. Traffic difficulties had been solved in the simplest fashion by turning back the omnibuses. The police eliminated themselves by seeking dark corners and smiling out over the scene.

ON THE WESTERN FRONT

In Paris the rejoicings extended over several days. It was most notable among Alsatians who were greeted with enthusiasm everywhere. Paris awoke for days as late as November 17, after night revelings, to repeat previous scenes of jubilation. Crowds thronged the streets shouting *"Vive la France!"* *"Vive les Alliés!"* and singing the "Marseillaise." Huge American lorries filled with doughboys and poilus were acclaimed by crowds. Traffic was unable to pass down main thoroughfares, business was at a standstill, for the day was a national holiday for everyone. While crowds cheered in the streets, aeroplanes flew above doing acrobatic feats and dropping leaflets, encouraging the celebration. The whole of Paris manifested the utmost joy. Flags floated everywhere, and everybody had on some sort of bunting. It was literally impossible to walk on some of the streets, nor could one find a seat in any restaurant. On the steps of the Grand Opera poilus with trumpets played the French national anthem, while a hundred thousand sang Rouget de Lisle's hymn to liberty. From every side street parades marched past, only to get lost in the throng. American officers and soldiers, caught in the whirlwind of excitement, were carried away bodily in triumph.

Midinettes, draped from head to foot in the national colors, danced round the nation's heroes and kissed them. Doughboys marched with French girls on their arms. Opposite the statues of Strassburg and Lille in the Place de la Concorde thousands stood with bared heads singing the "Marseillaise." British soldiers sang their own anthem, and Americans sang theirs. Press photographers took pictures without end. Stuffed effigies of the Kaiser, the Crown Prince and leaders of the German military party were carried around, while people shouted "Down with the Kaiser!" "Down with the Crown Prince!" "Down with Germany!" The only safe way of getting a meal was to go to a café early in the morning and remain there for hours. If you left your seat scores would be waiting to take it. It seemed impossible that there could be such crowds in Paris, but suburbanites had flocked in by the hundred thousands. If all this could be done now, what would Paris not be when the poilus marched down the Champs Elysées and under

the Arc de Triomphe. Important boulevards were lighted
again as before the war. Until long after midnight the
people's voices filled the air with laughter. With linked
hands the masses whirled around every American soldier
whom they met. All conventions were laid aside. Young
and old were kissing and being kissed—happy over their
freedom from the burden of war. They sang not only
French tunes and English songs, but American favorites,
like "Over There" and "Dixie." Scenes like these were such
only as Thomas Carlyle could have fitly described in the manner he employed in his "History of the French Revolution."

Accepting the armistice terms Germany could fight no
more. Great masses of enemy troops would soon occupy
broad belts of her territory. The war thus ended in sub-
jugation as effected by the armies under Foch, by the
blockading fleets of the Allies, and, in a real and important
sense, by the diplomacy of President Wilson, who had
demonstrated to the German people that the Hohenzollern,
and the false and faithless men about him, had long been
the great obstacle to peace.

Only four months and eleven days before Germany accepted the armistice terms, Count von Roon, a member of
the Prussian House of Nobles, had delivered himself un-
officially of an ultimatum of terms upon which Germany
would consent to peace. Until its conditions were realized,
he said, there should be no armistice and no cessation of
submarine warfare. The conditions in detail were: the
annexation by Germany of Belgium, including the Channel
coast as far as Calais; the annexation of the Briey and
Longwy Basins and the Toul, Belfort, and Verdun regions
eastward; the restitution to Germany of all her colonies, including Kiaochow; Great Britain to cede to Germany such
naval bases and coaling stations as Germany desired; Great
Britain to cede her war fleet to Germany, to restore Egypt
to Turkey, and the Suez Canal to Turkey; Greece to be re-
established under the former King Constantine; Austria
and Bulgaria to divide Serbia and Montenegro; Great
Britain, France, and the United States to pay all of Germany's war costs, the indemnity being a minimum of

$45,000,000,000, they also to deliver raw materials imme-
diately; France and Belgium to remain occupied at their
own expense until the conditions were carried out.

Such was Prussian belief in herself as late as July 1,
1918—two weeks and three days before Foch struck his blow.
While the defeated German armies were making their way
backward across the Rhine, there came to President Wilson
a cry for an early conclusion of peace because starvation
faced the war-torn empire. Germany, that once had boasted
that she would throw a circle of iron about the British
Isles and starve British people into submission, was now
begging not alone for peace, but for bread.

© KEYSTONE VIEW CO.

THE POILU IN METZ

Within a few months of the pulling down of the equestrian
statue of Kaiser Wilhelm I at Metz, this mud-covered French
soldier, with one foot on a German helmet, was set up in its
place on the same pedestal

FATHER AND SON IN METZ

The upper statue is of the Emperor William I; the lower one the Emperor Frederick, who, after reigning ninety-eight days, was succeeded by William II. Both statues were hauled from their pedestals as soon as the French got possession of Metz after the armistice was signed

251

ON THE WESTERN FRONT

To have lived to see November 11, 1918, filled up the measure of happiness for uncounted millions. The thrill which ran through the American people vibrated in the hearts of men everywhere. It was more than a great military victory that the world was celebrating. It was the majestic triumph of great moral ideas. Two systems of government, rather than two armies, had been locked in a death-grapple for four years, and the system which now lay in irreparable ruin had long been an anachronism and an offense in this modern world of which the breath of life was liberty and free self-expression. It was clear now that the subjects—or victims—of German military autocracy had never really believed in it, altho they were forced to submit to it. The speed and joy with which they seized an opportunity to throw off the hated bonds were fresh proof of the terrorism in which they had been held, soul and body.

Most Americans took pride in their President, whom all nations were acclaiming. By him, at least during a year and a half, the nations' hope and the world's desire had been given singularly apt and powerful expression. No American President in his lifetime had ever entered into such a heritage of world-wide fame as had the man who, years before, was simply an American teacher, Woodrow Wilson. Fit to stand with him were our commanders in the field and on the sea. Unpretentious, modest, but terribly resolute and efficient, General Pershing had been an ideal head of our army in France. Nor would Americans soon forget the splendid qualities shown by Field-Marshal Haig, the British Commander-in-Chief, whom the hurricane could batter but could not break. Of the Supreme Commander, Marshal Foch, it was only necessary to say that he had made for himself an immortal name. To the highest military genius he had united a mind and spirit that compelled admiration to the verge of idolizing. The fact that not one vulgar or braggart word had come from him in the course of his magnificent successes, showed possession of the good taste of a true gentleman and the poise of a firm-set soul. In Ferdinand Foch was realized the poet's vision of the Happy Warrior, "whom every man in arms would wish to be."

Over the other side charity might be induced to draw a

veil. Autocracy had died ignobly. Even that bit of imperial tinsel of an older generation, Napoleon III, had cut a better figure after the first Sedan than the German Kaiser William II after the second. Napoleon at least had sought to die at the head of his troops, but William II slunk away into exile. The swaggering monarch who had thought he

© WESTERN NEWSPAPER UNION.   FRENCH OFFICIAL PHOTO.

FRENCH AND AMERICAN OFFICERS SALUTING
OUR FLAG IN ALSACE

made the world tremble at his empty oral threats, who used to speak blasphemously of being the vice-regent of the Almighty, had departed from the imperial scene like a discharged hostler. What might not the accusing spirit of Bismarck have said to one who had made such fool's work of the splendid inheritance which the creator of German unity had left to the Hohenzollerns!

With the signing of the armistice the third of the great wars of modern Europe came to an end. With the struggles of the Reformation, the wars of the French Revolution and the Napoleonic era this World War, altho it was far greater than any of these, would hereafter have to be classed. Like them it was a struggle against tyranny, ending in the triumph of the forces of liberalism. In the wars of the Reformation mankind won religious freedom. In the upheaval of the French Revolution the civil liberties of men were established. In the conflict of 1914-1918, the rights of peoples, large and small, to live their own lives, to preserve their own ideals, to follow out their own destinies, were vindicated. The German had said in his heart: "There is no God but the god of violence; there is no law but the law of the sword; there is no people but the German people, who, because they are strong, shall rule the world." As a consequence, mankind for more than four years had fought the Germans, until Asia, Africa, and Europe—from the capes of Good Hope and the Horn to the Arctic Sea at Archangel, from the coast of Chile eastward around the world to the China Sea—became scenes of gigantic struggles with them, while America sent millions to fight them in France in order to preserve American ideals and American liberties. Some millions of men had died, some thousands of towns and cities had been wrecked and many provinces ravaged. Since other barbarians in another and far-off age had burst upon the Roman Empire, scattered its treasures, wrecked its temples and destroyed its civilization, the earth had seen no devastation and ruin such as the Germans wrought. The pathway of their armies in Europe could be traced by smoking ruins of recent conflagrations and the cold ashes of towns that had lain dead for four years.

Unlike other militarists, the Germans had brought nothing but the sterile doctrine of force to the regions they overran. They enslaved people, wasted fields, and wrecked monuments. No consideration of humanity, of international law, of what we once called Christian sympathy, tempered their violence or moderated their barbarity. Unorganized civilization had finally conquered their organized barbarism. No defeat in history was more complete and never was a faith in ultimate justice more completely vindicated. The Germans began this war with every advantage that long preparation, skilful leadership, and infinite organization could produce. They had the weapons and the machinery, and they were halted by no regard for human or divine laws. They had power, unlimited willingness to employ it, and they employed it for four years and a quarter, but in the end they failed and their machine was "in the scrap," their nation sinking into chaos, while Belgium, Serbia, Roumania, the little states they had subdued, were returning into the sunlight of the world. Only the allies of Germany had been ruined, only their people had been brought to the brink of chaos. All their armies had been beaten, their generals mastered, their preparations surpassed, their machinery distanced. German Kultur was exposed as the mere handmaid of military brutality, powerless when intelligence was aroused and armed and organized to cope with it.

Allied fleets within a few days after the signing of the armistice were in Constantinople, and while the guns of great warships were pointing threateningly toward St. Sophia, the Sublime Porte announced that the ancient city, so long invulnerable, had fallen. Constantinople, in the long past had been under sieges, among others by Avars, Arabs, Bulgars, Varangians, Crusaders, and Turks, but usually she had beaten off all their attacks. Three times only had her walls been scaled, twice by Crusaders in 1203, and 1204, once by the conquering hordes of Mohammed II, who put an end to the Greek Empire of the East and began the long era of Turkey-in-Europe. Hostile armies had twice camped within sight of the city in recent years—Russians in 1878 when they penetrated as far as San Stefano; and the Bulgars in 1912 when they were battering at the Tchataldja lines.

The presence of Allied fleets at Constantinople now was visible evidence that the Ottoman Empire had fallen, that the Sick Man of Europe had drawn his last painful breath and that the century-long régime of Turkish brutality was over. Suffering races in the Levant would acclaim the event as the dawn of a new era, in which they might control their own destinies, unhampered by reactionary and brutal masters, and win for themselves a place among modern nations. Now would be unlocked the gates to the Black Sea, and immediate relief could be given to long suffering Roumania; now it would be possible to save the tortured remnant of the Armenians; now was clear the way to southern Russia where there was pressing need of Allied assistance in overthrowing the German régime in the Ukraine and in establishing a "government of the people." The day when the Allied fleets passed through the Dardanelles would long be celebrated in the Near East as marking the passing of an old and the beginning of a new world epoch.

After an eventful month the war had ended as President Wilson was aiming to make it end; the armistice was signed, Germany was in revolution and the Kaiser was a fugitive in Holland. Then a little story was made public. "What will be the effect, what do you hope to accomplish, by your three inquiries of Germany?" was asked of Mr. Wilson by a friend after one of his much criticized armistice notes was published. "This will bring a revolution in Germany," replied the President. "Her people are ready to overthrow their present rulers in order to get peace." Wilson's bold prediction had been fulfilled. He had had in his possession more information as to conditions in Germany than the public had, the most of it confidential. He knew that when the German request for an armistice came, Germany was on the road to collapse, and his inquiries helped along the collapse by showing the German people that what stood between them and the peace they so longed to see, was their imperial and military masters who had brought on the war and who had so conducted it as to array against them a world of enemies no longer willing to have anything to do with them, except on the field of battle.[4]

The hand of an American, only a little while before an instructor of youth and the head of a great university, who had long been a student and writer of history and was now the head of a great State, had rung the death-knell of a powerful, centuries-old dynasty that had been guilty of fouler crimes than had ever before blackened the reign of any king. It was a marvel unmatched in human chronicles

[4] David Lawrence in a Washington letter to The *Evening Post* (New York).

that this unassuming gentleman who had never worn a sword in his life, should have been able to write the word that toppled from his ancient throne, in a far-off land, the world's greatest military despot, one who had never publicly appeared without a sword, and who through a long reign had frequently rattled one, or had threatened to rattle one whenever he wanted something and could not get it by fair means. An American pen had stilled those proud and grandiose threats of this wickedest of men who had long strutted about Europe with a spiked helmet and a gleaming saber.

FRENCH OFFICIAL PHOTO.

THE FRENCH FLAG FLYING FROM STRASSBURG CATHEDRAL

At Treves, on January 15, 1919, Marshal Foch was asked, "But was not the armistice concluded too soon?" "It was not possible to do otherwise," answered the Marshal, "because the Germans gave us everything that we asked for at once. They satisfied all our conditions. It was difficult to ask more. Doubtless any general would have preferred to continue the struggle and to have had battle when the battle which offered itself was so promising, but a father of a family could not help thinking of the blood that would be shed. A victory, however easy, costs the lives of men. We held the victory in our grasp without any further sacrifice. We took it as it came. The German High Command was not ignorant of the fact that it faced a colossal disaster. When it surrendered everything had been prepared for an offensive to which it would infallibly have succumbed. On November 14 we were to attack in Lorraine with twenty French divisions and six American divisions. This attack would have been supported by other movements in Flanders and in the center. The Germans were lost and they capitulated. There is the whole story."

Germany having failed to comply with important conditions of the armistice, new armistice terms were imposed by Marshal Foch in January. They provided first, for retribution for the murder and ill-treatment of Allied prisoners in Germany; second, that the machinery and goods stolen by Germany from France and Belgium should be at once given up, it being pointed out that France alone had 500,000 men who would be out of work until this machinery was returned; third, that German gold should be moved from Berlin to a safe place, probably Frankfort, and protected from Bolshevism in Germany while en route, while certain other property was to be surrendered; fourth, that Germany give over shipping, of which she was believed to have 4,000,000 tons, to carry food supplies to countries in Europe in need of them; fifth, that any U-boats on the stocks be handed over to the Allies for their disposal, or be destroyed, and no more submarines be built. Marshal Foch informed the Supreme Council on February 17 of the acceptance by the Germans of the conditions for still another renewal of the armistice. He appeared in person before the Council and announced the acceptance and the signing by the Germans at 6 o'clock the evening before.

Ludendorff late in February, 1919, was quoted as saying that events as early as August, had shown that the value of some units in the German army had depreciated and that an improvement was not to be expected, in view of the fact that the war "had broken the will of the people at home." When afterward the ground became more shaky, he had informed the German Government that it was no longer possible to make Germany's enemies desire peace by means of war and that the war therefore should be ended quickly. After the collapse of Bulgaria, he had demanded that the German Government make an offer of peace. He said the Emperor had been kept informed of the entire situation, and after August 8 "recognized that Germany could not win the war." August 8 was the date of the Albert-Montdidier offensive.

Early in March, 1919, Ludendorff made another statement to a Swedish newspaper in which he was reported to have said that the military power of Germany had now "vanished forever." He attributed the causes of the German defeat not to Foch or his armies but to "the deficient strategy of Moltke," to "the defective direction of Falkenhayn," to the poor information supplied by the German intelligence service, and particularly to "the inability of Austria to help Germany on account of the tenacity of the Italian army." If Austria had been able to release even a small number of her divisions to help Germany on the Western Front, the war would have been won by the Central Empires before America would have had time to send reinforcements to the Allies. Ludendorff admitted the part tanks had played in his defeat.

He stated further that the position of the Central Empires had really become precarious as far back as when Italy abandoned her neutrality and joined the Allies, which was in May, 1915, but their position became altogether disastrous in June, 1918, when Diaz foiled the Austrian offensive on the Piave, where the Austrians had employed their best troops and all their resources. After that failure Ludendorff favored making immediate peace proposals.

Emperor William telegraphed his objections and urged that the Austrian Army be placed under the German command, but Emperor Charles refused to sign a decree for that purpose. Ludendorff's statement was psychologically interesting for its failure to give the slightest hint that he had been out-fought and out-generaled by Foch.[5]

[5] Principal Sources: William L. McPherson in The *Tribune* (New York), The *Times*, The *Journal of Commerce*, The *Evening Post*, The *World*, The *Evening Sun*, The *Wall Street Journal*, New York; The Berlin *Vossische Zeitung*, The *Social Demokraten* of Stockholm.

BRITISH OFFICIAL PHOTO.

BRITISH, AMERICAN AND FRENCH ARMISTICE
COMMISSIONERS AT SPA

II

A REVOLUTION IN GERMANY IN WHICH KAISER, KINGS, AND GRAND DUKES LOSE THEIR THRONES—THE SPARTA-CAN INSURRECTION

November 6, 1918—April 16, 1919

BETTER proof was not needed for the saying that no such word as "impossible" can be found in the psychology of nations than the revolution which overwhelmed Germany during the armistice negotiations. The assumption had been constantly made, and generally accepted, that, even under stress of defeat, poverty, and hunger, the German people would not revolt. Bismarck had pointed out that, in order that German patriotism should be active and effective, it required dependence upon a dynasty; independent of a dynasty it had rarely come to the rising point; German love of the Fatherland had need of a prince on whom to concentrate attachment. But now it was shown that reverence for the Hohenzollern dynasty could not survive a hopeless defeat of the army on which the existence of the dynasty had been staked in 1914.

When William II ascended the throne, he found a prosperous Germany, comparatively sane and pacific, but, after thirty years of his rule, Germany now confronted the world, isolated, distraught, friendless, and bankrupt. The great middle class—manufacturers, merchants, shopkeepers—who had long been under the spell of Kaiserism, militarism, and pan-Germanism, were beginning to realize the depth of their folly and to see with some clearness to what pass it had brought them, and what was the price they would have to pay for any further pursuit of those mad ambitions which all Germany before and during the war had tolerated and most Germans had approved. The bill was a heavy one and could be liquidated only by patient toil and rigorous self-denial.

There had been for many months—for quite a year in fact—definite statements from Holland and Switzerland and from returning travelers, some of them Americans, that deep discontent prevailed in Germany, and that demands for peace were growing more and more insistent. Bread riots, naval and military mutinies, had had to be supprest vigorously and sometimes with bloodshed. Ludendorff's great offensive of 1918 was well understood to have been in response to a wide popular demand for peace. That last great effort of the fast waning military power was officially called a "peace offensive," an effort to force peace with the German sword. When, therefore, the German Chancellor, in October, begged President Wilson to ask the European Allies for an armistice, it was evident beyond question that the situation at home had become so critical as to have got quite beyond the control of the military power. Every sign appeared of a German wish that an armistice should be arranged at once. Henry C. Emery, a former professor at Yale, who had been in Russia for one of the large New York trust companies and was taken to Germany as a prisoner early in the year, finally got out of the country in October when conditions economically were such that a suit of clothes cost from 1,200 to 1,500 marks, handkerchiefs 12 marks each, collars 8 marks, and an ordinary dinner 20 marks. No linen could be secured and paper was being used as a substitute for cotton in curtains and table-linen, even in the best hotels.

Early in the summer, when it began to be realized that the Ludendorff offensive had failed to secure the promised peace by force, Mr. Emery discovered a restlessness among working people that was not yet discoverable among the more well-to-do and educated classes. Each succeeding week brought him a growing conviction that great masses of the people were thoroughly sick of the war and of their rulers. Before he left men would talk quite openly in the Unter den Linden of a necessity for the Kaiser's abdication. Mr. Emery remarked to a member of the Reichstag that in August people were afraid that President Wilson would insist on the Emperor's abdication, "but in October they seemed afraid he wouldn't." It was generally understood that

PHILIPP SCHEIDEMANN PROCLAIMING A GERMAN REPUBLIC

The building shown is the Reichstag; the statue is one of Bismarck

the Kaiser had lost his grip and that Ludendorff had long been the dictator of Germany. Within a few weeks Mr. Emery saw the Kaiser fall from his pedestal as a national hero and become the most execrated man in the empire. Early in October, a rather conservative journalist had remarked to him, "The lamp-post he will hang on is already picked out."

When the military machine went to pieces, a few Pan-Germans even could be found who turned against it, believing they had been deceived. In spite of a general sense of humiliation, the faces of people "looked brighter and a sense of relief went through them, because the long nightmare of oppression and misrule was over." Truths, as they came to be told and read with avidity, brought about a great revulsion of feelings, in which were degrees of shame and remorse which Mr. Emery never expected to see. Before an armistice could be effected, members of the crew of the battleship *Kaiser*, at Kiel, had mutinied and hoisted the red flag. Officers attempting to defend the German flag had been overpowered, and two of them, including the commander, were killed. The red flag had also been hoisted at Warnemunde, a seaport of northern Germany, and again in the port of Rostock, on the Baltic. Kiel practically passed into the hands of a Soldiers' Council formed on Russian lines. The uprising spread to many cities, until several parts of the empire fell completely into the hands of revolutionists. Not only was the German navy ripe for revolution, but the Rhine Provinces became panic-stricken at the prospect of a shifting of military operations to German soil. The German Government in these circumstances had to accept any terms it could get from the Entente in an effort to save the existing régime. Germany was going the way of Russia toward collapse and dissolution and the only hope of saving the dynasty lay in concluding peace at any cost, because the German armies now in Belgium, Luxemburg, Lorraine, and Alsace, were needed at home to prop the tottering thrones of kings, grand dukes and reigning princes.

Maximilian Harden dated the German military collapse from August, 1918—as did Ludendorff in his statement published in April, 1919—and adopted a current version of the cause as a "sudden loss of military morale and a complete breakdown of the whole system of lies and artificial optimism." Harden said Albert Ballin had been called in by one of Ludendorff's satellites as early as August as the only man who could go to the Kaiser and tell him the truth; but Ballin early in the war had been virtually banished from the Emperor's presence because he had recommended immediate peace negotiations. At that time, said Harden, "there

was a terrible scene, and a lady's fan threatened the cheek of the great ship-owner, the only German who had defeated England in her worldfield and yet had won and kept British confidence." Ballin was finally induced to make an effort to see the Kaiser and so traveled for this purpose to Wilhelmshohe. The Kaiser would not see him alone, insisting that their conversation should take place in the presence of the chief of the Emperor's Civil Cabinet. The interview over, Ballin went away, but he had accomplished nothing. Not many weeks after making this effort for peace Ballin died

KURT EISNER
Bavarian Premier under the revolution. Assassinated in Munich in 1919

suddenly from a stroke of apoplexy. He had not lived to see the armistice carried into effect.

Ballin was one of the few men in Germany who long before August, 1918, had seen the catastrophe coming. Even before war was declared on Russia he had tried to prevent war. During the crisis of July, 1914, he had gone to England and talked with Grey and Asquith and in Germany "tried in vain to illuminate the minds of the blind ones in Berlin," said Theodore Wolff.[6] With all his expert knowledge, he had warned against the submarine campaign and

[6] Editor of The *Berliner Tageblatt*.

against a breach with America. Later, he had continued to warn the Kaiser against further efforts to win the war, but in vain. The clique that ruled the hour treated Ballin with contempt and kept him at a distance. For years he had been the foremost shipping man in Germany as head of the Hamburg-American line.

Ludendorff's next move was to tell Admiral von Hintze, the Foreign Secretary, that he must bring about peace; but weeks went by without Hintze making any progress. Meanwhile the number of German deserters continued to increase until in September it was more and more clear that the morale of the army was breaking down. In October Ludendorff demanded definitely that Germany should ask for an armistice, a demand which broke in upon the Reichstag and the German people, said Hardin, "with the violence of an unexpected thunderstorm." Even the military and naval world did not know at the time that the demand had come from Ludendorff, but attributed it to "cowardly bourgeoisie" and to Jews and then conceived the plan of sending out the fleet "to fall upon the English" and, if need be, "die in honor." Harden described this naval scheme as the definite beginning of the revolution, which no political party had had anything to do with planning. Some of the stewards at Kiel overheard conversations that the navy was about to be sent out "to attack and go under." As the word was passed along among men on the ships a resolve was taken and in Harden's words this resolve was: "We will neither oppose the will of the Government nor let our lives be thrown away for a cause which can no longer be saved in this way. We will do everything that is necessary for defense of the coast, but we will not make an attack which the civil authorities regard as no longer necessary and even as harmful, and which would be bound to befog afresh the aim of getting peace." Harden described how the sailors then got control of the ships and how the spirit of revolution spread inland until all Germany was aflame.

In general the outbreak was at first marked by good order. In few places did rioting occur, councils having appealed for order on the ground that any turmoil would endanger the movement of food supplies. In Berlin there was some machine-gun and rifle firing and a few persons were killed and wounded; but otherwise the revolution seemed like some great popular holiday with enormous crowds parading the streets. The public having been disarmed, soldiers kept order, after having torn off their military insignia and obtained red flags.

Rumors soon got afloat that the Kaiser had abdicated, or would soon do so, but they were denied officially. Then it was said semi-officially that he was willing to become "the hereditary president of Germany." On November 7 an ultimatum as to the Kaiser was sent to Prince Maximilian, the Imperial Chancellor, by the managing committee of the Socialist Party, and Philipp Scheidemann, the Socialist member of the Cabinet, without portfolio, was sent to Spa with a demand for the Kaiser's abdication and an immediate change in the Prussian Government in conformity with the views of the majority of the Reichstag. Next day, at the conclusion of a great popular meeting in Munich, a republic was proclaimed in Bavaria, and during a sitting in the Diet Palace a decree was passed deposing the Whittelsbach dynasty. Several thousand persons were present, by invitation from the Socialist party. The future of the whole social and political order in Germany was now in peril. Hamburg, Bremen, Wilhelmshaven, Lübeck and other German ports were in the hands of revolutionists, and a Socialist republic, following the Russian model, was being proclaimed in North Sea and Baltic ports. The High Seas Fleet having been seized by the mutineers, the whole German coast line from Heligoland to Memel was open to an Allied naval attack. On November 9 a definite statement was made by Prince Max that the Kaiser had "decided to renounce the throne"—nothing more precise than that, however. That the Kaiser actually had abdicated did not appear from any official statement made either by or for him.

From all parts of the empire came reports of the astonishingly rapid spread of the revolution. In Munich even the garrison found itself compelled to take orders from the new powers. The movement then spread to Hanover, where all trains bound for the front were stopt and soldiers and officers on board were disarmed. Oldenburg, Schwerin, and the whole province of Mecklenburg were next to go. In the Rhine industrial region the movement "spread like wildfire." From Essen, the home of Krupp, people fled toward Holland, and at the Krupp works thousands of workers were dismissed and others ordered to stop work. In seven, short days the German people had effectively burst the fetters of an autocratic rule which had bound them for generations. Kaiserism, for the time at least, was dead, and there was little doubt that a German republic would be called into existence.

The edifice that was crumbling before our eyes had seemed only a year before on the point of becoming the most stately structure of arbitrary power the world had beheld since Imperial Rome rose to her zenith under the Antonines. Buttressed on one side by command of the Baltic, it was holding on the other, through the subject government of the Ukraine, complete control of the Black Sea and, with a helpless Austria, a still faithful Bulgaria and a Turkey which apparently remained a formidable military organization, all three at its beck and call, it had driven a solid wedge across southern Europe into Asia, whose potentialities were such as no man could foresee. Prussia apparently not only had within her grasp the hegemony of Europe, but was settling firmly into a position from which its royal house might dominate the world.

George Renwick [7] learned "on good authority" in Amsterdam that the Kaiser had "made a determined effort to stave off abdication," that he had gone to headquarters "with a deliberate intention of bringing the army around to his side, and in this had failed miserably." His main support consisted of a number of officers, nearly all of Prussian regiments, who with two regiments had placed themselves at his disposal, but to do anything with such small support "was seen to be Gilbertian." During the night of November 8 he called the Crown Prince, Marshal von Hindenburg and General Gröner for a consultation at Spa, that lasted a couple of hours, and during which both officers strongly urged him to bow to the inevitable. Hindenburg said that "any more delay in coming to a decision to

[7] Correspondent of The *Times* (New York).

abdicate would certainly have the most terrible consequences and lead to serious events in the army,'' and declared that he refused to be responsible for the outcome. Gröner supported him, but when the conference broke up the Kaiser "remained unconvinced of the advisability of abdication.'' An hour or so later he came to a definite decision, however, after several communications had reached him from Berlin and after another short and stormy talk with Hindenburg. Meanwhile his son-in-law, the Duke of Bruns-

© INTERNATIONAL FILM SERVICE, N. Y.

GERMAN SOLDIERS ON THEIR WAY HOME

wick, for himself and his heir, had abdicated, this "Brunswick's Fated Chieftain'' having been forced to do so without fighting. A republican movement in Brunswick had been noticed even before one got in motion at Kiel.

The greater part of Berlin by November 10, the day before the armistice was signed, was in control of revolutionists, and Friedrich Ebert, a Socialist, was in command as Chancellor. Revolt was spreading with rapidity. A Workmen's and Soldiers' Council was administering municipal government, the red flag floating over the royal palace and Brandenburg Gate and the former Crown Prince's palace was in possession of revolutionists. Outside the palace was seen an old woman who had been employed inside the building all her working life now complaining that, "since the Kaiser has gone, that cursed Liebknecht has slept two nights in his bed." Her intense indignation at this unwelcome event "made listeners laugh." Prince Max, in announcing the abdication of the Kaiser, or at least his "decision" to abdicate, had said a bill "should be brought in for the establishment of a law providing for the immediate promulgation of general suffrage and for a constituent National Assembly, which would settle finally the future form of government of the German nation and of peoples who might be desirous of coming within the empire."

On November 10, King Friederich August of Saxony was dethroned, as well as the Grand Duke of Oldenburg, and the Grand Duke of Mecklenburg-Schwerin abdicated. By this time the revolution seemed to all intents and purposes an accomplished fact. Fourteen of the twenty-six States, including all the four kingdoms and all other important States, were in the hands of revolutionists and the twelve small States not yet affected could not hope to stay their progress. Hindenburg had placed himself and the army at the disposal of the new government and said he had taken this action "in order to avoid chaos." On November 13 the abdications of Leopold IV, Prince of Lippe, and Duke Edward of Anhalt were reported, the latter resigning the throne in favor of his son Joachim Ernest. Then Prince Friedrich of Waldeck-Prymount voluntarily relinquished his government; Grand Duke William Ernest of Saxe-Weimar abdicated "in order to prevent civil war"; republics were proclaimed in Württemberg and Hesse; a new government was constituted in Baden under the presidency of a Socialist; Prince Leopold of Lippe-Detmold renounced his throne; and in Hesse revolutionaries declared the Grand Ducal lands confiscated and all hereditary entails abolished.

Amid the crash of the Hohenzollern and Hapsburg thrones, little noise was made by the collapse of petty kingly, ducal, and princely houses. Besides the two kaisers, three kings had gone to the scrap-pile, seven or eight princes,

FREDERICK III, KING OF SAXONY

LUDWIG III, KING OF BAVARIA   WILLIAM, KING OF WÜRTTEMBERG

ERNST, DUKE OF BRUNSWICK

THE GRAND DUKE OF HESSE   THE GRAND DUKE FREDERICK OF OLDENBURG

FREDERICK, THE GRAND DUKE OF MECKLENBURG-SCHWERIN

DETHRONED GERMAN KINGS AND GRAND DUKES

271

and too many dukes and grand dukes to be counted easily. History would probably devote a paragraph to each exit by rulers of Bavaria, Saxony, Württemberg, Baden, and Brunswick, but scarce a line to the Ernsts and Adolfs, Friedrichs and Augusts, who had held sway over the Anhalts and Waldecks, Lippes and Reusses; or to lesser ones of hightitled nobility. So passed into oblivion one of Europe's most interesting vestiges of medievalism, a system of microscopic sovereignties, humorous or historically picturesque, or anachronistically repellent. About these principalities hung an aroma of distance in time and space that had made revolutionary Socialism seem impossible.

History had long refused to look on these sovereigns, posing so grandiosely, as persons heroic or even romantic. They had first defined their character after the Thirty Years' War, when most of them became local despots. Their morals were notorious; every little tyrant had his intriguing court and his mistresses *a la* Augustus of Saxony and George of Hanover. Liebnitz declared that "they thought it beneath their dignity to improve their minds." Some few did play a noble part in the history of German thought and art; such, for example, as the Weimar dukes, who made for Goethe a pleasant and familiar society. There were also some great houses which had founded universities, patronized theaters and orchestras, and rewarded musicians and poets, but in any time of revolution they had appeared at their worst. When Napoleon or Bismarck clanked a sword, their eagerness to get into line was pitiful. But when, in November, 1918, Democracy toppled over the King of Prussia, they all had to fall down together like a line of wooden dominoes. Following is a list of the emperors, kings and princes who had lost their thrones in the course of this war:

The Khedive of Egypt, Egypt, November 16, 1914.
Czar Nicholas, Russia, March 17, 1917.
King Constantine, Greece, August 28, 1917.
King Ferdinand, Bulgaria, August 12, 1918.
King Boris, Bulgaria, November 3, 1918.
Kaiser Wilhelm II, Germany, November 9, 1918.
Kaiser Karl, Austria-Hungary, November 14, 1918.

THE PRESIDENT OF THE GERMAN REPUBLIC AND HIS CABINET

Left to right—Dr. Otto Landsberg, Minister of Justice; Philipp Scheidemann, Premier; Gustav Noske, Minister of Defense; Frederick Ebert, President, and Herr Wissel, Minister of Commerce

Duke Ernst, Brunswick, November 11, 1918.
King Nicholas of Montenegro.

The following rulers were reported to have abdicated in the week of November 11, 1918:

King Ludwig III, Bavaria.
King Wilhelm II, Württemberg.
King Friedrich August, Saxony.
Grand Duke Friedrich II, Baden.
Grand Duke Friedrich Franz, Mecklenburg-Schwerin.
Grand Duke Friedrich August, Oldenburg.
Grand Duke Wilhelm Ernst, Weimar.
Grand Duke Adolf Friedrich VI, Mecklenburg-Strelitz.
Duke Charles Edward, Saxe-Coburg-Gotha.
Duke Edward, Annhalt.
Duke Ernst II, Saxe-Oldenburg.
Duke Bernard, Saxe-Meiningen.
Prince Leopold IV, Lippe.
Prince Heinrich XXVII, Reuss.
Prince Friedrich, Waldeck.
Prince Adolf, Schaumberg-Lippe.
Prince Guenther, Schwartzburg-Rudolstadt.

There was no intention of confiscating private property belonging to these princes, but most of them had been lavish in bestowing upon favorite firms and tradespeople the title of "purveyors to the crown," which warranted purveyors in carrying escutcheons emblazoned on their signs. Within a week of the revolution there were not many houses on which workmen had not been busy taking down emblems that were once the pride of all ambitious Germans. Hotels, places of amusement, and similar establishments, even those named after Hohenzollerns or other royalists, had hastened to remove these signs. The famous Kaiser Kaffee on the Friedrichstrasse in Berlin became merely a "Kaffee." From the tile hall in a restaurant, built of fancy tiles from the Kaiser's private works in Kalinen, William's costly bronze bust was removed. The public, however, took little interest in the disappearance of these outward signs of a glory that had so suddenly departed.

The payment of large annuities to members of the Hohen-zollern family was suspended by the government. Mecklenburg abolished all payments to members of its Grand Ducal house, among which were nearly 200,000 marks annually to the former Crown Princess's mother, Anastasie, who was greatly rich otherwise, and used to spend most of her income in France and at Monte Carlo. Duke George of Mecklenburg, who before the war had lived on a ranch in Arizona (or Texas), and whose adventurous flight from America as a stoker on an ocean liner once caused a sensation, was also

FORMER KING LUDWIG OF BAVARIA'S NEW HOME
IN SWITZERLAND

cut off. Little Mecklenburg saved 700,000 marks annually by stopping these payments.

While the new German Government was being formed, power passed into the hands of a Socialist triumvirate—Ebert, Scheidemann, and Landsberg. Unity had been achieved between the Majority and the Independent Socialist parties, under which the Government was to consist of members of both. Liebknecht appeared to have championed the extreme Socialist, or the almost Bolshevist, cause, but was losing support. In a forthcoming election all persons of both sexes who had reached the age of 20 years were to vote in an election that would decide the future form of government for Germany. There seemed little doubt that Germany would have a republican form of government, tho it was in doubt whether there would be one or many republics in the fatherland. Negotiations were being held with Bavaria and other States, with a view to common action, but many in Bavaria desired separation. Pan-German papers in Berlin, like the *Kreuz Zeitung,* which a short week before had been breathing fire against the Socialists, were now appealing to the public in lamb-like tones to support the powers that were. Skeptical observers at the same time inclined to think that Germany was still "playing possum."

© G. G. BAIN.

KARL LIEBKNECHT

The Independent Socialists carried all before them in Berlin, forcing moderates to permit all power to be centered in the Workmen's and Soldiers' Council. A compromise cabinet was decided upon, which meant a Soviet Government, with the Independents growing in power and the bourgeois excluded from the government. The entire German northern fleet and the island base of Heligoland were now in the hands of the Soldiers' Councils, while a Soldiers' Council had been formed at the front and would submit its demands to Hindenburg who remained at Main Headquarters and adhered to the new Government. When Field-Marshal von Mackensen and his advance guard of 2,000 men arrived at Grosswardein in Hungary, on their way home from Roumania, and first learned of the revolutionary events in Germany, Mackensen's soldiers greeted the announcement of the Kaiser's abdication with prolonged cheers.

The movement continually spread, with Königsberg, Frankfort-on-the-Main, and Strassburg in control of the Soviets, but with as yet no further disorder. Imperialism was for the time no more, even in a mild form. There had been no renewal of bloodshed. Fewer than 1,000 in all had been killed. All news agencies, telegraph and telephone wires were under control of the revolutionists.

"But yesterday the word of Cæsar might have stood against the world," and now Cæsar was begging bread, and, what was worse, begging it from those who had conquered him, begging from the United States who less than two years before had been told by Germany that she could send only one ship each week to one English port, along a route which Germany herself prescribed. Fourteen armies were about to move upon the Rhine, there to wait until Germany carried out the peace terms that the Entente would impose upon her. A new "watch on the Rhine" was to be maintained by the "degenerate" French, the "contemptible" British and the "dollar-chasing Yankees." Only a week before Germany had been destroying French cities, even up to the day of the armistice; and now she had discovered that she was simply adding to her bill of expenses with every house her soldiers smashed. German prisoners were to re-build those houses, and Germany was to pay for the work. Most remarkable of all, the Germans were begging the Allies to protect German troops while they evacuated Alsace-Lorraine—that is, to protect them from the civil population which they had been assuring the world for forty odd years was loyally German. Thus had Zabern been tremendously avenged. No more would young officers strike down harmless cobblers for failing to show them respect— no more in any town of Lorraine or Alsace. In Rhenish Westphalia uniforms were being torn from soldiers, fights occurring between royal and Socialist soldiers and Socialists were disarming frontier guards. A ban was put on "Die Wacht am Rhein," and on "Deutschland Über Alles." War work in Essen stopt.

By November 18 tranquillity was reported to have been

established. In Berlin and throughout the provinces determined efforts were being made to consolidate the many authorities which had been set up. The Ebert government appeared to be firmly in the saddle, the extreme Socialist element under control. The army, so far as could be seen, was against Bolshevism. Work was being resumed; cafés and restaurants were open. Prussia passed under a purely Socialistic Government, the Federal Council having ceased to exist. Both Prussian houses had been abolished and the Reichstag was no more. Even the stern, pompous official was gone, suavity ruling instead of sternness. Alongside aristocratic officials worked sailors from Kiel. Most officials, even ministers of State, had dropt uniforms and donned civilian clothing. In place of a stern military censor at the post-office, one met the gentle-mannered wife of a well-known Socialist. Herr Ebert and Herr Haase shared the Chancellor's palace. Ordinary soldiers came and went where once were arbitrary counts and sword-bearing barons.[8] *Vorwärts* of Berlin declared that the report was true that the German fleet had been ordered out on October 28 for a final battle, to be fought until the last ship was sunk. Pan-Germans had believed that such a battle would reanimate the German people with the spirit of 1914. When reports that a sacrificial battle was intended got abroad, it spread like wildfire, and the mutiny followed. This, said the *Vorwärts*, confirming Harden, "was the real spark that kindled the revolution."

People and parliament in Luxemburg were expected soon to demand the abdication of the Grand Duchess, who was considered a symbol of German intrigue. Members of the liberal party desired the grand duchy transformed into a republic attached to France or Belgium. The Grand Duchess, on learning of this as the general opinion of her people, replied that she was ready to abdicate after a general vote had been taken on the question, but not before. Most of the inhabitants at the beginning of the war were either sympathizers with France and Belgium or were neutrals. Dissatisfaction with the German occupation had

---

[8] Cable dispatch from George Renwick to The *Times* (New York).

grown as the years passed, because the Germans behaved much as they had always behaved in occupied territory. The Luxemburgers had interpreted the Grand Duchess' lenient behavior, after her first protest against the German entry in 1914, as having been dictated too much by memories of the time when her dominion was part of the German Confederation. The last straw had come in 1918 when she gave her consent, whether voluntary or enforced, to the betrothal of one of her sisters to Crown Prince Rupprecht of Bavaria. This feeling was abetted by activities on the part of an element that vigorously sympathized with France and Belgium, and, fed by evidences of a collapse in the government, promised to result in a violent upheaval when the Germans left and the Americans came in. General Pershing had prevented this for a time while his army of occupation was responsible for order, but by January 11 the revolution was consummated. The Grand Duchess left the country and her government formally announced that she would renounce her throne if the people so desired.

After the Grand Duchess abdicated, the population, numbering about 200,000 was described as gravely divided as to whether one of her sisters should succeed to the throne or a republic be established. Within a few days one of the sisters was accorded the succession. Apart from dislike of the Germans, the causes of the change were economic. Before the war, Luxemburg, an independent state, had been included in the German Customs Union. As the chief industries were iron and iron ore the natural economic connection was .with the power which held the iron and coal of Lorraine and the Saar Valley. Iron-workers and the commercial classes as an outcome of the war became strongly favorable, therefore, to a new orientation in economic policy, the great majority being in favor of some form of customs union with France. There was no question of any closer connection. All Luxemburg stood together for independence. The events of four years had only strengthened the desire of the little State for complete freedom. Whatever might be the flag, republican or ducal, autonomy was its blazon. What the movement meant was recognition that the economic reconstruction of western Europe was at hand.

The people of Luxemburg had read the signs of the times and meant to be prepared.

The hurly-burly of events in Germany had been astounding. Events of tremendous import followed each other with a rushing impetus. With Imperial Germany prostrate, the Kaiser in flight and the whole Hohenzollern dynasty apparently cast into the limbo of defunct royalty, a Socialist, formerly a saddler, was holding the reins of power at Berlin and preparing to lay the foundations for a Democratic Republic—surely there had been material enough crowded into one

AT AN UNDERGROUND STATION IN BERLIN
Government troops are using flame-throwers to protect the station

brief week to keep historians busy. Some of the chief points in these developments stood out clear. The Hohenzollern idol had been demolished by the battering-ram of Socialism. The ground on which the idol had stood had months before been undermined by President Wilson's declaration that no peace treaty, signed by a Hohenzollern, would be accepted by the powers warring against Germany. That had been "a monkey-wrench thrown into the autocratic machine." Then came the blows of Foch shattering the vast military machine that supported the idol, followed by the request for an armistice.

It had been the fashion during the war to speak of German Socialists as having sold themselves to the Kaiser, but close ooservers of Socialist leaders, or of their speeches in the Reichstag, had not entirely subscribed to that judgment. Socialists had tried to prevent the war, but had failed. Once the war began they decided to support it, as a war of defense, but their party leaders rejected all annexations as proposed by the worshipers of military power, criticized military aggressions, and at the same time pushed their demands for a Democratic suffrage in Prussia. The Brest-Litovsk treaty was never agreed to by them. They never ceased to denounce it as contrary to the spirit of the Reichstag resolution of July, 1917, and as a serious obstacle to peace, as well as an injury to Germany. President Wilson, in the meantime, continued to influence the German people with his notes. After his fourteen conditions were announced, on January 8, 1918, Socialists began to pay serious attention to his utterances. They saw in them a hopeful opening for peace and inwardly approved of his wish to oust Wilhelm II. Their whole attitude toward the Kaiser, up to the time when the war broke out, had been one of more than cold indifference; he had treated them as his enemies, and they had reciprocated his aversion in full measure. During the war there had been little or no criticism of him from them, but their latent opposition remained. They were only waiting for their opportunity—so they and their apologists declared.

Under the hammer strokes of Foch in July, August and September, the temper of the people had changed rapidly. They saw all their hopes of victory dashed to the ground. While their lines were crumbling in France and Belgium, the food situation at home was becoming more distressing than ever, and the Junkers were doing the suffrage bill to death. When the Main Committee of the Reichstag met on September 24—a meeting looked forward to on all sides as certain to mark the beginning of a new era—it was obvious to everybody except Chancellor von Hertling that a radical transformation of the government was at hand. By the end of that momentous week, Hertling saw he was at the end of his resources and so resigned and induced the Kaiser to issue his decree of September 30 stipulating for the establishment of parliamentary government.

In agreement with the majority parties of the Reichstag, Prince Max had been made Chancellor on a platform adopted by Socialists, Catholics, and Progressives. Socialists for the first time accepted important Cabinet positions, and nearly all the new ministers were selected from the Reichstag. Not a month elapsed before it became obvious that this coalition was inadequate to deal with the new situation. Germany's plea for peace, made when Prince Max took office, together with the rapidly progressing breakdown of Germany's military power, fostered the development of the most radical views. This had showed itself first at Kiel on November 3 with the mutiny in the navy. Socialist leaders then grasped the chance to set their battering-ram in full operation. As the Kaiser had more clearly than ever become a grave obstacle to peace, Socialist managers sent to Prince Max an ultimatum demanding his abdication. On Thursday, November 7, he refused on the ground that "he could not at that moment of peace undertake the terrible responsibility of handing over Germany to the Entente and delivering up the country to anarchy." William had not yet learned that a Germany purged of the Hohenzollerns would fare better with the Entente than if he remained in power, and that he in particular was no adequate protection against anarchy. He was predestined by his character to misread the situation.

The revolutionary movement made great progress everywhere. The vocabulary of revolutionary Russia came into vogue, and Workmen's and Soldiers' Councils quickly got possession of leading cities. Not only the navy but the army deserted the sinking ship of militarism and kaiserism until William had to yield and on the 9th the world was officially told that he had "decided to abdicate." At the same time Prince Max turned over the government to Friedrich Ebert, chairman of the Socialist caucus of the Reichstag. Other crowned heads of Germany bowed to the inevitable. The King of Bavaria anticipated William by a day, being deposed on the 8th by the Diet, which proclaimed a Republic.

After William quit other dynasties followed rapidly, some voluntarily, others under compulsion, and by November 13, when the King of Württemberg and the grand dukes of Hesse and Saxe-Weimar renounced their thrones, the last royal and princely house had been overturned. At the same time Karl, Emperor of Austria, found that, altho filled with unalterable love for his people, he was not willing to be a hindrance to their free development, and left his country for his country's good. German Austria was waiting to be admitted as a State into the new German republic which the Socialists were about to set up. Thus ended what would probably be regarded as the most momentous week in modern history. Crowded within its brief space came the termination of the greatest war of all time, the overthrow of dynasties that had had their birth in the Middle Ages, and the inauguration of a new order in two of the greatest States of Europe.[9]

In Berlin, after a week of revolution, a casual visitor would not have been aware that the city had been the storm center of a gigantic political upheaval. The public were anything but excited, their war-weary nerves apparently no longer capable of responding to thrills, no matter how inspiring. No casual visitor could have formed the faintest idea of the series of tremendous earthquakes that had shaken Germany to her foundation and caused all her petrified princely idols to tumble from lofty heights into shattered ruins, perhaps never to rise again. A week before Berliners had gone to bed under an absolute monarchy. When they awoke next morning they found themselves in a radical republic, the revolution an accepted fact, and everybody, to outward appearances, going about his business. Intelligent people were thankfully recognizing that none but the Social Democratic Party could have saved the situation from the utter chaos to which the Kaiser's criminally selfish attitude had seemed to have led the German people. So far the Socialist Government had made good. It had been fair in its attitude toward employees of the former *régime*, leaving as many as possible in their old positions. Despite tremendous difficulties things were going smoothly.

[9] William C. Dreher in The *Tribune* (New York).

With some apprehension, however, the press and the Government was watching the swelling tide of uniformed humanity that was beginning to flow back from the western frontier. It had already inundated Westphalia and would soon reach Berlin. Everything imaginable was being done to prevent another catastrophe and to lead the great flood into proper channels, but the question was, would the impoverished and exhausted people be able to accomplish it. Supplies were being brought together wherever found. To

FIRING ON A CROWD IN BERLIN FROM A ROOF-TOP

civilians all distant travel was barred; every locomotive, every car was reserved for the home-coming soldiers. The former Crown Prince's palace and the Bundesrath, or *House of Nobles*, in which the fate of the whole population used to be decided, had been prepared for the reception of those that could not find room in already overcrowded barracks and whom the war had deprived of their homes. Around Cologne, Berlin, and other great cities cordons of soldiers were being formed to divert the flood into harmless channels. Watchmen no longer carried sabers in Berlin, but went about unarmed waiting to be furnished with rubber clubs. There had been astonishingly few cases of robbery. Among autos employed in patroling the city were some that formerly belonged to the Kaiser. Their horns, sounding imperial notes familiar to all Berliners, created no little astonishment and mirth when heard doing a different duty.

People showed little curiosity as to the fate of their former rulers. The Kaiser's wife, who had obtained permission to join her husband in exile, was still in the Neue Palast at Potsdam, waiting until the railway congestion caused by the demobilization should permit her departure. The former Crown Princess and her children, and the wives of other Hohenzollerns, Prince August Wilhelm and Prince Eitel Friedrich, the latter a despoiler of a French château, were with their mother in Potsdam, under custody of the Potsdam Council of Soldiers and Workers. Former Grand Admiral von Tirpitz, promoter of the *U*-boat atrocities, had managed to escape to Switzerland shortly before the revolution broke out. His appearance had been greatly altered, the long flowing whiskers that had distinguished him so significantly having been closely cropped. Tirpitz had collected enormous funds, especially from Rhenish industrial circles, for promoting Pan-German aims and from other sources had drawn millions to be used in corrupting newspapers. Perhaps 90 per cent. of the people were now demanding that he be court-martialed for the part he had played in the *U*-boat war.

People in Berlin had been quite taken by surprize by the tremendous upheaval which was practically over before they knew where they were. When its seriousness and magnitude were realized high hopes were roused, but afterward a great deal of indifference set in. The popular mind had become thoroughly confused by political maneuvering and endless appeals until most people were content sullenly to await events. Former popular heroes were forgotten, all save one. With little talk about the former Kaiser and Crown Prince, with Ludendorff's name seldom heard, and other military figures now become men of the past—if Berlin had any hero left, it was Hindenburg. Where por-

A SPARTACAN BARRICADE IN BERLIN

Spartacans fired from this barricade on Government troops
sent to disperse them

SPARTACANS MOUNTING A MORTAR IN BERLIN

Shells are seen in the foreground. One of the men has a shell ready for
insertion in the mortar

traits of the Kaiser hung on walls, one now saw the grim old Field-marshal who retained a strong place in people's affections. He alone among the chief leaders had not run away. He was still with the army.

Within a month Central Europe was in a condition of chaos in which it was difficult to discern clear outlines. Former Austro-Hungarian subjects were in hopeless bewilderment; they did not know to what State they belonged, to which new legislature they should apply, or who would visé their passports. When they wrote to friends at home, they were not certain of the name of the country to which the letters should be addrest. States were seething with rival claims. National conflicts and social disorders had taken the place of war. The chief impression one received in Berne was one of depression and exhaustion in Teutonic Europe with complete absence of the ordinary essentials of civilized life. The Czechs were the only people who made no particular complaints, but, altho well organized and economically strong, they were in continual conflict with their Austro-German and Magyar neighbors. Czechs were occupying Slovak territory in Hungary. There was great danger that trains and trams would cease running; that factories would be idle and gas, electricity, and water supplies be cut off.

From the beginning the new order of affairs in Germany became subject to violent controversies and feuds. Ebert, Haase, and their comrades in the first Cabinet of six, styling themselves the People's Commissioners, and having proclaimed a republic, assumed to exercise supreme authority. But the executive committee of the Soldiers' and Workmen's Council, organizing a Soviet Government after the Russian Bolshevik plan, insisted that the six were merely its agents and were subject to its authority. In addition, Karl Liebknecht, Rosa Luxemburg, and other extreme Socialists organized a "Spartacus" party, so named from the gladiator who led a famous servile revolt in ancient Rome, which for a time seemed likely to overawe the capital and gain supreme power through mob violence. On November 25 an agreement was reached between Ebert's government and the Soldiers' and Workmen's Council, under which the supreme power of the German

Socialist Republic was to be vested in the latter and to be exercised through its Executive Committee. A national conference of deputies from the Soldiers' and Workmen's Councils of all the states was summoned at Berlin on December 16, and it was tentatively agreed to have on February 16, 1919, a general election for delegates to a Constituent Assembly which should determine the permanent future government of Germany. For the purposes of that election the empire was to be divided into thirty-eight districts, with from six to sixteen deputies each, according to population.

Meantime symptoms of disintegration appeared. Kurt Eisner, who had been the Bavarian Prime Minister and practically the head of the Government of that State since the deposition of the dynasty, gave notice of a complete breach of relations with Prussia and the Berlin Government, "owing to the efforts of Berlin to deceive the people by withholding the truth about conditions." In this he seemed to be almost unanimously supported by Bavarians of all parties. The Liberal Party of Baden likewise issued a proclamation demanding a complete separation from Prussia and from the Berlin Government.[9a]

On February 11 a German National Assembly having been elected, Ebert was chosen President of the German state by a vote of 277 out of 379. Spartacan agitation was then still growing in Berlin, especially in the barracks of troops. Ebert, in a speech accepting the Presidency, denounced the Allied armistice terms and declared that "we shall combat domination by force to the utmost from whatever direction it may come." Demobilization of Germany's old army had been completed. About 100,000 men, however, were to be kept on the Eastern Front. At length a press campaign was started against the armistice and the expected peace conditions of the Entente. Murders, fighting, and plundering meanwhile continued in various parts of Berlin. Many Spartacans were made prisoners and summarily executed. Germany's war costs were given out as more than $46,500,000,000, in an announcement by the Minister of Finance. The conditions as laid down in the Treaty of Peace were denounced by the German press and by many public men. "No German can sign such terms,"

[9a] "The American Year Book for 1918" (D. Appleton & Co.).

Vorwärts declared. "No more shameless mockery of President Wilson's fourteen points can be imagined," said the *Lokal Anzeiger*. Complete anarchy reigned in Munich; all work had ceased, trains were not running, and robbers were looting houses and threatening banks.

Politicians in Cologne early in December took a step forward toward separation from Prussia at a mass meeting which, with great enthusiasm, unanimously adopted a resolution, to "undertake the construction of a new German State composed of the Rhineland and Westphalia." Recognized leaders were asked as soon as possible to arrange a proclamation of "an independent Rhenish Westphalian Republic as a part of Germany." About 5,000 men and women were present at this meeting, most of them belonging to the old Centrist Party. The Republic set up in Brunswick was one of the most novel in Germany; its President, a former mender of old clothes, and its Vice-president a juggler, who, until two weeks before the revolution, had performed at a café, while a woman who could hardly read or write was minister of education. The Duke, Ernest Gunther of Schleswig-Holstein, brother of the Kaiserin, had discovered that feudalism was bad and that he was really an honest democrat. At a mass meeting he said he was ready with his person and his wealth to serve the new Government. Most of the Hohenzollern princes had accepted the new situation, altho reluctantly, and other German princes having become quite resigned, were trying to make themselves useful to the Republic. The most conspicuous among them was the Prince of Reuss, of the younger line, who was in Gera acting as a theatrical manager of the former Court Theater which was widely known for its architectural features.

"I remained at the head of the army," said Hindenburg late in December, "because I considered it my duty to remain in order to save my country from chaos. After the army gets home and is demobilized my duty will be done. I am getting to be an old man, and I am ready to retire." As for Mackensen, he was interned in December in Castle Foth, near Budapest, as the "guest" of Count Ladislau Karolyi. He asked bitterly whether the German military

THE PALACE IN BERLIN AFTER THE BOMBARDMENT

authorities knew of "the shameful treatment" meted out to him. "They do," was Count Karolyi's reply. "Then I am really abandoned," said Mackensen, as tears came into his eyes. The scene was described as "extremely painful." Mackensen and his staff had arrived at the Budapest station only to find it guarded by 200 soldiers under a Hungarian revolutionary officer, Major Geroe.

Late in December thousands of demobilized soliders were crowding the central thoroughfares of Berlin wandering about dejectedly, or trying to earn a living by selling cigarets, newspapers, postcards, or crude Christmas toys. Berlin heard the shouting and singing of poverty-stricken street venders and saw beggars in rags, most of whom a few weeks before were soldiers in the Kaiser's Army. Restrictions on drinking and dancing having been removed, another class of the population took advantage of their liberty and tried to show that Berlin was light-hearted. One newspaper had advertisements announcing the re-opening of no fewer than twenty-eight establishments, described as cabarets, bars, or wine-saloons, all in the center of the city. Thirty other advertisements were of dancing-places, where five o'clock tango-teas were served. The frivolous section of Berlin danced and enjoyed itself as if a grim and tragic doom were not hanging over the country; as if no enemy were on the frontiers; as if there were no famine to be feared; as if celebrating a victory. Hundreds of dancing-places were overcrowded daily. Dancing, eating, and drinking went on unchecked till 4 and 5 o'clock in the morning, money being spent in an incredible way by people who had earned fabulous wages under the revolution. Many who once had twenty marks a week now had forty marks a day. [10]

Then came what was sometimes called the Second Revolution, during which the world thought Germany might look for what had occurred in Russia after the Bolsheviki overthrew Kerensky. In a riotous demonstration sailors on December 24 undertook to take the Castle stables, attacking from the west side of the Castle; with machine-guns and rifles when field-guns were brought into position and fire opened. Shots struck where the White Hall was situated, but did not do

[10] Amsterdam dispatch from George Renwick to The *Times* (New York).

much damage. Other guns, directed against heavy doors on the east side, shattered them to pieces, and the balcony from which the Kaiser made his famous "I no longer know any parties" speech in August, 1914, was destroyed. Government troops entered the palace, finding the north and east sides in the hands of sailors who had persuaded several formations of infantry to desert the Government. For nearly two hours the sailors held the whole of the Bruder-

© PRESS ILLUSTRATING SERVICE.

FUNERAL IN BERLIN OF DR. LIEBKNECHT AND
ROSA LUXEMBURG

strasse and parts of the Breitestrasse, in both of which they occupied buildings as points of vantage, and placed machine-guns in convenient doorways and show windows. A great deal of firing occurred on the north and east sides. Government troops attacked the royal stables and a cannonade ensued, lasting about a quarter of an hour. After a white flag had been flown from the window of the stables, and another from the balcony of the castle, fire subsided and negotiations for capitulation took place, but without result.

About this time the Guard Cuirassiers, marching through Franzoesische-strasse, reached the scene of disorder with field-guns. In a desperate attempt to drive off Government troops sailors placed machine-guns on the roofs of the stables, but shots fired by Government troops put the guns out of action, casualties on the roof numbering sixty-four. In addition to damage to other buildings, the cathedral was badly scarred. One of the marble columns forming the background of the monument of William I. was completely shot away. The interior of the palace was damaged heavily, royal apartments having been transformed into a revolutionary habitation. Signs of confusion and neglect were everywhere. In the private dining-room of the former emperor were the bodies of five sailors who were killed in the fighting. That more persons were not killed was considered extraordinary in view of the extent of the promiscuous shooting that occurred on both sides. Kurt Eisner, the Bavarian premier, described these proceedings as "pure comedy."

Two months after the armistice was signed [11] Berlin and some other parts of Germany were in such a state of unrest that the power of the new Government to keep its hold seemed in peril, and a state of civil war was proclaimed. Sanguinary encounters had occurred in many localities. Terrible confusion existed, parties clashing at almost every street corner. After the third day of what seemed a new revolution the city reached a state of utter disorganization and lawlessness with what might have been called fortresses at various points where guns thundered and sputtered forth missiles night and day. Some of these points were held by the Government and some by the extremists who called themselves Spartacans; others changed hands twice or oftener within twenty-four hours. The worst shooting occurred in Unter den Linden, where a furious fusillade opened on people "who ran for their lives in all directions, or dropt to the pavement, hoping to escape." With the

[11] Cable dispatch from Berlin to The *Times* (New York). Zurich dispatch to *L'Information* of Paris.

fusillade mingled the boom of large guns. At the Brandenburg Gate large guns were put in position by Government troops. The Spartacans made attempts to seize the Chancellor's palace, but were driven back with the loss of thirty killed and forty-five wounded. Chaos prevailed and the city was reduced to a state of siege.

By January 10 Chancellor Ebert was believed to have become master of the situation. Hindenburg was in Potsdam, having arrived two days before. When the Government decided to use arms in suppressing the insurgents, the situation had changed at once. Cavalry and Prussian Guards were massed at all gates; Government forces recaptured public buildings; martial law was proclaimed and reinforcements poured into Berlin. As part of the Government defense, fifteen men were stationed on top of the Brandenburg Gate with machine-guns, silhouetted against the sky. Now and then desperate Spartacans would get on the roof of a building overlooking the Wilhelmplatz and start firing at soldiers below. At first the Government was not rigorous enough. Instead of taking insurgents prisoners, an officer on duty would simply disarm them, and sometimes would permit them to walk away. But on January 13 several leaders were taken prisoners with 1,000 of their followers; military material was captured, including 100 machine-guns, 1,200 rifles and 1,000 bombs. After that the Government got control of the situation, recaptured the Spandau arsenal, and cleared Spartacans out of the Tiergarten.

When the *Vorwärts* building, after being shattered by Government artillery, was stormed and captured by Government troops, 125 dead were found in the building. About 300 Spartacans were killed and 700 wounded in the last fighting. The total of their dead reached 1,300. Sooner than the most optimistic expected, their power was broken, but more than 1,000 harmless pedestrians had been killed or wounded within a week. Unter den Linden, Brandenburg Gate, and the Royal Castle one night had all resounded with reports of hand-grenades, answered by Government's machine-guns and larger field-pieces stationed at the gate. Only at the peril of being wounded could one cross Unter den Linden. In Jerusalemersstrasse, Markgrafenstrasse, and Charlottenstrasse hardly a building escaped damage from Leipzigerstrasse to Bellealliance Platz. About every third shop-window in the center of Berlin was pierced by bullets, which must have been fired by Spartacans from housetops and dark corners. [12] By January 13, the backbone of the insurrection had been broken. The Spartacans had evidently lost heart. Fortresses held by them were surrendered unconditionally. The most they could now do was to loot stores and rob delivery-wagons.

On January 17, Dr. Karl Liebknecht, leader of the Spartacans, and Fräulein Rosa Luxemburg, his chief colleague, who had been taken prisoners two days before, as the result of a general order issued to the Government troops that they be arrested, were killed. Liebknecht met death while trying to escape from his captors by a dash through the Tiergarten, Fräulein Luxemburg was killed by a crowd which dragged her from a motor-car and pounded her to death. No trace of the body was found afterward. The fate of these two had "something of divine justice in it," said the *Tageszeitung*. The *Lokal-Anzeiger* remarked that Liebknecht had "brought his fate upon himself," while "the murder of Rosa Luxemburg showed how tremendous must have been the indignation which seized the people of Berlin as the result of criminal activities." The press in general declared that she had fallen a victim to the basest passions which she herself had awakened. But the Pan-German *Deutsche Zeitung* and the radical *Tageblatt* agreed that Liebknecht was an "honest fanatic."

Reports of an election for the National Assembly in January showed that the Majority Socialists had a plurality, with a total of 161 votes. The next highest number was returned by the Christian People's Party, (the former Centeristes, which had 88. The Majority Socialists and Democrats, supported by an overwhelming majority of the people, were now in position to dominate the German National Assembly. The elections assured a democratic republic, freed of monarchial or Bolshevist influences. Extremists on both wings had been heavily defeated. Pan-Germans had

[12] Berlin dispatch to The *Times* (New York).

been overwhelmed by the Democrats and the Spartacans had failed to reach any of their objectives. In February the Assembly, meeting at Weimar, elected Ebert Provisional President.

Kurt Eisner, the Bavarian Premier, was assassinated in Munich in the last week of February. There were two

A ROOM IN THE BERLIN PALACE WITH A MACHINE-GUN
IN THE WINDOW

distinct upheavals in the Bavarian capital succeeding each other within twenty-four hours. One was a counter-revolutionary conspiracy leading to the assassination of Eisner and the other a Spartacan uprising ostensibly provoked to avenge his death and resulting in the shooting of Minister Auer and Clerical Deputy Oesel of the Bavarian Diet. A plot of the Monarchists and the military-party to do away with

Eisner had been planned some time before. Eisner's attitude at the Berne Socialist Congress, where he fearlessly exposed the war-guilt of the Central Powers had sealed his doom. Eisner solemnly declared that he had documentary evidence in his possession proving that the German General Staff continued, even then, to entertain secret relations with Lenine and Trotsky and the Russian Soviet Republic. Fear of the terrible revelations this solitary German statesman might make had armed the assassin's hand against him.

During the night preceding his assassination, a social gathering of officers belonging to the Bavarian Life Guard Regiment took place in the club rooms of the famous corps. In reality it was a meeting held in order to designate the officer who should shoot Eisner. A dice-box was produced and officers tossed dice to determine which of them should undertake to rid Germany of her accuser. The lot fell to Count Arco Valley, a distant relative of the Wittelsbach family, the late rulers of Bavaria. After the murder there was found upon the Count, who was shot by Eisner's followers but was not yet dead altho lying seriously wounded in a Munich hospital, a proclamation entitled "Down with Kurt Eisner! Long live the Wittelsbach!" A Munich butcher named Peters shot down Auer, Timm, and another.

Political developments in Germany were long confused, and there were frequent outbreaks in large cities, with bloodshed, especially in Berlin, but one thing seemed certain among all others, the Hohenzollern at least had been cast out for good and all. Attacks upon the credibility and integrity of the former Kaiser continued to be unsparing. His fairy-tale about having been sent away to Norway by his Ministers in July, 1914, and kept in ignorance of what was going on, was punctured by proof that his telegraphic communication with Berlin was extraordinarily heavy all the time he was away. Evidence was coming out that he not only read and approved of incriminating dispatches, as to Serbia and Russia, but wrote "impulsive" comments upon them. [13]

[13] Principal Sources: William L. McPherson in The *Tribune* (New York), The *Evening Post* (New York), William C. Dreher in The *Tribune* (New York), The *World*, The *Journal of Commerce*, The *Times*, New York; Associated Press dispatches.

III

THE KAISER AND CROWN PRINCE IN FLIGHT TO HOLLAND—CHARLES OF AUSTRIA ABDICATES

November 9, 1918—March 15, 1919

T HE flight of the Kaiser and Crown Prince to Holland took place while Germany was already in revolution. The request for an armistice did not cause the revolution; on the contrary it was fear of a revolution amounting to conviction that led the German Government to ask for the armistice. The Kaiser's flight occurred two days before the armistice was signed, that is, on November 9. His journey began at Spa, in eastern Belgium near the German border, which had been the Great Headquarters of the German army. The circumstances in which he was prevailed upon to go were related in much detail a month afterward in a statement made by "a personage in the entourage of William II." As late as November 8, according to this statement, the Kaiser at Spa was still saying: "I do not think of abdicating. I ask every officer to resist to the end, and as the Highest War Lord I must hold out also. The crassest Bolshevism will break over Germany if I go, and there must be a strong hand to save her from chaos." Next day "long distance discussions" with him took place. These were understood to be with Berlin.

One of the first of the war lords to make his appearance that day in the imperial villa at Spa was Hindenburg, who, after an audience with the Kaiser, had a discussion with high staff officers, each army having been ordered to send to Spa five or six representatives for the purpose of stating in writing their views as to the continued loyalty of their troops to the Kaiser's government. At a second audience Hindenburg laid before the Kaiser the verdict of these officers, "which was almost unanimous that the troops were to be depended on against the enemy, but would not fight against their comrades.'' Meantime, more urgent telephone messages came from Berlin, some saying, the Kaiser must abdicate, others ''asking whether he had not already abdicated.'' After further discussion an answer to Berlin was formulated, in which the Kaiser was said to have abdicated as German Emperor, but not as King of Prussia. After this had been communicated to Berlin, a reply came back saying: ''It is too late. We have already published news of the abdication.'' That afternoon the Crown Prince arrived at Spa with the intention of returning to his army later on the same day and the Kaiser said to him: ''Tell the troops it is not true that I have abdicated as King of Prussia.'' Hindenburg, accompanied by Gröner, Ludendorff's successor, and Hintze, the Foreign Secretary, then saw the Kaiser a third time, and shortly afterward Admiral Scheer arrived. Representations were then made to the Kaiser that he should also renounce the Prussian throne. As the Kaiser left the audience chamber, he was heard to say to Graf Schlodien, who was waiting in the ante-room: ''You have no longer a Highest War Lord,'' and passed on alone to his workroom.

In the evening of that day men in the Kaiser's nearest circle urged him to go to Holland, but he refused. ''They want me to flee,'' he said to others, ''but I will not go.'' Still later he remarked to his Adjutant: ''I am so fearfully ashamed, I can not do it; I can not go away. If there be but one faithful battalion here, I will remain in Spa.'' Reports then came that the Bolsheviki were in Herbesthal, not far away, and that troops were threatening Spa. Still he would not consent to go, but did agree to preparations being made for his going, having remarked to those about him: ''I have always known before what to do, but now I can not help myself.'' One of his adjutants was asked to give his views and replied: ''If I personally had to decide, I would remain; for if the troops will not defend your Majesty, we can form a bodyguard of officers and with them can occupy all the posts.'' At 10 o'clock the same evening Hintze urged the Kaiser's departure. ''Once more, your Majesty,'' he pleaded, ''in a few hours it may be too late,'' meaning by this to make reference to disquieting reports coming from Berlin and other towns. It was not until then that the Kaiser made the momentous decision.

At first, Castle Brühl, near Cologue, was thought of as a place of sojourn. There was also a suggestion that the Kaiser join the Crown Prince and his army. But the roads were no longer open to Brühl, and reports came in that the roads to the Crown Prince's army were not safe. Having considered the probability that the Entente would never conclude a peace with him, the Kaiser finally declared: "I will go to Holland to make it easy for my people to obtain peace. If I went to Germany it might be assumed that I wished to form a new party and effect a rising in my favor." He also considered that, from the moment when he laid down his position as the Highest War Lord, he was without power of command and had become purely a private person. As troops would not fight against their rebellious comrades, his army had virtually abandoned him in his emergency. Hence any possible reproach that "he had abandoned the army fell to the ground." Moreover, he felt released from the duty of making political decisions for the empire, since the new Government using his powers had published his abdication.[14] Of the conduct of the Crown Prince when the Kaiser made his decision, it was declared in an earlier statement, that he "cried like a baby," a statement that did not appear to be questioned anywhere.

Next day, which was Sunday, the former emperor crossed from Belgium into Dutch territory through the Belgian town of Visé, one of the frontier places where a German army first entered Belgium after stiff resistance in August 1914. Ten automobiles conveyed him and his suite all of whom were "bristling with rifles and other arms, with the Kaiser in uniform." As they crossed to Eysden, the frontier town in Holland, the Dutch sergeant on guard refused them further passage. One of the Kaiser's generals assured the guard that everything had been arranged with the Dutch Government, that the Kaiser was expected, and that he had come solely as

---

[14] This statement was made public in this country by Leonard Spray, a correspondent of The *Times* (New York), who cabled it from Rotterdam on December 15th.

a private person, his status being that of a plain citizen asking hospitality. Being only a non-commissioned officer, the sergeant finally allowed himself to be overcome by the plea and so the Kaiser was permitted to enter the country. The higher Dutch officials, when they heard what had happened, thus found themselves face to face with a *fait accompli,* but it was for a time questionable whether the Kaiser could be allowed to pass on further. Finally it was decided to treat the party as ordinary soldiers, their arms to be taken from them, and they to be interned. People in the locality generally remained quiet, altho some of the Belgians cried out *"En voyage à Paris?"* ("On the way to Paris?")

At that time, 8.30 in the morning, mists were still hanging low over the Meuse valley. For half an hour the Kaiser, who never before in his life had waited, was obliged to remain in front of a barbed wire barricade. He got out of his automobile and paced the ground up and down while many customs formalities were being gone through with, including a thorough examination of each auto for smuggled goods. While the officials were looking after various forms to be filled in, some of which had to be debated before the men could make up their minds what to do, the former Kaiser and his suite, weary with the delay, set out on foot for the Eysden station, a twenty minutes walk distant from the frontier line. There they expected to find a royal train in waiting; but through some mishap, the train did not arrive until an hour and a half afterward. The Kaiser was in the uniform of a general, with officer's cap and sword. Thus attired he had walked to the station, his eyes "staring straight ahead." After the imperial party had been formally interned, and while William was walking up and down the Eysden station, hardly any one had taken any notice of him, until the wife of the landlord of a public house nearby said to her husband: "It is the German Kaiser; look at his left arm"—that arm being shorter than the other.

After the special train came in, it appeared that the men in charge had received no instructions as to where beyond Eysden the train should go, and so they were obliged to inquire of the Government at the Hague, which meant another long wait. The train did not start till 9.30 o'clock,

when the whole party of fifty-one persons began their long
journey to the castle of Count Bentinck at Amerongen, in
northern Holland, between Arnheim and Utrecht. The rest
of that day they spent on the train, guarded by Dutch
troops. The train stopt at times, as at Maestricht, where
a tremendous crowd had gathered, including 2,000 Belgian
refugees, who hooted vigorously. A month later an attendant
of the Kaiser, who had been in his service for more than
twenty years, wrote an account of the Kaiser's journey into

THE KAISER'S REFUGE IN HOLLAND
Amerongen House, or "Castle," lies in northern Holland,
not far from Arnheim

northern Holland.[15] "Our experiences," he said, "were
simply indescribable. Every single station we passed
swarmed like an ant-heap with people endeavoring to surpass each other in howling, hissing, holding up their hands,
showing their tongues and spitting." In one of the long
waits the fallen monarch entered into conversation with
peasants who had gathered at the place, asking of them if
they knew how many degrees of frost had occurred during

[15] Published in *Vorwärts* under the heading "William the Last."

the previous night, an incident which in England and in this country recalled Shakespeare's words as spoken by Wolsey to Cromwell:

> "The third day comes a frost, a killing frost;
> And—when he thinks, good, easy man, full surely
> His greatness is aripening—nips his root,
> And then he falls, as I do."

Maarn, the station for Arnheim, near which was the Bentinck residence, Amerongen, was reached at 2.35 o'clock, motor-cars being in waiting. Count Bentinck met William as he descended from his compartment, greeting him with a low bow. The imperial fugitive wished it understood that his journey was not in the nature of a flight; he had merely left Germany to "facilitate the work of the new Government and rid it of many embarrassments which his presence might cause." As the party consisted of about fifty persons the majority had to be lodged at country hotels near the castle, which is a fine old place with luxuriously adorned apartments. Louis XIV of France had spent a night there in 1672. It was renowned among historic houses in the Netherlands, the estate a large one, with a wonderful avenue of trees, known as the Middachten-Allee, leading up to the house. From the windows one looked across a valley to the River Yssel, which flows into the Rhine and thence to the North Sea beyond Rotterdam. Two days before forty large cases containing various treasures, including the crown jewels, had arrived at the castle. There were sixteen officers in the fallen Kaiser's personal suite.

The Kaiser's presence put up to officials in Holland a problem that was said to "beat the Dutch." Public opinion at first favored sending him back to Germany. The difficulty was complicated by uncertainty as to his real status. He was installed in the left wing of the house and next day took a walk, accompanied by officers, and later went motoring, followed by a car containing Dutch officials. Among those who accompanied him to Holland were Generals von Plessen, von Gontard, von Drankelberg, von Lintoff, and von Grimmam, Count von Moltke, Surgeon-General von

Miesser, Major von Hirschfield, Count von Plann, and five captains. General Onnen of the Dutch army asked all to give their paroles. Having taken down the name of Count William Hohenzollern, he allowed Count William to retain his personal property only. All non-personal property brought to Holland had to be confiscated, as was customary in internment cases.

On November 12, Emperor Charles of Austria abdicated

CHARLES OF AUSTRIA IN EXILE IN SWITZERLAND
The former Emperor is shown with his cane, the other men being companions

and a part of German-Austria was proclaimed a republic. Charles and his family withdrew to a residence about fifteen miles east of Vienna. When, during the war, Charles succeeded Francis Joseph as Emperor, he was described as an amiable, but far from extraordinary, young man, who as Archduke had chiefly attracted attention in Vienna by a suburban habit of taking out his youngest born in a perambulator. Portraits of him showed nothing of the "character" that was supposed to reside in the face of a war lord. But now this slim and mild-faced young Austrian stood out as much the better man of the two Teutonic emperors. From the first moment of his accession, Charles had seemed earnestly to labor for peace—out of self-interest, to be sure, but yet with an intelligent foresight ·of events that was denied to his cousin of Hohenzollern. When defeat was followed by the storm which was now cleansing the whole of Central Europe of hereditary sovereigns, he did not run away like the possessor of the famous "mailed fist," but remained in his own country, apparently ready to take chances with fortune. He had bowed his head to the tempest which had made such a clean sweep of other royal Teutonic heads, and his words of abdication were accepted as more sincere than the usual language in such documents. The last of the Hapsburgs made a pathetic figure, but he carried with him into history little of the taint of criminality which adorned the late ruler and his advisers in Germany. Before the spring was far advanced he was heard from as having made Switzerland his home.

That William of Hohenzollern was somewhat of a burden to his hosts soon became obvious. All his prestige as a vice-regent of Heaven, or even as a man of unusual mental gifts, had departed. He was now a broken-down outcast, an exposed charlatan, held in some circles in as low estimation east of the Rhine as anywhere else. In Germany his flight was looked upon as a rather poor performance, especially as he had crossed the frontier without his consort or any other member of his family. Holland soon was agitated by the question whether he really had abdicated. No abdication proclamation had been published, nor had he taken leave of his people or his troops. His action might well be taken to indicate that his abdication was a sham—that he had "a string tied to it." His ignominious flight was regarded in London as a grand climax to the tragedy of autocracy, as it had now been played out on the European stage.

The whereabouts of the Crown Prince remained in doubt for days. He was at first said to have been assassinated and then was said to be staying at the residence of the Governor

of Limbourg, at Maastricht, having crossed the Dutch frontier in an automobile accompanied by a dozen intimate military associates. When he arrived at the Dutch frontier, his
first request had been for something to drink, and a big
glass of Dutch beer was given to him. No less did he appreciate an offer of cigarets, saying he had left Spa without bringing with him anything to smoke. He chatted with
Dutch guards, while his companions "maintained a frigid
attitude toward everybody." He had a lot of luggage, all
personal effects, but was greeted in silence by a crowd whose
curiosity appeared to amuse him greatly. He had taken a
circuitous route into Holland from Spa, in order to avoid
mutinous troops, his party traveling in three motor-cars.

They were held up at the frontier because all were armed
and an internment was ordered, but when it became known
that one of the party was the former Crown Prince, they
were disarmed and detained until a Dutch official could arrive from Maastricht and take the prince to his home,
holding him under guard with his suite pending instruction
from The Hague. When darkness fell the fallen prince,
accompanied by Dutch officers, went for a stroll about town
in civilian clothing, but was entirely unnoticed by the
people who thronged the streets. He had been accompanied
into Holland by three officers and ten soldiers armed to the
teeth. They crossed the frontier at such high speed that
sentries could not stop them. Chauffeurs said they had
never driven so fast in their lives before. The one-time
prince was drest in field-gray, wore all his medals and decorations, and looked deprest—"in fact, like a drowned rat,"
said an eyewitness. Smoking cigarets and in his familiar
insolent manner, he said of the new German republic: "Germany is lost! All is lost and all are crazy!"

When the former Crown Prince arrived at the Zuyder Zee
fishing-town of Enkhuyzen, on November 21, where he was
to be interned, he received a different welcome from that
which he had encountered anywhere else in Holland. As
he descended from the railway-car, wearing a sheepskin coat,
howls of execration arose from a crowd gathered outside
the station—an outburst that seemed actually to perturb
him. As the Government yacht which was to have taken

him to Wieringen, his future abode on a neighboring island, grounded in a fog, a little tugboat was substituted. Affecting indifference, he stept on the gangway leading to the tug, lighted another cigaret as the tug cast loose, and then disappeared in the fog amid angry shouts from the populace.

The hamlet of Osterland, on the island where the former heir to the imperial throne was to be interned, consisted of a score of small farmsteads and fishermen's huts, a bleak and lonely spot some distance from a Dutch naval station. The humble two-story residence of the local pastor at Osterland had been leased for his residence for six months, furnished, a simple little house off the beaten track and hardly ever visited by strangers. The hamlet itself was inhabited for the most part by mussel fishermen, who, after their experience with German *U*-boats during the war, viewed the outcast's advent with anything but favor. To the furnishings of the parsonage, which were very simple, had been added a small billiard-table and a bath-tub. In an adjoining Bible-classroom building, where were installed the former Crown Prince's guard, one of the pictures on the walls was of the Prodigal Son. As a lonely retreat this island suggested St. Helena, but it was recalled that the young man had long been a collector of Napoleonic relics.

Cyril Brown [16] described how two hundred loose-breeched, saboted Dutch fishermen, two local policemen, a Burgomaster, and half a dozen newspaper men, silently watched the former Crown Prince land at 1.30 on a bitter cold and cheerless afternoon on that dismal island in the Zuyder Zee. The "has-been Crown Prince," as the Dutch called him, landed from a fifty-foot Dutch Government boat, the *Noord Holland,* and cut a pathetic figure as he posed conspicuously in the stern, trying to keep up appearances as he gazed on the deadly dulness of the shore-line, his sheepish grimaces plainly forced. He wore a green Alpine hat with a feather, an old winter sheepskin coat with a beaver collar, and twirled a pair of gray suede gloves in lieu of a cane.

With cries of "beggar!" from the Dutch at Enkhuyzen, his port of debarkation, still ringing in his ears, he looked pitifully self-conscious on the boat, as if dreading a hostile

[16] Correspondent of The *World* (New York).

reception on the island, but he feigned rather unsuccessfully an air of nonchalance while puffing a cigaret and forcing himself to be jocose with his nervous entourage. As the boat warped to the pier on the island he saluted stiffly and seemed greatly relieved when the assembled fisherfolk hurled no invectives at him, but he had an absolutely silent reception. He was not permitted to land until the Dutch lieutenant, his chaperon for the internment, had surveyed the scene and called out in German words that meant, "All right, you can get busy now." He then leaped ashore, dashed across a narrow roadway "like a frightened jack-rabbit" and got into a waiting ramshackle two-horse, sea-going cab, the best the town could boast. He looked shyly from one of its windows and tried to salute and bow to the fisherfolk. When the natives failed to respond to courtesies from their unwelcome guest, he checked himself.

Leaving his suite to look after his baggage, he directed the cabman to go at full speed to the parsonage which had been assigned for his use. Arriving there, after a drive of nearly an hour, a fresh shock awaited him. It probably brought home to him more vividly than had anything else the depth of his fall. He saw that his house of detention was a mean two-story brick structure which would pass for "an extremely modest tenement in furthest Bronx." The impression it made was tersely exprest by a German orderly who afterward pointed out the bedroom of his chief to Mr. Brown, saying, with a sob in his voice: *"Es ist traurig,* damn it." (In plain English, "This is tough," etc.) As Mr. Brown saw it afterward a hallroom in a Bronx flat would have been quite sumptuous in comparison with this chamber, which was done in dingy dark-green paper. It had a single bedstead with an iron frame, a small dresser, an oil-stove, and in the center a tiny table, adorned with a photograph of the former Crown Princess in an oval gold frame, two photographs of the former Kaiser in wooden frames, an atomizer, and some shabby writing material. Such lodgings would be "dear in New York at $5 a week."

The adjutant had been assigned to an equally modest room immediately at the back. Downstairs was a cold hall, a very small dining-room, and an adjoining room having a shabby billiard-table. The dining-room had a table set for four persons, with two sets of wine-glasses. The house was flanked by a brick church and a parochial school. The only view looked out on the cheerless expanse of the gray and gloomy Zuyder Zee. Wieringen is one of the world's jumping-off places. The island is about eight miles long, with its widest diameter four miles, and in 1918 had a population of 3,000. No kind of amusement was to be had, not even a "movie" show. Fishermen got their recreation in taverns. Walking and talking with his own companions seemed to be about the only activities that would be possible for the interned Hohenzollern.

As the Government boat scraped the end of the island's pier, George Renwick [17] had a good look at the "victor of Longwy," that frontier French town taken by the Crown Prince's army in August, 1914, after a siege of twenty-one days, and the author of the "Frischer, Froehlicher Krieg" ("Free, Happy War"). As the fallen prince was standing on deck with his companions, Mr. Renwick was only two or three yards away and noted how he had changed since Mr. Renwick had seen him last in Berlin. He "looked even more inane than ever, more like *Simplicissimus's* cartoons of him, but he was heavier under the eyes and his face had a somewhat bloated look." He still wore "his toothbrush mustache," and his effeminate hands toyed with his inevitable cigaret. Mr. Renwick could not help thinking that only about six months had passed since the world read the Kaiser's pompous message beginning: "This morning William stormed the Chemin-des-Dames." The stormer of the Chemin-des-Dames was now scrambling into a carriage that was nothing but a dilapidated "growler." No soldier presented arms to him, not a single cheer was raised, nor a single hat doffed. Half a dozen portmanteaux were brought ashore and Major von Mueller, the Prince's Adjutant, having followed him in entering the carriage, the vehicle went off at a funereal pace past scores of fishing-boats, most of them long laid up on account of the *U*-boat war, and some of which had been under submarine fire. No one appeared interested enough to follow the slow-paced

[17] Correspondent of The *Times* (New York).

vehicle and the little crowd went off about its business.
"Did you see his coat?" said a quaint old fishwife. "It still
has the blood of war on it."

At the parsonage no sentry stood before the door. The
adjutant rang the bell and a Dutch manservant appeared
and admitted the strange little band of refugees. The
billiard-table was an old French one, the cloth of which
had been cut several times and badly mended. Some previous

© PRESS ILLUSTRATING SERVICE.

BRIDGE ACROSS THE MOAT AT AMERONGEN
One of the men seen on the bridge is the Kaiser, the others
belong to his suite

owner had apparently had the habit of putting down a
lighted cigar or cigaret on the edge of the table which was
burned in places. A sorry array of cues stood near-by and
the balls were much the worse for wear. The former Prince
was about to undergo a Gilbertian punishment by playing
"on a board untrue with a twisted cue, and elliptical
billiard-balls." He was not expected to leave the island

except by special permission of the Home Office at The Hague and was supplied with food-cards the same as an ordinary citizen would be.

"I hope that when peace is signed America will remember that she and Germany were once friendly," said Frederick William, in an interview obtained while on his way to his island home. "I am unable to make any formal statement," said he, "as my mouth has been closed by orders. I do not know how long I shall stay in Holland, where I have been accorded nice treatment. My future depends on the revolution. I hope to see Germany again, but must be patient. My only knowledge of events has been obtained through the newspapers. I have not seen my family for weeks. My father, I am told, also lives in Holland. I have not heard anything regarding my wife, my children, or my friends. But have I any friends left? The food in Holland is good, but I eat very little. I wish to retain my slender, sportsman's figure." He added that he had made plans to dictate his war memoirs. Offering the correspondent a cigaret, he terminated the interview with "greet America for me."

Meanwhile his wife, the Crown Princess Cecilie, remained in Berlin. On November 16 she assembled her household attendants in the throne-room and addrest them as follows: "You know how things turned out. The time to separate has now come. I hope you will entertain pleasant remembrances of us. My heart breaks. Farewell, my trusted friends. May God bless you." She then shook hands with each and presented each with a small gift, saying, "I can't give more for the present." She expected to visit her sister, the Queen of Denmark, and to reside permanently with her children near Copenhagen, close to her mother, the Grand Duchess Anastasia. The former Kaiserin was reported at this time to be so seriously ill in Potsdam that the doctors opposed her joining her husband, who had been telegraphing daily for her to come. All members of the Hohenzollern dynasty were expected to leave Germany soon.

Thus far the Berlin government had sent no communication to the Allies, or to the United States, concerning the Kaiser's reported abdication. No abdication document bearing the Kaiser's signature was in existence, so far as the outside world knew—nothing but a statement that he had "decided to abdicate" and another that he had made a *"thron verzicht,"* a renunciation of the throne. The word *"abdankung,"* meaning "abdication," had not been used. Wilhelm apparently still regarded the German throne as his. A few days later he was spending most of his time in bed because of an illness following a severe chill with which he had been suddenly stricken. Two officers took turns in reading novels and newspapers to him. He had not left the grounds of Amerongen since he arrived, but began each day with a walk and then attended a religious service conducted by Count von Bentinck or the Count's son. A day might close with another walk in the gardens. The pastor of the village church dined with the former Emperor's party and local notables visited the castle.

The Bentinck family emphasized the fact that they had received William only at the request of the Dutch Government. It appeared by November 18 that the former Emperor had not been actually interned, but was regarded as a distinguished foreigner who had sought refuge in Holland and so had a claim to protection. He, therefore, was presumably free to go where he chose, but the fact that his suite had been actually interned restricted his movements. Members of his suite had surrendered their swords to Dutch officers, having previously surrendered other arms. From investigation in western Germany a correspondent [18] at The Hague had found considerable German hostility to the former Emperor and his eldest son. When William entered Holland a thousand German soldiers had been pursuing him to the frontier and requested that they be allowed to pursue him further, but they were turned back by Dutch frontier guards. The correspondent did not believe the former Emperor could go again to Berlin in safety, no matter what guaranties he might give, while the former Crown Prince was so universally hated that his life in Germany "would not be worth an hour's purchase." Some of the Dutch newspapers advocated the expulsion of the troublesome visitors, fearing that Holland might get into difficulties if they did not soon depart.

[18] Of The *Daily Mail* (London).

Prince Maximilian of Baden, the former Chancellor, on November 18, revealed what he called "some interesting things." The German people, he said, "by the formation of a popular government, had been liberated from the dictatorship of Ludendorff and would never tolerate another." As to an abdication, the Emperor had "hesitated to sign," altho "a decision due to his own initiative might have spared the empire serious convulsions." His hesitation, however, "must not be interpreted against him, as certain influences had worked on him to persuade him that his abdication would be the signal for a collapse." Fears were exprest in England that as Wilhelm had not actually abdicated, he might again "bestride the world like a Colossus." But obstacles stood in the way of his doing that—the armies of the Allies, the German people, and the former Kaiser himself. Wilhelm might have thought of himself as still "holding a string" to his alleged abdication, but whether he did so or not was unimportant because an Emperor who had run away was not an Emperor, and was likely to think twice before incurring a second chance to run away from danger. Eight large Allied armies were then marching into Germany which had been disarmed and was begging for peace. These armies represented nations who were as one in their stern determination that German autocracy should never again be a world menace. In Amsterdam it was understood, on November 29, that the former Kaiser would soon leave Amerongen Castle for a sanatorium near Arghem, to undergo treatment for shattered nerves. He was reported as subject to fits of weeping, and unable to write at times, owing to spells of trembling in his hands. His condition recalled again the prophecy of Charles M. Schwab made a year before, when addressing some discontented workmen at a government shipyard: "If you men remain loyal to your job, we shall make the Kaiser take his medicine lying down."

On November 28, on a raw, misty morning, Augusta Victoria, wife of the former Emperor, arrived in Holland from Potsdam to join her husband in Amerongen Castle. She was placed in charge of Count von Bentinck by a captain of rural gendarmerie, who, under orders, had escorted her across Holland from Zevenaar, the Dutch frontier-station.

Her baggage was large enough in amount to indicate a prolonged stay, and included a number of wicker-baskets and
boxes marked "Imperial cellars." She wore a plain dark
tailor-made velvet dress with a hat and veil which offset an
abundance of silver hair. No official reception for the former
Kaiserin took place. Count von Bentinck pointed out his
delicate position as a reason for declining to answer questions about her. He said the Dutch Government was the
host, and that he had no right to make known the details
of the daily life of his visitors. The meeting of the former
Emperor and Empress was described by a Dutch correspondent of the London *Daily Express:*

"The gates were thrown open, the drawbridge was lowered with
a noise of chains and iron bars that sounded very medieval, and in
the courtyard before the castle an elderly man in a gray military
cloak was seen at a distance, walking slowly, leaning on his stick.
It was the former Kaiser. As the former Kaiser's car was driven
into the courtyard, the ex-Kaiser threw down his stick and, before
the valet was able to do so, opened the door and handed out his
wife. The two shook hands and then threw themselves into each
other's arms, the ex-Kaiserin falling upon her husband's shoulder
and crying like a child. The gates then closed and further view
was shut out."

Statements showing that the former Kaiser had sought to
escape responsibility for bringing on the war were made
in an article by Dr. George Wegener that now appeared in
the Cologne *Gazette,* as based on a conversation with the
Emperor just before he fled from Germany. The former
Kaiser attempted to shift the blame to Bethmann-Hollweg,
the former Imperial Chancellor, and von Jagow, the former
Minister of Foreign Affairs. "Against my will, they sent
me to Norway," he was quoted as having said. "I did not
wish to undertake the voyage because the gravity of the
situation, after the murder of Archduke Francis Ferdinand,
was clear at first sight. But the Chancellor said to me:
'Your Majesty must take this voyage in order to maintain
peace. If your Majesty remains here, it undoubtedly means
war, and the world will lay to your charge responsibility
for the war.' Then I undertook the voyage. During all

this time I received no reports from my Government concerning events. Strictly speaking, I only learned from Norwegian newspapers what was occurring.''

From this statement it appeared that William, who had looked upon his crown as a trust from *"Unser Gott,"* who had boasted how "I go my way" regardless of passing views and opinions, and who considered himself the chosen instrument of his Maker for the promotion of the welfare of a chosen people, had allowed his servant, Bethmann-Hollweg, to send him out of his country at a time of supreme international crisis. For a man supremely powerful as he had been, and as he boasted himself to be, it was hard to see how his mere presence in Berlin in July, 1914, could have meant war. His statement that it would have done so, implied that he could not have been trusted to prevent war; that he was unable to control the emotions roused in himself by the killing of Francis Ferdinand and by the possibilities of the Austrian ultimatum to Serbia, and in consequence his ministers had put him out of the country in order to keep things quiet. There was not a word in' all his statements about the Potsdam Conference of July 5, 1914—which had been held before his visit to Norway, and at which further Teutonic territorial aggression, or war as the alternative, had been determined upon by representatives of Germany and Austria. It was decided at this conference that the Kaiser should go to Norway, in order to put suspicion to sleep—in order, moreover, that Poincaré and Viviani, then on their way to Petrograd, might be caught unprepared for the crisis the conspirators intended to create. The Kaiser had been sent to Norway, not to maintain peace, but to satisfy the world that Germany was innocent of the crime of starting the war, and as much surprized at the sudden gathering of a storm as were the other Powers.

The world, however, could not forget Dr. Muehlon's statement that, at the Potsdam Conference, the Kaiser promised to stand by Austria through thick and thin. Nor could the world forget Dr. Muehlon's report of his conversation with Krupp von Bohlen, who told him how the Kaiser reiterated "with an almost comical insistence" that this time "no one should call him irresolute"; they could not say again that he was "afraid to draw the sword." Further evidence was before the world in Henry Morgenthau's account of Baron Wangenheim's report to him of the conference itself, at which the Baron was present. The world knew to its own satisfaction that Bethmann-Hollweg and Jagow, however deficient they were in appreciation of the obligation of a pledged word, could not have started a World War just of their own volition. Bethmann-Hollweg formally denied that the former Kaiser had been sent to Norway by the German Government, or that he had been sent there in order that he might not interfere in the European crisis that was impending.

Kurt Eisner, the Bavarian Premier, declared in a speech on December 5 that he intended to publish documents of the German Foreign Office to prove that William was responsible for the war. "Comments on certain documents showed that the Kaiser caused the war," he said, and three months later Eisner was assassinated. Dealing with Eisner's speech, the *Tageblatt* of Berlin said it was true that notations on certain documents often bore signs of the well-known impulsiveness of the Emperor, and were more compromising for the Emperor than for those who had drawn up the documents. With reference to the Kaiser's statement that in three weeks spent in Norway he was informed of events only through the Norwegian newspapers, a local newspaper in Norway, the *Morgensbladet,* now gave particulars of an ordinary day's work gone through with by the Emperor at that time:

"The Kaiser during his stay was busier at work on board his yacht than during any previous visit. His visits ashore were remarkably less frequent and briefer. His telegraphic correspondence was very heavy. He passed several hours daily in wireless communication. When the imperial yacht lay in one of the fjords, where the height of a mountain prevented wireless telegraphy, a first-class torpedo-boat appeared daily to deliver and receive his telegrams and mail. The majority of the telegrams received by him were known to be in cipher."

Approximately three weeks after he fled from Spa, that is on November 28, William definitely renounced all his

future rights to the crowns of Prussia and Germany and
released all officials and officers from their oaths of fealty.
He signed this abdication at Amerongen, in a document
which, however, said nothing about other members of the
Hohenzollern house. Its form indicated that his previously
exprest intentions of abdicating had amounted to temporiz-
ing with the Allies. To all practical purposes he was now
a prisoner still, confined behind iron gates and high brick
walls, and devoting himself to religious meditation. He
could not put his hat on to go for a walk like a private
person except when guarded. A squad of three uniformed
police stood at the main gateway of Amerongen, a reserve
squad was stationed in a porter's lodge, and another policeman guarded the bridge over the moat. When, on November 30, the "act of renunciation," as his abdication was
called, was issued in Berlin, it was described as having been
issued "in order to reply to certain misunderstandings
which had arisen with regard to the abdication." It read
as follows:

"By the present document I renounce forever my rights to the
crown of Prussia and the rights to the German Imperial crown. I
release at the same time all the officers and soldiers of the Prussian
Navy and Army and of contingents from confederate States from
the oath of fidelity they have taken to me, as their Emperor, King,
and supreme chief. I expect from them, until a new organization
of the German Empire exists, that they will aid those who effectively
hold the power in Germany to protect the German people against
the menacing dangers of anarchy, famine, and foreign dominion.

"Made and executed and signed by our own hand with the Imperial seal at Amerongen, November 28th.   "WILLIAM."

The Crown Prince continued to be described as maintaining a "gleesome manner," but, after having said he would
not talk for publication, he developed a month later a pronounced attack of "I-told-you-so." Most Germans had for
years denied that there had ever been a defeat on the Marne,
or had maintained that what occurred there was merely "a
movement of strategy"; but the Crown Prince, on December
5, declared [19] that the German position after the Marne was

---

[19] To an Associated Press correspondent.

"hopeless," that Germany there "lost the war." "I tried
to persuade the German High Command to seek peace," he
said, "even at a great sacrifice, going so far as to give up
Alsace-Lorraine," and in consequence was told to "mind my
own business and confine my activities to commanding my
armies." In this interview he added that, if the German
Government should decide to form a republic similar to the
United States or France, he would be "perfectly content to
return to Germany as a simple citizen ready to do anything

MOUNTED POLICE ENTERING AMERONGEN

to assist the country." He would even "work as a laborer
in a factory." While conditions appeared chaotic, he hoped
things would right themselves. "I was convinced early in
October, 1914," said he, "that we had lost the war," but
Germany would not have lost it "if the chiefs of our High
Command had not suffered a case of nerves." What finally
brought about the downfall of the German military power,
he declared, was the revolution, as induced by four years

of hunger among civilians and troops in the rear, together with the fact that overwhelming numbers were being gathered at the front by the Entente Powers since America's entry into the war, and this had undermined the confidence of German fighting forces. "My soldiers, whom I loved and with whom I lived continuously, and who, if I may say so, loved me, fought," he said, "with the utmost courage to the end, even when the odds were impossible to withstand. They had no rest. Sometimes an entire division numbered only 600 rifles. These were opposed by fresh Allied troops, among whom were American divisions containing 27,000 men apiece."

After the Kaiser left Germany for Holland the former Crown Prince said he had remained with his group of armies and had asked if they desired him to retain his command. As they replied negatively, and he could not continue to lead armies under orders from the Soldiers' and Workers' Council, he went to Holland, but "with the greatest regret after having participated in trench-life for so long." He had not been in Germany for a year, and from the beginning of the war had taken only three or four fortnight leaves. Other points in the interview were these:

"Contrary to all statements hitherto made abroad, I never desired war, and thought the moment inopportune. I was enjoying a stay at a watering-place when mobilization was ordered. My father, also, I am sure, did not desire war. If Germany had sought the best opportunity for making war, she would have chosen the period either of the Boer war or the Russo-Japanese war. From the beginning I was certain that England would enter the conflict. This view was not shared by Prince Henry and the other members of my family. You English clamor to get father and me away from Holland. We are down and out, and my father is a broken man. Isn't that enough punishment? I quarreled with my father in regard to Great Britain. I told him the British would be against us. He never believed this, and would not take into account that possibility. People have credited me with war-like intentions. But I was only a soldier with the desire to see the army kept thoroughly efficient, and I worked hard to bring this about. People blame me with the failure at Verdun. But I refused twice to attack there with the troops at my disposal. On the third occasion my attack was successful for the first three days, but I was not properly supported.

I thought that the Verdun attack was a mistake. We should have attacked to the eastward of Verdun, where there would have been great probability of success."

He was rather bitter toward the German High Command, which he thought was responsible for numerous mistakes, including the offensive of 1918. Ludendorff had been the mainspring of Germany's warlike activities, while Hindenburg was "a mere figurehead." Ludendorff and his staff continually underestimated the enemy's forces and never believed that America's contribution of soldiers was as great as it actually proved to be. With regard to air-raids on unfortified cities, the submarine warfare, the bombardment of Paris, and the deportation of women from occupied districts to work in Germany, the fallen Prince said he had always entirely disagreed with these policies. The air-raids on London and other towns, and the big gun used against Paris were "useless militarily, and, in fact, silly." Orders issued to submarine commanders were interpreted differently by various officers, who often went much too far in following them. Regarding air-raids, he had suggested two years before that an international agreement should confine air activities to an actual war-zone, but his opinion was disregarded and he was again told that his job was to command his armies. German diplomats before the war had made "awful mistakes," and been unable to see the viewpoint of the countries where they were stationed, and they misread opinion in other countries. The former Crown Prince finally renounced his right to the Prussian and German thrones on December 1, in the following document:

"I renounce formally and definitely all rights to the Crown of Prussia and the German Imperial Crown, which would have fallen to me by the renunciation of the Emperor-King, or for other reasons. Given by my authority and signed by my hand; done at Wieringen, December 1, 1918. "WILHELM."

"You see that window? It is there that he sits writing, writing, as if he were in a hurry, hour after hour," said a Dutchman at Amerongen to George Renwick [20] on December

[20] Correspondent of The *Times* (New York).

2. Mr. Renwick through the misty atmosphere could see the window indicated, which looked out over flatlands toward the sunset. It had been "a dull, mournful day, and the castle, lying behind its ancient moat and broad, well-tended gardens, looked as depressing as a prison, but fascinating." Villager after villager passed by without turning his head. Slow-paced people who lived near the place, when asked if they had seen the ex-Kaiser, nearly all answered "No." His appearances in and outside the grounds became more ⌐⌐d more rare. While the whole world was still discussing ⌐⌐s fate, the village which harbored him was forgetting his presence and had all but lost interest in him. And yet not since it was possible for men to look on St. Helena when it held Napoleon had such a vision been presented to men's eyes as that which one had in that stately Dutch castle, now the prison-house of the last royal and imperial ruler of Prussia and Germany.

Mr. Renwick could not help recalling opportunities he had had of seeing the Kaiser in Berlin, when to have thought he could possibly fall from his dazzling position would have seemed the maddest of hallucinations. Imperial, keen, and alive he had always looked in Berlin. "I wonder what he looks like now," Mr. Renwick said one day to a man at the castle who had come much in contact with him. "Looks like?" was the reply. "Why, he looks dejected. He wore an air of relief when he came, but that soon went, and even the cheery ex-Kaiserin can not now rouse him from his moodiness. She is really acting something like a heroine. Tho ill, she tries to occupy his thoughts and make him look on the bright side of things; but in vain. More and more he keeps himself apart from the household. Less and less does he feel inclined to go about."

To the main entrance to the castle, callers and members of the household would come and go looking opprest with the tragedy of all that had happened. Some would come in a travel-stained motor-car with a portmanteau covered with German labels. The former Kaiserin and her ladies from day to day would return silently to the gate after a walk outside. Visitors might look over the grounds, but were kept at a distance from the house, and altogether away from that side where the former Kaiser's suite of twenty rooms was situated, which, before his arrival was so suddenly announced, were being prepared for Belgian refugees. As darkness fell, Mr. Renwick went to look at that window again. All other windows save that one were then dark. It was in that room that he had signed his abdication. While sitting there, "he might yet receive an imperious command such as no man on earth ever received before." To an Associated Press correspondent who early in December called at the castle and asked for an interview, the fallen monarch replied:

"I am a private citizen and while in Holland will not make any statement whatever for publication. You must fully realize my position. I am threatened on all sides with criminal charges, which, if brought, I must face. Therefore I must reserve any statement until charges are actually brought. Also I owe a certain loyalty to the present German Government and can not make a declaration which might compromise others."

The Kaiser's private fortune in cash, mostly deposited in banks, was estimated at 20,000,000 marks, or $5,000,000, and his annual income therefrom as $250,000. The new government had declared that his private landed property would not be seized, but that Crown domains would pass to the State treasury. Of some ninety forest, farm, park, and other estates and castles, only seven were Crown domains, all the others being private. The private estates included Bellevue Palace in Berlin, and Monbijou Palace within whose grounds was St. George's English Church. In Potsdam he had thirteen palaces. Wilhelmshohe was his and he had also Cassel, where King Edward paid him his last visit, and where Napoleon III was confined after Sedan. Other palaces and estates were in Coblenz, Wiesbaden, Charlottenburg, and elsewhere. He owned an experimental farm at Cadinen, a shooting-box and forest at Rominten, near the eastern frontier, house property at Trouville, and the Achilleion Palace at Corfu. His cash was largely savings made by Frederick William III—calculated in 1840 at about $3,750,-000. After 1871 his grandfather received $1,125,000 as a sort of war-bonus from the indemnity paid by France. This sum, it was conjectured, France might ask to have returned to her. He had received $2,500,000 from the State for the ground where the Royal Library stood in Berlin, and for the Old Opera House of Kroll. From that sum he derived the funds he spent in improving the royal stables in Berlin, from whose subterranean passages officers for two days had resisted a mob during the revolution.

Reports from the moated castle of Amerongen on December 8 were that William had become more isolated from the world than ever. Not for some days had he been outside the grounds and then only for a walk in the garden with an escort at his side and a policeman near by. Day by day he remained in his study alone writing. Sheet after sheet of foolscap was covered with what many thought was his reply to the world's arraignment of him. His private correspondence outward was heavy, but out of proportion to the number of letters that reached him. Strange whispers got abroad, as that Amerongen would soon be free of its unwelcome guest, or that he had suffered a complete physical breakdown. The exile gave much time to reading world-news, which was placed before him daily in concise form from German newspapers. Everything was marked that contained any reference to the future of the two Hohenzollerns, father and son. While the world was drawing up its terrible indictment, he had not failed to do homage to the Christmas spirit. For him, his consort and their entourage, a Christmas tree was set up in the suite set apart in the castle. With his own hands he helped place it in position and light the candles, and standing beneath it handed presents to his companions. Tragi-comedy was played out as it might have been in the Prussian court, but in strictest privacy. Not even members of the Bentinck family set foot in the rooms where it was staged.[21]

By the middle of January, it was reported that the imperial exile was having repeated chills—due to overheating himself while engaged in "his favorite exercises of sawing and chopping wood." He had been accustomed in Germany before the war to do this work as an exercise. This and

[21] Cable dispatch to The *Times* (New York) from Amerongen by Leonard Spray.

another form of exercise he undertook at Amerongen—to dig an irrigation channel in the flower-garden, but this brought on a chill and a sojourn in his apartment. He had become increasingly irritable under the restrictions imposed upon him as an interned person. This feeling had been augmented by the gradual departure from Amerongen of many of his old servants, who found life in Holland unbearable under the circumstances imposed. Dutch domestics were filling their places, but they did not attain to the same perfection of attention and obeisance as the Imperial servants had acquired. For years the latter had been accustomed to foresee every requirement of their sovereign. It was believed that before many weeks the entire German personnel would have disappeared, and the former monarch, who never had done any of the simple things in life for himself in the way of dressing, would thenceforth be cast on his own resources. His recent ailments had had a marked effect on his physical and mental condition. The damp climate had affected his ear and throat, and he had become generally run down. His wife acted as his nurse. She was now in fairly good health herself, and went out occasionally to tea.

Late in February, 1919, the former Emperor was reported from Weimar to have appealed to the German Revolutionary Government for money. He had already been forced to borrow 40,000 guilders from his host, and as he could not continue to be his debtor, he asked for at least a portion of his private fortune. The Government agreed to the request but instituted a detailed investigation to determine what portion of his fortune really was his, and what portion belonged to the Government. The investigation showed that he might legally claim 75,000,000 marks as his own, but the Government decided to allow him temporarily only 600,000 marks to meet existing indebtedness and future expenses. These disclosures put an end to a belief that the former Emperor had been able to take large sums of money with him to Holland.

On March 15, the former Kaiser completed the sawing into logs of the thousandth tree he had attacked since he took refuge in Count von Bentinck's castle. A few logs from this tree were converted into souvenirs, and as marked in red ink, were presented to members of the Bentinck family and others who had assisted him in his work for ten weeks. Expert sawyers in the neighborhood computed the value of the wages which he would have earned had he been paid at trade-union rates, as about $30 for the whole period, or an average of 50 cents a working day of three hours.

Harold Begbee,[22] who visited Amerongen in April, described the place as "a castle only in name." It was rather an unimpressive, somber, brick-red house, standing in so thick a companionship of trees that it looked "expressly made for a ghost story by Edgar Allan Poe." The piece of land on which it stood was so small as to give little room for a garden; set in a wood, it was surrounded by shrubbery, with outbuildings quite close to it, "just as the castle itself is quite close to village houses." The better part of the space belonging to the castle was occupied by water in a moat extending around its walls, with still another moat, separating it on the north from the village and on the south from water meadows that stretch away to a confluent of the lower Rhine, along whose course had passed in recent weeks many transports bearing British troops on their way homeward from Germany.

Count Goddard Bentinck, on Sunday morning, November 10, when the Kaiser crossed the Dutch frontier at Eysden, had been confronted by a domestic crisis, half his servants being down with influenza, and the other half recovering from it. He had expected to have a shooting party at the castle a few days later, and after attending church in the morning and eating his dinner at noon, had decided to put off the shooting party for want of efficient household help. That same afternoon he had a telephone call from the Governor of the Province of Utrecht, in which the castle is situated, telling him the Kaiser had fled from Germany and crossed the frontier, that he had been held up by Dutch soldiers and that the Government was suddenly confronted with a critical situation out of which it might get some

[22] Correspondent of The *Daily Chronicle* (London), and *The Times* (New York).

help provided Count Bentinck would oblige it by receiving the Kaiser at his castle for a few days, the Government meanwhile turning about to see what it could do with its unexpected guest.

To this inquiry Count Bentinck replied that it was impossible for him to receive the Kaiser and his suite, owing to his domestic crisis, but the Governor brushed that aside as a thing not worthy to be mentioned in such a world-important situation. Count Bentinck agreed to consult his children, who, on reflection, thought the matter might be managed in some way, and so it was that next day the Kaiser and his suite were received into Amerongen, and Count Bentinck had to provide dinner for forty-five persons. At the time of Mr. Begbee's visit, those two days had lengthened into twice as many months, with the problem of the ex-Kaiser's domicile still unsettled. The world had been led to believe that Count Bentinck offered the Kaiser the hospitality of his home as an old and intimate friend. This was not true. Count Bentinck had merely seen the former Emperor once before—not as Emperor, but in the days when he was simply Prince William, and not even a Crown Prince. The two men, host and guest, met, therefore, as absolute strangers on November 11. After the former Kaiser had been a week at Amerongen, the Empress arrived from Germany, and Count Bentinck found himself now called upon to provide dinner for sixty-two persons.

Since those November days, the imperial staff had declined in April to a general, an adjutant, and a doctor; the suite of the Empress to one lady. The fallen monarch walked daily about the castle grounds. One might see him, said Mr. Begbee, after breakfast "drest in plain clothes, with a cloak thrown over his shoulders, striding forward, his head up, his arms swinging, the whole body of the man still electric with that nervous energy which made him something of a whirlwind in former days." His eye had kept its fire, his lips their firmness, his voice its ring, but there were changes—"his hair white, the pointed beard he had grown adding ten years to his appearance, and all the boisterous hilarity which sometimes made his friendliness a little difficult to bear, now gone."

ON THE WESTERN FRONT

The end of that reign, as one felt it in that Dutch village, Mr. Begbee thought "tragic enough." The once puissant and medieval Emperor, "who made himself the mouthpiece of God, and whose sword would flash from its sheath on occasion like some terrible lightning that threatened thrones and nations with destruction, now sat regularly on one side of a hearthstone, talking of Freemasonry and shaking his white head over the world's lapse into atheism—on the other side of him, often struggling for breath, the former Empress, whose one task it was to comfort and sustain her fallen lord in his broken fortunes, her own heart crying out in secret for the presence of her children and grandchildren, from whom she felt herself eternally parted." Discussing the world across their fireside, these two "were more remote from the great world than the village policeman who lounged in front of the castle gate; they were prisoners, and the jailer who turned the key on their liberty was the outer world whom they were discussing in their prison cell." Whatever the world's verdict on his part in the war, no one knew better than this fallen man that "for the rest of his existence he would have to live the threatened life of an outlaw." A strong tide in the affairs of men had borne him out of the ocean of great trafficking and cast him up as a piece of broken wreckage on the shore of a remote and friendless sea.[23]

[23] Principal Sources: The *Vorwärts* (Berlin), The *World*, The *Evening Post*, The *Times*, New York; The *Daily Mail*, The *Daily Express*, London; The *Evening Sun* (New York), Associated Press dispatches.

IV

THE SURRENDER OF GERMANY'S BIG SHIPS AND SUBMARINES—OUR NAVY IN THE WAR

November 21, 1918—December 27, 1918

IT was to the wars of Rome and Carthage, two hundred and fifty years before the Christian era, that one had to turn for a parallel to the great naval surrender which on November 21 destroyed all German hopes of ever wresting control of the seas from Great Britain. After Scipio's victory over Hannibal at Zama, the Carthagenians accepted a peace by the terms of which all their battle-fleet, save ten galleys, was surrendered to the Romans, and so perished the last serious challenge by any organized state to Roman world supremacy for several centuries. In 1918 it was much less than a generation since the Kaiser had issued his challenge to the British, in that historic speech in which he declared that the future of Germany lay "on the seas." From that hour to the outbreak of the war, German naval officers had constantly drunk to *"Der Tag"*—"The Day" when British mastery of the sea would be destroyed.

It was less than two and a half years since the Kaiser, in visiting his battle-fleet in harbor, after the Jutland fight, had arrogantly proclaimed that Germany's goal had been attained, the decision of Trafalgar abolished. But from that hour onward the German fleet never again risked battle with the British. When all had been lost on land, sailors of Germany's battle-fleet had in fact mutinied rather than follow the example of Cervera at Santiago and go out to certain destruction rather than surrender. Whatever the immediate results at Jutland were, its consequences were the same as those of Trafalgar; sea-power remained in control of the British. From a post north of the British Isles the great British fleet still maintained its guard, while behind its screen a merchant fleet, and lesser warships continued to convoy millions of Allied soldiers to France and far eastern scenes of battle until, starving at home, overwhelmed by masses of fresh troops constantly brought to battle-fronts from every quarter of the globe, Germany's military power had been slowly worn down until nothing was left for it but to go to Senlis and in a railway car surrender to Foch.

When, on August 1, 1914, the British battle-fleet, already mobilized, moved to its battle-station in the North Sea, the war at sea was already lost to Germany. Within a few brief months the last of German ships at sea was sunk or forced to intern, and the German flag disappeared from ocean waters. The British navy had taken Germany by the throat and continued to hold her there until sufficient Allied armies could be organized to perform their task of defeating her on land. The submarine was the deadliest thrust made by Germany after her defeat at the Marne, but this thrust the British navy had met, with aid from the French and American navies. The sea phase of the war, however, was the British share. How well it had been performed we now saw when the pick of Germany's fleet surrendered and sailed to British ports a captive. Here was a new vindication of all that Admiral Mahan had asserted of sea power in days before the conflict. It was an ultimate demonstration of the real war power of Great Britain. Her fleet had saved the world, her fleet had won the war, not by a Trafalgar or a Salamis, but after four years of ceaseless pressure by an unbroken blockade, without decisive battle. And now that German fleet was to surrender on the most ignominious terms known in modern naval history. None of us knew just what the phrase "freedom of the seas" meant, but we knew quite well what freedom of the world meant; in the German surrender we had spread before us an impressive demonstration of how that freedom had been preserved.

What might be reckoned the most dramatic incident of the armistice, and historically the most impressive of the war was this surrender off the Firth of Forth to a naval force consisting of the British Grand Fleet with French and American squadrons. Among the surrendered ships, whose ultimate fate was to be determined at the peace conference, were ten dreadnaughts of about 25,000 tons displacement, most of them built since 1911, and six battle-cruisers, including the *Hindenburg* and *Derfflinger,* of even greater displacement and the very latest additions to the German Navy. Germany was not to recover any of these ships; her colonies in all parts of the world were gone; her foreign trade, that had bade fair before the war to drive Great Britain and the United States from profitable markets, was no longer more than a memory, and her mer-

© UNDERWOOD & UNDERWOOD, N. Y.

THE BRITISH FLAGSHIP "QUEEN ELIZABETH"
As she appeared at the surrender of the German fleet. On her right is
Vice-Admiral Beatty's destroyer, *The Oak*

chant marine only a surviving nucleus. A great naval and commercial fabric that had been built up with a vast expenditure of money and labor now lay helpless and dismantled. Nothing in the empire of Germany was imperial now.

With little actual fighting, her heavier ships scarcely engaged at all, Great Britain's fleet during the war "had ridden at anchor on the north coast of Scotland, apparently doing nothing, as idle as painted ships upon a painted ocean." But in reality this fleet was exerting irresistible and decisive power, and now it moved out to accept, without firing a gun, the surrender to it of German cruisers and dreadnoughts. The last act became not a fight, but a mere naval parade, and yet it as truly told the tale of what sea-power was as could have done a gigantic naval battle with scarred victors sailing home in triumph. This majestic proof of British might at sea was proof also of the wisdom of the British war policy. British statesmen for generations had had to make a choice, since they could not make themselves both invincible on the sea and formidable on land. As practical men, they knew their choice lay between a great navy and a great army, for they could not maintain both. With large foresight and a clear measuring of probabilities, they decided to insure their safety by making their island and the Empire safe at sea. Men had cried out in 1914 against British unpreparedness, but we had seen that Britain had prepared herself with the surest armor that was available to her statesmen. All that time England had been held in light esteem in Berlin. In land fighting her army had been dubbed "contemptible," and her fleet Berlin thought could be kept at bay by mines and torpedoes. Wisdom had been justified of her children. Military experts in Germany had sorrowfully to admit that the British had been wiser than they. Germany's steady refusal to consider British proposals of naval disarmament was now seen to have been for twenty years one of the blackest of reproaches to German statesmanship. Germany's "future on the sea" had been sedulously preached and she had built a powerful navy costing hundreds of millions, but all now squandered, her future on the sea reduced to a trip to British ports to make a complete surrender.

Captain Persius, a leading German naval critic, chose the occasion to publish some revelations regarding the German fleet. He declared that all hope that the German fleet would be able in a second Jutland battle to beat the British rested on "mere bluff and lies" issued by German naval authorities. In August, 1914, Germany, he said, had about one million tonnage in warships, while Great Britain had more than

© INTERNATIONAL FILM SERVICE, N. Y.

THE SURRENDER OF SOME OF THE GERMAN *U*-BOATS OFF HARWICH

331

double that. Owing to mistakes of Admiral von Tirpitz, the German material, such as it was, was quite inferior to the British. In the battle of Jutland the German fleet had been saved from destruction partly by good leadership, but in part also by favorable weather conditions. Had the weather been clear, or had Admiral von Scheer's leadership been less able, the destruction of the whole German navy would have taken place. Long-range British guns would have completely smashed the lighter-armed German ships. As it was, the losses of the German fleet were enormous, and in June, 1915, it became clear to every thinking man in Germany that the Jutland battle must remain for Germany the last general naval engagement of the war.

Two years before the war ended, an order had been issued terminating the construction of battleships in order that material might be used for making *U*-boats. In the meantime, so great a scarcity of material had arisen that it became necessary to disarm a number of battleships and use the guns elsewhere. In this manner, at the beginning of 1916, twenty-three battleships had been disarmed, as well as one newly built cruiser. At the beginning of 1916, the German navy consisted only of dreadnoughts and battleships of the *Helgoland, Kaiser* and *Markgraf* types, and some few battle-cruisers. All the ships which von Tirpitz had constructed from 1897 to 1906 had been destroyed.

Only a small percentage of Germany's submarines were actively operating at any given time, said Captain Persius. In January, 1917, for instance, when conditions were favorable for submarine work, only 12 per cent. were active, while 30 per cent. were in harbor, 38 per cent under repairs, and 20 per cent. "incapacitated." Submarine crews could not be sufficiently educated and trained for the work, and they looked with distrust upon the weapon. In the last few months it was difficult to get men for the work, as experienced seamen looked upon that kind of warfare as political stupidity.

Germany, as a naval power, ceased to exist on November 21, 1918. A minutely detailed program of submission, as laid down by Admiral Beatty, the commander of the British fleet, was carried out strictly according to plan. The German warships, strung out in a single column almost twenty miles long, appeared at the rendezvous at the appointed time and were led up to the Firth of Forth between twin columns of Allied ships, which overlapped the Germans at each end. That night the German ships were anchored in the Firth under guard as prisoners. A surrender on such

WHERE THE GERMAN WARSHIPS AND SUBMARINES
WERE SURRENDERED

a scale had no precedent. Altho the wonderful spectacle looked like a peace review and evoked little enthusiasm, a haze blotting out the horizon, American and British officer could scarcely credit the evidence of their eyes. Men, animated by the spirit of Lawrence's "Don't give up the ship," or Nelson's "England expects every man to do his duty," could not have conceived of such an ignominious fate as that to which the great German sea force was submitting. For the most part, officers and men were silent as they realized that they were witnessing the climax of Germany's downfall. Naval men seemed to feel a sort of contemptuous pity for a fallen giant who had refused to fight. The surrender automatically raised the United States to second position among naval powers.

The German ships that morning were sighted at 9.20 o'clock, following the light cruiser *Cardiff* as a British pilot. The Allied fleet, extending over a line fourteen miles long in the Firth of Forth, had begun to weigh anchor at one o'clock that morning. When the moon shone brilliantly out of a clear sky, battle-cruisers led the way, followed by dreadnoughts, Beatty's flagship, the *Queen Elizabeth* (*"Big Bessie"*), leading in the northern column. American warships fell into line behind Beatty's craft, balancing a British squadron similar in power on the opposite file. The rendezvous was approximately fifty miles distant. The ships gaged their speed so as to arrive at the appointed place at 8 o'clock. When dawn broke, the sea was covered with mist, which reduced the visibility to less than 8,000 yards. Eyes straining through the murky haze finally discerned off the starboard bow, the *Cardiff*, trailing an observation kite balloon. Close behind her were the first of the German ships, the great battle-cruiser *Seydlitz*, which was flying the flag of Commodore Togert. After her came four others of the same type, the *Derfflinger, Von der Tann, Hindenburg,* and *Moltke,* moving along three cable lengths apart. Immediately following them were nine dreadnoughts, the *Friedrich der Grosse,* flagship of Rear-Admiral von Reuter; the *Koenig Albert, Kaiser, Kronprinz Wilhelm, Kaiserin, Bayern, Markgraf, Prinzregent Luitpold,* and the *Grosser Kurfuerst.* Three miles astern of the battleships came seven light cruisers, the *Karlsruhe,* bearing the ensign of Commodore Harder; the *Frankfort, Burnberg, Brummer, Köln,* and *Bremen.* Then after another gap of three miles German destroyers came steaming in five columns abreast, with ten destroyers to a column.

Six miles separated the Allied columns. Squarely between them the *Cardiff* brought up her charges, all steaming at the stipulated speed of ten knots. As ordered, their guns were iu regular fore-and-aft positions. Until all the major ships had been swallowed up in the enveloping Allied columns of ships, the latter never for a moment relaxed their watch. Over the Germans circled a British dirigible, acting as eyes for the Allied ships, which, altho the fog had lifted, were still too distant for accurate observation.

When the leading German ship reached the western end of the flanking columns, Allied ships put about in squadrons, and, quickly reforming their lines, proceeded to escort the enemy into the Firth of Forth. By noon the last wisp of fog had disappeared, and a splendid view of the vast array of war-craft was obtained. Holding steadily to its course, the great fleet reached May Island at two o'clock, and the captive Germans were piloted to the anchorages assigned and then British ships from the southern column closed in as guards as the northern column steamed on to regular anchorages higher up the Firth. Inspection parties from the British fleet boarded the Germans to make sure that all conditions of the armistice had been observed. Part of the German crews were retained for maintenance work, but the remainder were returned to Germany.

Admiral von Reuter, of the German fleet, protested against the order of Admiral Beatty requiring the German flag to be hauled down after the ships came to anchorage. He pointed out that internment in a British harbor, under the terms of the armistice, was equivalent to internment in a neutral port, where, in accordance with precedent, flags should be allowed to remain hoisted. In his opinion, the order to strike the flag "was not in keeping with the idea of chivalry between two honorable opponents." Admiral Beatty, in reply, called attention to the fact that the armistice had merely suspended hostilities, that a state of war still existed between Germany and the Allies, and that, in such circumstances, "no enemy vessel could be permitted to fly its national ensign in British ports while under custody."

Scapa Flow, the place to which the German warships were taken after their formal surrender by the Germans off the Firth of Forth, east of Edinburgh, is an almost entirely landlocked bay in the Orkney Islands, north of Scotland—an ideal place for ships to ride at anchor without danger from high seas. In its longest distance Scapa Flow extends over 15, or perhaps 20 miles; in its breadth about 8 miles. On all sides it is surrounded by islands, alongside which most entrances to the bay are narrow. The Orkneys are 73 in number at low water, and 56 at high water. Only 29 of them are inhabited. They were visited by the Romans soon after the occupation of Britain, following the visits which Julius Cæsar made. The name Orkney is believed to be a corruption from the name bestowed upon the islands by the Romans. Irvings who lived in the Orkneys were the ancestors of Washington Irving.

One of the German accounts of the surrender described Great Britain as having "done its best to make an imposing demonstration in sending its most modern ships and most modern destroyers." The British had received the Germans "with the greatest mistrust, having cleared for action and had torpedoes ready in tubes." Then "a thick girdle of light and heavy fighting forces was rapidly thrown around us, and we were caught." The account went on:

"There were still some men who, with the officers, felt deeply this day of ignominy and humiliation and who, in impotent rage against the enemy and those responsible for this ignominy, did their duty to the fatherland to the last. Anchor was cast in the Firth of Forth, and the Inspection Commissions boarded the ships, led by superior officers. Polite, cold, scornful—thus did the British officers and men bear themselves toward us. We were not treated as if we were interned, but like prisoners. In the evening we lowered the flags which hitherto no British guns had been able to lower, and were not permitted to replace them—a superfluous wounding of our feelings on the part of the British. No place could be more God-forsaken than Scapa Flow." [24]

The day before this great spectacle King George made a visit to the American flagship *New York,* the royal ensign being hoisted to the mainmast as soon as he stept aboard. Seeing his standard snapping in the breeze above the Stars and Stripes, he exprest his appreciation. With the Prince

[24] Printed in The Hamburger *Nachrichten.*

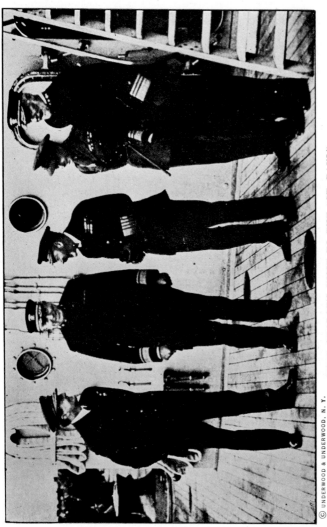

KING GEORGE'S VISIT TO THE "ST. PAUL"

Left to right—Admiral Beatty, Admiral Rodman, King George, Prince of Wales, Admiral Sims

VI.

of Wales, Admiral Beatty, and other members of the visiting party, King George was received by Admirals Rodman and Sims and other American officers. A tour of the ship was made between long lines of marines standing at attention, sailors manning the rails, and then the visitors went below to the Admiral's cabin, where they remained for half

SCAPA FLOW IN THE ORKNEY ISLES, WHERE THE GERMAN
SHIPS WERE INTERNED

Scapa Flow is a bay almost land-locked by islands, its dimensions some 15 by 8 miles. Here the ships were sunk six months afterward by the German admiral in command of them

an hour, formalities being abandoned. Admirals Beatty, Sims and Rodman were in high spirits. Good-natured bantering kept the whole party in fine humor. It was an interesting manifestation of the cordial and intimate relations that had cemented Great Britain and the United States. King George voiced the brotherly feeling between the two navies, with a suggestion that arrangements be made for joint maneuvers every year by the American and British fleets. His proposal was quickly and heartily seconded by the American officers. As the visit came to an end and the King entered the royal barge, an order came from an American officer on the bridge to sailors and marines, ''Three cheers for the King of England!'' These cheers brought an answering cheer from men on distant ships of the American squadron. Seventy German warships then lay in sulky silence in the Firth of Forth.

On November 20, a first batch of twenty German submarines were surrendered; more than eighty others remained to be handed over before the end of the week. After steaming some twenty miles across the North Sea from Harwich, five light-cruisers, headed by a British flagship, steamed toward the Dutch coast, followed by other ships in line. Under a shining moon great vessels were going forth to take part in the surrender of submarines. Just as a red sun appeared above the horizon the first submarine appeared in sight, and soon twenty were seen accompanied by two destroyers, which were to take the crews back to Germany after the transfer. All lay on the surface, their hatches open, their crews on deck. They were flying no flags, and their guns, in accordance with the terms of the surrender, were trained fore and aft. A bugle sounded, and all the British crews took up their stations ready for any possible treachery. Then, the leading British destroyer, in response to a signal, turned and led the way toward England, the submarines following. As each cruiser turned and steamed toward Harwich the surrender became an accomplished fact.

On June 21 German officers and sailors, forming the complements of the German ships at Scapa Flow, sank most of them. All the battleships and battle-cruisers, excepting the *Baden,* and numerous smaller craft were sunk, or went ashore in a half-sunken condition. Eighteen destroyers were beached by tugs, and four kept afloat, but the remainder went under. Crews took to boats and rowed toward shore; some swam ashore and other were rounded up. The sinking had been carefully arranged by the German officers. Explosives having been removed, the only means of destroying the fleet was by opening the seacocks. The ships went down slowly, with the German flag, which the crews had hoisted, showing at mastheads. Under the terms of the armistice—which did not permit British guards aboard—the crews had been composed entirely of Germans. What an hour before had been a stately fleet, riding calmly at anchor, was now an array of reeling and rocking battleships, whose doom

© UNDERWOOD & UNDERWOOD. N. Y.

AT THE SURRENDER OF THE GERMAN *U*-BOATS
The crew from a German boat is boarding a British destroyer off Harwich, to be taken to a German warship for transport to Germany

was written in their movements. Here a destroyer would disappear amid a cloud of steam, there a battleship would take her last plunge and disappear in a tumult of spray. One would settle down by the stern, another would heel over until only her keel showed above the water. The *Der-flinger, Hindenburg, Von der Tann, Moltke,* and the *Seyd-*

litz, the pride of the German navy, settled down beside each other. The last mentioned turned turtle, and her keel remained showing above the water.

The officers and men were taken aboard the *Victorious,* the deck of which soon became crowded with men and bundles. One officer went aboard wearing his sword and seemed to expect an impressive ceremony when handing it over. Responsibility for scuttling the ships belonged to Admiral von Reuter, who was made prisoner, and the remainder of the crews interned. The scuttling might prove to be not a bad thing in its results, since it removed a vexing question which had led to differences of opinion among the Allies, but the act itself was a violation of the laws of war. The terms of the armistice, signed November 11, 1918, provided that the German battleships, battle-cruisers and other vessels should be interned, "only caretakers being left on board," and that "no destruction of ships should be permitted before evacuation, surrender or restoration." Pending the conclusion of peace, they were to be held in neutral, or Allied, ports in the care of German crews. To this obligation Germany had bound itself by solemn pledges.

Germany had never had enough submarines, according to Captain Persius, who now said there were 126 in April, 1917, and 146 in October, 1917, while in February, 1918, the number had dropt to 136, and in June, 1918, to 113. As hardly more than 12 per cent. of these had been in active service at any one time, this strikingly confirmed Admiral Sims' earlier statement that not more than a dozen submarines had ever been cruising at one time in the North Atlantic sea-lanes. Tirpitz and his successors in the Admiralty had grossly deceived the German public about the extent and efficiency of their submarine campaign.

Rear-Admiral Hugh Rodman made an interesting statement of the work of the American fleet in the North Sea in cooperation with the British, just after our fleet of some 30 warships arrived in New York on December 27. He told how on arrival in British waters the fleet had found themselves able to coordinate and cooperate with the British. They adopted British signals and methods of communication with their plans of maneuver and tactics; took a share in the work of patrol, of search in protecting convoys, in mining and other duties. Sometimes the British were commanded by British, sometimes by Americans.

After the first operations, the Americans were assigned to one of the two places of honor and importance in the battle-line. As one of the two so-called fast wings "they would take station sometimes at the head, sometimes at the rear of the whole battleship force, when going into action." On one occasion they came within a few miles of cutting off from its base and engaging the German fleet, the disposition being such that the American battleship division "would have been in the van and led the way into action, had the enemy not avoided the action and taken refuge behind his defenses, as usual, before we could catch him." It was the policy "to go after the enemy every time he showed his nose outside of his ports; no matter when or where, whether in single ships, by divisions or his whole fleet; out we went, day or night, rain or shine (and there was mighty little daylight and much less shine in the winter months), blow high or blow low, and chased him back in his hole." Toward the end, he "rarely ventured more than a few miles from his base; but immediately we would start after him and back he would go in his hole, and haul his hole in after him." Every inducement was offered to the Germans to come out. Inferior forces were sent into the Heligoland Bight to induce him at attack; "valuable convoys were dispatched, apparently without protection, and other devices to tempt him out, but he would not come." Such expeditions, of course, were well guarded, "and we were ready to pounce on him with unseen forces."

New York paid tribute to the sailors and marines of the Sixth Battle Squadron of thirty warships which arrived in the harbor on December 26, from service in the North Sea. A large contingent of the men, accompanied by sailors from other warships that escorted the battle squadron across the seas, about 5,000 in all, took part in a parade down Broadway and Fifth Avenue. In the crowds that gathered were many relatives who caught glimpses of lads whom they had not seen for several months. Thousands braving the snow, intermittent rain and cold, nipping wind, stood along the water-front on Riverside Drive, and by the warmth of their welcome brought grins of appreciation to the faces of the homecoming veterans of the sea. Crowds had begun to gather at the Battery as early as 6 o'clock in the morning awaiting the arrival of the battle-fleet. The parade was reviewed in front of the Public Library by Secretary of the Navy Daniels and Henry T. Mayo, Commander-in-chief of the American fleet. The greatest enthusiasm came from friends and relative in the throngs that lined the streets. Cigarets, fruit and candy were tossed to the marchers from sidewalks and windows. A battle that was never fought had won the war.

Many tried to form an appreciation of what Allied navies did to save the world during the four war years. Fundamental and magnificent had been that watch in the North Sea, hour after hour, day following day, through storm and sunshine, without halt or rest, to fight a battle that was never fought by that sixty-five mile column of ships. Admiral Rodman made it clear how compelling and controlling was the threat that never came to action, yet upon which, of necessity was based the whole battle of tactics of the Allied fleets, indeed the whole grand strategy at sea. The relation of sea-power to history, to the safety of Democracy, spoke in those grim fortresses of the deep that held the seas against the Germans. But Admiral Mahan was no longer living to see his contention once more brilliantly demonstrated.[25]

[25] Principal Sources: The *Tribune,* The *Times,* The *Evening Post,* New York; The *Tageblatt* (Berlin), The Hamburger *Nachrichten,* Associated Press dispatches.

V

ALSACE-LORRAINE RECOVERED, BELGIUM EVACUATED AND THE RHINE VALLEY OCCUPIED BY THE ENTENTE

November 11, 1918—December 16, 1918

WHEN the Germans capitulated on November 11, Foch as has already been stated elsewhere, had had the stage set and the orders given for a drive on Metz a few days later along both sides of the Moselle. His operations on November 9 and 10 had been preliminary to this major attack, which had had excellent chances of success. The Franco-American advance to Sedan had cut the German supply-line, so that the German command no longer had a way in which to get troops eastward to save Metz. After the Metz drive Foch expected to launch another drive in the south toward Mulhausen, in Alsace, for which preparations had also been made. On this frontier was Castelnau, hero of the Grand Couronné battle of 1914, and commander of the French offensive in Champagne in the autumn of 1915. Foch had also planned attacks by French and English troops in the west and north, his ultimate object being to drive out of France the German army and to bottle it up with only Liége as a gateway of escape.

But without these campaigns the victory was complete. Four months after German hosts had gravely menaced not only Paris but the Channel coast, and British communications, the Allies were marching toward German cities on the Rhine, toward the Belgian capital, Constantinople, Bucharest, Sofia, and Trieste, and had taken possession of the great German High Seas Fleet as a pledge of peace. French troops were soon to enter Metz, and Strassburg, the British to move across the Rhine Province into Cologne, British naval forces to enter Constantinople, Americans to march down the Moselle and cross the Rhine from Coblenz to Ehrenbreitstein.

When fighting ceased on November 11, the most advanced section on the Western Front was held at Thann in Alsace by a French army under Castelnau, including American troops, among whom were the Fifteenth New York Infantry, a negro regiment, and some Senegalese French troops. On November 11 the whole valley about Thann was bedecked with French, American and British flags, and merry with clanging of bells, which for four years had been rung only for the dead. Elsewhere all through recovered Alsace the joy of the people was contagious and profoundly impressive. French was spoken everywhere. All traces of Teutonic occupation had vanished. One looked in vain for even a tradesman's sign in German. If Alsace had not been truly French, no such transformation would have been possible. From the tower of the cathedral of Thann floated the Tricolor, while men below, outside the edifice, celebrated the victory. From miles around people had gathered inside to pray and listen to M. le Curé, who, speaking in the local patois, told how the God of battle had blessed France and the Allies because their cause had been that of justice and liberty. After the service the curé was unable to make his way back to the altar, so dense was the crowd of officers, peasants, and American soldiers who thronged nave and transept and packed the choir.

The reoccupation of Alsace-Lorraine was accomplished with growing enthusiasm as forces penetrated farther east toward the Rhine. Near the old German frontier the rejoicing became greatest and the manifestations most picturesque. After Château-Salins, Metz, and Sarrebourg in Lorraine and Mulhouse in Alsace had been reached, Colmar and Zabern opened their arms and poured out their hearts to their "liberators" with an ardor that exceeded the earlier welcomes. The smallest villages and rural districts showed how their loyalty to the French had been deepened, rather than diminished, by long separation. In Zabern streets were planted on both sides with evergreens. More bunting was flying than the entire region was supposed to possess after four years of dearth in cloth of all sorts. Zabern on the border of Alsace and Lorraine was tranquil and peaceful enough to merit its name of the "town of roses."

AT THE STRASBOURG CELEBRATION

Left to right—Marshal Joffre, Marshal Foch, General Humbert, Field-Marshal
Sir Douglas Haig, General Pershing, Marshal Pétain

VI.

FROM THE ARMISTICE TO THE CONFERENCE

Some of the flags that Alsatians put out had been made from strips of calico; others from silk that dated from the Second Empire and had now been brought from hiding-places where it evaded the Germans for nearly fifty years. In this region of Alsace, where German was supposed to be not only the principal but almost the only tongue spoken, French officers and men were everywhere treated to the joyous surprize of being saluted in French. It was not Parisian in its accent, but quite understandable, and it was uttered with a sincerity that provoked tears. Strassburg, the fine Alsatian capital became one fluttering mass of red, white, and blue. When automobiles arrived with officers in advance of troops, the officers were taken out and carried in triumph into the city. Troops followed arm in arm with civilians in national costume. In the evening, under torch-light, were seen long lines of horizon blue soldiers interspersed with men and women in gay Alsatian colors, ribbons stretching from curb to curb, men and women singing, dancing, and seemingly oblivious to the sharp cold. Next day the great clock was set to French time, so that it might beat in unison with clocks in the capital of France. The de-Germanization of the town had for its first phase a frantic renaming of business houses. Every few yards was soon seen a white cotton band with a French name on it hastily draped over some German name or some German trade-mark. One now read of the *"Café de Paris"* and the *"Restaurant de la Marne,"* while houses had in their windows cards on which was written, "A French house dating from before 1870."

No words could picture the first entrance of French troops into Mulhouse, nor express the wild joy of the people who crowded the streets to applaud their liberators. Flowers, tobacco, and cockades were thrown to soldiers as they marched. French troops had also occupied the Gravelotte forts south of Metz, the great iron mines centering at Briey, and Altkirch. It might be some time, however, before smoke would again arise from the Briey blast furnaces and betoken the forging of plowshares where for two years the Germans had made swords. Fifteen hundred civilians greeted the troops at Briey. Outwardly Briey showed few indications of the war, buildings being intact, but there were German signs everywhere, pointing to ammunition-dumps and headquarters.

The entrance of Pétain into Metz, Castelnau into Colmar, and Fayolle and Gouraud into Strassburg, the hardly less moving return of Hirschauer to his native city of Mulhouse at the head of a French army, formed ceremonies marking the restitution to France of her "lost provinces," and were necessarily military in character. When the entry into Metz occurred on November 18, it marked the return to France of a city that had always been French, but was

FRENCH OFFICIAL PHOTO.

MARSHAL PÉTAIN IN METZ

Pétain is the man on the white horse and is watching a march pass. In this square, but not shown in the picture, is a statue of Marshal Ney

torn from France under a German argument that possession of it was necessary to the furtherance of German military purposes. Tours, Orléans. and Paris itself were not more French than Metz. From 1562 it had been a part of French national soil, the countryside in a wide circle inhabited then as now by French-speaking people. Because it was a fortress guarding the road into the heart of France the Germans in 1871 had taken it, but thousands of its inhabitants had emigrated to France, some of whom opened family tombs in order that the bones of their ancestors might be taken away to rest in French soil. Metz and Thionville under the Germans had become the most intensively fortified places in Europe, perfect symbols of German aggression and the Prussian doctrine of force.

On the forts of Metz, crowning the circle of hills above the city, French flags now came out. Foch and Pétain had brought the tricolor back to the land of Ney and the Kellermanns, of Rapp and Kléber, a land once called "the nursery of French generals." French flags on the cathedral were more than signals that "the day of glory had arrived;" they were final evidence that mere settlements by the sword after all may be of brief duration. The German Empire in its might had trampled on the liberties of a few hundred thousand people. Its rulers had mocked at the claims of right and justice, its soldiers had maintained frontiers with the sword, and now the German Empire had fallen, the Prussian sword was broken, and down the Verdun road into Metz marched the armies of France and the United States. When Pétain, commander-in-chief of the French armies, made his formal entry, he appeared for the first time as a Marshal of France, in what proved to be one of the most picturesque demonstrations ever carried out in Lorraine.

From early morning all roads leading to Metz were crowded with Lorrainers. People long unaccustomed to hearing any other tongue than German, had begun many days before to brush up their French in preparation for the occasion. The majority probably had a perfect acquaintance with no other tongue than German, but little of that language was heard in the streets of Metz that day. Other things German disappeared, including statues of German rulers. William I on horseback was toppled off his pedestal to the ground, while Frederick III, who for long years had pointed a menacing finger at France from the pedestal upon which he stood, was also brought down with a rope thrown around his neck. On the façade of the cathedral one saw William II in chains. Years before Germans had taken from a statue of the Prophet Daniel its head and had substituted for it the Kaiser's own head. William now wore chains on that cathedral front, and from his piously raised hands hung a placard which read "*Sic transit gloria mundi.''* No Americans appeared in the triumphal march into Metz, because a ceremony which meant so much to France was left exclusively to the French. From a tower at the portal, however, the Stars and Stripes were flying, and fifty or more Americans who came to see the ceremony were received as welcome guests. It would have been untrue to say that all Metz was gay. Some Germans still remained there, and tried to put a good countenance on the situation. They mingled with throngs out of doors, but their faces were mostly seen in open windows, from which they peered with curiosity and interest. Germans in the streets were not molested.

When Marshal Pétain appeared on the Esplanade mounted on a fine white charger, followed by his entire staff with a few American and British officers attached, a shout went up that drowned the whirr of a dozen or more airplanes flying overhead. Crowds surged forward, breaking the line of guards in places to get a glimpse of the victorious commander. He advanced and took up position in front of the statue of Ney to review the troops. In the march past, pretty Lorraine girls brought a blush to the cheek of many a poilu by giving them unexpected embraces. Aged women who had known Metz before it was German, threw kisses to poilus and cried out thanks from open windows along the line. Young girls and children wore the ancient Lorraine costume, with frilled head-dress and bright petticoats. Streets and cafés were thronged with French officers and soldiers, who paid for their food and drink in francs in houses where only marks had been known for nearly fifty years, and were welcomed everywhere. It was a remarkable fact that in the whole city not a single hostile act occurred. German soldiers in Metz, or men who had been German soldiers and still wore the gray uniform, walked arm in arm with poilus in horizon blue, the French tricolor upon their breasts. They were Lorrainers of French blood who had been forced into the German army and at last had escaped, declaiming with flashing eyes against *"les Cochons,"* who made them fight their own flesh and blood.

Metz on December 8 had another great ceremonious occasion when it received President Poincaré and representatives of every branch of the French Government. Martial music was heard as it had been heard every day since the entrance of Pétain's army. In a sense the visit of Poincaré meant more than the formal military occupation had meant. People understood it as the real official French entry. A vast throng continually cheered Poincaré, Clémenceau, Joffre, Pétain, Haig, and Pershing, all of whom were in the official party. A notable feature was the formal presentation to Pétain of his baton as a Marshal of France, which evoked tremendous cheers. Clémenceau gave Pétain the accolade. During the review American troops had the honor of leading the line. The regiment marched by in columns of eight, the Star Spangled Banner wildly cheered. At the city hall Clémenceau handed to the Mayor the keys to the city, which the Germans had failed to get when they captured it in 1870, and which had ever since been preserved by a descendant of one of the defenders.

Marshal Pétain was attended by Castelnau, Fayolle, and Gouraud as he drove through Strassburg a few days after his entry into Metz. He was followed by the flower of the French army. Walter Duranty [26] motored 600 kilometers from Brussels to see the pageant. The impressive sincerity of the crowds proved to him beyond doubt that the heart of Alsace still beat true to France. After the generals in automobiles followed picked battalions of the Colonial Army, led by Zouaves with red shoulder-straps, flanked on either side by a long file of girls in Alsatian costume. Then came a little band of veterans of the war of 1870. The pageant was a fine demonstration of the military power that had borne the brunt of war, upheld the Allies in defeat, and had the lion's share in the final campaign to victory. With snappy marching-step, poilus swung along, blue wave after blue wave for a full hour—infantry, cavalry, and artillery, their physique as fine as their equipment. All along the route crowds cheered them to the echo. In Brussels the occasion had been the triumph of King Albert; in Strassburg it was the poilus' triumph.

Pétain was greeted warmly as he passed in an open automobile, followed by cars carrying the other generals.

[26] Correspondent of The *Times* (New York).

After the military review, Alsatian societies went through the streets, the chilly air ringing with sounds until a late hour that night. It was recalled how, on September 28, 1870, Strassburgers had emerged from cellars and caves where they had sought refuge from Prussian shells, to see a white rag flying from the ruined tower of the cathedral. For seven weeks they had suffered every misery of a city under siege. To their prayers for milk for children the Prussian high commander had sent back the taunting reply,

GENERAL DE CASTELNAU ENTERING COLMAR IN ALSACE

"Surrender, and then you can have milk for your babies." To their plea that besiegers should turn guns upon fortifications and not on churches and houses, the Germans, then the same barbarians that they had been in Belgium and Northern France, answered with a storm of shells until scarcely a building in the city escaped injury from bombardment. When Pétain entered, the city was no longer Strassburg, but *Strasbourg*. It had taken forty-seven years to make that change in the spelling of the name. More than

50,000 Alsatians in that time had given up their homes rather than suffer under Prussian lordship. Their descendants had now come back, and peasants were flocking in from the Vosges and the Rhine plains, men in somber black, with long hidden French flags on their breasts, streamers of tricolors on their hats, and women with black bow head-dresses, manifold and multi-colored petticoats.

Strasbourg's welcome to Poincaré, Clémenceau, and other official representatives of the French Government took place on December 9. Crowds filled gayly beflagged streets and waves of enthusiastic cheers passed along the thoroughfare as the veteran soldiers of France were reviewed. A drizzling rain failed to dampen the enthusiasm of throngs, who cheered wildly whenever Poincaré or his colleagues appeared. Pershing and Mr. Sharp, the American Ambassador, were there, and received cries of *"Vive l'Amérique!"* while Haig was welcomed by cheers for Great Britain. The ceremonies began when Poincaré went to the monument of Desaix, the general who defended the passage of the Rhine against the Austrians in 1794, and placed a wreath before it. The whole square was aflutter with flags and bunting, while everybody carried French flags or wore Alsatian colors. Later the official party went to the cathedral, where *Te Deums* were sung. From there Poincaré went to the City Hall, and received the keys of the city. In the afternoon came a review of troops. The French officials then went to Colmar, where similar ceremonies followed, and next day went to Mulhouse.

On November 12 German troops began to evacuate France and Belgium. They had left Namur by November 16, and the city soon slipt back into the groove it occupied before the war. Namur had fared better than towns nearer the fighting line. The forts still remained about as they were after the bombardment in the first month of the war. Only the railway-station and some neighboring buildings had suffered from bombing. Otherwise the town was practically unchanged. As soon as the Germans left Namur, Brussels had a couple of days of wild celebration, people dancing and singing through the streets all night. When the British arrived there was a renewal of the celebration. Residents told how the Germans had put English prisoners to work in places that might become military objectives to British bombers, such as the railway-station, which was provided with dugouts only sufficient to protect the German soldiers stationed there. As a result, a considerable number of British had been killed by their own comrades. In the last days of the occupation, marked depression prevailed among the German troops because British propaganda dropt from

GERMAN TROOPS ARRIVING HOME

airplanes and eagerly read, had convinced them of Allied victories and German failures, and especially of the failure of the submarine campaign.

By November 22 German soldiers were anxiously marching from battle-fronts to trains for Berlin, in order to "see the revolution," seizing railway-trains formerly used to convey troops to different parts of the front, and forcing engineers to take them to the capital. Roofs, platforms, and even brake rods became loaded with soldiers, many of whom were injured when trains passed through tunnels. There was a good deal of rejoicing among them over the war's end. Shouts of "Long live the Republic!" and "Peace forever!" were what civilians got in return for cheers. The largest German force marching through the Rhine Province was the army under General von Hutier, consisting of 500,000 men and 150,000 horses. At night many regiments marched with music and song, carrying Chinese lanterns with which people had provided them.

On the Meuse, within a few days after the signing of the armistice, were seen many barges which as pleasure boats in peace time, traversed the river regularly. Down stream to Namur from Huy now went these boats crowded with liberated prisoners—French, British, and Italian—who were going to Namur to board trains on their homeward way. Thousands of others were seen tramping along roads, back from the German lines, in small groups, keeping company in ties of comradeship made on the way, sharing bread and having common memories of misery. Going outward and westward from Namur, were other thousands, pushing on to some goal of the heart's desire, with packs on their shoulders pressing hard, their tired feet stumbling over stones and ruts, bound for Manchester, Shropshire, Padua, Mantua, Poitiers and Toulouse. One could seldom tell by their clothes to what country they belonged, for many were in German prison-camp uniforms, with long black coats and round black caps, or in German tunics such as had been served out to them after six months of captivity. French and Italian soldiers might wear British khaki, British soldiers odd garments representing other nations, picked up on the way, or doled out to them in German camps. Some still wore the clothes they had been taken in long before, now stained and tattered after months of captivity, or one might meet Cossacks in gray Astrakhan caps and long-waisted coats above heavy boots, Chasseurs Alpins in blue bonnets and knickerbockers, or Belgians in "slacks" and tasseled caps. Each had a story to tell which fitted into the grim drama of this war. "We had a bad time," said one of them. "They starved us so that we had to stew nettles and mangel-wurzels to keep ourselves alive, and many of us died. They worked us hard to the end, and when we could not work they lashed us." Two men said they had been harnessed to carts and made to drag a transport during the German retreat.

Along roadsides were scattered many non-human things which told of the tragedy of an empire and the fall of great ambitions—material of war that had been left behind by the Germans according to the terms of the armistice. Hundreds of German guns, limbers, ambulances, airplanes and transport wagons could be seen. In a field might be found a German aerodrome, or an airplane factory, with enormous hangars built in brick, and big work-shops, all abandoned to the British. Airplane wings lay piled up with Iron Crosses painted on them, or complete airplanes were standing as if ready for flight as pilots left them. Belgian children were playing with long-muzzled anti-aircraft guns elaborately camouflaged, or peeping innocently into the barrels of long-range "heavies." All the way to Namur were trails of derelict guns and transports abandoned in flight. Many wagons and motor-trucks were overturned, some of them burned, others smashed; but even when they stood whole and unbroken, they had a sorry look, for the German transport had become worn out and had been patched up in a makeshift way.[27]

GEN. SIR WILLIAM ROBERTSON
Robertson commanded the British Army of Occupation on the Rhine

German newspapers published long descriptions of how their vanquished armies were coming home in good order, with the utmost speed. Two armies on November 23 were marching through Cologne, the city lavishly decked for the occasion, the troops welcomed with enthusiasm by crowds,

[27] Cable dispatch from Philip Gibbs to The *Times* (New York).

which remained in the streets from early morning till midnight, when the march through the city was halted. Infantrymen were gaily decked with flowers. Cavalrymen went along singing. Horses, cannon and wagons were decorated with evergreens. In Cologne and most other places the old German flag did not wave to greet the home-coming warriors, Soldiers' and Workers' Councils having given orders that it must not be displayed. The Dusseldorf Council issued an order that "criminal imperialism has so greatly dishonored the Prussian and German colors that they are now completely inappropriate for worthily greeting returning soldiers." When the German flag was run up on the Town Hall in Cologne, the Council hauled it down. Newspapers in an issue which contained a statement by Hindenburg that the German Army was not in condition to face the French, printed pathetically extravagant eulogies of the German Army. "The spirit of 1914 still lives in these men," said the Cologne *Gazette*. "The army we see to-day has not lost the struggle." "Greet our Unbeaten Army," was a headline that appeared in many papers.[28]

American forces had the task of demolishing barriers which guarded the old German front east of Verdun. These last included pillars of reinforced concrete stretching along the front for two miles, the pillars three feet apart across roads and fifty feet apart across the country, and connected by 2-inch cables. Engineers placed a few blasts of dynamite under each pillar, and so made the roads passable. After that gangs working in relays toiled to dig up immense steel rails and concrete foundations six feet underground, the rails extending five feet above the ground, with concrete poured around them. Each pillar was five feet square and stood eight feet above the ground. The pillars apparently had been constructed a year or more before, as each was camouflaged by reeds growing in nearby swamps, the concrete scarcely noticeable from the distance. At Mars-la-Tour, just at the edge of the village, Americans encountered barriers of tanks, some of which were half completed. A few blasts of dynamite put them out of commission. At Etain the Germans had barriers made of logs chained together on

[28] Cable dispatch from George Renwick to The *Times* (New York).

four wheels, the logs movable like a gate. On these barriers the Germans had installed ingenious devices to remove wheels from beneath logs, which they would drop across the road at the main entrance into Etain. This log barrier was just at the western entrance, the logs acting as a check in the event that mines failed to destroy a bridge.

In the American march to the Rhine, complicated problems arose. Supplies, guns and ammunition for more than 200,000 men had to be moved along three main roads. The army started on a fifty-three mile front, the front growing

THE MAIN STREET IN MARS-LA-TOUR
Mars-la-Tour was the scene of an important battle during the Franco-Prussian War. It lies fourteen miles southwest of Metz

narrow slightly as the troops moved forward. Few traces of war were seen. Trenches, barbed wire, shell-holes and leveled towns were absent; unused fields, dirty streets, looted houses, and a scarcity of civilians were about all the signs one saw of the four years' curse that had rested upon these villages and open-farm fields. Men in fighting trim went along roads with measured step, patrols in front, while lumbering cannon, ammunition trains and ambulances groaned over roadways. It looked like war, but was not war. What made the march exciting was not the marching itself, but the towns reached and what the troops saw there, the celebrations, the tears of joy of the delivered French people, the cries of little children, the prayers of aged priests. Of all that one saw in Montmédy, the most striking was the constant stream of released prisoners and civilians coming back from Germany. Just outside of Montmédy a company of the 6th Marines was seen marching to the tune of a mouth organ played by a six-foot-two soldier from Brooklyn. When Pershing's forces halted on the Longwy-Briey line, they had completed the first stage of a march from the Meuse over an historic route leading through Luxemburg and down the Moselle to the Rhine at Coblenz.

Systematic destruction of machinery had taken place in the Briey Valley. Stocks of iron ore and steel had been requisitioned and officers and men had organized a destruction of plants. German manufacturers had come and picked out certain pieces of machinery which they wanted in their own plants and shipped them to Germany. The demolition of blast-furnaces, steam-engines, boilers, tools, gearings and electric-lighting fixtures, not connected with the actual working of the mines, followed, employees of the plants being compelled to aid in the devastation. In the meantime the exploitation of mines had been kept in full swing. Prisoners to the number of 15,000 had been put to work with hardly any rest and under terrible discipline until the output of the mines became larger than in peace times, and so enabled the Central Powers to hold out. The Germans had concentrated there some 500 heavy guns and 7,000 machine-guns for defense.

In the minds and hearts of the 200,000 men who formed the American Army of Occupation, two never-to-be-forgotten days were the first forty-eight hours of their march toward Germany. It yet remained for them to cross the German frontier and reach the valley of the Rhine, but those first days were such as would be remembered longest, because our men then had the experience of marching across country and up roads, foot-free, for fifteen kilometers, after having previously had to fight for days for the privilege of going half a mile. What delighted them most was to go ahead without fighting over roads that led into vain, boastful, fallen Prussia. Moreover, they had the great joy of freeing innocent women and children, old men and invalids, from years of bondage; the joy of having little children sit upon their knees and laugh happily over their first good meal in weary months, and the joy of welcoming back comrades who had been captured by the enemy. Such joys were sweet, and had never before been known. Men realized what their country meant when they saw their own flag waving aloft with the flags of France and Belgium.

Any doughboy would have said that the thing which gave him most pride was the home-made American flags he saw. Probably none among those women of France and Belgium. makers of these flags, had ever heard of Betsy Ross. They had never known that one of the heroines of American history almost a hundred and fifty years before, had won fame by doing just what they had been doing. Here were many Betsy Rosses in the restored lands of France and Belgium. And at the same time they had their own flags, for they had kept them hidden for four years, in cellars and chimney clefts, in holes, buried in gardens wrapt in silk, against the return of a great new day. It was only two or three months since they had received word that Americans were fighting their way toward them. Every now and then they had seen an American prisoner, an American wounded soldier, and had heard Germans talk of American "swine." Then they began secretly to make American flags against the coming of the day of their deliverance. From school books they got the design, and then sacrificed their finery lovingly, as Betsy Ross had sacrificed hers. The sewing went on, and when the great day came, by the side of French flags in French towns, and Belgian flags in Belgian towns, they flew their home-made Stars and Stripes. In a parade in America these rather crude flags might have aroused a smile, but flown from house-tops and churches in northern France and southern Belgium, they were solemn emblems that told the story of America in the war. Some of the stripes were lacking, and there never were stars enough, but stripes were there and stars were there, and they were lovely things for an American to look upon.

By November 21, the progress of the American Third

Army [29] across Luxemburg had taken on the nature of a triumphal procession, through villages filled with cheering people, down streets lined with American flags. On the right, in Lorraine, the popular joy at sight of Americans knew no bounds. Crossing the border, the army passed Petange; then Sanem, Eschau, Budersburg, and in Lorraine went ten kilometers beyond Fontoy. The feature of the day was the reception of Americans in Luxemburg, the duchy a blaze of color with its own red, white and blue and Stars and Stripes. Luxemburgers put out the best they had to eat. Luxemburg that day was all American. People said they were glad the Germans had gone, hoped they would never come back, and added profuse assurances that American faces looked good to them. Twenty-four hours before, the Grand Duchess had seen long columns of gray-clad German soldiers depart for their own country after an occupation of her country for more than four years. Now the American Army controlled every road, city and village in Luxemburg. It was impossible to doubt the sincerity of the welcome. The Grand Duchess and members of her Cabinet exprest gratification that Americans had come to take the places of those whom they had been forced to tolerate.

Popular approval found expression in a great demonstration when the people sighted General Pershing, and again when the dusty column of American soldiers moved through the streets. Prior to the entry of the troops Pershing, in a proclamation, had assured the public that the American Army would remain only as long as was necessary, and while it was in Luxemburg would conduct itself in conformity with the civil law. The proclamation was distributed among troops as well as among the population. The Grand Duchess, a slightly built little woman, was seen attired in a simple silk dress, and appeared even younger than her twenty-three years. She had no doubt of the honest and helpful intentions of the Americans, and repeatedly exprest her gratitude.

Pershing entered Luxemburg ahead of his troops, greeted by thousands of cheering Luxemburgers, with the blowing

[29] Cable dispatch from Edwin L. James to The *Times* (New York).

of sirens and the ringing of church- and school-bells. School children tossed flowers in the pathway, and to each soldier presented a bouquet of chrysanthemums. Almost every building flew the Luxemburg flag, with here and there an American banner, and every once in a while the picture of President Wilson could be seen always coupled with that of Marshal Foch. Some forty societies participated in the parade. When Pershing and the Grand Duchess stood on the balcony of the Grand Ducal Palace, they saw in the

GRAVE OF A GERMAN OFFICER AT MARS-LA-TOUR

square below the duchy's whole army, 300 strong. While the 18th United States Infantry passed, squares and streets were filled with a cheering crowd. After Pershing's car reached the palace, he greeted cordially the frightened little Duchess.

Among many rumors that had been afloat just before the Americans arrived, was one that the people of the country wanted the Duchess to abdicate; another that they wanted her to stay, while some wanted the Duchy annexed to France or Belgium, and others to have it stay where it was. News of the revolution in Germany had come thick and fast across the border, and excitement was intense. Crowds had gone through the streets shouting "Abdicate! Abdicate!" But when Pershing appeared with the Duchess cheers were heard for her and cheers for him. All discontent and ill-humor seemed to vanish as the Stars and Stripes passed through. The celebration continued into the early hours of the next day, but there was no violence. Next morning an incipient revolution seemed to be "all off." Luxemburg was effusive in its welcome. The Americans' passage was, however, an incident only in the march to the Rhine that had now set in.[30]

The German frontier was crossed from Luxemburg at several places on November 23, by American Signal Corps units and ambulance workers, who now entered Rhenish Prussia. The front lines of the American Army rested along the Luxemburg-German border on the Sauer and thence along the Moselle. Germans apparently had been withdrawing according to schedule, everywhere singing and whistling as they marched. The American Army itself crossed the Sauer and Moselle on December 1, spread out on a front of ninety kilometers. The final part of their trip to the Rhine was begun in cold, clear weather, the front line held by the First, Second, Third and Thirty-second Divisions, moving in battle order with all arms. Trèves was the first important city occupied. Here Pershing's advance headquarters were established. The people received the Americans with no outward sign of hostility, but as if hardly able to believe this visible proof of German defeat. In the advance into Germany there had not been a clash. Towns and villages were occupied quietly and methodically, with guards stationed everywhere and the Americans taking every precaution. Germans simply stood in doorways and watched them pass without a word to one another. The country seemed wrapt in depression. No trace of a German army in force was seen.

On December 2, after a first night's sleep on German soil, American troops were ready at dawn to resume their march toward the Rhine. Once across that river they were

[30] Luxemburg dispatch from Edwin L. James to The *Times* (New York).

to take up a line some sixty miles long, with an arc of a circle extending eastward and having Coblenz as the center, the radius eighteen miles in length. This circle, pivoting upon Coblenz, protected one of the bridgeheads which the Germans had conceded in the armistice. The Americans were traveling from seven to nine miles each marching day, with a day or two of rest at intervals. A policy of moderation was adopted toward the German people. In his first proclamation, Pershing told them we were not making war on civilians, and that they would be disturbed as little as possible, so long as they did not disturb the American soldiers. Leniency, however, was predicated on good behavior. No abuses of kindness could be overlooked. Shops were allowed to be kept open, restaurants to do business, street cars to run, newspapers to be issued. In other words, there was to be no interference with the ordinary life of the German city.

Germans soon became less sullen toward the Americans, and often stopt them on the street to say they had relatives living in the United States. Within a few days an abnormally large proportion of the people seemed to have relatives in the United States, and the number increased hourly. Whenever one saw a doughboy in an idle moment, one was apt to see a group of little children about him talking German. Especially interesting was the entry of the Thirty-Second Division into the zone north of Trèves, many being from Michigan and Wisconsin and speaking German. From this region many emigrants had gone to America. In one town five out of eight families questioned said they had relatives in the United States. One of the Americans who was a captain, on reaching a town in this region, found his uncle was the Mayor. When asked why the Americans had come into the war, the Americans usually replied that it was to rid the world of Prussian militarism. Economic conditions were better than had been supposed. As one looked at lovely vineyards that covered hillsides, one recalled in contrast the barren and ravaged hillsides of the right bank of the Meuse, north of Verdun. The sight of spick and span Saarburg, recalled the ruins of Grandpré. For every German village in excellent condition one thought of some fearful ruin in France. Trèves, in all its unharmed prosperity, brought back a memory of Reims.

Coblenz had passed under complete military control by December 8, the municipal authorities cooperating with the Americans. At the western ends of bridges that here cross the Rhine, American sentries were posted, German soldiers doing duty at the eastern ends. American sentries could see from these bridges the lights of the great fortress of Ehrenbreitstein on its rocky promontory across and 400 feet above the river. Several regiments of German soldiers were still quartered there. Four bridges here spanned the Rhine, two in the city, one north and another south of it. As the Americans marched into the city, the last division of the German Army had got only a few kilometers beyond the Rhine, and was moving in orderly fashion, but with the spirit of a holiday rather than that of a defeated army. Almost every man had a rosette or a sprig of green in his cap. Many trucks and wagons had on top of them quantities of Christmas greens. In two days a city of 90,000, finding that the Americans were not going to be severe, so warmed up socially that Americans were treated as if they were friends rather than enemies. One afternoon an American party took tea at a fashionable hotel, then dined at another, attended the opera "Mignon" in the evening, and, when the opera was over, spent an hour at a large café, where an excellent orchestra played American tunes, including "Dixie." Defeat, however, had not yet subdued the Germans. While they regretted the sinking of the *Lusitania*, this was not because the act had been inhuman, but because it was a mistaken policy and had brought America into the war. Nor were the Germans sorry for the war. Many were sorry that the war had stopt, but it was only because they believed Germany might eventually have won.

On December 16 the American Army reached its final objective, on an arc of thirty kilometers' radius, from the Coblenz bridgehead. The French had taken over a considerable part of the same sector. When American infantry reached their last destination the Third Corps, First, Second and Thirty-Second Divisions were across the river, the

Fourth and Seventh Corps remaining on the west bank. Headquarters were set up at Coblenz with the Second Army, in support of the army of occupation, established at Luxemburg. It had been a business-like operation, this march of 200 miles in a month with the occupation of some 5,000 square miles of German territory having about a million population. All had been done without friction with the Germans, who seemed to appreciate the treatment they received, which was represented as "in a class by itself." On all sides one heard Germans say how glad they were that the American Army had come into their territory. The local authorities were allowed to conduct their civil affairs under American supervision, a policy which was expected to make a minimum of interference so long as things ran smoothly.[31] The Forty-second Division established headquarters at Ahrweiler. The Third passing through Coblenz, evoked praise for the fine appearance of the men and wagons, and especially the mounted 76th Field Artillery with their gray horses. The Thirty-second Division had come into position, and the Third was marching northward to Berncastel. The Eighty-ninth was near Bitung, and the Ninetieth near Wittlich. Soon all the American troops had fitted into their permanent stations and settled down to garrison duty.

On December 13, the same day on which the French entered Mainz, the first Americans crossed the Rhine. Three French divisions were sent out to take the southern part of the American sector on the east bank of the river, and one American division, the Third, composed of Regulars, was sent south to take over part of the French bridgehead at Mainz. The First, Second and Thirty-second American divisions comprised the force which crossed the river. It was raining at the time and just getting light when the troops started to cross, the American flag waving and bands playing. German people came out to see this first crossing of the Rhine by hostile troops in more than a century. The crest of the once formidable Ehrenbreitstein looked down in impotence on men in khaki who silently went their way. The area to be occupied across the river,

[31] Cable dispatch from Edwin L. James to The *Times* (New York).

in the form of a semicircle, had a thirty-kilometer radius. Outside of it was a ring ten kilometers wide, a neutral zone policed by Germans not in the military force.

Fawning upon the Americans took many forms. Americans had only to enter a café to get the best table and the best attention without asking for it, or really wanting it. Forthwith the orchestra would play American tunes. Invitations were given to dinner. It was frequently insisted that American people were not really angry with the German people; the President did not like Wilhelm or Tirpitz, but then neither did the Germans like them now. President

COURTESY OF THE MARINE CORPS RECRUITING PUBLICITY BUREAU.

MARINE PATROL-BOAT ON THE RHINE AT EHRENBREITSTEIN

Wilson never had had anything against the German people. All of which showed how the German people had not yet realized the meaning of the words "reparation" and "restoration." The German, as seen in war, was a curious, thickheaded person. In war he could not be a gentleman, but he had an inextinguishable faith in the virtue of an appeal made by him to the gentlemanly instincts of others, hoping to secure more generous consideration for himself than he had ever dreamed of giving others. The German at war, having power, was brutal and merciless; when beaten, he began to be obsequious.

In Belgium and the invaded districts of France the world had seen the German in his first mood. Allied soldiers in the Rhine valley were now seeing him in his second. His politeness and humility took the form of an appeal to the magnanimity of his conquerors, but there was no repentance, no regret, no acknowledgment of German wrong-doing. While he called on Heaven to witness and pity his misfortunes, he ignored the four years of martyrdom which he had inflicted on Belgium and northern France. What he was most loth to think of was reparation. He wanted to be let off and to forget his crimes. To his mind the German Army had done no wrong in ravaging Belgium and tearing out the heart of northern France. Still as unrepentant as he was in August, 1914, his chief thought was to escape the consequences of his wrong-doing, and he was now trying to make America his agent in bringing about his escape. His pride was still of a kind not humbled; his arrogance not cured. Nor could it be until his pocketbook had been reached and emptied. Germany's lack of realization of the wrongs she had done left the world sick at heart. The world looked in vain for the faintest expression of regret for German atrocities. The simple reason was that the German mind was too Prussian to realize that Germany had done anything wrong. Wrong, when done by a German, was not wrong, because done for the State which could not do wrong. Only other States could do wrong.[32]

British and Belgian forces moved eastward through King Albert's kingdom, to take up positions on the Rhine from below Coblenz northward to the Dutch frontier, with Cologne as their destination. They were to follow the path which the armies of Kluck and Bülow had taken in 1914, when they came through Liége and went across Belgium to win their first battles with the French and British at Charleroi and Mons, and thereafter to make their mad dash into France only to find defeat in September on the Marne. Cologne for the British, Coblenz for the Americans, Mainz for the French, that was the arrangement, which in general

[32] James E. Lough in The *Times* (New York).

took account of fronts held by the respective armies when the armistice was signed. It gave to each an easy and independent line of communications from its old front to its new one. With Coblenz and "Fair Bingen on the Rhine" under American governors was supplied one of the oddest incidents in American history.

The march of British troops to Cologne led them through scenery different from anything they had met on marches through France and Belgium. It was perfectly German in character. From Malmédy to Montjole and from Montjole to Duren, on the way to Cologne, men climbed steep hills covered with fir forests, and along edges of deep ravines round which narrow tracks wound in sharp curves, perilous for transport, dipping down into villages, as old-fashioned as those in pictures in Grimm's "Fairy Tales," snuggling in valleys below high sand-stone cliffs. Troops marched through the great forest of Duren, dark and mysterious in its depths, between long glades of tall, straight-columned firs, with sweeping green foliage above masses of scarlet bracken. All was silent in those woods. No living thing stirred as the British went by, and glanced sideways up glades through which the sunlight slanted. One might have met women in such a forest, or red-capped gnomes, or the wolf which said "Good morning, my dear," to Little Red Riding Hood. Beyond this forest a cliff fell steeply down to a stream rushing swiftly over boulders. It was a wild country for men to pass over. Motor-lorries side-slipped on the edge of ravines, and only the skill of drivers saved them from toppling over. Pack mules trudged up slowly, and men, with rain splashing on waterproof-capes and with tunics already soaked, went silently through the forest over hills, breathing hard because of the steep climbs. Packs weighed heavy and the march was long.[33]

The British crossed the Rhine at Cologne on December 9 just as a paddle-wheel river steamer was putting out into the stream crowded with customary freight and civilian passengers, as if nothing unusual had occurred. Within twenty yards of the boat's side, as she steamed away, was a British machine-gun so placed as to be able to keep a line

---

[33] Cable dispatch from Philip Gibbs to The *Times* (New York).

on the water-side. A stranger might have come and gone through many parts of the city itself and not been aware that anything unusual was afoot. Had he gone to Newmarket, however, he would have seen a hundred German ammunition wagons and gun-carriages which had been parked there as a hostage for the Allies, and in front of the bronze statue of Emperor Frederick—father of William II— a long six-inch gun, tipped on its side and lying in the street. Otherwise Cologne was more civilian than ever, because no German officers in uniform were seen. While a certain number of gray uniforms still remained, every man had taken off his military buttons and other badges of his regiment and service. Streets were thronged and shops brilliant and luxurious to look upon. On December 14, British cavalry passed through Cologne, crossed the Hohenzollern bridge, went beyond the Rhine and took possession of the bridgeheads.

The passing of cavalry over the bridge was an impressive sight, another historical episode of this war. To Germans the Rhine was the river of their life. Down its tide for centuries had drifted all the ghost memories of their race, its water sacred to them as the fount from which national legends, folk-songs, and sentiment deep in their hearts had come forth. In military history the Rhine had been their last line of defense, the moat around the keep of German strength. When British troops rode across that bridge and passed beyond to further outposts, it was the supreme sign of German defeat. Altho a proud people, the Germans did not show by word of bitterness the emotion they must have felt. Many did not come out to see the actual crossing, and altho many people were in the streets through which the cavalry rode, there were only small groups at each end of the Hohenzollern Bridge, a massive structure of German character, with castellated towers at each end like those outside some medieval fortress. At the city end on pedestals were enormous equestrian figures of William I and his son. Below one of these, General Plumer, commanding the Second British Army from Flanders, which had fought many battles since the first of Ypres, stood in the midst of other generals and the Staff Officers of his corps and received the salute of the cavalry as they rode across the Rhine. Hardly once during two hours did Plumer give his arm any rest as he stood there rigid, his hand to his cap, an ordeal for any man. Plumer saluted each colonel, corporal, trooper, horse-gunner, bugler, or signaler, with all the honor he could give them on this last ride to their journey's end.

A guard of honor of lancers, with red and white pennons at their lance tips, was on one side of the bridge below the statue of William I., sitting there motionless, as if made of bronze, like the imperial horsemen, except when their beautiful animals pawed the ground or tossed their

BRITISH OFFICIAL PHOTO.

BRITISH TROOPS CROSSING THE BRIDGE AT COLOGNE
Cologne Cathedral is seen in the rear

heads. Officers rode with drawn swords, and, as they came
near the saluting base, turned in their saddles and shouted:

BRITISH OFFICIAL PHOTO.

A BRITISH PATROL ON THE RHINE

"Carry swords," and then, to the escort squadron: "Eyes
right," when every trooper turned his head sideways, making a gleam of steel helmets. Lancers and dragoon guards
and hussars, with horse-artillery, in which each gun was
polished as a pretty toy for pageantry and not for death,
passed in a steady stream which took two hours to flow by
across that bridge. Down below on the quay side was another procession headed by two German officers in full
uniform, with a white flag on the front of their motor-car,
and behind them a long line of other cars with the German
eagle painted on panels. They had come into Cologne under
a flag of truce to deliver up cars, according to the terms
of the armistice.

Mr. Gibbs,[34] after leaving the British lines, went to Aix-la-
Chapelle, where he saw the entry of the Belgian army of
occupation. They came, some with bugles playing, officers
with drawn swords, men marching through at a quick pace
with colors flying. The Germans were shocked beyond
measure when the Belgians promulgated as an ironclad rule
that civilians should step off sidewalks and uncover when

[34] Correspondent of The *Times* (New York).

370

Belgian officers approached, and that hostages should be given. Having protested to the Armistice Commission, they were told that the rules were exactly the same, even to the printed words, as those which the Germans had laid down at the time of their occupation of Brussels in 1914. This gave the Germans an additional shock. They offered as a defense the plea that the Belgians had brought the rules down upon themselves by firing upon German troops, while people in Aix-la-Chapelle had never injured the Belgians. It appeared that the Belgians had not intended to maintain the rules they had posted in derision in Aix-la-Chapelle. Next day other orders were posted. The German people, however, knew the meaning of defeat as soon as they saw the Belgians enter.

General Mangin, who had resumed command of the French army occupying Lorraine, by December 6 was preparing to enter Mainz, to establish the bridgehead there as stipulated in the armistice terms. He addrest an order of the day to

ⓒ COMMITTEE ON PUBLIC INFORMATION.

THE FIRST AMERICAN HORSE TO DRINK FROM THE RHINE

his troops, in which he paid a tribute to the fine discipline shown by them in marching through Alsace and Lorraine. the order added:

"You will now continue your triumphant march toward the Rhine. Nobody can ask you to forget the abominations committed by the enemy. It is not in revenge for German barbarism that you can now fight against the enemy; you would be beaten in advance. You will remain worthy of your great mission and your victories. You will remember that, during the wars of the Revolution, the armies of the Republic behaved in such a way that the Rhine populations asked to be incorporated into France and that the fathers of those you will now meet once fought side by side with your fathers on the battlefields of Europe. 'No stain on the laurels of the Tenth Army' must be the watchword of all."

The entry of Fayolle and Mangin into Mainz on December 14 created a profound impression on that part of the population that did not remain indoors. It was one of the most memorable ceremonies of the occupation, in which the people maintained greater reserve than the inhabitants of other towns occupied by the French. Many houses and buildings were tightly closed. A large proportion of the people seen in the streets were women and children. In the old Grand Ducal Palace, after a review Fayolle and Mangin were presented to the authorities, who exprest a hope that the French would cooperate with them in maintaining order and keeping the economic life of the region going. Fayolle, in reply, reminded them that the war imposed on France by Germany in 1871 was one of the most cruel and unjust in history. He drew a picture of the devastation in France and Belgium in this war, and the distress of families without shelter, their goods, products and manufacturing machinery having been carried into Germany and their soil made a desert. He recalled how, after repeated defeats since July 15, the Germans had been obliged to ask for an armistice. He assured them that, however natural reprisals might appear, Germans had nothing to fear from the troops of occupation, either for their persons or possessions, so long as they accepted the French ccupation in a proper spirit. The German authorities listened with respectful attention to a translation of Fayolle's address and a short talk by Mangin, who assured them of the cooperation of the army in maintaining the regular course of life in the occupied region.

© UNDERWOOD & UNDERWOOD. N. Y.

THE BRITISH ON THE RHINE
A crossing of the river is about to be made. The equestrian statue represents Kaiser Wilhelm II

The real invasion of Germany had taken place. Belgian, British, French, and American troops were on German soil, in an occupation the end of which no man could forecast. One year before such an invasion would have shaken the foundations of the German Empire, the whole fabric of which had dominated Continental Europe for forty years, conditioned upon a single fact—military power. Prussian domination had reared something which the Holy Roman Empire could not supply, nor Austria, inheriting an estate dissolved by Napoleon I, could guarantee. The Prussian failure was now revealed. Roads of invasion that had been followed by Louis XIV and Napoleon were filled again with the armies of a great invasion. This was a fact of enduring historical importance, because it offered final proof that the whole theory and faith which were exprest in the German Empire had been wrong. It was impossible to exaggerate the value of this demonstration. The German for four years had occupied Lille, St. Quentin, and Laon; he had planned to annex Flanders and French Lorraine; and now Trèves, Coblenz, Aix-la-Chapelle, Cologne, and Mainz were in possession of Entente garrisons. Meanwhile Alsace-Lorraine had been lost and Prussian Poland was destined to pass to other hands.

Suddenly and at a leap the Rhine once more was making history. For a period the famous river had ceased to be German. Allied forces occupied its west bank from Switzerland to Holland, while other Rhine territory to the east had become for the time neutral. The Germans had surrendered the whole of their principal waterway, their proudest geographical possession, their most romantic river, so rich in associations, racial, territorial, and sentimental. No river in the world bore the same relation to a country that the Rhine bore to Germany. No river had been more loudly celebrated in German song. In the world there was no natural spot so fervently acclaimed by tourists. By taking possession of the German part of the Rhine, the Allies had delivered besides a strategic and necessary blow at their enemy, something more, for in one sweep they had struck at the deepest and most fundamental symbol of German pride. The German race from time immemorial had invested the waters of the Rhine with so much glamor that a draught of it would now have been the bitterest they could taste. The long "watch on the Rhine," and to points far beyond it, had been interrupted; the song which celebrated that watch had become untuned. It was not only a spiritual humiliation, but a retribution for forty years of infatuation of mind and brutality of body.

The Rhine was one of the great geographical landmarks of Europe. The Romans were never wholly comfortable until they had established themselves on its banks and beyond. Mainz had always been a commanding military site; it was one of the first places on the river at which a Roman camp was established. It had always been a commanding military site. Ever since Cæsar came the Rhine has had a full and crowded history, as the most important river in Europe, a cradle of good architecture and art; a home of religion, learning and beneficent invention; the stage and background of a thousand legends and romances; the most northerly, as

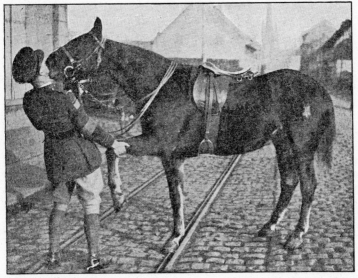

(c) CANADIAN OFFICIAL PHOTO.

CANADIAN STAFF OFFICER SAYING GOOD-BY TO HIS
HORSE IN FRANCE

well as one of the richest, of the nurseries of the vine; with a flourishing industrial area. All that fair tract, the richest spiritual, almost the richest material, inheritance of Germany, had now been temporarily handed over to the custody of the Allies. To the English, the surrender of the Thames from Lechlade to Gravesend could hardly have meant more. The Rhine was no mere geographical conception; it was an integral part of the German soul. By the Rhine above Bingen stands a colossal statue of Germania, commemorating the year 1870, and near enough to the river for inclusion within the 30 kilometer radius from the bridgehead at Mainz; but its owners had no grounds to fear for its safety in Allied hands.

On December 11 Berlin welcomed the return of the German army in crowds such as had not been seen since the funeral of Kaiser William I. The Prussian Guard and other soldiers marched through the Brandenburg Gate, gay with evergreens and flags, past millions of rejoicing people. Band after band played, and from balconies flowers were thrown. Premier Ebert, fearing no rebuke, reviewed the parade in a silk hat, which he removed when making a speech. "No enemy overcame you," said he. "You protected the land from invasion, sheltered your wives, children, and parents from flames and slaughter, and preserved the nation's workshops and fields from devastation." Ebert did not say how in Belgium, France, Serbia, Poland, and Roumania these same men had stolen, burned, ravaged, destroyed, and dishonored. On the contrary, "You can return with heads erect," said Ebert. By December 17 the scenes of enthusiasm which had marked the home-coming of troops were ending. Men had been coming home at the rate of 10,000 a day, and every day Ebert had taken his place on a rostrum opposite the French Embassy and addrest the home-coming men, while bands played martial music and crowds cheered and waved handkerchiefs. Even "Deutschland über Alles" was played and sung as cavalry, infantry, and artillery swept by. Regimental flags were crowned with laurel wreaths, men wore evergreens around steel helmets and tunics, and guns were covered with flowers. Berlin "went dancing mad." At fifty cabarets dancing at first went on all the afternoon and until 9 o'clock at night; then the edict closing halls at 9 o'clock was removed and the dancing went on all night, with cabarets packed to suffocation with women in expensive toilettes, soldiers and civilians dancing and drinking wine that cost $10 a bottle. "We are trying to forget," said a Berliner.[35]

[35] Principal Sources: The *Times* (London), The *Sun* (New York), Associated Press dispatches; The *Tribune,* The *Times,* New York.

THE FIRST RAISING OF THE AMERICAN FLAG ON THE RHINE

VI

VISITS BY PRESIDENT WILSON AND OTHER LEADERS TO EUROPEAN CAPITALS

November 28, 1918—January 18, 1919

BETWEEN the signing of the armistice and the meeting of the Peace Conference, there was much activity among the Entente Powers preliminary to the formal assembling of the delegates in Paris and Versailles. Not only was there discussion of the terms to be imposed on Germany, but several notable visits were made by heads of Governments, statesmen and military chiefs to Paris, London, and Rome, among them visits by King George, King Albert, King Victor Emmanuel, President Wilson, Marshal Foch, and Premier Clémenceau, King George being the first to visit another country.

King George went to Paris on November 28. After a dinner had been served in his honor at the Elysée Palace, a reception took place at the British Embassy, where he bestowed upon Marshal Foch the Order of Merit, Foch being the only Frenchman on whom that decoration had ever been bestowed. "I am happy," said the King, "to give the highest distinction of which I can dispose to the eminent soldier who has conducted the Allied armies to victory." The British Order of Merit was instituted by King Edward VII in 1902. While rarely given and in a sense exclusive, it carried with it no title or personal precedence. At this reception, the first fête that had been given in Paris since the signing of the armistice, women appeared in gay-colored toilettes, which, combined with the scarlet robes of Cardinal Amette, Archbishop of Paris, and Cardinal Bourne, Archbishop of Westminster, contrasted strikingly with the khaki and horizon blue uniforms of officers and the black clothes of civilians. It was an occasion that had been familiar enough in the Paris of other

378

days, but had been almost forgotten in the Paris of wartimes. Marshal Joffre was there in the black tunic and red trousers of the battle of the Marne period.

On December 1 a group of Allied civil and military leaders visited London for a conference over peace questions, one of which was understood to be the ultimate fate of the former Kaiser. Besides Marshal Foch, the visitors included Premier Clémenceau, Premier Orlando of Italy, and the Italian Foreign Minister, Sonnino. The highest military honors were paid them, the ceremonial marked by a display such as London had never seen since the war began. Indeed, the setting provided at the railway station, when the guests arrived, outdid in splendor of pageantry anything London had ever accorded even to a visiting sovereign. Charing Cross was transformed into a blaze of color. At each end of the platform hung two enormous Union Jacks. At twenty paces from a 500-foot-long crimson carpet covering the platform stood a double line of khaki-clad men, the tallest in the British army, forming a hollow square, lined by the multi-colored uniforms of officers who had come to greet the great French Marshal. When the train, bearing a tricolor on the engine, drew in, the first to alight was Foch. The Duke of Connaught, uncle of the King, stept forward with extended hand to welcome him. Then Premier Clémenceau stept from the train and was received by the Duke, while Foch became engaged in an earnest conversation with Lloyd George. The Italian Premier and Foreign Minister were also greeted by the Duke of Connaught and other high officials. An inspection of the guard followed, Marshal Foch giving close attention to the troops. When this was over, he turned to an officer of the guard and said: "Never have I seen troops dearer to my heart."

Outside the station and from distances far away, cheers of welcome were heard, a medley of joyous sounds such as London had seldom known. The vast volume of it was British, but Americans did their part, giving a full assortment of cheers and calls, and waving the Stars and Stripes. As Foch's carriage drove out of the station, so thunderous an outburst greeted him that he seemed to have been taken off his guard as he failed to give the salute in acknowledgment. Tears gathered in the great soldier's eyes at that supreme moment, after which he soon became a soldier again—precise and clock-like with the salute. Troops lined the route to the French Embassy,. where Clémenceau was taken and the hotels where others were lodged. During roars of cheers, Foch kept his hand at salute almost constantly. Among the cries was "Good old Tiger!" for Clémenceau. Men of long experience never remembered London crowds so unrestrainedly enthusiastic. They were thickly massed along the whole route, rising superior to the depressing influence of dismal, gray, damp weather. Many cheered themselves hoarse, giving a true ring of boundless admiration and gratitude to the organizers of victory.

While in London Marshal Foch made one speech in a manner described as "very much like a soldier talking to his friends, chest out, head well back, with one leg thrust forward, suggesting the elastic posture of a fencer as he moves slightly and regularly at the knee as if about to lunge." Foch's main point was that he had done nothing. "The Boches attacked," said he; "I said I would stop them. When they were stopt, I attacked them. Well, every one did what he could, and after some time we were all attacking along the 400 miles of front—the French, the English, the Americans, the Belgians, and we all went for them." Then the Marshal ceased speaking and raising both hands, pushed forward with them and his body in one movement. "Victory," he continued, "is an inclined plane. We pushed them, all of us, and they simply had to retreat and retreat again." Then the Marshal made a slightly downward movement with his hands, moving elastically at the knee in unison. "And after that," said he, "we simply kept pushing and pushing, and they went back, and we were simply on the point of getting—" At this point he waved his hands and added, "Then they asked for an armistice, and they accepted all our conditions." At this point Foch's shoulders, hands, and eyebrows went up, and the Marshal merely remarked as if he had been understood, "Well—!" The impression every one got when he sat down was of the great shock it had been to the Marshal that the enemy surrendered.

FROM THE ARMISTICE TO THE CONFERENCE

When the Congress of the United States assembled on December 2, President Wilson went before it with a speech in which he paid an eloquent tribute to Americans who had served in the war, and announced his intention of going to Paris two days later to take part in the peace deliberations. He said of his trip:

"I welcome this occasion to announce to Congress my purpose to join in Paris the representatives of the governments with which we have been associated in the war against the Central Empires for the purpose of discussing with them the main features of the treaty of peace. I realize the great inconveniences that will attend my leaving the country, particularly at this time, but the conclusion that it was my permanent duty to go has been forced upon me by considerations which I hope will seem as conclusive to you as they have seemed to me.

"The Allied governments have accepted the bases of peace which I outlined to the Congress on the 8th of January last, as the Central Empires also have, and very reasonably desire my personal counsel in their interpretation and application, and it is highly desirable that I should give it in order that the sincere desire of our Government to contribute without selfish purpose of any kind to settlements that will be of common benefit to all the nations concerned may be made fully manifest.

"The peace settlements which are now to be agreed upon are of transcendent importance both to us and to the rest of the world, and I know of no business or interest which should take precedence of them. The gallant men of our armed forces on land and sea have consciously fought for the ideals which they knew to be the ideals of their country; I have sought to express those ideals; they have accepted my statements of them as the substance of their own thought and purpose, as the associated governments have accepted them; I owe it to them to see to it, so far as in me lies, that no false or mistaken interpretation is put upon them, and no possible effort omitted to realize them. It is now my duty to play my full part in making good what they offered their life's blood to obtain. I can think of no call to service which could transcend this."

President Wilson's decision to make this trip aroused at the time a somewhat acrimonious controversy. It was not only the first trip a President had ever made to Europe while in office, but there was a feeling that it was not properly the part of a President to become a delegate to a

Peace Congress, but rather the part of persons whom he should appoint. Another phase of the opposition centered around neglect of the duties of his office at home. After he had made his speech in Congress, as quoted above, there was added to these criticisms a feeling that he had refrained from taking Congress and the people of the country into his confidence on a matter in which they were vitally interested—that is, he had decided on his own initiative to go and had really said very little to explain to them why he was going. The speech was received in Congress with an unusual lack of anything like a demonstration. Probably it was a correct statement which the Washington *Post* made in saying that "For good or ill, President Wilson leaves for Europe without the united support of the American people." There were, however, representative organs of public opinion which had nothing by way of criticism to offer. Even some which were severe critics of him in other matters, and even hostile to him politically, maintained that a President ought not to be placed at a disadvantage at a time like this through faultfinding among his own people.

Among these was the Philadelphia *Public Ledger,* which did not see how matters could be in any way helped by what it called "a barrage of political criticism, discounting Mr. Wilson's prestige in Paris." Mr. Wilson had made himself "the foremost spokesman of the forward-looking Liberals of Europe," and if he had not decided to go to Europe that paper believed that "long-submerged millions on the plains of Czecho-Slovakia and Jugo-Slavia, in Poland and even in Russia would have felt that a powerful friend on whom they had confidently counted, would be absent." Eventually this critical feeling seemed almost completely to disappear, and notably so after the plan for a League of Nations was adopted unanimously in Paris at the conference. Weeks afterward, however, bitter criticism flared up again, mainly in the United States Senate, but of that episode passages in the chapter on the Peace Treaty in Volume X of this work gives details.

President Wilson sailed for Brest on the United States steamship *George Washington,* the former North German-Lloyd liner, on December 4, and so became the first President of the United States who ever visited Europe while in office. His departure from New York was witnessed by thousands from the waterfront of Manhattan and Staten Island. Craft in the harbor joined in a noisy farewell, the like of which New York had perhaps never before seen. With Mrs. Wilson at his side, he stood on the bridge of the great transport waving his hands and tipping his hat time and time again in response to the parting tribute. The *George Washington* was escorted down the harbor by five destroyers. Off Staten Island the super-dreadnought *Pennsylvania,* the flagship of Admiral Mayo, Commander-in-Chief of the battle-fleet, and a dozen or more destroyers, all under orders to escort the liner to a point about 100 miles east of Sandy Hook, a few to return, met the President's ship.

With the first break of day at Brest, on December 13, fleets of warships and merchant craft brought out their colors and drest ship with long lines of streamers, among them French cruisers in war-paint at anchorage, and a score of French destroyers about them. Near at hand loomed the big Atlantic liner *France,* which had been in use as a hospital ship during the war, but was about to resume her transatlantic service. American destroyers, naval yachts, and small craft glided about the harbor. Further off lay flotillas of merchant ships, transports, freighters, and quaint Breton fishing craft. Two American freighters were engaged in unloading army supplies, and an American transport was preparing to take more troops homeward. It was a scene stirring in its activity and glowing with color. From early morning a fleet of airplanes had hovered over the entrance to the harbor, keeping an outlook for the approaching fleet. On shore there was equal animation, with vast throngs of Bretons, in picturesque head-gear, packing streets and massed along quays and terraces overlooking the harbor. French and American soldiers lined streets and took assigned positions along the Cours Dajot, a handsome promenade leading from the commercial harbor to the city, and over which President Wilson was to pass. The whole city was a mass of bunting, the Place President Wilson hung with streamers and mottoes. The entire Presidential route was lined with Venetian masts, flags, and trans-

THE "GEORGE WASHINGTON" WITH PRESIDENT WILSON
ON BOARD

parencies. About nine o'clock the French cruiser squadron, consisting of the *Admiral Aube*, the *Condé*, and *Montcalm*, with a number of destroyers, moved out of the harbor, amid the screech of sirens, to meet the incoming fleet off shore.

The entrance to the harbor is a narrow strait, a mile wide, with forts that crown towering cliffs on each side. Through this avenue the imposing pageant moved, each of the fourteen forts contributing its cannonade to which the ten American battleships answered gun for gun. As the first fleet neared the inner harbor, land-batteries and assembled war-craft took up the thunderous salute, while quays, hills, and terraces rang with cheers from enthusiastic crowds. At the same time all war-craft, merchantmen, and transports drest ship and manned yards, while the strains of the American anthem, mingling with the roar of guns and the shouts of vast crowds, could now and then be heard. The battleship squadron escorting the *George Washington* entered the harbor precisely at noon, the President's ship moving through lines formed by battleships. She dropt anchor as the first rays of sunlight for the day fell across her side, and illuminated on shore a huge reproduction of Bartholdi's Statue of Liberty. Under the booming of saluting guns from the Château of Ste. Anne, which has walls dating from Phenician times, the *George Washington* steamed to anchorage in the Brest roadstead, escorted by ten American battleships, twenty-nine destroyers, five French and one Italian warship, each thundering the Presidential salute.

With an agile step the President debarked at the municipal pier, to receive a spectacular welcome from a picturesque assortment of Breton women in native costumes, Red Cross nurses, French marines and Colonial troops, including Spahis, Turcos, Senegalese and Cochin-China contingents. Red Cross women presented flowers to the President and Mrs. Wilson. Through a lane formed of 20,000 doughboys an open motor-car in which the President sat with the French Foreign Minister, Stephen Pichon, and Mayor Hervagault of Brest, traversed the hilly streets of the town. Wilson was hailed everywhere as "the champion of the people's rights and of international justice." In his ears were dinned cries of "Hurrah for Wilson!" *"Vive le*

Président Wilson!" "Vivent les Américains!" Many Breton
girls tossed flowers into the car. The President, in response
to a greeting from Minister Pichon that France welcomed
him "to help her settle the terms of peace," said with
marked significance: "We will settle that together." In
response to an address from the Mayor of Brest, the President said he had come to "join counsel with your own public
men in bringing about a peace settlement which shall be
consistent alike with the ideals of France and the ideals of
the United States."

The Presidential train soon left for Paris, reaching the
Bois de Boulogne Station at 10 o'clock next morning. One
got his first emotional thrill out of the occasion from the
slowness with which the locomotive, draped with an American flag, moved into the station in order to bring the door
of Mr. Wilson's car to an exact halt at the red-carpeted
platform, where President Poincaré, Madame Poincaré, and
Premier Clémenceau were standing to greet the nation's
guest. President Wilson was the first man to step out of
the car. Platform greetings followed, but were brief and
informal. Five minutes later the Presidents of the French
and American Republics, sitting together in an open carriage
drawn by two horses, began an historic and moving episode
in a city that for centuries had known great ceremonial
pageants. Following in the second carriage were Mrs.
Wilson, Miss Wilson, Mme. Poincaré, and Mme. Jusserand.
Thirty-six thousand soldiers—the flower of the French
army—lined the avenues from the Dauphine Gate to the
Murat Mansion, which, during their stay in Paris, was to be
the home of the President and his wife. Alpine Chasseurs
and Zouaves, fresh from the battlefields of Champagne, and
Colonial troops, from whose uniforms the mud of the
Somme had only a few days before been removed, occupied
the post of honor. Gently but firmly these men kept order
among enormous crowds, which prest forward in eagerness
to have a closer look at the guest of France.

The night of President Wilson's arrival was declared to
be a greater night in Paris than "Armistice Night," the
city ablaze with illuminations, boulevards filled with crowds,
dancing, singing, and throwing confetti. The Place de la

Concorde was turned into a great dancing pavilion, where American soldiers were favorite partners for French women. "America" was the predominating word in Paris that night. David Lawrence [36] declared that the demonstration "was only a partial manifestation of our real hold on the Entente nations." Mr. Lawrence had trailed behind Mr. Wilson's automobile during many processions in the United States; had been with him in the campaigns of 1912 and 1916 and on other journeys, but "never had any body of people shown by incessant applause and outbursts of cheering the same emotion and the same enthusiasm that he witnessed as he followed a few feet behind the President's carriage through the center of Paris." It was "a thrilling exhibition of the fraternity of the great French nation for the republican people far across the seas." Another observer, Henry White, a member of the American delegation to the Peace Conference, said he had seen most demonstrations in Paris in honor of sovereigns and Presidents since 1867, but had never "witnessed anything approaching the welcome given President Wilson." Mr. White had served in Paris not only as the American Ambassador but as Secretary of Legation through several administrations. President and Mme. Poincaré gave to President and Mrs. Wilson, after their arrival in Paris, a luncheon at which notable speeches were made by the two Presidents.

Next day being Sunday, the President went out quietly to the tomb of Lafayette in the Picpus Cemetery, after a morning service. No ceremony had been arranged there, and he was accompanied only by a secret service man and a French officer, who had been assigned to him as a personal aide. The President, removing his hat, entered the tomb carrying a large floral wreath, which—contrary to a custom by which, in Paris, a florist delivers a wreath and the donor later makes the visit and leaves his card—Mr. Wilson insisted on carrying himself. On his card he had written: "In memory of the great Lafayette, from a fellow-servant of liberty." As he placed the wreath on the tomb, he bowed his head and stood silent before the resting-place of

---

[36] Washington correspondent of The *Evening Post* (New York), who had gone to Europe to report the President's visit.

the famous Frenchman. As his arrival had been entirely
unannounced, the aged gate-keeper was almost too much
disconcerted to unlock the gates when he learned who his
caller was. News of the visit spread rapidly to the adjoining convent and as Mr. Wilson left the cemetery, he passed
through lines of aged nuns who had come out to pay their
respects to him.

After the President had been in Paris four days, the cele-

PRESIDENT WILSON IN PARIS

The picture shows a crowd which had gathered in the Place de la Concorde
to see him pass

bration was still going on, boulevards as crowded as ever.
The throngs that waited outside the Murat mansion where
he had his Paris home, did not lessen. Whenever he appeared the cheering seemed as spontaneous as ever. When
he and Clémenceau were seen together, they "seemed as
happy as two boys." Clémenceau, as one commentator said,

"had probably expected to see a Moses with tablets of stone, but found instead a human being, with a fine sense of humor like himself." One source of the President's success in Paris was his sincere, frank enjoyment of it all. His smile made a hit because it came obviously from the heart. There was a reception at the American Embassy with President and Mrs. Wilson and President and Mme. Poincaré the guests of honor. The company which assembled for dinner included many prominent figures in French life, and at the reception which followed were gathered several hundred persons of various nationalities representing the many official, military, and diplomatic groups then gathered in the French capital. The spacious marble staircase of the Embassy was lined with palms, while salons and dining-rooms were filled with palms and flowers, the decorations including a tasteful blending of the American and French colors. In Berlin news of his arrival was displayed prominently, and his utterances were scanned carefully. Newspapers, formerly foremost in attacking his policies, said they "had been deceived." [37]

A letter from the Pope was presented to the President on December 18 by Monsignor Gerretti, Papal Under Secretary of State, pleading for assistance on behalf of opprest nationalities, and especially Armenia and Poland. The Pope hoped for a just and durable peace through enlightened action, and asked the President to help new States to realize their ambitions, regardless of race and religion. The letter was a reply to a former letter from President Wilson to the Pope thanking him for his congratulations on the part taken by the United States in the war. Monsignor Gerretti had intended to present this letter in Washington, having been delegated to attend Cardinal Gibbons' jubilee in Baltimore, but he was recalled from England when about to embark after it was learned that the President would soon be in France.

In the great amphitheater of the University of Paris (the Sorbonne) the President on December 21 received a degree conferred in recognition of his work as a jurist and historian. This was the first time in the history of the univer-

---

[37] Cable dispatch from Charles H. Grasty to The *Times* (New York).

sity that it had bestowed on any one an honorary degree. President Poincaré, the presidents of the Senate and Chamber of Deputies, the diplomatic corps, other men in the government, including the highest civil and military authorities, were present at the ceremony. In his speech accepting the honor, the President gave his conception of a league of nations. "The task of those who are gathered here, or will presently be gathered here," he said, "to make the settlements of this peace, is greatly simplified by the fact that they are the masters of no one; they are servants of mankind. And if we do not heed the mandates of mankind, we shall make ourselves the most conspicuous and deserved failures in the history of the world." He concluded by saying that just a little exposure "would settle most questions," and if the Central Powers "had dared to discuss the purposes of this war for a single fortnight, it never would have happened."

President Wilson, accompanied by Mrs. Wilson, Rear-Admiral Grayson, and a small party, left Paris on the night of December 24 for a week's trip, which was to take him to American Army Headquarters at Chaumont and to England. He reached Chaumont, which was not far from St. Mihiel, on Christmas morning, and received a most cordial welcome from the people of the town. From Chaumont America's part in the war had been directed. General Pershing, M. Lévy-Alphandery, Mayor of Chaumont, and other officials, were on the platform to receive him and Mrs. Wilson, who were to pass through a salon hung with red tapestries and flags and enter a courtyard, where a company of the 109th French Infantry and a company of the 102d American Infantry had been drawn up. When the President, as the train drew in, raised the curtain of a window in his car, the first person he saw was an American doughboy on guard, who gravely came to salute, and the President smilingly gave him a "Merry Christmas." From his train, the President, along the way to Chaumont, had seen on every hand evidence of America's participation in the war—great piles of supplies, American soldiers swarmed on locomotives, and boxcars, and in treetops and every other point of vantage from which to get a glimpse of him, and shouted "Merry Christmas."

Gusts of raw wind came over the hills that day from a battle-front in the tranquil distance. All along the roads over which the Presidential party now traveled in motor-cars to a reviewing field, thousands of privates and officers had come unbidden. Young and old shivered while standing in muddy roads, or leaning from windows as they waved tiny American flags in tribute to the representative of a nation that was looked upon as a savior of France in the supreme crisis of the war. The day, in spite of snow, slush, and overcast skies, was one never to be forgotten by those who had a part in it. The chief event was a review of 10,000 picked men, all of whom had seen active service. A stand had been erected in the center of an open field near the town of Humes. It was an inspiring scene that greeted the President's eyes as he reached the stand and looked around upon grim soldiers standing shoulder to shoulder, forming solid masses clad in khaki and wearing steel helmets. Nothing could dampen the feeling of enthusiastic patriotism among the Americans present.[38]

Ambassador and Madame Jusserand, who had accompanied President and Mrs. Wilson to Chaumont, left for Paris that night at the same time that Mr. Wilson's train started for Calais on his way to London. The train next morning came to a stop on the quay at Calais, where British troops were awaiting his coming; opposite them a detachment of French soldiers in steel helmets. At one end of the quay was a working-party of German prisoners of war who gazed with curious eyes at the ceremonial that marked the arrival of the man who was Commander-in-Chief of the land and naval forces of the United States. The day was full of sunshine, and the air almost balmy. As the Channel boat moved out a squadron of eight British airplanes appeared in sight and hovered over and around the ship during her passage to England. Sometimes these ships of the air flew close to the boat, and then would flit away, return and circle around the vessel. French destroyers, flying the American flag at the mainmast, composed the escorting

[38] Paris dispatch from Richard V. Oulahan to The *Times* (New York).

fleet, and accompanied the boat to midchannel, where they turned sharply about to give way to a British flotilla of seven destroyers sent to escort the ship to Dover. It was a beautiful sight as the British destroyers, dividing so as to pass the boat on each side, quickly turned, each seemingly on a pivot, and took up the same direction as the ship.

To a salute of forty guns, the strains of many bands, the

U. S. OFFICIAL PHOTO.

PRESIDENT AND MRS. WILSON AT THEIR CHRISTMAS DINNER
ON THE AMERICAN FRONT IN FRANCE

whirr of aeroplanes darting overhead and thunderous cheers from huge crowds, the President, on reaching London, where he was met at the station by the King and Queen, walked through a miniature arch of triumph surmounted by a gilded American eagle. Emerging from the station he passed lines of an American guard of honor in his progress through the heart of London, while seated on the right hand

WILSON AND POINCARÉ IN PARIS

VI,

of the King in a royal coach drawn by four horses with scarlet-coated footmen riding in front and back of the carriage. Multitudes of cheering people, numbering nearly one hundred thousand were in Trafalgar Square, the majority waving American flags. The President scarcely replaced his hat from the moment when he first lifted it in response to the wild cheering that marked his journey through London streets.

Two standard-bearers and the King's imposing escort cavalcade preceded the procession. Roofs and balconies in Piccadilly were packed with sightseers. When the center gate at the top of Constitution Hill opened a passage for the President, he was the first uncrowned head to pass officially through that gateway on the route to Buckingham Palace, which was lined with khaki-clad girls belonging to the Women's Army Auxiliary Corps, blue uniformed members of the Women's Royal Naval Service and wounded Tommies. A row of masts encircled the gateway to the palace where the Union Jack and Old Glory were seen floating as the party approached and drove up to the grand entrance, brilliant sunshine adding to the glory of the scene, a picture of perfect harmony. After the palace was entered, the demonstration outside grew so tumultuous that the glass doors behind the scarlet-draped balcony of the palace were seen to open and the President, King, Queen and Mrs. Wilson appeared. That was the great moment of the day. The President stood there facing a multitude which stretched down the Mall to the Admiralty, half a mile distant, and overflowed St. James's Park on one side, and the Green Park on the other. Only a corporal's guard could hear the President's brief speech, but the people had demanded that he show himself, and gave him a greeting more clamorous than any other guest of the nation had commanded within the memory of oldest Londoners.

No more regal setting was ever seen in Buckingham Palace than that which greeted President and Mrs. Wilson when they were escorted into the banquet hall on December 26 for a State dinner. Prior to the dinner they had been escorted from their apartments to the great White Drawing Room, where the Royal family had gathered with their other guests. After these guests were presented, the dinner party proceeded to the dining hall, which is 200 feet long by 75 feet wide, and approached through a great hallway, richly furnished and decorated with paintings and porcelain. The banquet hall had a throne at one end, the main table being so arranged that the backs of President Wilson and King George were toward the throne. The permanent decorations were strikingly simple. The only work of art on the walls

MRS. WILSON AT THE AMERICAN LADIES' CLUB IN MAYFAIR

Names, left to right, are: Countess of Strafford, Lady Harcourt, Mrs. Curtis Brown, Mrs. Wilson, Mrs. Wright

was one Gobelin tapestry, but there had been brought from vaults to the banquet a great collection of solid gold plate and huge gold ornaments valued at fifteen million dollars. One of the three buffets held pieces of plate actually too large, or otherwise too cumbersome, to be used, and including a piece of great size that had been taken from one of the ships of the Spanish Armada. In color, the gold-laden table blended with the decorations which were white and gold, with a crimson carpet and upholstering to match, the crimson effect being further carried out by the exclusive use of poinsettas as floral decorations. In the balcony at the end of the room was a military orchestra not hidden from view by floral or other decorations. The attendants were in full state-dress, heavy with gold lace. Other guests than President and Mrs. Wilson had preceded the Royal Family and Ambassadorial guests into the banquet hall, and when the chief guests entered, they rose and remained standing.

Every royal formality which had attended great occasions at the British Court for two or three hundred years was carried out. President Wilson and Queen Mary led the procession, preceded by officials of the palace splendidly costumed, bearing wands, walking backward and making obeisance to the guests. Immediately behind the President and the Queen came King George and Mrs. Wilson, followed by members of the Royal Family. At the head of the table were seated twelve persons, with King George in the center. President Wilson sat at the King's right and Mrs. Wilson on his left. To the right of President Wilson was Queen Mary and then the French Ambassador, Princess Christian, the Spanish Ambassador and Princess Patricia, daughter of the Duke of Connaught. At Mrs. Wilson's left sat Princess Mary, the Italian Ambassador, Princess Beatrice and the Japanese Ambassador. The American Ambassador, John W. Davis, had the first place at a side rectangular table on President Wilson's right.

It fell to the lot of Mrs. Wilson's negro Washington maid, Susie, to carry off the honors for creating the most humorous incident connected with this dinner. When the gold plate had been brought out for the banquet, one of the royal servants thought Susie would be imprest by it, and so taking her in, asked what she thought of it, to which she replied that the Wilson's had "quite as good at the White House." "There is no gold plate at the White House," said Mrs. Wilson to Susie, when she afterward heard what Susie had said. "I know that, ma'am, but I was not going to let them know it." Queen Mary said to Susie at parting that she hoped she had been made comfortable during her stay, a remark which Susie reported to Mrs. Wilson, adding: "You must always ask your guests at the White House if they are comfortable." Susie after the dinner had the place of honor at the upper servant's table.

On December 28, with all the ceremony of ancient times, the President received the welcome of the City of London at the Guildhall. A page from the past was the pageant there unfolded, amid which the representative of America seemed like an anachronism. That this ancient ceremony should have furnished the setting for a speech by the President in which he pictured the vision of a new world, no longer under the rule of the sword, and no longer concerned with the balance of power, was one of the remarkable features of a historic occasion. The President's statements were more definite than any he had made up to that time in Europe, and plainly were intended to convey, not only the purpose of his visit, but some idea of the fruits of his momentous conference the day before with the leaders of British State policy. The men who sat on the Guildhall platform were a composite of the political, intellectual, and military genius of the British Empire. The President never made a more graceful address than the one he delivered before that audience, the like of which no American President had ever faced before. Behind him was all the quaint pageantry of the past—red and blue robed aldermen and commoners, men wearing wigs of ancient shapes—while before him in vision was the future in which a new world order was to take the place of the old. Britons applauded rapturously when, speaking of that epoch-making meeting between representatives of the two greatest democracies of the world, the President exprest his delight that their minds had moved along the same lines and that the ground had been cleared, as they already were in harmony as to basic principles. Cheers that shook the old walls of the Guildhall followed that remark.

At Carlisle, on the Scottish border, on Sunday, December 29, in falling rain, street crowds cheered the President all the way to a hotel, where prominent citizens were waiting to receive him. He had gone to Carlisle to visit the place where his maternal grandfather had lived as pastor of a church. He visited a house his grandfather had built, in which his grandfather had taught school, and in which his mother had lived for a while. At the crowded Lowther Street Congregational Church, where his grandfather had been pastor, the congregation rose as he entered and was conducted to the front pew, while the organist played "The Battle Hymn of the Republic." In his speech in the church, the President said:

"I believe, as this war has drawn nations temporarily together in a combination of physical force, we shall now be drawn together in a combination of moral force as much as physical force that has defeated the effort to subdue the world. Words have cut as deep as swords. The knowledge that wrong has been attempted has aroused the nations. They have gone out like men for a crusade. No other cause could have drawn so many of the nations together. They knew an outlaw was abroad and that the outlaw purposed unspeakable things. It is from quiet places like this that the forces are accumulated that presently will overpower any attempt to accomplish evil on a great scale. It is like the rivulet that gathers into the river and the river that goes to the sea. So there come out of communities like these streams that fertilize the conscience of men, and it is the conscience of the world we now mean to place upon the throne which others tried to usurp."

On December 30 Manchester made President Wilson a freeman of the city. Manchester men, women and children, and many from elsewhere in Lancashire, cheered him continuously during the five hours in which he made a sort of democratic progress from one point to another, the general atmosphere intimate and friendly. People often got near enough to shake hands with him. Even the ceremony of conferring the freedom of the city upon him had about it an atmosphere of homely simplicity. It was more like a college commencement than a formally staged ritual. People even sang "For He's a Jolly Good Fellow," which could hardly have been done at a state banquet in Buckingham Palace, or in the Guildhall of London. In a speech which was the most important he had made to Englishmen in England, he declared that the United States would "join no combination of Powers which was not a combination of all of us." Its reception showed that it was not lost upon its hearers. No other audience in Europe had absorbed his utterances so understandingly, or had so quickly responded to every point as this Manchester audience. "We are with you, Mr. President!" was a cry that resounded in the streets when the President drove from the inspection of the ship-canal, which was built to facilitate the landing of American cotton, to the City Hall, where he received the freedom of the city. No incident of his English visit was

PRESIDENT WILSON AND THOMAS WATSON

Mr. Watson, aged 90, was a survivor of Mr. Wilson's grandfather's Sunday-school at Carlisle

more impressive than this welcome to the heart of industrial England.

The President and Mrs. Wilson left London December 31 by a special train for Paris. King George, Queen Mary and the Duke of Connaught having accompanied them to the station. Premier Lloyd George was on the platform and the Scots Guards formed a guard of honor, while the band of Irish Guards played. As Queen Mary and Mrs. Wilson, followed by President Wilson and King George, left the waiting-room for the royal saloon which had been decorated with flowers, the band played "Over There." After crossing the Channel, a special train for Paris was taken, and President and Mrs. Wilson, on arrival, went directly to the Murat mansion.

The President left Paris for Italy on New Year's Day. A change made in the schedule had brought the Italian visit forward, in order that the preliminary peace conference might begin on or about January 10. Aboard the Royal train at the Italian border, the President was met by representatives of the King. The train was the acme of luxurious comfort. It consisted of nine coaches in charge of the King's personal staff. In the center was the President's car, its exterior of dark blue emblazoned with the royal arms, its interior a combination of mahogany and blue satin. All the way down to Rome the journey became a triumphal procession. Mountaineers and villagers swarmed around stations, many having come from distant hills and valleys to pay homage to America, shouting *"Vivas!"* waving hats, handkerchiefs and flags, and forming picturesque groups, which were emphasized by brilliant sunshine, a blue sky and green, luxuriant landscapes. When the train arrived at Turin, the President was met by the Prefect of the province, the Mayor, the General commanding the troops there, and other dignitaries, the station decorated with the Italian and American colors. Everywhere in the city the Stars and Stripes flew beside the Italian Tricolor.

A tremendous cheer went up in Rome as the train stopt in front of the waiting-room, which had been transformed into a gaily decorated parlor, carpeted with rich coverings and replete with rare flowers. As the President alighted on a rug-covered platform, he was heartily greeted by King Victor Emmanuel, Queen Elena, and the Duchess d'Aosta. When the presentations had been made, the President and King chatting merrily walked to the edge of the platform

ON LEAVING BUCKINGHAM PALACE

Left to right—Mrs. Wilson, Queen Mary, President Wilson, King George, Princess Mary

and inspected troops accompanied by the Prince of Udine, Ambassador Page and Ambassador Cellere. As the carriages left the station, the President received a rousing greeting from British and American officers, and representatives of every American military mission in Rome grouped about the exit. The commander of the garrison gave an order which hundreds of officers repeated and more than 5,000 soldiers presented arms. One of the largest crowds modern Rome had seen now massed behind the troops and gave the President the city's welcome. A group of returned emigrants greeted him in English. Several squadrons of airplanes flew overhead, church bells were rung and guns from forts boomed out the royal salute.. Crowds thronged the streets and adorned the windows of every building. The street demonstration continued long after the party reached the Quirinal. A crowd massed outside cheered for several minutes, and brought the Wilsons to the balcony of the palace.

An American contingent of fifty men, drawn from troops who had been in the final Italian offensive, had taken part in the parade. From the front had come representatives of the King's Brigade, who were famous as formidable fighters. Besides veteran troops from the Piave and Grappa fronts, many aviators had been summoned to Rome, their machines being decked with Italian and American flags. A huge Caproni triplane of the type used for bombing purposes, flew among smaller machines. One of the most daring of Italian aces thrilled crowds by looping the loop above housetops. Rome seemed transformed into a fairy city of waving flags, green festoons, and decorations of all descriptions. Brilliant sunshine and a blue sky made the scene typically Roman. Every shop decorated its windows with the American flag. Photographs of the President dominated everything. Hundreds of Austrian cannon, exposed in different squares, were decorated with American and Italian flags. Streets were crowded with soldiers wearing steel helmets.

In Rome, on January 3, President Wilson went through probably the hardest single day's program he had had since he arrived in Europe. He visited the Queen Mother, had conferences with Premier Orlando and Foreign Minister Sonnino, gave an audience to the Council of the Royal Academy of Science, was received at the Houses of Parliament, was the guest of honor at a state dinner given by the King, and ended the day with a reception in the Capitol, where he was made a citizen of Rome.

The President's last formal appearance before leaving Rome was when from the American Embassy he drove to the Vatican to visit the Pope. The demonstration on this occasion reached unprecedented heights. Hours before the time set for his arrival across the Tiber, the immense Piazza di San Pietro was completely filled. It can hold more than 200,000 people, and presented an imposing sight. Opposite the entrance rose the Church of St. Peter—the Cathedral of the World, as it is sometimes called, tho St. Peter's is not technically a cathedral, St. John's Lateran being the Pope's cathedral as Bishop of Rome,—while the colonnades on either side were thick with people. When the President appeared at the entrance, a great shout arose. He was momentarily taken aback, as he had not expected another great demonstration. Then his smile broke forth, and his hat continually waved in response to salutations. He remained some time in the Vatican, but the crowd did not tire with waiting, and on his return gave him another rousing cheer. The Pope had given him a handsome mosaic reproducing a picture by Guido Reni of St. Peter, and made in the Vatican grounds at an ancient mosaic factory. It was a yard square in size. In a tour of Rome the President visited the Forum, on entering which he was met by the archeologist, Professor Giacomo Boni, who presented him with branches of laurel and myrtle. The Forum, Palatine and Capitoline hills were black with people who had climbed ruins, broken columns and arches, and who acclaimed America as the modern champion of a civilization which had had its birth in that place two thousand five hundred years before.

From Rome the President went to Milan, where it seemed as if all the inhabitants and all the people of the city and the surrounding countryside had jammed themselves into the public places, until squares and all thoroughfares were choked with humanity. The President's motor-car was forced to crawl and edge its way about with the greatest difficulty, and was in constant danger of running people down. Balconies, roofs, and all other vantage points were black with people, the route plastered with pictures of President Wilson and quotations from his speeches. At the City Hall the freedom of the city was conferred upon him. He went

© COMMITTEE ON PUBLIC INFORMATION.

MILAN'S WELCOME TO PRESIDENT WILSON
An assembled crowd awaiting his arrival

to La Scala, dined at the palace and received delegations. Secret service men declared they had never taken any President through such crowds in America as Milan had turned out. While orderly, they were wild with enthusiasm. The President's tour was accompanied by a continuous roar of "*Vivas!*" in which every individual seemed to share.

Turin gave the President another tumultuous welcome. Thousands flocked into the streets and rent the air with cries of *"Viva,* Wilson, God of peace!" and similar expressions. After a round of receptions, which included conferring the freedom of the city upon him, he went to a luncheon at which the Cardinal was present, and visited the university, where an honorary degree was conferred upon him. The most picturesque feature of his visit was the gathering of more than a thousand mayors from cities and towns of Piedmont to greet him. They came from hills, fields and valleys. Virtually every little crossroad community was represented, as well as large cities. Each mayor wore a sash made in the national colors. The mayors represented every condition of society. Among them were prosperous bankers, merchants, cultured citizens, shy countrymen. and typical blacksmiths, each an official representative of his community. The President was now a citizen of Turin, Milan, Genoa and Rome—an unprecedented honor. Nothing like those Italian scenes had been seen in Europe in modern times. The President had plainly conquered Italy.

On January 20, two days after the Peace Conference held its formal opening session in Paris, President Wilson became a guest of the French Senate at a luncheon in the Luxemburg Palace. It was a most elaborate function, in the sumptuous setting of one of the finest of Old World palaces, with 300 guests in the throne-room of the Bourbon kings, now used for the first time for a dinner since, a hundred years before and more, Napoleon had there banqueted his generals on returning from a campaign. The Republican Guard, in snow-white uniforms and gleaming helmets, lined the marble staircase as President Wilson ascended it. The guests had their coffee in the Salon Victor Hugo, where two brilliant groups were formed, one with Marshal Foch in the center, the other with President Wilson, premiers and foreign delegates crowding around. The President received military honors again when he departed. Notable passages in his speech were these:

"We know the long period of peril through which France has gone. France thought us remote in comprehension and sympathy, and I dare say there were times when we did not comprehend, as you comprehended, the danger in the presence of which the world stood. There was no time when we did not know how near it was, and I fully understand, that throughout these trying years, when mankind waited for the catastrophe, how the anxiety of France must have been the deepest and most constant of all, for she did stand at the frontier of freedom. She had carved out her own fortunes through a long period of eager trouble. She had done great things in building up a great, new France. And just across the border, separated from her only by a few fortifications and a little country whose neutrality, it has turned out, the enemy did not respect, lay the shadow cast by the cloud which enveloped Germany—the cloud of intrigue, the cloud of dark purpose, the cloud of sinister design. This shadow lay at the very borders of France.

"And yet it is fine to remember here that for France this was not only a peril but a challenge. France did not tremble. France quietly and in her own way prepared her sons for the struggle that was coming. She never took the initiative or did a single thing that was aggressive. She had prepared herself for defense, not in order to impose her will upon other people, but had prepared herself that no other people might impose its will upon her.

"This is a new, awakened world. It is not ahead of us, but around us. It knows that its dearest interests are involved in its standing together for a common purpose. It knows that the peril of France, if it continues, will be the peril of the world. It knows that not only France must organize against this peril, but that the world must organize against it."

President Wilson, on February 3, delivered an address in the French Chamber of Deputies, having as auditors President Poincaré, the Presidents of the Chamber and the Senate, large numbers of members of both Houses of Parliament, and the personnel of the French Cabinet. The audience insisted on hearing the President's address standing. Even Poincaré, Clémenceau and Dubost remained standing. This seemed to embarrass the President, who made gestures that the Deputies remain seated, but they shouted: "We will hear you standing." The President turned to M. Deschanel, begging him to request that the deputies be seated, but he only shrugged his shoulders, as if utterly helpless.

The peace conference having assembled on January 18, and within a month completed the preliminary part of its work, the President on February 14 sailed from Brest for home on the *George Washington,* expecting to return in a few weeks. The argument for his going to Europe looked stronger now than it did when he sailed in December. The crucial test in the controversy as to his going had been the fact of his proposal for a League of Nations. The result in Paris already had been unanimously favorable to the League, and this result had to be admitted as being largely the result of his personal presence and labors in Europe, the presumption being strong that the adopting of the League plan could not have been brought about had he not been personally on the ground in Paris.

President Wilson's voyage home ended in Boston on February 24. After making a speech to a great crowd, he went by night train direct to Washington, signing on the train the new Income Tax Law by which $6,000,000,000 was to be raised for war expenses. Following days were spent in Washington in consultation with Senators and members of the House, in signing bills and making appointments. His last day was spent in New York, where he delivered a speech with Former President Taft on the same platform, both speaking in support of the League. Next day (March 5) he again sailed for Europe on the *George Washington,* duly arrived at Brest and proceeded to Paris to resume work in the peace conference. Of the work of the peace conference from January 18 until the draft of the treaty was presented to the German delegates at the Grand Trianon in Versailles early in May, and of the final conclusion of peace in the Hall of Mirrors at the Palace of Versailles, an account in several chapters will be found in Volume X.

President Wilson's long-promised visit to Belgium did not take place until June 19. Guided by the King and Queen, he was taken through some of the deepest horrors in treeless wastes of "Flanders Fields," brightened only by red poppies. He saw the utter ruin of Cloth Hall at Ypres, saw a dozen tanks, with their sides dashed in and sunk deep in the mire at Poelcapelle, and took lunch in what was once a glade in the forest of Houthulst, where 10,000 Belgians had fallen in the last offensive. The automobile tour ended at Zeebrugge, when the party went to Brussels, where formal ceremonies were held amid great enthusiasm. Visits were made to Louvain and Mechlin, and Cardinal Mercier was presented to him. At Louvain, amid the ruins of the university library, a degree was conferred upon him. In one of his speeches he referred to the Cardinal as the true shepherd of his flock, the majesty of whose spiritual authority awed even the unscrupulous enemy himself, who knew that he did not dare lay hand upon this servant of God.[40]

[40] Principal Sources: The *Manchester Guardian* (London), The *Evening Post,* The *Times,* New York; The *Evening Public Ledger* (Philadelphia), The *World* (New York), Associated Press dispatches.

THE BATTLEGROUND IN
BELGIUM, FRANCE
and ALSACE-LORRAINE

Farthest Advance of Germans, 1914	—— —— ——
Hindenburg Line, 1917	· · · · · · ·
Farthest Advance of Germans, 1918	+ + + + + +
Final Battle Line, Nov. 11, 1918	· + · + · +
(Neutral Zone along the Rhine)	ʃ 10 KM ʃ
Principal Railroads	————
Principal Canals	————
Forts	★

Scale of Miles

0   10   20   30   40   50   60

COPYRIGHT, 1919, BY FUNK & WAGNALLS CO., NEW YORK
THE MATTHEWS-NORTHRUP WORKS, BUFFALO, N. Y.